The Acquisition of Diminutives

Language Acquisition & Language Disorders

Volumes in this series provide a forum for research contributing to theories of language acquisition (first and second, child and adult), language learnability, language attrition and language disorders.

Volume 43

The Acquisition of Diminutives: A cross-linguistic perspective
Edited by Ineta Savickienė and Wolfgang U. Dressler

The Acquisition of Diminutives

A cross-linguistic perspective

Edited by

Ineta Savickienė

Vytautas Magnus University

Wolfgang U. Dressler

University of Vienna

John Benjamins Publishing Company

Amsterdam / Philadelphia

∞ TM The paper used in this publication meets the minimum requirements of American National Standard for Information Sciences – Permanence of Paper for Printed Library Materials, ANSI Z39.48-1984.

Library of Congress Cataloging-in-Publication Data

The acquisition of diminutives : a cross-linguistic perspective / edited by Ineta Savickienė and Wolfgang U. Dressler.
p. cm. (Language Acquisition & Language Disorders, ISSN 0925–0123 ; v. 43)
Includes bibliographical references and indexes.
1. Language acquisition. 2. Grammar, Comparative and general--Diminutives. I. Savickienė, Ineta. II. Dressler, Wolfgang U., 1939-

P118.A1423 2007
401'.93--dc22 2006052653
ISBN 978 90 272 5303 3 (Hb; alk. paper)

John Benjamins Publishing Co. · P.O. Box 36224 · 1020 ME Amsterdam · The Netherlands
John Benjamins North America · P.O. Box 27519 · Philadelphia PA 19118-0519 · USA

Table of contents

Introduction 1
Ineta Savickienė, Wolfgang U. Dressler

CHAPTER 1
Form and meaning of diminutives in Lithuanian child language 13
Ineta Savickienė

CHAPTER 2
Diminutives in Russian at the early stages of acquisition 43
Ekaterina Protassova, Maria Voeikova

CHAPTER 3
The acquisition of diminutives in Croatian 73
Marijan Palmović

CHAPTER 4
Diminutives in Greek child language 89
Evangelia Thomadaki, Ursula Stephany

CHAPTER 5
The role of diminutives in the acquisition of Italian morphology 125
Sabrina Noccetti, Anna De Marco, Livia Tonelli, Wolfgang U. Dressler

CHAPTER 6
The acquisition of diminutives in Spanish 155
A useful device
Victoria Marrero, Carmen Aguirre and María José Albalá

CHAPTER 7
A longitudinal study of the acquisition of diminutives in Dutch 183
Agnita Souman, Steven Gillis

CHAPTER 8
Diminutives and Hypocoristics in Austrian German (AG) 207
Katharina Korecky-Kröll, Wolfgang U. Dressler

CHAPTER 9
Acquisition of diminutives in Hungarian 231
Péter Bodor, Virág Barcza

CHAPTER 10
Diminutives in Finnish child-directed and child speech 263
Klaus Laalo

CHAPTER 11
The (scarcity of) diminutives in Turkish child language 279
F. Nihan Ketrez, Ayhan Aksu-Koç

CHAPTER 12
Acquiring diminutive structures and meanings in Hebrew 295
An experimental study
Anat Hora, Galit Ben-Zvi, Ronit Levie and Dorit Ravid

CHAPTER 13
Diminutives provide multiple benefits for language acquisition 319
Vera Kempe, Patricia J. Brooks, Steven Gillis

Conclusions 343
Ineta Savickienė, Wolfgang U. Dressler

Subject index 351

Introduction

Ineta Savickienė and Wolfgang U. Dressler

1. Diminutives are commonly viewed as a characteristic of child speech (CS) and child-directed speech (CDS), but this has never been studied in a cross-linguistic way with adequate quantitative analyses nor in a qualitatively adequate manner, notably with reference to recent theoretical developments in the study of diminutives and their related evaluative (or alterative) classes of augmentatives and pejoratives (cf. Dressler & Merlini Barbaresi 1994, 1997, 2001; Jurafsky 1996; Corbin et al. 1999) and in reference to hotly debated issues in inflectional morphology or word formation and its acquisition (as focussed, e.g., in Clahsen 1999; Clahsen et al. 2003). We intend to do both, especially in order to show how and why diminutives emerge as the earliest category of derivational morphology in nearly all languages and of morphology as a whole in many languages.

2.1 Early research in baby talk (BT) noted that diminutives or hypocoristics are not only more frequently used in BT than in adult-directed speech (ADS) but also play a role in the development of the child's grammar. For example, Rūķe-Draviņa (1959) reported that Latvian has a rich variety of diminutive suffixes in ADS with these suffixes used even more commonly in BT.

2.2 Interesting results from experimental research on the acquisition of morphology, diminutives included, came from the morphologically poor English language. J. Berko in her classical study in 1958 showed how children from the age of 4 until 7 master English morphology and the derivation of diminutives. She observed that 50% of adults produced diminutives with several English suffixes (**wuglet, *wuggie, *wugette*), but none of the children used a diminutive suffix. 52% of children formed analytical phrases like *baby *wug* and *little *wug*. One interesting case was observed when two children said **wig*, employing sound symbolism where a narrow vowel stands for a small animal (1958: 168).

2.3 According to Ferguson (1977: 224), the 'most prominent expressive feature of BT probably is the hypocoristic affix.' The statement is supported by research into a number of languages investigated in this study (Dutch, Greek, Italian, Lithuanian, Russian, Spanish, a bit less in Austrian-German, Croatian, Hebrew, Hungarian, Turkish), which has demonstrated that diminutives are especially frequent when talking to children. It stands to reason, then, that due to the direct influence of CDS, diminutive suffixes are among the first morphemes that a child acquires.

2.4 In their longitudinal and experimental investigation of Italian diminutives, Bates and Rankin (1979) found, in a first phase of development, "no evidence of either understanding or an attempt to encode size or value concepts" (1979: 35). They claimed that, in a later phase, denotative (or semantic, i.e. size-related) concepts emerge, with pragmatic (or connotative or value-related) concepts acquired even later, such as metaphoric and interpersonal speech in general. It should be noted that Bates and Rankin incorrectly classified Italian diminutives as inflectional, rather than derivational morphology. Although diminutives are inflectional morphology in Bantu languages, and diminutives in other languages may share some properties with inflections, diminutives in Italian and in all of the other languages studied in this volume are derivational (cf. Dressler & Merlini Barbaresi 1994).

2.5 Dressler (1994), Dressler and Karpf (1995) have claimed that diminutives are also acquired early because they belong to non-prototypical derivational morphology, which is easier to acquire than prototypical derivational or inflectional morphology. Due to their early acquisition, diminutives may have some properties of extra-grammatical and marginal morphology, such as truncations, applicability to bases other than nouns, preservation of the gender of the base noun in the diminutive derived from it. This proposal has been integrated into a model of development from pre- over protomorphology to morphology proper established within the *Crosslinguistic Project on Pre- and Protomorphology in Language Acquisition*.[1] In this model premorphology precedes the child's detection of morphology (as indicated by the emergence of mini-paradigms, i.e. incomplete paradigms consisting at least of three contrasting, freely used contrasting paradigm members, see Kilani-Schoch & Dressler 2002; Bittner et al. 2003), protomorphology starts with the first generalisations of morphological patterns (usually beginning already before age 2), morphology proper (or modularized morphology) starts to resemble adult morphology, cf. Dressler (1997), Voeikova and Dressler (2002), Bittner, Dressler and Kilani-Schoch (2003).

2.6 In her experimental study, Dąbrowska (2006) administered an inflection formation test with nonce words, half of which resembled diminutives, to Polish adults and to three groups of Polish children (aged between 2;4 and 4;8). Especially young children did better on diminutives than simplex nouns (but not in neuters) and substituted simplex nouns more often with diminutives than vice versa. Dąbrowska interpreted this pattern as evidence for the greater impact of low-level schemas than of general rules of inflection. Unfortunately she specifies neither the properties of diminutive inflection schemas (which include vowel-zero alternation in the masculines and morphophonological rules of palatalization in the feminines) nor of the errors committed nor does she discuss the advantages and disadvantages of different schema approaches (totally omitting the most elaborated one of Köpcke 1993, 1998). On other research on saliency see § 6.1.

3.1 With this volume we intend to innovate in several respects: we will look closely into the difference between diminutives and hypocoristics and into the gradual transition between them and explicate how young children differ in this categorization from adults. Diminutives are derived from common nouns, and in many languages also from adjectives, adverbs, etc. (cf. Dressler & Merlini Barbaresi 1994; Nieuwenhuis 1985; Grandi 2002). Hypocoristics are derived from proper names, either by diminutive suffixes or a subset of them (e.g., *Jonny* vs. **John-let, Annie, Annette*) or by reduction (e.g., *Pete, Mike, Liz*) or by other suffixes or by a combination of such operations. Finally there is, especially for children, the special category of common-noun diminutives used as hypocoristic names for caretakers, such as *mummy, daddy, granny*, which behave like names also in other respects, i.e. pragmatically or in some languages syntactically, e.g., in German by feminine nouns taking the masculine and neuter genitive *-s*, as in *Maria-s Haus, Mutter-s Haus, Mutt-i-s Haus* 'Mary's / Mother's / Mummy's house' vs. *der Mutter Haus* 'the mother's house.'

3.2 Furthermore, we will attempt to transcend cross-linguistic juxtaposition of languages (i.e. of the time course of diminutive acquisition) towards a real typological analysis. We will relate the acquisition of diminutives to typological properties of the morphology of the target languages (from most agglutinating Turkish to introflecting Hebrew and strongly vs. weakly inflecting-fusional Indo-European languages) and to the properties of diminutives intermediate between prototypical derivational and prototypical inflectional morphology. Wherever there are sufficient data we will try to support our findings by statistical analysis.

3.3 Another typological criterion is morphological richness in the domain of diminutives. Beyond the question of whether diminutives are accompanied by augmentatives and/or pejoratives in their inventories, languages differ in the number of diminutive operations – in our languages: the number of suffixes, especially productive suffixes. Such differences may (but need not) be paralleled by the generality of application of these rules, i.e. by the conditions of their application (e.g., whether a given suffix may also be attached to adjectives and adverbs or how it is restricted in its application to different types of nouns). Finally the higher or lower degree of productivity may be paralleled by higher or lower frequency of usage. Such differentiation between generality, consequences for type frequency, token frequency and productivity makes most sense if one defines productivity in Schultink's way, as translated by van Marle (1985: 45), as "the possibility for language users to coin, unintentionally, a number of formations which are in principle uncountable" (cf. Dressler 2003; Dressler & Ladányi 2000). Finally, a language may have, among diminutive formation rules, a default, i.e. the rule normally used, in contrast to rules used under specific conditions only, as in English the default *-y/-ie*, in contrast to the non-default suffixes *-let, -ette* (more on default in Clahsen 1999). In this volume, the main question will be the impact of such typological differences, as manifested in the input, on the emergence and development of diminutives in the children's output.

4. Usually, the term diminutive is interpreted as a category, which expresses smallness and endearment. Most research (cf. Grandi 2002; Kiefer 2004) views smallness as the basic meaning of diminutives, with connotations associated with emotions and assessment dealt with as pragmatic extensions of this basic semantic meaning (but see the counter-arguments in Dressler & Merlini Barbaresi 1994: 141ff). In contrast, others view pragmatic meanings attached to speech situations and speech events as basic (cf. Sifianou 1992; Dressler 1994; Dressler & Merlini Barbaresi 1994, 1997; Jurafsky 1996; Gillis 1997; Stephany 1997). Here, evidence from our 'Crosslinguistic project on pre- and protomorphology in language acquisition' has supported the assumption that the acquisition of at least some pragmatic connotations of diminutives (i.e. morphopragmatics) precedes their semantic meanings (morphosemantics, see Dressler & Merlini Barbaresi 1997, cf. the publications on diminutive acquisition in Dressler 1997b and Gillis 1998). Can this be seen as external evidence for the priority of pragmatic over semantic meanings of diminutives (cf. Dressler & Merlini Barbaresi 2001)? Or even for the semiotic view (cf. Morris 1971) of semantics being a decontextualized and thus more abstract subpart of pragmatics as opposed to the view that pragmatic meaning involves a secondary application and adaptation of semantic meaning to speech situations (cf. Kiefer 2004)? In any event, the importance of pragmatic meanings of diminutives sets them apart from nearly all other types and categories of word formation.

However, in early phases of the emergence of diminutives, children often seem to use base nouns and their diminutive derivations indiscriminately, i.e. without any apparent difference in meaning. Moreover, no meaning differences among the competing suffixations from the same basis have been ascertained. This challenges Eve Clark's (1993, 1995) Principle of Contrast (cf. Dressler 1994, 1997a). This principle states that 'children will assume that differences in form mark differences in meaning' and that 'different forms necessarily have different meanings. So if the meanings of two forms are the same, one form must be eliminated' (Clark 1995: 394). Another problem for this principle is children's frequent use of two different diminutives/ hypocoristics derived from the same base without any tangible meaning difference. Some of the chapters will discuss solutions to this problem.

5.1 It has been claimed that diminutives may simplify the acquisition of inflectional noun morphology and may therefore be preferred to their base nouns (Olmsted 1994; Laalo 1998; Kempe & Brooks 2001; Kempe et al. 2001, 2003, Savickienė 2001, 2003). But both connected claims have not been thoroughly checked or supported by sufficient quantitative data or by statistical analysis. For example, the transfer from an unproductive and opaque opposition of the base noun in number and case into a productive and transparent one of the corresponding diminutive would predict a difference in the time course of acquisition. For example, the opposition between Sg. and Pl. in the declension class of It. *ami[k]o*, Pl. *ami[č]i* is both unproductive and morphotactically opaque, whereas the respective opposition between its diminutive Sg. *amichetto* and Pl. *amichetti* (with identical [k]) is both productive and transparent. Accordingly, the productive and transparent opposition may be acquired earlier than the unproductive and opaque one, and in this way diminutives may facilitate the acquisition of morphology (cf. Kempe & Brooks 2001) and strengthen the salience of productive and transparent morphological patterns. Notably, in such cases, the time interval between the emergence of the two partners of the opposition should be ceteris paribus (i.e. after removing frequency effects and other confounding variables) smaller for diminutives than for their simplex bases. Moreover children may prefer transparent and/or productive inflection of diminutives over opaque and/or unproductive inflection of their respective bases.

5.2 However, if the simplex and its diminutive belong to the same productive and transparent class, then there should be no such shorter time course of acquisition for diminutives nor a preference for diminutives. This can be checked both within the same language and cross-linguistically. For example, Turkish has nearly no such difference between base nouns and diminutive nouns, whereas Hungarian, another agglutinating language, does. Such differences in the time course of the emergence of form oppositions and mini-paradigms (cf. Bittner, Dressler & Kilani-Schoch 2003) and in the token frequencies of diminutives used will be both checked statistically within single languages and compared cross-linguistically.

5.3 It will be discussed whether and to what extent such declensional class distinctions can be seen as an instance of the distinction between a default and non-default class and between regular and irregular morphology (in the sense of Clahsen 1999; Clahsen et al. 2003; Marcus 2000) and how this shift from the latter to the former class in early diminutive acquisition can be analyzed in terms of dual-mechanism hypotheses. Do native speakers of Turkish have a very differently distributed dual-mechanism in inflectional morphology, because nearly everything is done by the rule mechanism, which leaves nothing to irregular stored morphology, and does this explain why Turkish morphology is acquired much earlier (cf. Aksu-Koç & Ketrez 2003) than the morphology of other languages? And is there among early emerging diminutive formations evidence for a dual-mechanism account, in the sense of extracting rules only for some diminutive formations, whereas the other suffixations are merely stored in the lexicon (cf. Clahsen et al. 2003)?

6.1 We will also explore whether diminutivization has effects on other domains of language. For example, it has been suggested that diminutivization might regularize patterns of metric stress thereby simplifying the problem of word segmentation (Jusczyk 1997; Kempe et al. in press) and of identifying structural patterns at the right edge of words, making them more salient (cf. also Dąbrowska 2006 in § 2.6). In other words, can diminutives be used as bootstrapping devices (cf. Weissenborn & Höhle 2001)?

If diminutive derivations are more salient, they should have preferential status in the speech of children despite their greater formal complexity, insofar as diminutive nouns are longer than their corresponding base nouns (in contrast to truncated hypocoristics, see above) and are morphologically derived (sc. after children have detected their morphological make-up).

6.2 In this book, we will not study in depth the question of whether diminutives facilitate conversational interaction and the acquisition of discourse strategies (cf. King & Melzi 2004; Melzi & King 2003), although the pragmatics of caretakers' facilitation strategies in the use of diminutives is included in most chapters. Another socio-pragmatic question that several chapters of this volume will touch (Bodor & Barcza; Korecky-Kröll & Dressler; Laalo; Protassova & Voeikova) but not discuss at length is whether girls use diminutives more than boys (cf. Berko Gleason et al. 1990).

7.1 Going beyond previous cross-linguistic publications on the acquisition of diminutives (most advanced in Gillis ed. 1998), this volume combines: 1) eleven longitudinal studies on spontaneous child-caretaker interactions in single languages (based on parallel data collection, transcription and morphological coding according to CHILDES methodology, cf. MacWhinney 2000); 2) two experimental papers on Hebrew and on the contrast between Russian and Dutch. The two experimental papers have included, supplementing and checking the longitudinal dimension by comparison with the transversal one.

7.2 The languages represented are: the strongly inflecting-fusional Indo-European languages Lithuanian (Baltic), Russian (Slavic), both rich in diminutives, and, less rich in diminutives, the Slavic language Croatian, then Greek, which is rich in diminutives but less strongly inflecting-fusional in noun morphology, the two weakly inflecting-fusional Romance languages Italian and Spanish, both rich in diminutives, and the two Germanic languages Dutch and Austrian-German, of which the first is much richer in diminutives but even more weakly inflecting-fusional than the other. Non-Indo-European languages are represented by the mainly agglutinating Finno-Ugric languages Hungarian and Finnish and by the strongly agglutinating Turkish, and finally by the introflecting Semitic language Hebrew.

8. The longitudinal chapters are based on intensive work done during the last ten years. They have a broader coverage and address a greater number of topics more systematically than could be done in previous studies published in the volumes edited by Dressler (1997b), Gillis (1998), Voeikova and Dressler (2002).

Main points of the chapters are:

8.1 I. Savickienė's paper *Form and meaning of diminutives in Lithuanian child language* discusses the acquisition of diminutives in its quantitative and qualitative aspects. Diminutives in Lithuanian present an interesting case not only from a morpho-pragmatic point of view (which is shared with other chapters of this volume), but also from an inflection-class perspective: the Lithuanian child's frequent use of diminutives is also due to the fact that it facilitates the acquisition of declensional noun endings by restricting the number of paradigm patterns to three instead of the traditional twelve declensional classes.

8.2 E. Protassova and M. Voeikova in their paper *Diminutives in Russian at the early stages of acquisition* explore the acquisition of diminutives within the context of "mother-child" interaction, comparing two case studies of children exemplifying different cognitive styles and strategies of language acquisition. They report the frequent use of diminutives in child-directed situations as a characteristic feature of CDS and child speech, which is explained by pragmatic and structural reasons, e.g., diminutives usually move from the unproductive and marginal declensional classes to the productive ones. The authors analyze the data of two Russian children and claim that the frequency of diminutive usage varies markedly across families.

8.3 The paper by M. Palmović *The acquisition of diminutives in Croatian* shows that diminutives are a prominent feature of CDS in Croatian. According to the data of the Croatian child language corpus, children acquire them early, i.e. before the age of 2 years. Although phonologically more difficult, diminutives help children to detect morphology, make paradigms more transparent and reduce the number of noun classes. Diminutive formation in Croatian is a productive model of derivational morphology. The range of meanings of diminutives is wide, i.e. from smallness to pejorative and irony, depending on the word that is diminutivized and the context.

8.4 In their contribution *Diminutives in Greek child language* based on extensive longitudinal data of one child (1;8 – 3;0), E. Thomadaki and U. Stephany show that the richness of diminutive endings characteristic of the Greek language is reflected in the array and frequency of diminutives found in early child Greek. From the age of 2;3 on, the six most frequent diminutive suffixes occurring in the child's speech follow the type frequency of CDS quite closely. The most frequent diminutive suffix (*-aki*) occurs in a high number of singular and plural forms both type- and token-wise from 1;9 on. Since this type of diminutives does not allow case distinctions it cannot facilitate the development of case. Pragmatic rather than semantic reasons seem to be involved in the choice of diminutives as opposed to simplex nouns at an early age.

8.5 Next comes a joint paper by S. Noccetti, A. de Marco, L. Tonelli and W. U. Dressler *The role of diminutives in the acquisition of Italian morphology*. Diminutives are very productive in Italian and their formation is one of the first morphological operations that children acquire. The quantitative and qualitative analysis is focused on four children's development of diminutives from the beginning of premorphology to morphology proper. The analysis shows a close parallelism between mothers' and their children's use of diminutives, both in their variants, in the syntactic categories to which they are attached, and in the semantic domains selected for diminutivization. But it also stresses children's overgeneralizations and use of idiosyncratic constructions, as well as the relation between the acquisition of diminutives and augmentatives.

8.6 Another joint contribution by M. J. Albalá, C. Aguirre and V. Marrero, *The acquisition of diminutives in Spanish: a useful device*, is based on quantitative and qualitative analysis of two corpora of longitudinal spontaneous speech data. It shows diminutivization as a highly productive morphological mechanism, mastered very quickly at a very early stage, which plays an important role as a forerunner for the rest of morphology. The Spanish diminutive system reinforces this fact because of the phonological saliency, high productivity of diminutivization of nouns and adjectives, highly regular suffixation and transparency (form-meaning biuniqueness).

8.7 A. Souman and S. Gillis, in the paper *A longitudinal study of the acquisition of diminutives in Dutch,* analyze diminutives in the corpora of three children in their third year of life and show that diminutives appear from early on and occur with high frequency in the language of the children. They show that the order in which the allomorphs emerge in the children's language, reflects the frequency of the allomorphs in the parental input. Furthermore, CDS is compared to the frequency of diminutives in Dutch ADS. It turns out that the claim with a long-standing history, that diminutives are typical for CDS, is indeed correct: the Spoken Dutch Corpus contains significantly less diminutivized nouns than a corpus of CDS. Moreover, the frequency distribution of the diminutive allomorphs is the same for CDS and ADS in terms of types (lemmas), but in the actual usage (tokens), differs significantly.

8.8 According to the paper by K. Korecky-Kröll and W. U. Dressler *Diminutives and hypocoristics in Austrian German (AG)*, hypocoristics and diminutives emerge simultaneously with plural and compound formation and the first inflection-form oppositions in verbs. Pragmatic and semantic meanings emerge simultaneously, although there is a preponderance of pragmatic meanings. Even though diminutives are relatively rare in German, even in more diminutive-prone Austrian German, individual variation between the two investigated Viennese children is considerable.

8.9 P. Bodor and V. Barcza in the paper *Acquisition of diminutives in Hungarian* present an investigation which is the first real transcription based on a longitudinal study of the acquisition of Hungarian. The data show that the two children investigated in this study followed their own particular paths while acquiring diminutive suffixes. Most probably this was influenced by the input of their families. Grammatical productivity did not exert an unequivocal effect on the sequence of acquisition: both children started with unproductive suffixes, whereas the grammatically most productive suffix was produced later. The analysis indicates that diminutive suffixes did not convey the semantic meaning of "smallness"; in addition, a positive emotional evaluation of a pragmatic value of diminutives was not clearly present in the analysed conversations.

8.10 K. Laalo in his paper *Diminutives in Finnish child-directed and child speech* shows that diminutives in Finnish CS and CDS are interesting not only from the morphopragmatic perspective but also from the morphophonemic one: using diminutives is one way to avoid some complex stem alternations. Finnish diminutives generally have a more transparent inflection pattern than their corresponding base nouns, and the process of diminutive formation thus includes a shift to a more transparent and productive inflection class.

8.11 F. N. Ketrez and A. Aksu-Koç in their study *The (scarcity of) diminutives in Turkish child speech* report that diminutive morphology is not one of the early acquisitions in Turkish child speech (1;3–2;0) although the language has a number of productive diminutive morphemes. The authors attribute the scarcity of diminutives and hypocoristic forms in child speech to their infrequent use in the input speech and the complexity of the diminutive formation in the language, which does not have properties that could facilitate word learning.

9.1 The chapter *Acquiring diminutive structures and meanings in Hebrew: an experimental study* by A. Hora, G. Avivi-Ben Zvi, R. Levie and D. Ravid presents the acquisition of diminutives in Hebrew as a part of later language development, that is, linguistic acquisition during the school years. The experiments described in the chapter indicate that the morphological, semantic, pragmatic, and cognitive knowledge involved in producing and explaining Hebrew diminutives is acquired mostly between the ages of 9 and 12. This path of acquisition is presented in the paper against the background of juvenile diminutives, a simplex device ushering in morphology in very young Hebrew-speaking children.

9.2 V. Kempe, P. J. Brooks and S. Gillis in *Diminutives provide multiple benefits for language acquisition* summarize a body of experimental research showing that diminutives, which are pervasive in the child-directed speech registers of many languages, provide a number of cues on different levels of linguistic analysis that are useful for language acquisition. The studies that are reported demonstrate how experimental methods can be used to test hypotheses about the role of diminutives in first and second language acquisition. Focus is on Dutch and Russian.

Notes

1. The *Crosslinguistic Project on Pre- and Protomorphology in Language Acquisition* is coordinated by Wolfgang U. Dressler, sponsored and partially financed by the Austrian Academy of Sciences, in part also funded by the Austrian "Fonds zur Förderung der Wissenschaftlichen Forschung" (projects P 10250-SPR and P 13681-SPR). These have also been sources of funding for the work on several chapters of this volume.

Acknowledgments

We want to thank Ursula Stephany and other volume contributors for their helpful comments on earlier version of the *Introduction* and *Conclusion* chapters, and Patricia Brooks for her revision of English.

References

Aksu-Koç, A. and Ketrez, F. N. 2003. Early verbal morphology in Turkish: Emergence of inflections. In *Mini-paradigms and the emergence of verb morphology*, D. Bittner, W.U. Dressler and M. Kilani-Schoch (eds), 27–52. Berlin: De Gruyter.

Bates, E. and Rankin, J. 1979. Morphological development in Italian: connotation and denotation. *Journal of Child Language* 6: 29–52.

Berko, J. 1958. The child's learning English morphology. *Word* 14: 150–177.
Berko Gleason, J., Perlmann, R. Y., Ely, R. and Evans, D. W. 1990. The baby talk register: Parent's use of diminutives. In *Handbook of Research in Language Development using CHILDES*, J. L. Sokolov and C. E. Snow (eds), 50–76. Hillsdale, NJ: Lawrence Erlbaum Associates.
Bittner, D., Dressler, W U. and Kilani-Schoch, M. 2003 (eds.). Development *of Verb Inflection in First Language Acquisition: A Cross-Linguistic Perspective*. Berlin: Mouton de Gruyter.
Clahsen, H. 1999. Lexical entries and rules of language: A multidisciplinary study of German inflection. *Behavioral and Brain Sciences* 22: 991–1060.
Clahsen, H., Sonnenstuhl, I. and Blevins, J. P. 2003. Derivational morphology in the German mental lexicon: A dual mechanism account. In *Morphological Structure in Language Processing*, H. R. Baayen and R. Schreuder (eds), 125–155. Berlin: Mouton de Gruyter.
Clark, E. 1993. *The lexicon in acquisition*. Cambridge, England: Cambridge University Press.
Clark, E. 1995. Later lexical development and word formation. In *The handbook of the child language*, P. Fletcher and B. MacWhinney (eds), 393–412. Oxford: Blackwell.
Corbin, D., Dal, G., Fradin, B., Habert, B., Kerleroux, F., Plénat M. and Roché, M. (eds.). 1999. La morphologie des dérivés évaluatifs [Forum de morphologie (2e rencontre), Toulouse 29–30 avril 1999. Special issue]. *Silexicales* 2.
Dąbrowska, E. 2006. Low-level schemas or general rules? The role of diminutives in the acquisition of Polish case inflections. *Language Sciences* 28: 120–135.
Dressler, W. U. 1994. Evidence from first phases of morphology acquisition for linguistic theory: extragrammatic morphology and diminutives. *Acta linguistica Hafniensia* 27: 93–105.
Dressler, W. U. 1997a. Zur Entstehung der Distinktivität in der Kindersprache. In *Polyphonie pour Iván Fónagy*, J. Perrot (ed.), 127–136. Paris: Harmattan.
Dressler, W. U. (ed.). 1997b. *Studies in Pre- and Protomorphology*. Wien: Verlag der Österreichischen Akademie der Wissenschaften.
Dressler, W. U. 2003. Degrees of grammatical productivity in inflectional morphology. *Rivista di Linguistica* 15: 31–62.
Dressler, W. U. and Karpf A. 1995. The theoretical relevance of pre- and protomorphology in language acquisition. In *Yearbook of morphology 1994*, G. Booij and J. Van Marle (eds), 99–122. Dordrecht: Kluwer Academic Publishers.
Dressler, W. U. and Merlini Barbaresi, L. 1994. *Morphopragmatics. Diminutives and intensifiers in Italian, German, and other languages*. Berlin: Mouton de Gruyter.
Dressler, W. U. and Merlini Barbaresi, L. 1997. Morphopragmatics. In *Handbook of Pragmatics*, J. Verschueren et al. (eds). Amsterdam: Benjamins.
Dressler, W. U. and Ladányi, M. 2000. On contrastive word formation: German and Hungarian denominal adjective formation. In *Words: Structure, meaning, function*, Ch. Dalton-Puffer and N. Ritt (eds), 59–74. Berlin: Mouton de Gruyter.
Dressler, W. U. and Merlini Barbaresi, L. 2001. Morphopragmatics of diminutives and augmentatives: on the priority of pragmatics over semantics. Diminutives and intensifiers in Italian, German, and other languages. In *Perspectives on Semantics, Pragmatics and Discourse*, I. Kenesei and R. Harnish (eds), 43–58. Amsterdam: Benjamins.
Ferguson, Ch. A. 1977. Baby talk as simplified register. In *Talking to children: Language input and acquisition*, C. A. Snow and Ch. A. Ferguson (eds), 209–235. Cambridge: Cambridge University Press.
Gillis, S. 1997. The acquisition of diminutives in Dutch. In *Studies in Pre- and Protomorphology*, W. U. Dressler (ed.), 165–179. Wien: Österreichischen Akademie der Wissenschaften.

Gillis, S. (ed.). 1998. *Studies in the acquisition of number and diminutive marking.* [Antwerp papers in linguistic 95]. Antwerp: Universiteit Antwerpen.

Grandi, N. 2002. *Morfologie in contatto: Le costruzioni valutative nelle lingue del Mediterraneo.* Milano: FrancoAngeli.

Jurafsky, D. 1996. Universal tendencies in the semantics of the diminutive. *Language* 72 (3): 533–578.

Jusczyk, P. W. 1997. *The discovery of spoken language.* Cambridge, MA: MIT Press.

Kempe V. and Brooks, P. J. 2001. The role of diminutives in Russian gender learning: Can child-directed speech facilitate the acquisition of inflectional morphology? *Language Learning* 51: 221–256.

Kempe, V., Brooks, P. J., Gillis, S. and Samson, G. (in press). Diminutives facilitate word segmentation in natural speech: Cross-linguistic evidence. *Memory and Cognition.*

Kempe, V., Brooks, P.J., Mironova, N. and Fedorova, O. 2003. Diminutivization supports gender acquisition in Russian children. *Journal of Child Language* 30: 1–15.

Kempe V., Brooks, P. J. and Pirott, L. 2001. How can child-directed speech facilitate the acquisition of morphology? In *Research on Child Language Acquisition: Proceedings of the 8th conference of the International Association for the Study of Child Language*, M. Almgren, A. Barrena, M.-J. Ezeizabarrena, I. Idiazabal, and B. MacWhinney (eds), 1237–1247. Medford, MA: Cascadilla Press.

Kiefer, F. 2004. Morphopragmatic phenomena in Hungarian. *Acta Linguistica Hungarica* 51: 325–349.

Kilani-Schoch, M. and Dressler, W. U. 2002. The emergence of inflectional paradigms in two French corpora: An illustration of general problems of pre- and protomorphology. In *Pre- and Protomorphology: early phases of morphplogy development in nouns and verbs*, M. D. Voeikova and W. U. Dressler, 45–59. Munich: Lincom Europa.

King, K. and Melzi, G. 2004. Intimacy, imitation and language learning: Spanish diminutives in mother-child conversation. *First Language* 24(2): 241–261.

Köpcke, K. M.. 1993. *Schemata bei der Pluralbildung im Deutschen.* Tübingen: Narr.

Köpcke, K. M. 1998. The acquisition of plural marking in English and German revisited: schemata vs. rules. *Journal of Child Language* 25: 293–319.

Laalo, K. 1998. Diminutives in Finnish child-directed and child speech. In *Studies in the acquisition of number and diminutive marking* [Antwerp papers in linguistic 95], S. Gillis (ed.), 138–148. Antwerp: Universiteit Antwerpen.

MacWhinney, B. 2000. *The CHILDES Project. Tools for Analyzing Talk.* Third Edition. Mahwah, NJ: Lawrence Erlbaum Associates.

Marcus, G. F. 2000. Children's overregularization and implications for cognition. In *Models of language acquisition: inductive and deductive approaches*, P. Broeder and J. Murre (eds), 154–176. Oxford: Oxford University Press.

Melzi, G. and King, K. A. 2003. Spanish diminutives in mother-child conversations. *Journal of Child Language* 30: 281–304.

Morris, Ch. 1971. *Writings on the general theory of signs.* Hague: Mouton.

Nieuwenhuis, P. 1985. Diminutives. PhD dissertation, University of Edinburgh.

Olmsted, H. 1994. Diminutive morphology of Russian children: A simplified subset of nominal declension in language acquisition. In *Alexander Lipson: In memoriam*, 165–207. Columbus, Ohio: Slavica Publishers Inc.

Rūķe-Draviņa, V. 1959. *Diminutive im Lettischen.* Lund: Håkan Ohlsoons Boktryckeri.

Sifianou, M. 1992. The use of diminutives in expressing politeness: Modern Greek versus English. *Journal of pragmatics* 17: 155–173.

Savickienė, I. 2001. The role of diminutives in Lithuanian child language acquisition. *Linguistica Baltica* 9: 109–118.

Savickienė, I. 2003. *The Acquisition of Lithuanian Noun Morphology*. Wien: Österreichischen Akademie der Wissenschaften.

Stephany, U. 1997. Diminutives in early Greek. In *Studies in Pre- and Protomorphology*, W. U. Dressler (ed.), 145–156. Wien: Österreichischen Akademie der Wissenschaften.

van Marle, J. 1985. *On the Paradigmatic Dimension of Morphological Creativity*. Dordrecht: Foris.

Voeikova, M. D. and Dressler, W. U. (eds.). 2002. *Pre- and Protomorphology: early phases of morphology development in nouns and verbs*. Munich: Lincom Europa.

Weissenborn, J. and Höhle, B. (eds). 2001. *Approaches to bootstrapping: Phonological, syntactic and neurological aspects of early language acquisition*. Amsterdam/Philadelphia: Benjamins.

CHAPTER 1

Form and meaning of diminutives in Lithuanian child language

Ineta Savickienė

The aim of this chapter is to discuss the acquisition of diminutives from a quantitative and qualitative perspective. Diminutives in Lithuanian present an interesting case not only in terms of morphopragmatics (a feature which is shared by Lithuanian as well as other languages), but also from a language-specific point of view. We suggest that the early and frequent use of diminutives by the Lithuanian child is due to the fact that it facilitates the acquisition of declensional noun endings by restricting the number of paradigm patterns to 3 instead of the traditional 12 declension classes.

Introduction

Lithuanian is, at least in the realm of morphology, the most conservative of all living Indo-European languages, characterized by a very rich and complex inflectional morphology. The use of diminutives is rich in types and tokens, therefore, the study of diminutive formation is of a particular interest.

Cross-linguistically, the term 'diminutive' is interpreted as an item expressing smallness and endearment. However, one of the differences in the treatment of the term found in the literature is that the two senses are often separated. Most research views smallness as the basic meaning of the diminutive, whereas connotations, which are associated with emotions and assessment, are dealt with in the field of pragmatics (cf. Sifianou 1992; Dressler 1994; Dressler & Merlini Barbaresi 1994; Jurafsky 1996; Gillis 1997; Stephany 1997).

According to Lithuanian linguistic tradition, the study of diminutives does not distinguish between semantic and pragmatic senses characteristic of this type of noun; one reason for such a treatment is that these meanings are often very closely interrelated. The use of the diminutives may depend on the speech situation: they mainly occur in child-directed speech or are used to talk about small children. Adults use diminutives when they talk to good friends, parents or grandparents. It is obvious that the situations just mentioned are not formal situations; on the contrary, they relate to friendly or intimate exchanges, and Dressler and Merlini Barbaresi (1994: 218) refer to them as 'not serious' situations. Therefore, the prevailing meaning of diminutives is closely related to emotions, love and kindness in particular, when the addressee in a speech act is a dear person, especially a small child.

Research of the languages where an extensive use of diminutives was noted induced some scholars to advance the hypothesis to the effect that the use of diminutives simplifies the acquisition of nominal declension (Olmsted 1994; Laalo 1998; Savickienė 1998, 2001; Kempe et al. 2001, 2003).

The linguistic theory of morphological naturalness allows us to assume that children prefer productive to unproductive and transparent to non-transparent (opaque) morphology. In view of this, it is possible to hypothesize the following: first, children will produce relatively more diminutives if they are more productive and transparent than their respective simplex bases; second, children will produce more simplex forms if they are more productive and transparent compared to their diminutive derivatives.

To sum up, diminutives discussed in this chapter present an interesting case not only from a pragmatic perspective, but also from a language-specific point of view. We suggest that the Lithuanian child's early and frequent use of diminutives is due to the fact that it facilitates the acquisition of noun inflection.

1. Diminutives in Lithuanian

1.1 The Lithuanian language is characterized by a productive formation of diminutives from any noun via one or several competing suffixes. The most frequent and productive suffixes of diminutive formation are the masculine forms *-elis/-ėlis, -(i)ukas, -utis, -ytis, -aitis* and their feminine counterparts in *-ė: elė/-ėlė, -(i)ukė, -utė, -ytė, -aitė*. The unproductive suffixes do not occur either in input or output data.

Disyllabic nouns tend to be diminutivized more often than polysyllabic ones, e.g., *namas* 'house'– *nam-elis, nam-ukas, nam-ytis, saulė* 'sun'– *saul-ytė, saul-ulė, saul-elė,* but diminutives can also be formed from three- or four-syllable nouns, e.g., *saldainis* 'candy'– *saldain-iukas, saldain-ėlis, balionas* 'baloon'– *balion-ytis, balion-ėlis, balion-iukas, krokodilas* 'crocodile'– *krokodil-iukas.*

Noun diminutives provide the largest group of suffixed noun derivatives. Semantically this group consists of the names of animals, objects of everyday life, etc. Diminutives are not restricted to the names of physical entities; nouns denoting more abstract entities can also be diminutivized, e.g., *laikas – laikelis: Aš visai neturiu laikelio* 'time; I do not have time-DIM at all', *oras – orelis: Orelis šiandien nekoks* 'weather; The weather-DIM today is not good'.

A variety of suffixes are employed in the formation of diminutives from different lexico-semantic groups (at least three or four different suffixes can be attached interchangeably to the same lemma, e.g., *kepurė* 'cap'– *kepur-ytė, kepur-aitė, kepur-ėlė, kepur-iukė*, except for the group of abstracts nouns which are usually formed with the suffix *-elis/-elė (-ėlis/-ėlė)*, e.g., *nuotaika* 'mood'– *nuotaik-ėlė, sveikata* 'health'– *sveikat-ėlė, oras* 'weather'– *or-elis, darbas* 'work'– *darb-elis*).

Diminutives consisting of two subsequent suffixes are quite common in modern Lithuanian, e.g., *dal-el-yt-ė* 'particle-DIM-DIM', *žmog-el-iuk-as* 'man-DIM-DIM', *saul-ut-ėl-ė* 'sun-DIM-DIM'.[1] Double suffixation reinforces the pragmatic effectiveness or the meaning of smallness of the diminutive. Moreover, the number of subsequent diminutive suffixes in one word may amount to six. The greatest quantity and variety of diminutives can be found in folklore, whereas in modern spoken and written Lithuanian their usage is less frequent, except for the phenomenon of speech directed to children, dear persons or pets.

1.2 Hypocoristics, e.g., *Rūta – Rūt-elė, Rūt-ytė, Saulius – Saul-iukas, Saul-ytis* and special names in CDS, e.g., *mama – mam-ytė, mam-utė* 'mother-DIM', *tėv-elis, tėv-ukas* 'father-DIM' are very common as well. In hypocoristics, as well as in diminutives, all the productive suffixes are frequently used. Hypocoristics are more often formed from two-syllable nouns than from tri-syllabic ones. Hypocoristic truncations do not occur in our input and output data.

Hypocoristics as well as diminutives exhibit a gender shift. All the masculine noun bases, after diminutivization, retain the same gender, whereas feminine noun bases can be transformed to diminutives of masculine or feminine gender, e.g., *stalas* 'table:MASC' – *stal-iukas* 'table-DIM:MASC', but *kėdė* 'chair:FEM' – *kėd-utė* 'chair-DIM:FEM', *kėd-el-iuk-as* 'chair-DIM-DIM:MASC'; *Rūta – Rūt-ytė* 'Ruth:FEM, *Rūt-ukas* 'Ruth:MASC'.

1.3 Noun diminutive formation is very productive, but it is less so with adjectives (*balt-as – balt-utis* 'white'), ordinal numerals (*penkt-as – penkt-ukas* 'the fifth', with a class shift to nouns), some adverbs (*truputį – truput-ėlį* 'a little bit') and verbs (*šok-ti – šok-telėti* 'to jump'). The interjections, especially greetings, such as *labas* 'hello'– *lab-ukas, lab-utis, labanaktis* 'goodnight' – *labanakt-ukas, ačiū* 'thanks' – *ač-iukas* are often used in colloquial speech of adults.

There are other diminutive-like nominal derivatives with diminutive-like suffixes in Lithuanian but they are formed from verbs and not from noun bases, e.g., *myg-tukas* 'button' from *mygti* 'to press', *pieš-tukas* 'pencil' from *piešti* 'to draw', *trin-tukas* 'rubber' from *trinti* 'to rub' (7/35 in Rūta's speech, 10/43 in Mother's speech). Such nouns denote small objects, therefore children treat them as diminutives (it is most obvious in the case of back-formations).

1.4 Within the category of nouns diminutives show some processes of morphological simplification. The first and most important fact is that diminutives reduce the number of noun classes (see Table 1) with numerous endings and assign them to the masculine gender type of nominative *-as* or *-is*: Macroclass[2] I, microclasses 1 and 3. Nouns of the feminine gender type of nominative *-ė* occur only within one class, i.e., Macroclass II, microclass 3. Diminutives and hypocoristics only appear in the most productive declensional classes, i.e., I.1, I.3, and II.3. Since class II.1 is more productive than all the other feminine microclasses, but does not participate in diminutive formation (in contrast to microclass II.3), the dichotomy between productive and unproductive classes cannot be identified with a dichotomy between regular and irregular nouns or default and non-default classes.

Table 1. Noun classes with examples

Macroclass	Microclass	Gender	Ending of Sg. Nom.	Example
I.	**1 (product.)**	masc	-as	vyras 'man'
	2 (unproduct.)	masc.	-ias	kelias 'road'
	3 (product.)	masc.	-is, -ys	peilis 'knife'
	4 (unproduct.)	masc.	-us	medus 'honey'
	5 (unproduct.)	masc.	-ius	televizorius 'TV set'
	6 (unproduct.)	masc.	-is	dantis 'tooth'
	7 (unproduct.)	masc.	-uo	vanduo 'water'
II	1 (product.)	femin.	-a	ranka 'hand'
	2 (unproduct.)	femin.	-ia	vyšnia 'cherry'
	3 (product.)	femin.	-ė	bitė 'bee'
	4 (unproduct.)	femin.	-is	žuvis 'fish'
	(isolated p.)	femin.	-uo, -ė	sesuo 'sister'

Second, the use of diminutives helps to avoid stem alternations. This is especially obvious in the case of certain classes. For example, masculine nouns *vanduo* 'water' and *šuo* 'dog' (class I.7), and the feminine noun *sesuo* 'sister'(II.isolated paradigm):

(1) **Singular of simplex**

Nom.	*vanduo*	*šuo*	*sesuo*
Gen.	***vanden**-s*	***šun**-s*	***seser**-s*
Dat.	***vanden**-iui*	***šun**-iui*	***seser**-iai*
Acc.	***vanden**-į*	***šun**-į*	***seser**-į*
Inst.	***vanden**-imi*	***šun**-imi*	***seser**-imi*
Loc.	***vanden**-yje*	***šun**-yje*	***seser**-yje*

Singular of diminutive

Nom.	***vanden**-ukas*	***šun**-iukas*	*ses-ytė*
Gen.	***vanden**-uko*	***šun**-iuko*	*ses-ytės*
Dat.	***vanden**-ukui*	***šun**-iukui*	*ses-ytei*
Acc.	***vanden**-uką*	***šun**-iuką*	*ses-ytę*
Inst.	***vanden**-uku*	***šun**-iuku*	*ses-yte*
Loc.	***vanden**-uke*	***šun**-iuke*	*ses-ytėje*

The nominative singular of nouns belonging to these classes has no ending, just the stem which ends in *-uo*, but the other cases (e.g., genitive, dative, etc.) are based on another stem, i.e. *-en-*, *-un-* or *-er-*, and the appearance of a new element in a word changes it morphotactic transparency and hence causes difficulties to a child.

Also, if a noun in the nominative singular ends in *-tis, -tys, -dis, -dys*, in many other cases *t* and *d* change into *č* and *dž* respectively (morphonological palatalization). However, if the diminutive is used, no such changes occur (exemplified below). Consider the noun *dvirat-is* 'bike':

(2)

	Sg	Pl	DIM-Sg	DIM-Pl
Nom.	*dvirat-is*	*dvirač-iai*	*dvirat-uk-as*	*dvirat-uk-ai*
Gen.	*dvirač-io*	*dvirač-ių*	*dvirat-uk-o*	*dvirat-uk-ų*
Dat.	*dvirač-iui*	*dvirač-iams*	*dvirat-uk-ui*	*dvirat-uk-ams*
Acc.	*dvirat-į*	*dvirač-ius*	*dvirat-uk-ą*	*dvirat-uk-us*
Inst.	*dvirač-iu*	*dvirač-iais*	*dvirat-uk-u*	*dvirat-uk-ais*
Loc.	*dvirat-yje*	*dvirač-iuose*	*dvirat-uk-e*	*dvirat-uk-uose*

It can be concluded then that the inflection of diminutives is more transparent than the inflection of their bases.

1.5 It is worth pointing out that the Lithuanian accent is free. Sometimes different forms of the same word may carry the stress on different syllables. However, in the case of diminutives the suffix is always in a focal position by retaining stress. Consider in this respect the whole paradigms of the simplicia *akis* 'eye', *namas* 'house' and their diminutives *akýtė* 'eye-DIM:FEM' and *namùkas* 'house-DIM:MASC':

(3)

Singular				
Nom.	*akìs*	*akýtė*	*nãmas*	*namùkas*
Gen.	*akiẽs*	*akýtės*	*nãmo*	*namùko*
Dat.	*ãkiai*	*akýtei*	*nãmui*	*namùkui*
Acc.	*ãkį*	*akýtę*	*nãmą*	*namùką*
Inst.	*akimì*	*akýte*	*namù*	*(namukù)*
Loc.	*akyjè*	*akýtėje*	*namè*	*(namukè)*
Plural				
Nom.	*ãkys*	*akýtės*	*namaĩ*	*namùkai*
Gen.	*akių̃*	*akýčių*	*namų̃*	*namùkų*
Dat.	*akìms*	*akýtėms*	*namáms*	*namùkams*
Acc.	*akìs*	*akýtes*	*namùs*	*(namukùs)*
Inst.	*akimìs*	*akýtėmis*	*namaĩs*	*namùkais*
Loc.	*akysè*	*akýtėse*	*namuosè*	*namùkuose*

There is much less change or no change at all (as in *akýtė*) in the diminutives: only in three case forms the stress pattern changes, i.e. *namukù*-DIM:SG:INST, *namukè*-DIM:SG:LOC, *namukùs*-DIM:PL:ACC. Therefore, the exceptions in the stress pattern of peripheral cases which are acquired later, i.e., Sg. Inst., Loc., Pl. Acc. (Savickienė 1999), are not important at this phase of language acquisition.

1.6 The use of diminutives often depends on the speech situation: their highest frequency of occurrence is in child-directed speech. Unfortunately, there is no available source on the quantitative distribution of diminutives in ADS. Preliminary results are only available from the corpus of spontaneous conversations (the duration of exchanges is 186 minutes). The total number of noun tokens used in the dialogues is 2,954 and the number of diminutive tokens is 104, which makes only 3.5%.

3. Data

The following discussion is based on the analysis of data from a longitudinal corpus of a Lithuanian girl named Rūta. She is a first-born child of a middle-class family living in Vilnius. Her speech has been recorded in natural everyday situations by her mother, an educated philologist. Data collection[3] started in November 1993 when the child was 1;3 and continued up to 1996 when she was about 3;5. Recordings were made three or four times per week; they lasted about fifteen minutes each. For the present study we have chosen to analyze Rūta's speech covering the period from 1;7 to 2;6[4]. The corpus consists of almost 35 hours of recordings. The choice of the period was influenced by the fact that Rūta's onset of morphological development can be dated approximately around the age of 1;7 and continues until the age of 2;6, which marks the phase of morphology proper (Savickienė 2003).

The recorded speech was transcribed according to the requirements of CHILDES (MacWhinney 2000). Adult utterances were transcribed orthographically; the child's utterances, in addition, were transcribed phonetically.

4. The Development of diminutives in child language

4.1 In this section the analysis will focus on quantitative aspects of diminutives, hypocoristics and simplicia (for the absolute numbers see Table 2 and 3 in Appendix). As can be observed from Figures 1 and 2, Rūta has been using diminutives and hypocoristics since the very beginning of the recording (1;7). The spurt of diminutives was recorded one month later, i.e., at an early phase of word learning (1;8).

Thus at the beginning of lexicon formation, i.e. at 1;8, diminutives and hypocoristics (48%) are nearly as frequent as simplicia (52%). Diminutive tokens (Figure 2) even show a higher percentage of occurrence at the age of 2;0 and 2;2. The number of diminutive and hypocoristic types throughout the period is relatively stable (with the exception of 1;8, which is approximately 45% (Figure 1), whereas the frequency of diminutive and hypocoristic tokens increases during the period of 2;0 and remains at about 50% (Figure 2).

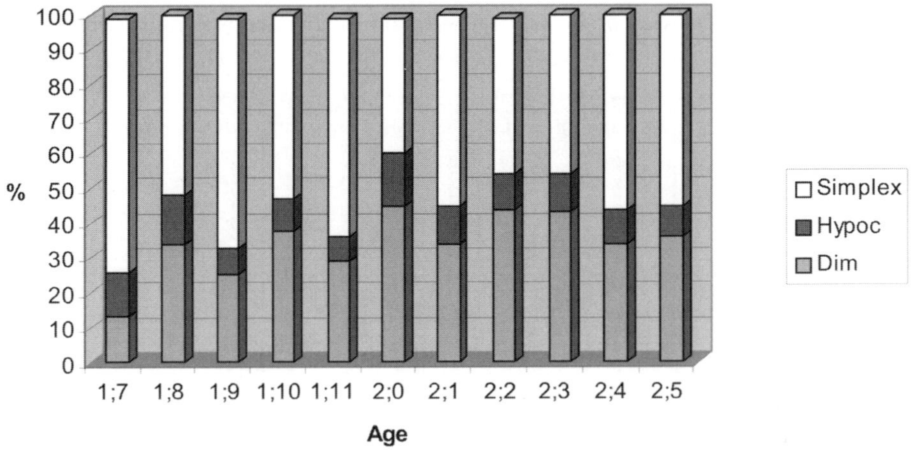

Figure 1. The frequency distribution of diminutive, hypocoristic and simplex types (%) in Rūta's speech (1;7–2;5)

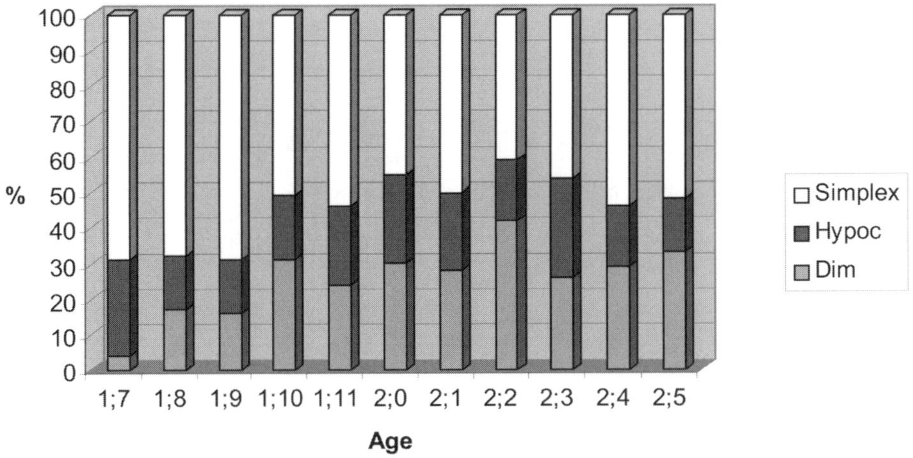

Figure 2. The frequency distribution of diminutive, hypocoristic and simplex tokens (%) in Rūta's speech (1;7–2;5)

4.2 It seems that the frequent use of diminutives and hypocoristics is characteristic of Lithuanian children and their mothers in the initial phase of language acquisition (unpublished observations on more than a dozen families). It is claimed in the literature that the period up to the age of three represents the 'peak' of diminutive usage and that in later periods this usage undergoes a sharp decline (King & Melzi 2004). The data analyzed here do not support this claim; in addition, it seems that the Mother uses diminutives and hypocoristics very often (see Figure 4) and we do not observe any decline.

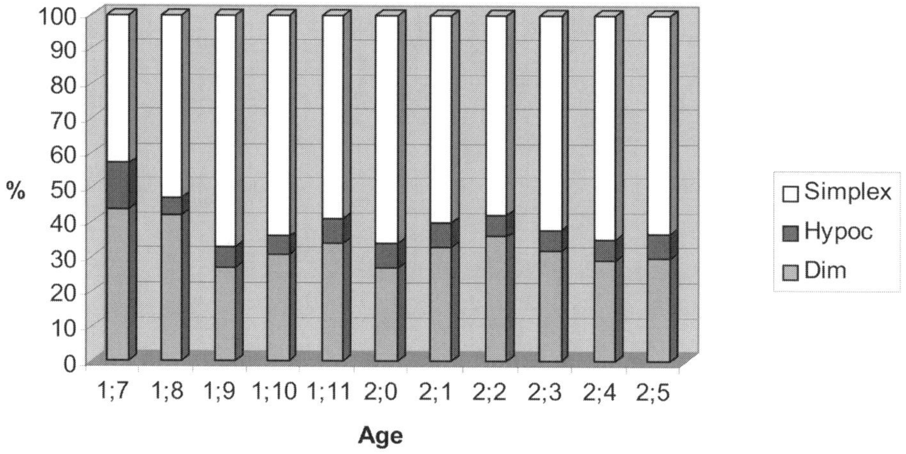

Figure 3. The frequency distribution of diminutive, hypocoristic and simplex types (%) in Mother's speech (1;7–2;5)

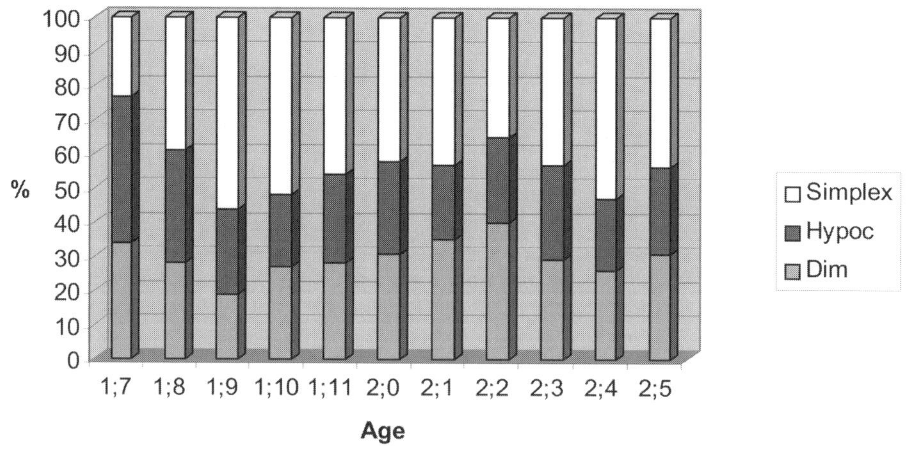

Figure 4. The frequency distribution of diminutive, hypocoristic and simplex tokens (%) in Mother's speech (1;7–2;5)

4.3 As can be observed from Rūta's data (see Figures 1 and 2), the average number of hypocoristic types is 10%, and the average number of tokens is about 20%. The average frequency of diminutives is 36% in types and 28% in tokens, the average frequency of simplicia is 54% in types and 52% in tokens. At the age of 2;0, 2;2 and 2;3 Rūta's speech shows an increased frequency of diminutives and hypocoristics (vs simplicia) both in types and tokens. The distribution of diminutive and hypocoristic tokens vs simplex tokens in the period of 2;0–2;6 is 52% vs 48%. If we compare the token frequency of diminutives and hypocoristics, we find among the latter a very frequent use of the girl's hypocoristic forms (*Rūt-ytė, Rūt-elė*) and Mother's name (*mam-ytė*). This may have facilitated the errorless acquisition of this class, i.e. II.3 (Nom. Sg. in *-ė*).

4.4 Figures 1–4 exemplify distribution of diminutive and hypocoristic types and tokens. We find that in both Rūta's and Mother's speech there are many more diminutives than is usually found in ADS (see § 1.6). What are the reasons for such a frequent usage of diminutives in the speech of Rūta and her mother?

Since diminutives are multisyllabic words, it may seem that they are difficult to produce, especially at a younger age. What could explain Rūta's preference for the phonologically more complicated words? A closer analysis of the Lithuanian noun declensional classes may be helpful in this respect.

As we saw in section 1.4, diminutives fall only into three, totally productive microclasses: microclass II.3 is reserved for the feminine gender, whereas the other two (I.1 and I.3) encompass masculine nouns (see Table 1). However, one masculine microclass – the most frequent one, with the nominative ending *-as* – is greatly preferred by Rūta. The predominance of this microclass is increased by the frequent use of the diminutive suffix *-uk-* which belongs to this microclass. Rūta simplifies the inflectional system by choosing one default diminutive suffix, *-uk-* for masculine and *-yt-* for feminine; both of them fall under the two most frequent microclasses, e.g., masculine I.1 *šuniukas* 'dog-DIM', *namukas* 'house-DIM', *ežiukas* 'hedgehog-DIM', feminine II.3 *sesutė* 'sister-DIM', *meškutė* 'teddy-bear-DIM', *bitutė* 'bee-DIM' (Savickienė 2003).

5. Formal aspects of diminutives

5.1 According to Bittner, Dressler and Kilani-Schoch (2003), the emergence of noun paradigms in a child's speech marks the starting point of detecting noun morphology. The first mini-paradigms with three contrasting forms in Rūta's data coincide with the beginning of protomorphology, i.e. 1;8 (Table 4). The first two-member mini-paradigms with verbs were found only one month later, i.e., at 1;9 (Wójcik 2003). It was observed that hypocoristic form oppositions develop into multi-member-paradigms, whereas diminutives establish only 2- or 3-member mini-paradigms (for examples, emergence and development of mini-paradigms see Table 5 and Figure 5 in Appendix).

Table 4. Frequency of mini-paradigms

Age	2-member mini-paradigm	True mini-paradigm (3 and multi-members)	Total	Total No of noun lemmas	Total No of noun tokens
1;7	–	–	–	15	52
1;8	1	2	3	56	339
1;9	11	9	20	163	1028
1;10	6	14	20	178	1174
1;11	5	6	11	140	863
2;0	9	12	21	126	1000
2;1	4	12	16	160	1010
2;2	6	20	26	156	1118
2;3	6	16	22	179	1158
2;4	7	13	20	190	1168
2;5	12	16	28	191	942

5.2 The analysis of the diminutive suffixes used by Rūta demonstrates that their choice and frequency is closely related to the respective usage by the Mother (see Table 6 for feminine nouns and Table 7 for masculine nouns).

Rūta's and Mother's usage is very similar: the most frequent suffix of the feminine gender is *-ytė*; the second is *-utė* and the third one is *-elė*, *-ėlė*. The most frequent suffix of the masculine gender is *-ukas* (more so with Rūta); then follow *-elis* and *-utis*.

The diminutive suffixes that Rūta and Mother use are among the most frequent ones that appear in spoken Lithuanian or fiction. According to Ambrazas et al. (1997), the suffixes *-elis* and *-elė* are the most frequent in newspapers, fiction, folklore etc. Mother's and, especially, Rūta's speech do not conform to this pattern: other suffixes, i.e., *-ytė* and *-ukas*, show the highest frequency and represent the default in Rūta's output. Thus, the most frequent and most productive suffixes *-ytė* and *-ukas* predominate in the girl's speech throughout the 1;7–2;5 period.

5.3 It is important to note that Rūta starts to use two or three different diminutive suffixes for the same lemma very early and without any difference in meaning, e.g., *t-elė, t-ytė* (*Rūt-elė, Rūt-ytė*) from Rūta (1;7); *mešk-iukas* (5), *mešk-utė* (6), *mešk-ytė* (1) from *meška* 'teddy-bear'; *med-ukas* (5), *med-utis* (1) from *medus* 'honey' (1;8); *kač-iukas* (1), *katin-ėlis* (1), *kat-ytė* (10) from *katė* 'cat'; *mašin-ėlė* (1), *mašin-ytė* (3) from *mašina* 'car' (1;9); *arbat-ėlė* (3), *arba-tytė* (2) from *arbata* 'tea' (1;10); *kišk-utis* (4), *kišk-ytis* (1) from *kiškis* 'rabit'; *rank-utė* (1), *rank-ytė* (1) from *ranka* 'hand' (2;0). These examples contradict Clark's principle of contrast (Clark 1995). This tendency is not usual in other languages where children learn diminutive suffixes one after another (Gillis 1997; De Marco 1998).

Table 6. Frequency of feminine nouns (types/tokens) relative to diminutive suffixes in Rūta's and Mother's speech (1;7–2;5)

Suffixes	**Feminine**							
	Rūta				**Mother**			
	Types		**Tokens**		**Types**		**Tokens**	
	No.	**%**	**No.**	**%**	**No.**	**%**	**No.**	**%**
-ytė	343	64	1933	76	252	53	3175	75
-elė	38	7	80	3	55	12	277	7
-ėlė	29	5	38	1	43	9	106	2
-utė	120	22	434	17	107	23	621	15
-ukė	1	0	1	0	4	1	4	0
-aitė	9	2	58	2	14	3	72	2
Total	540	100	2544	100	475	100	4255	100

Table 7. Frequency of masculine nouns (types/tokens) relative to diminutive suffixes in Rūta's and Mother's speech (1;7–2;5)

Suffixes	**Masculine**							
	Rūta				**Mother**			
	Types		**Tokens**		**Types**		**Tokens**	
	No.	**%**	**No.**	**%**	**No.**	**%**	**No.**	**%**
-elis	77	13	228	11	96	16	461	18
-ėlis	32	5	85	4	55	9	110	4
-ukas	434	74	1703	79	375	64	1640	65
-ytis	6	1	35	2	3	1	22	1
-utis	41	7	113	5	53	9	294	12
-aitis	0	0	0	0	1	0	1	0
Total	590	100	2164	100	583	100	2528	100

5.4 The formation of diminutives with two subsequent suffixes is quite common in modern Lithuanian. Our data do not show a frequent usage of diminutives with double suffixation in Rūta's or in Mother's speech, e.g., *ožk-yt-ėl-ė* from *ožka* 'goat', *diev-ul-iuk-as* from *dievas* 'god', *žmog-el-iuk-as* from *žmogus* 'man', *Rūt-ut-ėl-i* 'Rūta:VOC', *Rūt-yt-ėl-e* 'Rūta:VOC', *trup-uč-iuk-ą* 'a little', *žmog-el-iuk-as* 'man' (Rūta). Double suffixation reinforces diminutive meanings, at least pragmatically (see § 6).

It should be mentioned that up to the age of two Rūta had certain problems in pronouncing a longer word correctly. However, in spite of these pronunciation difficulties the diminutive suffix in Rūta 's speech has been retained, e.g., *teniùkas* (vandenukas) 'water-DIM', *teniùkas* (sausainiukas) 'biscuit-DIM', *kaliùkas* (auskariukas) 'earing-DIM', *etiùkas* (kamuoliukas) 'ball-DIM', *Týtė, Ūtýtė* (Rūtytė) 'Rūta-DIM' (valid until the age of two, due to the problems of pronouncing [r]).

5.5 Another related question to discuss is whether prosodic saliency is a potentially relevant factor since diminutives regularize stress patterns and thus simplify the task of segmenting the speech stream into words (Jusczyk 1997) thus making diminutives easier to identify. As our data show, diminutive suffixes are almost exclusively stressed (except in the rare instances, see § 1.5) and their word-final position makes them easy to be identified, distinguished and memorized by the girl. As a consequence of this (and in contrast to findings with children of many other languages), Rūta does not prefer trochaic diminutives, e.g., *niukas*, or diminutives with two trochees, e.g., *vandeniukas* 'water-DIM', but trisyllabic forms with a stress on the second syllable. The relevant examples are: *akýtė* 'eye-DIM', *duonýtė* 'loaf of bread-DIM', *kojýtė* 'leg-DIM', *lėlýtė* 'doll-DIM', *berniùkas* 'boy-DIM', *šuniùkas* 'dog-DIM', *kiškiùkas* 'hare-DIM'.

Thus, a salient feature of Lithuanian diminutives is that they represent word-final trochees, at least in the base forms and most case forms, and thus are easily identifiable by a child.

5.6 Since the beginning of recording and throughout the period of observation, Rūta used diminutives spontaneously. Even when her mother used simplicia, Rūta often used a diminutive (see example 9–11). This choice might be explained by the assumption that diminutives had predominated in Rūta's speech due to Mother's influence well before the recording started.

The examples below allow us to assert that Rūta has already acquired diminutive formation rules of adult language. She is not only able to spontaneously produce both simplicia and diminutives, but she also uses the diminutive in its correct, adult form; instances of incorrect diminutive formation were never noted even in the allomorphic distinction of *-elis* (with [æ]) being attached to disyllabic bases (*namas* 'house' → *nam-elis*) and of *-ėlis* (with [e]) suffixed to multi-syllabic bases (*balionas* 'ball', *krokodilas* 'crocodile' → *balion-ėlis, krokodil-ėlis*). The following examples illustrate Rūta's use of diminutives and simplicia for the same lemma in the same speech act, one immediately after the other:

(4) RŪT: *Statyk namą.*
build house:ACC!
'Build a house!'
RŪT: *Namuką.*
house-DIM:ACC.
'A house.' (1;10)

(5) RŪT: *Išsimaudė veidą.*
bathed face:ACC.
'She has bathed (i.e., washed) the face.'

RŪT: *Veiduką.*
face-DIM:ACC.
'The face.' (1;11)

Evidently, this early acquisition of diminutive forms is facilitated by the straightforward system of diminutive derivation in Lithuanian: to obtain a diminutive, any of the six masculine or six feminine diminutive suffixes can be attached to the root of the noun (e.g., *balionas* 'ballon', *balion-ėlis, balion-iukas, balion-ytis, balion-aitis* etc.). These diminutive variants are actually used in adult speech, but some of them not very frequently. Note that the common use of a certain diminutive suffix with a given lemma does not block the attachment of an alternative diminutive suffix (no synonymy blocking).

In cases when Mother used a new word in the basic form, at the beginning Rūta uses it in the same way, e.g., *žuvis* 'fish', *bitė* 'bee', *namas* 'house', *kiškis* 'hare', *saldainis* 'sweet', *mašina* 'car', *balionas* 'balloon'. However, all these words, with the exception of *namas* 'house', appeared as diminutives in Rūta's usage after just a few months. It is interesting to compare the relevant token frequencies: at 1;7 *žuvis* (5) – *žuvytė* (1) vs. *žuvis* (2) – *žuvytė* (5) at 2;4; at 2;3 *balionas* (24) – *balioniukas* (1) vs. *balionas* (7) – *balioniukas* (13) at 2;4; the same applies to *saldainis* (26) – *saldainiukas* (1) at 2;3 vs. *saldainis* (11) – *saldainiukas* (11) at 2;5.

One more example related to Rūta's preference for diminutives should be discussed. The first noun which appears in both forms, diminutive and simplex, is *batas* 'shoe'. At 1;7 Rūta spontaneously utters this word twice in the basic form. After a month the girl starts using the diminutive form as well, only the simplex is still more frequent, e.g., *batas* (4) – *batukas* (2) (1;8). However, from the period of 1;9 onwards the diminutive occurs more frequently, e.g., *batas* (1) – *batukas* (3) (1;9); *batas* (4) – *batukas* (5) (1;10); *batas* (3) – *batukas* (11) (2;0).

6. Productivity and transparency of diminutives

6.1 In Lithuanian all diminutives belong to productive inflectional classes, whereas many simple bases belong to unproductive ones. Thus, it is possible to compare the frequencies of diminutives having unproductive bases and those with productive ones. For this purpose we compare the ratio of the token frequencies of diminutives divided by their simplex bases (the other factor, that of transparency, remains equal). We found the following ratios [S = simplex, D = diminutive, p = productive, u = unproductive, t = transparent, o = opaque]:

D pt / S ut	D pt / S pt
3.81	2.08

The chi-square test shows a significant main effect: chi-square = 18.43, $p < 0.001$.

The results show that the girl appears to prefer diminutives to base nouns when this involves a switch from an unproductive to a productive inflection class.

6.2 We pass now to a discussion of morphotactic transparency/opacity. A non-transparent declensional class is one which includes an opacifying morphological or morphonological alternation of the type masculine Nom. Sg. *dviratis* 'bicycle', Gen. *dviračio* (with morphologized palatalization), as opposed to the transparent relation between diminutive Nom. Sg. *dvirat-ukas* and Gen. *dvirat-uko*. Let us compare the transparent and opaque simplex declensions with their corresponding transparent diminutives (keeping the variable of productivity constant). The respective ratios are:

D pt / S po	D pt / S pt
3.0	2.08

There are too few instances of opaquely inflected nouns and their diminutives in child speech for allowing statistical analysis. Nevertheless, diminutives are almost always preferred in such cases. This shows a tendency towards shifting from an opaque simplex declension to a transparent diminutive declension, but, because of the scarcity of pertinent data, the results of the chi-square test do not show a significant main effect: chi-square = 0.12.

6.3 Thus we can assume that the acquisition of diminutives simplifies the declensional system and thus facilitates its acquisition. Our results show that in Lithuanian those declensional classes which include diminutives emerge before those classes which do not include diminutives.

7. Semantics of diminutives

7.1 For a reliable analysis of diminutives, it is important to establish whether there are certain words that a child uses only as diminutives or only as simplicia, in contrast to words that appear in both forms. According to Clark's principle of contrast (1993, 1995: 394), a child relates difference in meaning to difference in form and vice versa. It follows that a child should perceive the two different forms of the same word – its basic meaning and the derived diminutive – as having two different meanings. In view of this we can predict that if a child has not yet perceived the basic semantic distinction of diminutives, that is, 'little, small' as opposed to 'normal-sized, large', and if he/she has not yet grasped the pragmatics of their usage, diminutives will not co-occur with their simplex base nouns.

Figure 6 summarizes the distribution of different noun types, i.e., simplicia (simplex), diminutives & hypocoristics (dim), and both forms, in Rūta's speech.

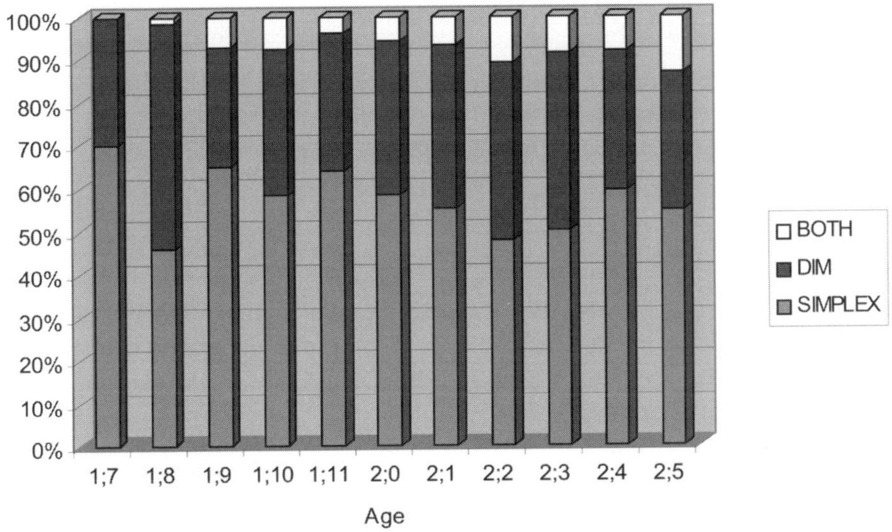

Figure 6. The distribution of noun types (percentage) used as either diminutive&hypocristic or simplex or both in Rūta's speech (1;7-2;5 period)

It can be seen from Figure 6 that Rūta uses the same noun either as a diminutive (approximately 35%) or as a simplex (approximately 55%). The average percentage of nouns used in both forms is rather low, just 8%; at the very beginning of recordings (i.e.1;7 – 1;8) this use amounted only to 3%, whereas since 2;2 onwards it increased almost to 12% (cf. § 5.1 on mini-paradigms). In contrast to types, the number of tokens of nouns that appear in both forms show different frequency of occurrences, i.e., diminutives are much more frequent. Some relevant examples are (for the time-course see § 5.5):

(6) *kamuolys* 'ball' (5) – *kamuoliukas* 'ball-DIM' (53),
koja 'leg' (2) – *kojytė* 'leg-DIM' (10),
ausis 'ear' (1) – *ausytė* 'ear-DIM' (10),
nosis 'nose' (1) – *nosytė* 'nose-DIM' (6),
batas 'shoe' (3) – *batukas* 'shoe-DIM' (11),
lėlė 'doll' (2) – *lėlytė* 'doll-DIM' (43), etc.

Rūta uses diminutive as well as simplex forms of the same noun to denote the same referent, i.e., she does not attribute different semantic meanings to different forms. Thus, Clark's (1995) assumption to the effect that different forms have different meanings is not corroborated by our data (cf. Dressler 1997b; Dressler & Merlini Barbaresi 1997). However, this does not exclude a difference in pragmatic meaning (see § 7).

7.2 The discussion of the semantics of diminutives entails answering the question whether Rūta uses diminutives in reference to small objects. In our examples where

Rūta uses both words, a simplex and a diminutive, there is no such difference in semantic meaning, e.g.,

(7) RŪT: *Turi, kamuolys, kamuoliukas, duok.*
have ball:NOM ball-DIM:NOM give.
'You got it, a ball, a ball, give it to me.' (2;1)

(8) RŪT: *Čia guli meška, meškiuka.*
here lies bear:NOM bear-DIM:NOM
'Here is a bear lying, a bear.' (2;2)

There are cases in our data where the girl repeats the noun used by Mother in a changed version, that is, she uses the simplex form of her mother's diminutive or, vice versa, she replaces simplicia by diminutives. Such a phenomenon is not easy to explain. The relevant examples are presented below:

(9) MOT: *Taigi jau nusiplovėm kojytę, nereikia plauti.*
well already washed leg-DIM:ACC no need to wash.
'We have already washed the leg, there's no need to wash it.'
RŪT: *Koją.*
leg:ACC.
'The leg.' (1;11)

(10) MOT: *Kas čia?*
'What is this?'
MOT: *Meška?*
bear:NOM?
'Is it a bear?
RŪT: *Meškutė.*
bear-DIM.
'A bear.' (2;5)

(11) MOT: *Labai gražus balionas.*
very nice balloon:NOM.
'It is a very nice balloon.'
RŪT: *Balioniukas, balioniukas.*
balloon-DIM balloon-DIM.
'A balloon, a balloon.' (2;4)

In view of the above it could be suggested that when the girl uses both forms of the word referring to the same item in the same speech situation, they do not exhibit any difference in semantic meaning.

It is interesting to note that the same tendency of referring to the same object by both a simplex and a diminutive form is very frequent in Mother's speech as well, but in these dialogues diminutives used by Mother have pragmatic meaning. Consider the following variations (always within the same speech situations):

(12) MOT: *Ar pieną gers?*
if milk:ACC will drink?
'Is she going to drink milk?'
RŪT: *Pieną.*
milk:ACC.
'Milk.'
MOT: *Ką darys su pienu?*
what will do with milk:INS?
'What will (Rūta) do with milk?'
MOT: *Gers pienelį mergaitė?*
will drink milk-DIM:ACC girl-DIM?
'Is the little girl going to drink the milk?'
RŪT: *Taip.*
'Yes.'
MOT: *Ar gersi pieniuką?*
if will drink milk-DIM:ACC?
'Are you going to drink the milk?'
RŪT: *Ne.*
'No.' (1,10)

(13) MOT: *Padainuok, kad jie užmigtų visi, arba pasek pasaką apie pelytę.*
sing that they would fall asleep all or tell tale about mouse-DIM:ACC.
'Sing a song so that they would fall asleep, all of them, or tell a tale about the mouse.'
RŪT: *Pasaką.*
'Tale.'
MOT: *Apie katytę moki pasekti?*
about cat-DIM:ACC know to tell?
'About the cat, do you know how to tell?'
MOT: *Pasakėlę?*
tale-DIM:ACC.
'The tale.' (1,10).

(14) MOT: *Gražiai lupk kiaušinukus.*
nicely peel eggs-DIM:PL:ACC.
'Nicely peel the eggs.'
RŪT: *Padėjau, padėjau kiaušinukus.*
put put eggs-DIM:PL:ACC.
'I put, I put the eggs.'
MOT: *Padėjai kiaušinukus?*
put eggs-DIM:PL:ACC?
'Did you put the eggs?'

MOT: *Duok, aš palaikysiu.*
'Give it to me, I will hold it'.
MOT: *Kas padėjo tokį kiaušinuką, putpelė?*
who put such egg-DIM:ACC, quail?
'Who laid such an egg, a quail?'
MOT: *Putpelės čia kiaušinukas.*
quail's here egg-DIM:NOM.
'This is a quail's egg.'
RŪT: *Viščiukas.*
chicken-DIM:NOM.
'A chicken.'
MOT: *Viščiukas sėdi.*
chicken-DIM:NOM sits.
'A chicken is sitting.'
RŪT: *Žiūri.*
'Looks.'
MOT: *Duodi ir viščiukui kiaušinio paragaut?*
give and chicken-DIM:DAT egg:GEN to try?
'Are you giving the egg to the chicken to try?' (1;10).

Rūta must have understood at a very early age that her mother uses both forms (simplex and diminutive) to express the same denotative meaning, without any difference in 'smallness'. To denote this meaning, the most frequent strategy is to use the adjective *mažas* 'small/little' either in combination with the diminutive itself, or separately (cf. Sinclair 1996; Gillis 1997; Stephany 1997). Consider the relevant examples:

(15) MOT: *O Rūtytė mažytė?*
and Rūta-DIM:NOM small-DIM:NOM?
'And what about Rūta, is she small?'
RŪT: *Mažytė, mažytė.*
small-DIM:NOM small-DIM:NOM.
'Small, small.' (1;8)

(16) MOT: *Mažytis vilkutis ar didelis?*
small-DIM:NOM wolf-DIM:NOM or big?
'Is the wolf small or big?'
RŪT: *Mažytis.*
small-DIM:NOM.
'Small.'
MOT: *Mažytis, mažytis, taip?*
small-DIM:NOM small-DIM:NOM yes?
'Small, small, right?' (1;8)

(17) MOT: *Kokio dydžio šuniukas tas mažas buvo?*
what size dog-DIM:NOM that small was?
'What size was that small dog?'
RŪT: *Matiuka (mažiukas).*
small-DIM:NOM.
'Small.'

(18) MOT: *O kas čia?*
'And what is this?'
MOT: *Kamuoliukas?*
ball-DIM:NOM?
'The ball?'
RŪT: *Kamuoliukas.*
ball-DIM:NOM.
'The ball.'
MOT: *Mažas, mažas.*
'Little, little.'
RŪT: *Ne.*
'No.'
MOT: *Didelis kamuoliukas?*
big ball-DIM:NOM?
'Is this ball big?'
RŪT: *Didis* [=didelis].
'Big.' (1;8)

(19) MOT: *O Akvilytė didelė ar maža?*
and Akvilė-DIM:NOM big or small?
'Is Akvilė big or small?'
RŪT: *Dide* [=didelė].
'Big'.
MOT: *Tu jau didelė?*
'Are you big?'
RŪT: *Dide* [=*didelė*].
'Big.' (1;9)

(20) MOT: *Ar didelis saldainis?*
'Is candy big?'
RŪT: *Didis (didelis).*
'Big.' (1;9)

Up to the age of two noun phrases consisting of adjective + noun are extremely rare. The examples 15–17 (with the adjective *mažas* 'small') and 18–20 (with the adjective *didelis* 'big') show that only the adjective ('small' or 'big') enables Rūta to emphasise the actual size of the object. Rūta never uses the diminutive for this purpose, even in the cases when she is referring to the 'ball' in its diminutive form. For the cases when Rūta used the adjective **dide* (fem.) **didis* (masc.) for *didelė, -is* 'big' (see examples 18–20), we assume the possibility of back formation (i.e., *did-is* from *did-el-is* as if it contained the DIM suffix *-el-is*). This would be a proof of a creative use of diminutive formation (adjective, not noun), however, no other cases of backformation were noted.

8. Pragmatics of diminutives

8.1 In order to understand the acquisition of diminutives in child language, it is important to analyze not only their derivation and semantics, but also their pragmatic functions. The use of diminutive suffixes in child language is mainly determined by pragmatics. As pointed out by Dressler and Merlini Barbaresi (1994: 224), diminutive suffixes are "firstly attributed to the nouns which describe the child, the parts of his body, or other objects which belong to that child".

8.2 The comparison of frequencies for diminutives and simplicia shows that with respect to diminutives, the most frequent lexico-semantic groups which appear in Rūta's speech are 'Animals', 'Toys' and 'Body parts' (see Savickienė 2003).[5] Diminutives dominate particularly in token frequency within the LSG 'Body parts', 'Toys' and 'Animals'. In contrast, nouns from groups such as 'Other things' and 'Food' occur mostly in the simplex form, which means that many new words (part of them used only just once) fall into this category. The group 'Persons' presents quite interesting results: the data show that Rūta uses a lot of simplex nouns (types). The majority of these are the names of Rūta's friends, relatives, and acquaintances. All the nouns denoting family relations are used by Rūta like proper nouns, e.g. mother, daddy, sister, grandma, and grandpa; they are assigned this function in the speech act and are used very frequently. Naturally, the hypocoristic form of Rūta's name makes up a large number of the hypocoristic tokens. It is characteristic of children to use their own name very frequently, especially in its diminutive form, and children can choose from several variants of their name. Rūta strongly prefers the diminutives *Rūtelė* and *Rūtytė* to the simplex and does not use other variants, such as *Rūtuliukas* and *Rūtužėlis* (gender shift to masculine) uttered by Mother. Such variant diminutive forms of names are used by people who are very close to each other; children, as a rule, do not use all of them while referring to themselves (Sifianou 1992).

Relevant research in other languages shows that hypocoristics are less frequent in a child's and his/her parents' speech than is the case in Rūta's and her mother's interaction. Moreover, they emerge relatively late, as research on child language in Russian (Voeikova 1998), Greek (Stephany 1997), Hebrew (Ravid 1998), or Italian (Ceccherini et al. 1997) shows. The neighbouring Baltic language, Latvian, however, demonstrates a frequent and early use of hypocoristics. This is especially relevant when children or parents address each other in a dialogue (see Rūķe-Draviņa 1976, 1982, 1993).

Hypocoristics are chiefly used to express warm feelings of love and kindness. Nevertheless, the basic forms of names in our data are not rare at all. Actually, the girl's name used by her mother in the base form acquires a different pragmatic value, e.g.,

(21) MOT: *Matai, vėl išpylei.*
'You see, you have spilt it again'.
MOT: *Tėvelis pyksta?*
father-DIM:NOM angry?
'Is father angry?'
RŪT: *Nepyta* [=*nepyksta*].
'He is not angry'.
MOT: *Nepyksta, kai Rūta pripila?*
'Isn't he angry when Rūta spills things over?'(2;2)

(22) MOT: *O ką tu čia darai?*
'And what are you doing here?'
MOT: *Nekratyk galvytės.*
don't shake head-DIM:GEN.
'Don't shake your head'.
MOT: *Rūta!* (2;1)

(23) MOT: *Negalima, Rūtyte, nukrisi nuo čia.*
not allowed Rūta-DIM:VOC will fall from here.
'You are not allowed, Rūta, you are going to fall down from here'.
MOT: *Rūta!* (2:1)

(24) MOT: *Ką čia padarei?*
'What have you done here?'
MOT: *Kalbėjau.*
'I spoke'.
MOT: *Nelįsk, nelįsk prie rozetės, Rūta!*
'Don't, don't get close to the socket, Rūta!'
MOT: *Negalima!*
'You can not do this.'(2:5)

(25) Situation: Rūta (2;5) made a mess of her toys in the room.
MOT: *Nu ką dabar tu padarei?*
'What did you do here?'
RŪT: *Oi, mačiau, mačiau šitą įdomų, žinok.*
'Oh, I saw, I saw that interesting (toy), you know'.
MOT: *Kai šitą nori ištraukt, tai mamytę pakviesk.*
when this want to take out then mother-DIM:ACC call.
'When you want to take it out, you should call your mother.'
MOT: *Išbarstei viską, oi tu Rūta, Rūta.*
'You have spilt everything, oh, my, Rūta.

In all the situations cited above Mother used the basic form of the name in order to discipline the girl, whereas in other situations Mother mostly uses the hypocoristic form to emphasize her love and tender feelings. Thus, the basic form of the name used in such situations acquires an entirely different – negative – pragmatic meaning. When Mother calls her daughter *Rūta,* she stresses the fact that the girl is doing something wrong and is not a good girl anymore.

Addressing her mother, Rūta also uses hypocoristics frequently. Consider examples 26 and 27 where the girl uses simplicia.

(26) Situation: Mother and Rūta (2;4) are playing together with Lego bricks.
RŪT: *Ateik čia, ateik!*
'Come here come!'
RŪT: *Statom statom!*
'Let's build, let's build!'
RŪT: *Mamyte, statom!*
mother-DIM:VOC build!
'Mummy, let's build!'
RŪT: *Mama!*
'Mother!'

(27) Rūta at 2;5.
RŪT: *Mama, mama, ajisk* [=užrišk] *mesiukai* [=meškiukui].
mother:VOC mother:VOC tie it up bear-DIM:DAT'.
'Mother, mother, tie it up for the bear.'
RŪT: *Mama, neužsimerk, žiūrėk.*
'Mother, don't close your eyes, look'.

Rūta's utterances clearly demonstrate that they reflect the demand directed to Mother to perform something, which is accompanied by an imperative verb form. In addition to the demand, a new nuance of discontent emerges indicated by the simplex form of the address. In the first utterance, the diminutive ('*Mamyte, statom!*') appears as the first item but the simplex ('*Mama!*') follows immediately. Moreover, the simplex is used with a specific intonation conveying impatience, irritation, and discontent; all these emotions express negative connotations.

Such difference in pragmatic meaning is evident only with respect to these two names, *Rūta* and *mama* 'mother'. It can be suggested then that in such cases hypocoristics appear as unmarked items, whereas simplicia are marked in terms of the pragmatic meanings they convey, such as seriousness, reproach, reprimand, or anger. This is a good example of pragmatic markedness reversal.

8.3 Another aspect of diminutive usage is related to situations which are unpleasant for the child. Rūta's mother uses diminutives and hypocoristics when she does not want to frighten the girl, or when she wants to alleviate the unpleasant situation, e.g.,

(28) MOT: *Rūtyte, eisim kirpti nagučius.*
Rūta-DIM will go to cut nails-DIM:PL:ACC.
'Rūta, we are going to cut the nails.'
MOT: *Reikia gerti vaistukus.*
necessary to take medicine-DIM:ACC:PL.
'It's time to take the medicine.'

What is meant by this usage is to convince the child that, for example, to cut nails or to take medicine is not terrible at all and that such activities do not hurt. An appropriate use of diminutives reduces the feelings of fear (i.e., mitigation) and encourages the child to carry out some unpleasant activity (i.e., the intended perlocutionary sequel).

8.4 Another interesting aspect of the diminutive usage by Mother when addressing Rūta is discussed below.
Situation: Rūta is leafing through a picture book.

(29) MOT: *Čia laputė ir vilkas.*
here fox-DIM:NOM and wolf:NOM.
'This is a fox and this is a wolf.'
MOT: *Lapė neša gaidelį.*
fox:NOM carries cock-DIM:ACC.
'The fox is carrying a cock.'

In the first case the diminutive *laputė* 'fox-DIM' and the simplex *vilkas* 'wolf' are used; this usage suggests that the fox is considered weaker in comparison with the wolf. In the second sentence we have the same referent *lapė* 'fox' used as a simplex, because *gaidelis* 'cock-DIM' in this situation is weaker than the fox and therefore it is the cock that deserves sympathy. Both utterances contain a hint as to who is better (in terms of sympathy); and better is the one who is marked with the endearment suffix.

Examples of diminutive formation in Rūta's speech within similar contexts were recorded as well, e.g., in talking with the father (FAT):

(30) FAT: *Nukrito.*
'Fell down.'
RŪT: *Numetei?*
'Did you throw it down?'
RŪT: *Dal* [=dar] *kengūrą.*
even kangaroo:ACC.
'Even the kangaroo.'
RŪT: *Kengūrytei skauda, skauda kakytę* [=kaktytę].
'Kangaroo-DIM:DAT hurts hurts forehead-DIM:ACC.
'The kangaroo's forehead hurts.'
FAT: *Panešiok kengūrytę, panešiok.*
hold kangaroo-DIM:ACC hold.
'Hold the kangaroo, hold it.'

RŪT: *Mažytė, mažytė, daug neskauda.*
little-DIM:NOM little-DIM:NOM much not hurt.
'Little, little, it does not hurt much.' (2;5)

31) RŪT: *Matai, meškiukas vargšiukas.*
see bear-DIM:NOM poor-DIM:NOM.
'You see, (this is) a poor bear.'
FAT: *Jį vargšą paliko, ar ne?*
him:MASC:ACC poor:ACC left no?
'Somebody left him, poor thing?
RŪT: *Taip.*
'Yes.' (2;5)

We see from the examples that caregivers and Rūta use diminutives when they speak about those who are weak, sick or helpless, i.e. when expressing sympathy for weakness. Thus, we could state that Rūta acquires this pragmatic meaning of diminutives only in the period of 2;4–2;5. This allows us to hypothesize that before, at an earlier age, the child was able to use only formal diminutive derivation rules without assigning them a definite meaning. Rūta's early indiscriminate use of simplicia and diminutives (more than one diminutive variant of the same bases) contradicts Clark's (1993, 1995) principle of contrast.

Therefore, Dressler's (1994) and Dressler's and Merlini Barbaresi's (1997) hypothesis to the effect that the pragmatic meaning of diminutives is acquired earlier than the meaning of 'smallness' is corroborated by Rūta's use of diminutives; on the other hand, the input shows systematic effects of pragmatic factors which allow Rūta to acquire pragmatic meanings of diminutives.

9. Concluding remarks

The analysis of our data allows us to draw several important conclusions.

1. Diminutives and hypocoristics in child language emerge during early (premorphological and protomorphological) periods. It is with the beginning of protomorphology (at 1;8) that Rūta starts using this nonprototypical type of derivational morphology productively.

2. Diminutive suffixes are the first morphemes that Rūta starts to use. She acquires diminutive suffixes earlier than inflectional endings (Savickienė 2003). Such early emergence of diminutive suffixes might be influenced by the transparency and frequency of diminutive morphemes. Morphological richness and productivity, transparency and saliency of diminutives in the input language make the acquisition and development of noun inflectional morphology faster and easier.

3. Contrary to Clark's (1993, 1995) principle of contrast, diminutive nouns and their basic forms are first used by Rūta side by side, without any perceptible difference

in meaning. Rūta starts to produce several diminutive suffixes simultaneously without any difference in meaning too.

4. The diminutive forms that appeared first and were used most frequently are derived from basic nouns belonging to the lexico-semantic groups of 'Animals', 'Toys' and 'Body parts' (with a different rank order for types and tokens).

5. The only perceptible differences of diminutive meanings are associated with pragmatic meanings starting with the age of 2;4; the notion of 'smallness' is expressed via the use of the adjective *mažas* 'small' as a part of a noun phrase. There is not yet any clear indication in the corpus that Rūta has acquired the semantic meaning of smallness for diminutives. It is due to their pragmatic meaning that diminutives are acquired first, since, in general, children acquire meanings contextually, in a pragmatic rather than semantic format.

6. Whereas the Lithuanian of adults cannot be considered to show a dichotomy of regular vs. irregular noun inflection or a default case within diminutive formation, the child Rūta exhibited a clear quantitative default in her use of diminutives for each of the two genders.

References

Ambrazas, V., Geniušienė, E., Girdenis, A., Sližienė, N., Tekorienė, D., Valeckienė, A. and Valiulytė, E. (eds.). 1997. *Lithuanian grammar*. Vilnius: Baltos lankos.

Bittner, D., Dressler, W. U. and Kilani-Schoch, M.(eds.). 2003. *Mini-paradigms and the emergence of verb morphology*. Berlin: Mouton de Gruyter.

Ceccherini, M., Serena, B. and Zocconi, E. 1997. Acquisition of diminutives in Italian. In *Studies in Pre- and Protomorphology*, W. U. Dressler (ed.), 157–163. Wien: Verlag der Österreichischen Akademie der Wissenschaften.

Clark, E. 1993. *The Lexicon in acquisition*. Cambridge, England: Cambridge University Press.

Clark, E. 1995. Later lexical development and word formation. In *The handbook of the child language*, P. Fletcher, B. MacWhinney (eds), 393–412. Oxford: Blackwell.

De Marco, A. 1998. The acquisition of diminutives in Italian. In *Studies in the acquisition of number and diminutive marking* [Antwerp papers in linguistics 95], S. Gillis (ed.), 175–192. Antwerp: Universiteit Antwerpen.

Dressler, W. U. 1994. Evidence from first phases of morphology acquisition for linguistic theory: extragrammatic morphology and diminutives. *Acta linguistica Hafniensia* 27: 93–105.

Dressler, W. U. (ed.). 1997a. *Studies in Pre- and Protomorphology*. Wien: Verlag der Österreichischen Akademie der Wissenschaften.

Dressler, W. U. 1997b. Zur Entstehung der Distinktivität in der Kindersprache. In *Polyphonie pour Iván Fónagy*, J. Perrot (ed.), 127–136. Paris: L'Harmattan.

Dressler, W. U. and Merlini Barbaresi, L. 1994. *Morphopragmatics. Diminutives and intensifiers in Italian, German, and other languages*. Berlin: Mouton de Gruyter.

Dressler, W. U. and Merlini Barbaresi, L. 1997. Morphopragmatics. In *Handbook of Pragmatics*, J. Verschueren et al. (eds). Amsterdam: Benjamins.

Gillis, S. 1997. The acquisition of diminutives in Dutch. In *Studies in Pre- and Protomorphology*, W. U. Dressler (ed.), 165–179. Wien: Verlag der Österreichischen Akademie der Wissenschaften.

Gillis, S. (ed.). 1998. *Studies in the acquisition of number and diminutive marking*. [Antwerp papers in linguistics 95]. Antwerp: Universiteit Antwerpen.

Jurafsky, D. 1996. Universal tendencies in the semantics of the diminutive. *Language* 72 (3): 533–578.

Kempe, V., Brooks, P. J. and Pirott, L. 2001. How can child-directed speech facilitate the acquisition of morphology? In *Research on Child Language Acquisition: Proceedings of the 8th conference of the International Association for the Study of Child Language*, M. Almgren, A. Barrena, M. J. Ezeizabarrena, I. Idiazabal, and B. MacWhinney (eds), 1237–1247. Medford, MA: Cascadilla Press.

Kempe, V., Brooks, P.J., Mironova, N. and Fedorova, O. 2003. Diminutivization supports gender acquisition in Russian children. *Journal of Child Language* 30: 1–15.

King, K. and Melzi, G. 2004. Intimacy, imitation and language learning: Spanish diminutives in mother-child conversation. *First Language* 24(2): 241–261.

Laalo, K. 1998. Diminutives in Finnish child-directed and child speech. In *Studies in the acquisition of number and diminutive marking* [Antwerp papers in linguistic 95], S. Gillis (ed.), 138–148. Antwerp: Universiteit Antwerpen.

MacArthur CDI. 1992–1993. The MacArthur Communicative Development Inventory: words and gestures; words and sentences. San Diego, CA: Singular Publishing Group.

MacWhinney, B. 2000. *The CHILDES Project. Tools for Analyzing Talk*. Third Edition. Mahwah, NJ: Lawrence Erlbaum Associates.

Olmsted, H. 1994. Diminutive morphology of Russian children: A simplified subset of nominal declension in language acquisition. In *Alexander Lipson: In memoriam*, 165–207. Columbus, Ohio: Slavica Publishers Inc.

Ravid, D. 1998. Diminutive *-i* in early child Hebrew: an initial analysis. In *Studies in the acquisition of number and diminutive marking* [Antwerp papers in linguistic 95], S. Gillis (ed.), 149–173. Antwerp: Universiteit Antwerpen.

Rūķe-Draviņa, V. 1976. 'Mama' and 'Papa' in child language. *Journal of child language* 3: 157–166.

Rūķe-Draviņa, V. 1982. *No pieciem menešiem līdz pieciem gadiem* [From five months to five years]. Stockholm: The Baltic Scientific Institute in Scandinavia.

Rūķe-Draviņa, V. 1993. *Latviešu meitene apgūst savu pirmo valodu* [The acquisition of first language by Latvian girl]. Rīga: Dio Nordik.

Savickienė, I. 1998. The acquisition of diminutives in Lithuanian. In *Studies in the acquisition of number and diminutive marking* [Antwerp papers in linguistic 95], S. Gillis (ed.), 115–135. Antwerp: Universiteit Antwerpen.

Savickienė, I. 1999. Lietuvio vaiko daiktavardžio morfologija [The acquisition of noun morphology in Lithuanian]. PhD thesis. Kaunas: VDU.

Savickienė, I. 2001. The role of diminutives in Lithuanian child language acquisition. *Linguistica Baltica* 9: 109–118.

Savickienė, I. 2003. The Acquisition of Lithuanian Noun Morphology. Wien: Verlag der Österreichischen Akademie der Wissenschaften.

Sifianou, M. 1992. The use of diminutives in expressing politeness: Modern Greek versus English. *Journal of pragmatics* 17: 155–173.

Sinclair, J. 1996. An international project in multilingual lexicography. *International journal of lexicography* 9 (3): 179–196.
Smoczyńska, M. 1998. Słowa i gesty. Inwentarz rozwoju mowy i komunikacji MacArthurów (wersja polska 2A) [Words and gestures. The MacArthur Communicative Development Inventory. Polish version 2]. Kraków: Katedra Językoznawstwa Ogólnego i Indoeuropejskiego Universitetu Jagiellońskiego.
Stephany, U. 1997. Diminutives in early Greek. In *Studies in Pre- and Protomorphology*, W. U. Dressler (ed.), 145–156. Wien: Verlag der Österreichischen Akademie der Wissenschaften.
Voeikova, M. D. 1998. Acquisition of diminutives by a Russian child: preliminary observations in connection with the early adjectives. In *Studies in the acquisition of number and diminutive marking* [Antwerp papers in linguistic 95], S. Gillis (ed.), 97–113. Antwerp: Universiteit Antwerpen.
Wójcik, Paweł. 2003. Early verb inflection in Lithuanian. In *Mini-paradigms and the emergence of verb morphology. A cross-linguistic perspective*, D. Bittner, W. U. Dressler and M. Kilani-Schoch (eds), 401–420. Berlin: Mouton de Gruyter.

Appendix

Table 2. The frequency distribution of diminutive, hypocoristic and simplex types and tokens (in absolute numbers) in Rūta's speech (1;7–2;5)

Rūta	Diminutives		Hypocoristics		Simplex	
	Types	*Tokens*	*Types*	*Tokens*	*Types*	*Tokens*
1;7	2	2	2	14	11	36
1;8	21	57	9	52	29	225
1;9	41	168	14	158	128	698
1;10	67	366	17	207	141	589
1;11	41	209	10	193	97	459
2;0	57	298	19	253	130	446
2;1	54	279	17	220	106	502
2;2	68	472	16	193	111	429
2;3	77	295	19	321	129	529
2;4	64	326	19	218	153	608
2;5	69	309	17	144	151	473

Table 3. The frequency distribution of diminutive, hypocoristic and simplex types and tokens (in absolute numbers) in Mother's speech (1;7–2;5)

Mother	Diminutives		Hypocoristics		Simplex	
	Types	*Tokens*	*Types*	*Tokens*	*Types*	*Tokens*
1;7	30	82	9	105	29	56
1;8	80	248	10	294	100	350
1;9	76	351	16	484	193	1067
1;10	113	550	19	425	238	1084
1;11	68	253	14	233	121	427
2;0	77	417	19	365	193	555
2;1	81	344	18	215	144	422
2;2	91	445	16	281	147	382
2;3	94	352	18	335	186	511
2;4	85	259	19	212	195	530
2;5	90	333	22	268	192	475

Table 5. Examples of Rūta's mini-paradigms (1;8–1;10)

Age	Lemma	Simplex	Category	Diminutive	Category	Translation
1;8	bitė	bitė	SG:NOM	bitutė	SG:NOM	'bee'
		bitę	SG:ACC			
	batas	batai	PL:NOM	batuką	SG:ACC	'shoe'
1;9						
	katė	katė	SG:NOM	katutė	SG:NOM	'cat'
				katytes	PL:ACC	
				katytė	SG:NOM	
				katytę	SG:ACC	
	mama	mama	SG:NOM	mamytė	SG:NOM	'mammy'
		mamos	SG:GEN	mamytę	SG:ACC	
		mamą	SG:ACC	mamytei	SG:DAT	
		mamai	SG:DAT	mamyte	SG:INS	
		mama	SG:VOC	mamyte	SG:VOC	
1;10	koja	koja	SG:NOM	kojytės	SG:GEN	'leg'
		kojos	PL:NOM	kojytę	SG:ACC	
				kojytės	PL:NOM	
				kojytėm	PL:DAT	
	arbata	arbatos	SG:GEN	arbatytė	SG:NOM	'tea'
				arbatyte	SG:INS	
				arbatėlę	SG:ACC	

* The table gives only a few cases of mini-paradigms, and only for the three months, i.e., 1;8–1;10, because the later periods have too many mini-paradigm examples to be presented in a table.

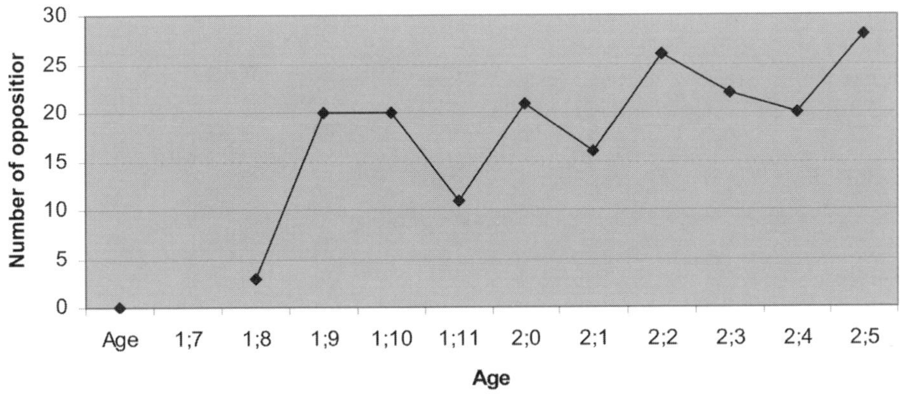

Figure 5. Emergence and development of mini-paradigms in Rūta's speech

Notes

1. A word with six diminutive suffixes *puod-el-ait-uk-ėl-yt-ėl-is* 'cup-DIM(6)' is known from folk tales. Such words are extremely rare in everyday usage.

2. On the distinction of Lithuanian noun classes according to the principles of Natural Morphology (Dressler 1994, 1997a, 1997b) see Savickienė (2003).

3. The Austrian Academy of Sciences (a grant to W. U. Dressler) supported data collection.

4. By 'period of observation' (referred to throughout the study) is meant the period from 1;7 to 2;6 unless stated differently.

5 According to 'MacArthur Communicative Development Inventory' (1992–1993) and Smoczyńska (1998), 16 lexico-semantic groups (LSG) of nouns have been determined, the most frequent of which are discussed in this work. The LSG of 'Other things' comprises those nouns that do not appear too frequently as diminutives and belong to the LSG 'Furniture', 'Vehicle', 'Clothes', etc.

CHAPTER 2

Diminutives in Russian at the early stages of acquisition

Ekaterina Protassova, Maria D. Voeikova

Two Russian children, a boy and a girl, were observed during the first steps of their use of diminutives. Having a different language proficiency and strategy of learning, the children under observation demonstrated a clear difference in the acquisition of diminutives: the early speaking girl Varja (as well as her mother) shows a high frequency of diminutives already at 1;6, whereas the later speaking Filipp reaches his maximum only about 2;0.

It is argued that the most important pragmatic function of consciously used diminutives in CDS as well as in CS is the creation of a familiar, personal world. The mothers try to familiarize the children with the surroundings, to make the world good for their children and to stress the relative smallness of the things that surround the children in contrast to those of grown-ups. Such distinctions are, in the Russian world, important both for the instruction and for the emotional comfort of a child.

In addition, diminutives play an important role in facilitating the acquisition of case system: in the early phases both children use more indirect case forms of diminutives than of simplex nouns. This may be explained by the fact that diminutives end with similar codas. After children get a good command of using nominal case suffixes, this advantage of diminutives is of no help anymore.

Introduction

Russian is known as a language with rich morphology and an elaborated diminutive system. Researchers such as Wierzbicka (1984) claim that diminutives are typical markers of Russian emotionality. It appears to be relevant to analyze whether the various diminutive types are equally represented in every single acquisition history, or whether they vary significantly. What provokes diminutive insertions and what is the context of their use? We argue that diminutives in child language have a general pragmatic value indicating intimacy and endearment, making the direct environment familiar and loyal to the child, helping her/him feel acquainted with objects manipulated or taken into account by caretakers (Protassova 1999, 2001a; Voeikova 1998). We will try to show that the diminutive system is under construction in this phase and that the phonological form of lemmas may influence the preference by caregivers and children either for a diminutive or for a simplex. Thus, early diminutives come into the mental lexicon of a child as inseparable units and are later reanalyzed, after a child has understood the pattern-building mechanisms. This stage is indicated by the increase and diversity of the child's diminutives and by back-formations.

Our paper describes diminutive patterns in adult Russian and studies the acquisition of diminutives by two Russian children, Filipp and Varja, at the very beginning of their development, from the first words to the first mini-paradigms. We juxtapose the findings and compare the acquisition paths. We will show that diminutives are used in a different way by the caregivers of our subjects and, therefore, play a different role in the language development of each child. Our goal is to assemble examples and comment them on various nuances that could allow us to realize peculiarities of diminutive use at this early age.[1]

1. Description of the adult target system

Diminutives are productively formed from Russian nouns by adding suffixes and combinations of suffixes to a stem (productive diminutive suffixes are given in Table 1), e.g. *syn-ok-Ø, syn-oček-Ø, syn-ulj-a* 'son-DimMasc' from the simplex *syn* 'son' (in colloquial Russian, also *syna, synočka* like formal feminines). Diminutives may also be formed from parametric and perceptual adjectives and adverbs, but these are not as frequent as noun diminutives. They may denote the same features as the corresponding simplex with the additional meaning of smallness or endearment, e.g. *bel-en'k-ij* 'white-Dim' means, in fact, 'white and small', or 'white and pretty (dear, attractive)'. It is not by accident that diminutive adjectives almost always refer to diminutive nouns (so to say *belen'kij* also implies to pick out *dom-ik* 'house-Dim' or *zaj-čik* 'hare-Dim' instead of the simplicia). Vinogradov regarded this tendency as "emotional agreement", saying that "evaluative forms are infectious" (Vinogradov 1947: 113). Most scholarly work has examined the semantics of diminutives in emotive language, including smallness, endearment, tenderness, special suffixes and higher pitch in intonation, and evaluative or expressive morphology. Surprisingly, it was often found that diminutivization does not relate to certain visual characteristics, as relatively small size or young age (Fentslova 1985; Polterauer 1981; Volek 1987; Wierzbicka 1980; Worth 1987). This brings us again to the non-linguistic question of whether child emotions (at least, some of them) are innate and develop under circumstances or whether they are learned, maybe together with certain verbal expressions or independently of them.

1.1 Diminutives from different parts of speech

It may be due to the emotional component that other parts of speech also are used in a quasi-diminutive form without any semantic indication of smallness. Several verbs in motherese may obtain diminutive suffixes. A good example is the verb *kuš-en'k-at'* 'eat-Dim' from *kuš-at'* 'eat'; *kuš-en'k-a-em, kuš-en'k-a-et* in 1Pl and 3Sg etc.[2] Other verb-like diminutives loose the verb markers and may not be conjugated (cf. *spat-en'ki* 'sleep-Dim:Pl', *rost-en'ki* – 'grow up-Dim:Pl') where the diminutive suffix *-en'k-* follows the infinitive marker. They are used in certain games and everyday rituals instead of the corresponding simplex infinitives. Even if not many examples were found in the corpus, this type of language play may still be used in a family-dependent way.

Uninflected words, such as particles, pronouns, interjections and the already mentioned adverbs, are also objects of diminutivization, e.g.: *netuški* 'no-Dim:Pl' from *net* 'no', *tutočki* 'here-Dim:Pl' from the adverb *tut* 'here', and *ajuški* 'ah-Dim' from the particle *a* 'what,' *xorošenečko* 'accurately-Dim-Dim' from the adverb *xorošo* 'well'. Typical of these forms is the suffix *-i* comparable to the false plural *-i* in exclamations such as *mamočki* 'lit. mommy-Dim:Pl' from *mama* 'mommy'. Thus, prototypical diminutives are nouns, and even if other parts of speech are diminutivized, it is due to the features of the objects under description and to the emotional attitude of the speaker to these objects.

Table 1. Productive diminutive suffixes of nouns

Masculine	Feminine	Neuter
-ik, -ok/-ek, (-onok/-jonok): *kot-ik, kot-ok* 'cat-Dim', *kot-jonok* 'baby-cat'	-k- (-ičk-, -on'k-/-en'k-, -ečk- /-očk-, -ušk-, -išk-), uš-: *lis-ka* 'fox-Dim', *lis-ička*, *lis-on'ka* 'fox-Dim'	-c-,-k- (-yšk-, -ušk-, -ečk-): *okon-ce, oko-ško* 'window-Dim', *soln-yško* 'sun-Dim'

Some of these suffixes are semantically specialized, e.g. *-onok/-jonok* serves to name small animals, e.g. *slonjonok* 'baby elephant' from *slon* 'elephant'[3]. The consonant *-k-* is a common part of most diminutive suffixes, except the suffix *-ce* in the neuter. Prototypical diminutive suffixes are combinations of the suffix *-Vk* with other suffixes, which are accompanied by historic changes of preceding consonants. The consonant *-k-* occupies a stable position before the vowel of the inflectional ending, thus changing all inflectional endings by the syllable *–kV*; compare the Nominative-Genitive opposition of simplicia and the corresponding diminutives: *dver'/dver-i* 'door-Nom/Gen' vs. *dver-ka/dver-ki* 'door-Dim:Nom/Gen', *ulic-a/ulic-y* 'street-Nom/Gen' vs. *uloč-ka/uloč-ki* 'street-Dim:Nom/Gen', and *stol/stol-a* 'table-Nom/Gen' vs. *sto-lik/stol-ika* 'table-Dim:Nom/Gen'. In the simplex bases, vocalic inflectional endings are preceded by various consonants that may make them phonologically opaque. Contrarily, the vocalic inflectional endings of the diminutives are always preceded by -*k*- and thus become phonologically clear and salient.

In suffixed diminutives some forms require a consonant alternation (*c* → *č*, *k* → *c*). The suffix vowels -*e*- and -*o*- in masculine diminutive suffixes are unstable, e.g. *petušok* 'cock-Dim:Nom' and *petuška* 'cock-Dim:Gen'. Thus, especially masculine diminutives may have an even less transparent inflectional paradigm than their simplex bases. The unstable -*e* and -*o* in diminutives allow the speaker to keep the same number of syllables in all forms of the paradigm. To the contrary, the vowel -*i* in diminutive suffixes remains intact in all forms (cf. *mjačik* 'ball-Dim:Nom' and *mjačika* 'ball-Dim: Gen'). Whether the maintenance of syllable number plays any facilitating role in the acquisition of forms is not clear. In most cases, diminutivization does not change the gender of nouns, but indeclinable neuter nouns of foreign origin become feminine, e.g. *taksiška prišla* 'taxi-Dim came: Fem'.

1.2 Diminutives and hypocoristics

The -*k*-suffixation is typical of diminutives but is not obligatory for hypocoristics which may not only be formed by the diminutive suffixes but also use the "truncation model" with and without suffixation, e.g. the quasi-suffixes -*ša* and -*nja* in *Saša, Sanja* from *Alexander*, or *Maša, Manja* from *Maria*, or a zero suffix accompanied by palatalization and a shift of the declension class: in *Kolja* from *Nikolaj*, and *Petja* from *Petr*. (The adding of -*a* ending with the preceding consonant palatalization changes the masculine 1st declension class into the masculine-feminine 2nd declension class.) Not all widespread Russian short names should be treated as hypocoristics unlike their diminutive derivatives; however, all of these forms have some semantic diminutive nuances, and children often make use of the whole scale, including non-shortened and rare variants and transpose the models acquired onto other examples. Thus, names of people may be considered as a very important field of morphological training. One common feature of diminutives and hypocoristics is the fact that they usually exhibit similar and predictable phonological sequences at the end of the word compared with the simplicia.

Normally, several diminutives or hypocoristics having different semantic nuances may be formed from one and the same noun, e.g. *set-ka* from *set'* 'net', or another diminutive (historically, a double diminutive) such as *set-oč-ka* 'net-Dim-Dim'. The first diminutive Dim-1 sometimes has a pejorative (depreciative) meaning. It may also replace the corresponding simplex, whereas the simplex gets another meaning and only the Dim-2 really means a small and/or beloved thing/person. In the given example the simplex *set'* 'net' is used in all possible meanings including 'net, network, system, scale' etc., the first diminutive is used to denote a string-bag of normal size and only the second Dim-2 really expresses the idea of endearment and/or smallness. The semantic nuance of endearment does not need any extra expression except diminutive suffixes. The pure idea of smallness is often expressed by the combination of diminutive suffixes with the adjective *malen'kij* 'small'. Thus the most common meaning of diminutives is endearment, and only the next important semantic feature is smallness.

The same tendencies are characteristic of hypocoristics: truncated forms are used for informal naming (*Filja* from *Filipp* or *Varja* from *Varvara*); forms ending in *-ka* are depreciative or strongly informal, whereas the addition of the second suffix makes them tender, e.g. *Fil'ka* 'Filipp-Dim', *Var'ka* 'Varvara-Dim' (depreciative) vs. *Fil-ečka, Fil-juša, Fil-juška, Fil-jušen'ka, Var-ečka, Var-juša, Var-juška, Var-jušen'ka* (tender). Not only personal names but also kinship terms and some names of animals may serve as a base for hypocoristics, e.g. *deda* 'grandfather-Hyp', *kisa* 'cat-Dim:Fem', *kotja* 'cat-Dim:Masc' etc. Masculine nouns take the inflectional ending *-a* that moves them to the 2nd (mostly feminine) declension class, but without gender shift. Normally, hypocoristics are shorter (have less syllables) than the given name, whereas diminutives mostly have one extra syllable (except feminine diminutives/depreciatives from *-a* nouns formed by *-k-*).

1.3 Diminutive grammar

Grammatically, all diminutives belong to the productive declension classes of nouns. Table 2 shows the regular shift of the declension class by diminutivization. Nouns belonging to productive feminine *-a* class 2 and masculine consonant class 1 usually do not change their class except for some rare masculine nouns that shift to the non-productive masculine *-a* class. This is a clear structural disadvantage that needs explanation. Feminine nouns of the unproductive consonant class 3 shift to the productive feminine *-a* class. This fact has been a reason for claiming that diminutives facilitate the system of Russian declension (Olmsted 1994; Kempe, Brooks & Pirott 2001; Kempe, Brooks 2005).

Table 2. Shift of declension classes by diminutivization

No change	No change	Disadvantage (opaque gender)	Advantage (non-productive → productive)
Fem Cl. 2 (+P) = Fem Cl. 2(+P)	Masc Cl. 1 (+P) = Masc Cl. 1(+P)	Masc Cl. 1 (+P) → Masc Cl. 2 (-P)	Fem Cl. 3 (–P) → Fem Cl. 2 (+P)
sobaka → sobačka 'dog-Dim'	mjač → mjačik 'ball-Dim' zajac → zajčik 'hare-Dim'	zajac → zajka 'hare-Dim' medved' → miška 'bear-Dim'	myš' → myška 'mouse-Dim' dver' → dverca and dverka 'door-Dim'

In general, Table 2 shows the strengthening of the 2nd declension class as a result of diminutive use. Other informal nouns may also contribute to the enrichment of the 2nd declension class. For example, some nouns of foreign origin remain indeclinable. They do not form diminutives in literary Russian; colloquial diminutives of these nouns, however, are feminine and belong to the 2nd productive class (cf. *metroška*-Fem from *metro*-Neut 'metro'). Such diminutives are very informal and occur mostly in the slang of children and teenagers. Nowadays, this diminutive type is growing in importance. Feminine diminutives like *apelsinka, pomidorka, morožka, suvenirka* 'orange-Dim:Fem*, tomato-Dim:Fem*, ice cream-Dim:Fem*, gift-Dim:Fem*' frequently occur instead of solely permissible previous masculine and neuter variants *apel'sinčik, pomidorčik, morožence, suvenirčik.*[4]

The majority of lexemes have a restricted number of diminutives which are normally used and may enter dictionaries as constant derivatives, even if in reality a much larger variety of them are used in spoken Russian. Besides, some very frequent words, like *malen'kij* 'small', *mal'čik* 'boy', and *devočka* 'girl' contain inseparable diminutive pseudo-suffixes. Children try to form false back formations from non-evident lexicalized diminutives, like **loga* < *ložka* 'spoon'.

1.4 Augmentatives and other related affixes

Augmentatives are formed from nouns and adjectives by suffixes which are attached to the stem such as *-ušč-/-jušč-*, *-išč-*(cf. *bol'š-ušč-aja sobač-išč-a* 'big-Aug:Fem dog-Aug' from *bol'š-aja sobak-a* 'big dog'). The suffix *-išč-* (with the corresponding consonant alternations) is accompanied by the inflectional ending *-e* for masculine and neuter, and *-a* for feminine nouns, and the suffix *-in-* has the ending *-a* for all genders (cf. *kozlišče* and *kozlina* 'goat-Aug:Masc' formed from the root *kozjol* 'goat-Masc').[5]

There are other suffixes and prefixes that attenuate the meaning of the words, expressing different degrees of quality or pejorative meaning. Other suffixes and prefixes denoting the degree of quality have an extenuating meaning, e.g. *gorelyj* 'burned down (completely)' vs. *pod-gorelyj* 'burned down (partly)', and *ryžij* 'red' vs. *ryž-evatyj* 'reddish'. Since all these forms are very productive in modern colloquial Russian, occasionally formed combinations (including prefixes and suffixes) can display a large palette of meanings, as e.g. *pod-syr-ovat-yj* 'having a tendency to be rough', from the adjective *syr-oj* 'rough', and *bol'š-evat-ist-yj* 'giving an impression of being too big', from the adjective *bol'š-oj* 'big'. However, these tiny nuances may only occur in the speech of little children after they get the first idea of the degree of quality expressed by prototypical diminutive suffixes. Semantic and emotional suffixes have a different representation in the input of our subjects: the mother of Varja uses a great variety of combinations of derivatives from the girl's name and also from some other animated nouns. The mother of Filipp, on the contrary, uses many diminutives but almost no augmentatives and other expressive derivatives from personal names except for the name of her son.

1.5 Diminutive use

A good command of using diminutive suffixes manifests language mastery. Nevertheless, native speakers repeatedly report that diminutives are overly loaded expressively and therefore may seem irrelevant, false, or in bad taste. Some native speakers frequently personalize their manner of speech by using diminutives or hypocoristics of proper names. According to the Academic Russian grammar (Švedova 1980: 208), the values expressed by diminutives are as follows: personal, evaluative, caressing, hypocoristic, and pejorative. It is stressed that the meaning of smallness is usually accompanied by the semantic nuance of endearment, but in many cases expressive meaning is the only semantic function of diminutives.

What meaning the speaker attributes to a diminutive depends to a greater degree on his intention and on context than on the semantic potential of a morpheme. The small size usually causes affection, and after some adjectives with the meanings 'small, nice, pretty' etc. the use of a diminutive suffix is highly expected. You can only say *malen'kaja ruka* 'little hand' about the small hand of an adult, whereas the hand of a child is supposed to be called *malen'kaja ručka* 'little hand-Dim'. Some diminutive forms are lexicalized but still not found in the dictionaries. Some are nominations for special things, e.g. *zajka* 'hare-Masc:Dim' serves as a tender name for a woman, therefore in some contexts it gets the illegal feminine agreement, *zajka moja* 'hare-Fem:Dim my-Fem', whereas in literary tradition it should remain masculine, as in the famous children's verse by A. Barto *Zajku brosila xozjajka, pod doždjom ostalsja zajka* ('The host has thrown her hare-Dim:Masc away, the hare-Dim:Masc remained-Masc under the rain').

The analysis of everyday spoken language demonstrates that child- or pet-centred situations as well as eating and taking care of one's body provoke the use of excessive diminutives even in adults. (This fact was stated in numerous studies on the Russian language.) They also mark irony and self-irony, insignificance of request, and politeness towards a customer rather than expressing smallness. Thus, the teacher addressing a group of pre-school children would not use the diminutive *ručka* 'hand-Dim'; she would use a simplex *ruka*, as it is prescribed in the official day care centre curriculum. However, coming closer to a certain child and especially wanting to appease, reassure or to set him/her at ease or at rest, she would certainly say *ručka* and name all surrounding objects in a diminutive form. The same is characteristic of adults in different intimate situations. If the interlocutor misinterprets this ambivalence, or if a caress is not taken intimately, a request may become an order, as in *Skoren'ko!* 'quickly+Dim'. The threat is expressed by the lexical choice itself, and the suffix definitely does not increase this threat, but rather mitigates it.

The pragmatic use of diminutives is due to the emotional closeness, and physical proximity, focusing on everyday use. The diminutivization manifests the idea of "things for us" versus "things for everybody / for the others". There is no study of priming effects for diminutives in Russian compatible with Clahsen et al. (2003), but in the Russian grammatical tradition, starting from the 19th century, several grammarians like Aksakov, Potebnja and Šaxmatov claimed that diminutive suffixes should be defined as inflectional rather than derivational, since they do not change the lexical meaning of the words and their gender assignment (Vinogradov 1947: 112–116). At the early phases of language acquisition, diminutives are item-based and may not yet be regarded as fully productive models. For both of our subjects we can only make some claims about the relation between diminutives and their simplicia based on the use of oppositions in the input and in the output. These data show that some of the diminutives never occur in oppositions, and replace the corresponding simplicia in child-centred situations.

The multiformity of diminutives outlines this phenomenon as a field of potential linguistic play; yet, they are neither universal nor compulsory, and some people, being perfect speakers of the language, do not employ them at all. It is a non-obligatory speech refinement.

2. Material

2.1 Previous studies on Russian child diminutives and augmentatives

The well-known diary study of the acquisition of Russian by Gvozdev reports that the first productive diminutives occurred in the speech production of his son Ženja at about age 1;9, next to the singular-plural and nominative-accusative distinction (Gvozdev 1961: 399ff.). Šaxnarovič and Jurieva (1990) claim that suffix formation in children develops rather early – they suggested the age 2;6 as the overall starting point – and stage by stage. They proposed the following sequence: 1) phonology-based orientation, 2) morpheme-based orientation, 3) real relationship to the object precedes the abstract representation of the surrounding world in the word. They found as well that children do not necessarily understand diminutive and augmentative suffixes as indicators of a real small or large size. Lepskaja (1997: 89–90) assumed that diminutives and hypocoristic words are semantically neutral in children's speech, and argues for this with numerous non-existent back-formations of the type **čaxa* from *čaška* 'cup', and **oduvan* from *oduvančik* 'dandelion'. In the same study, she observed superfluous childish suffixes in **sobač-on-oč-en'k-a* 'dog-Dim-Dim-Dim', and counted three times more diminutives in adults' child-directed speech than in their adult-directed speech. Diminutives also play an important structural role in facilitating the system of noun declension: when children were shown pictures of familiar and novel animals and were asked to describe them after hearing their names, they produced fewer agreement errors for diminutive than for simplex nouns (cf. Olmsted 1994; Kempe et al. 2003).

Andrews (1996, 1999) writes that the diminutive and endearing characteristics can sometimes overlap and in some cases be quite separate; the meaning is expressed by the appropriate context and intonation. Her data on the use of complex morphological substantive forms in CDS collected in St. Petersburg show that women were more likely to admit diminutives than men. However, the age effect (the older the subject, the less diminutives) was more statistically relevant than the gender effect. In her survey, she pointed out that *-k-a, -ik, -ok, -jonok, -očk-a* were the most popular suffixes in the specific family use.

The semantics of the productive augmentative in *-in-* also includes the idea of quantity, but it underlines the uniqueness of the object, a sort of definiteness, otherwise absent in the Russian language. Although these suffixes are not augmentative or "uniqueness" suffixes *per se*, they are used as such because the homonymous suffixes are mixed. For example, a girl aged about 3 years named a big toy pig *svinina*, while normally this means 'pork'. This suffix appears to be productive in colloquial Russian with hypocoristic animal names: *sobač(at)ina* for dog, *košatina* for cat etc. (Addressing an animal by the potential name of its meat makes it dear, a sort of rude tenderness.)

Previous research indicates that the regularizing features of diminutives enhance categorizations, first of all, for gender and declension. With the focus on the features of CDS vs. child-produced speech we may find what really can facilitate language learning.

2.2 The present study

Our subjects were the girl Varja investigated by E. Protassova from 1;6 to 2;10 and the boy Filipp investigated by M. Voeikova from 1;4 to 2;8.[6] Varja was an early-talking child; the age of development of Filipp corresponds to his biological age. Filipp was tested with the KID Scale (Reuter & Woznick 1966; Reuter & Gruber 2000; Čistovič & Šapiro 2000) at the Institute of Early Intervention in St. Petersburg at the age of 2;5. Both children were tape-recorded at least once a month, normally, once every 2–3 weeks. At the time of lexical spurt the corpus of Filipp reaches a high density level (more than 1000 utterances of the child per session from 1;5 to 1;9). The data for Varja are available in CHILDES. The observations on Varja's language development were documented also in a diary (about 500 000 signs), whereas for Filipp we rely on the tape recordings.

The children under investigation differed not only by sex and developmental level but also had quite a different strategy in acquisition. Varja was talkative and creative, whereas Filipp used a repetitive strategy and did not initiate the conversation, especially during the first sessions (1;4–2;0). The use of diminutives is also different: from the very beginning of tape recording, Varja often produces several different diminutives from one and the same word, her speech is emotional and she knows how she can express her emotions. Therefore we could not establish when the first diminutives occurred in her speech (Protassova 1997). Filipp uses diminutives as if they were the unique name for the object. There are no diminutive-simplex oppositions in his speech until 1;8, and even after they emerge, their number does not exceed 21 pairs, which means that more than 50% of all diminutives are used without an opposition (see the total number of diminutive types in Table 4 below). At the same time, Filipp starts to develop the system of noun declension and agreement between adjective and noun (Voeikova 1998). As we expect, a high percentage of diminutives in his speech helped him to cope with the system of nominal declension.

2.3 Frequency of diminutives in the speech of children and caregivers

This analysis aims to show whether there is a correlation between the number (percentage) of diminutives in the speech of children and their mothers and what phases in the acquisition and use of diminutives could be defined.

2.3.1 *Quantitative characteristics of diminutives: the case of Varja*

In general, diminutives are constantly growing in types, but diminishing in tokens per discourse unit. The majority of them is formed and used correctly, and there is no abuse of them. Varja uses a number of diminutives from the very beginning of the sessions; later on, they become more differentiated. The analysed data show that the number of diminutives depends on the subject of speech. Some concepts (such as body parts, meals, clothing, dolls and other toys) stimulate diminutive use. The variety of the items studied, both types and tokens, grows in both adult and child, and the child uses diminutivization more and more intentionally.

Table 3. Quantitative analysis: Varja and her mother. (Varja's sessions had the same time length, but were growing in word length from month to month)

Age	CHILD DIMINUTIVES			ADULT DIMINUTIVES		
	Proper Nouns: Types/ Tokens] TTR	Common Nouns: Types/ Tokens] TTR	Total Nouns: Types/ Tokens] TTR	Proper Nouns: Types/ Tokens] TTR	Common Nouns: Types/ Tokens] TTR	Total Nouns: Types/ Tokens] TTR
1;6	1/57/ 0.02	41/64/ 0.64	42/121/ 0.35	8/26/ 0.31	53/87/ 0.61	61/113/ 0.54
1;7	3/50/ 0.06	56/128/ 0.44	59/178/ 0.33	8/37/ 0.22	55/137/ 0.40	63/174/ 0.36
1;9	3/16/ 0.19	67/201/ 0.33	70/217/ 0.32	8/33/ 0.24	98/251/ 0.39	106/284/ 0.37
1;10	1/19/ 0.05	70/134/ 0.52	71/153/ 0.46	6/13/ 0.62	48/91/ 0.53	54/104/ 0.52
2;0	3/3/ 1.00	48/80/ 0.6	51/80/ 0.64	2/2/ 1.00	51/100/ 0.51	53/102/ 0.52
2;4	0	76/152/ 0.47	76/152/ 0.47	7/9/ 0.78	52/90/ 0.58	59/99/ 0.60
2;10	0	51/74/ 0.70	51/74/ 0.70	3/5/ 0.60	62/79/ 0.78	65/84/ 0.77

The proper names used by speech partners are mostly the names of the addressees, and they show a large scale of variants, especially for the name of the child. The self-given name of the child is *Aja, Ain'ka*, and it is picked up and repeated by adults. Still, in the adults' speech the most frequent hypocoristic noun is *Varen'ka* (a variant that has given birth to the above-mentioned self-reference), but also *Varjunja, Varjun'ka, Varčun, Varčuš, Varjušonec, Varčušon* (the last four being masculine), *Varjunečka, Varjuša, Varjušen'ka, Varčušečij* (this being a masculine adjective), and *Varjona*. The adjectives were only few in the sessions studied. In the first sessions, when the child had not yet acquired the personal pronoun of the first singular, self-reference was made mostly in a diminutive form (*Aika, Ain'ka*). In CDS, 3rd person singular reference was commonly made by diminutives (*Varen'ka, Varjuša, Varjušon* etc.).

Graph 1 shows the percentage of diminutives in the speech of Varja and her mother. There is a clear correspondence in the speech of a child and her caregiver: the percentage of diminutives decreases in both partners with the growing age of a child. Comparing these parameters to the ones of Filipp and his mother (Graph 2) we assume that Filipp never reaches the same density of diminutives as Varja demonstrated in the first phases of the period observed: maximal percentage for Filipp does not exceed 40%, whereas Varja starts with almost 60 % of diminutives both in types and in tokens. This may show that Varja's use of diminutives is intentional and may have another reasons than the one of Filipp.

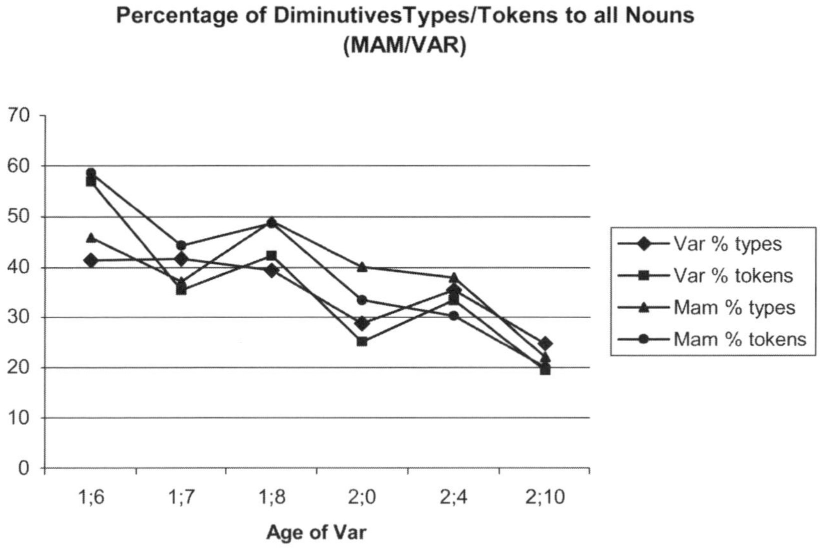

Graph 1. Diminutives in the speech production of Varja and her mother

The maximal percentage of diminutives in Varja's speech is registered in the very beginning of the observation. From that point on, she uses them productively. Her conscious use of diminutive patterns has much to do with emotional sphere and with the slight semantic nuances that she is able to express.

There is more imitation of the child's diminutives by adults than vice versa, i.e. adults pick up the word said by the child and repeat it: for example, the words for bread, bottle etc. The child cases of imitation (non-spontaneous uses) are rare. Thus, after having heard *top-top po dorožke* 'go-go along the road-Dim', a piece of a poem, the child says *top-top po doroge* 'go-go along the road', indicating that the diminutive was understood as another form of the same word. Instead, quite often a diminutive is used shortly after a base form (e.g. *kulič-kuličik* 'sand cake'), or the base form is derived from the diminutive. *Jagodki* 'berries-Dim' is a plural form of *jagodka*. It was pronounced as *jagyki* by the child at that time (according to her phonetics), and the base form should be *jagoda*, but the child says *jagyki, jagyk, jaga* deriving the plural form from the fictive masculine or a non-existent base *jaga* with unclear gender. In a couple of cases the child uses the base form after the adult has used a diminutive, as in adult: *jaičko* 'egg-Dim', child: *jaico* 'egg'. Almost all of these examples were found in the first session (1;6). Thus it is clear that the very first occurrences of diminutives must have appeared in the speech production of Varja before 1;6.

Among the diminutives used by both communicators are adjectives (names of colours, characteristics of softness, warmness, goodness), adverbs (with the meaning clean, fast, some) and sometimes verbs.

Nouns like *korzinka* 'basket-Dim', *knižka* 'book-Dim', *kosička* 'plait-Dim', *myška* 'mouse-Dim' are felt as if they were the adequate variant for everyday life. We did not find the correspondent dictionary base variants *korzina, kniga, kosa, myš'*. We count *jožik* 'hedgehog-Dim' as a base form, because it is doubtful that the child could hear the simplex *jož* with any frequency. *Trusiki* 'slip-Dim:Pl', plurale tantum, is the only form in the first sessions, but the base form *trusy* occurs afterwards; it was also first used and perceived as a diminutive. According to our analysis, the use of different suffix types reflects the general co-relation of the same suffixes in spoken Russian. (Those with *-n'k-* are the most common, then come those with *-čk-*.).

Diminutive nouns are more frequent than diminutive adjectives, next come interjections and adverbs. Diminutives are mostly used in the nominative and accusative, but also in the instrumental case. Filling in all the cells in the morphological tables demands that the child makes extensions, false starts, truncations and back-formations, some of them doomed as blind alleys.

2.3.2 *Quantitative characteristics of diminutives: the case of Filipp*

The sessions of Filipp had different lengths; therefore we give absolute numbers (Table 4), as well as percentages of diminutives in relation to all noun types and tokens for every age bracket (Graph 1). We counted separately the use of diminutives for common and proper nouns as well as the special vocatives formed from animal names and/or personal names. The use of hypocoristics in the speech production of the child was not extensive (the maximal number being 3 types and 8 tokens).

The first important change in the speech production of Filipp is at 1;7–1;8, when he proceeds from sporadic repetition of diminutives to their spontaneous production.

Then also the first simplex-diminutive oppositions occur. The quantitative characteristics of diminutive formation in the speech of Filipp becomes similar to the one of Varja after he reaches 2;0.

Table 4. Quantitative analysis: diminutives of Filipp and his mother

Age	CHILD DIMINUTIVES			ADULT DIMINUTIVES		
	Proper Nouns: Types/ Tokens/ TTR	Common Nouns: Types/ Tokens/ TTR	Total Nouns: Types/ Tokens/ TTR	Proper Nouns: Types/ Tokens/ TTR	Common Nouns: Types/ Tokens/ TTR	Total Nouns: Types/ Tokens/ TTR
1;5-1;6	4/6/ 0.66	6/14/ 0.42	10/20/ 0.5	8/40/ 0.2	180/493/ 0.37	188/533/ 0.35
1;7-1;8	3/8/ 0.38	20/32/ 0.62	23/40/ 0.56	6/16/ 0.38	236/478/ 0.43	240/388/ 0.62
1;9-1;10	1/1/ 1	55/117/ 0.47	56/118/ 0.48	3/7/ 0.43	154/282/ 0.55	157/289/ 0.54
1;11-2;0	0	45/75/ 0.6	45/75/ 0.6	8/11/ 0.73	131/223/ 0.59	139/234/ 0.59
2;1-2;2	0	111/239/ 0.46	111/239/ 0.46	8/20/ 0.4	255/445/ 0.57	263/465/ 0.57
2;3-2;4	4/11/ 0.36	107/229/ 0.47	111/240/ 0.46	14/38/ 0.37	157/267/ 0.58	171/305/ 0.56
2;5-2;6	3/3/ 1	76/160/ 0.48	79/163/ 0.48	2/4/ 0.5	115/222/ 0.52	117/226/ 0.52
2;7-2;8	2/2/ 1	94/206/ 0.46	59/121/ 0.49	6/13/ 0.46	187/290/ 0.64	115/193/ 0.60

At this time the number of diminutive tokens increases to 40 and the TTR becomes stable (approx. 0.40–0.50). At the same age, a real qualitative and quantitative change occurs. However, common nouns remain the main source of his diminutive formation. Also, the number of diminutives in the speech production of Filipp's mother is especially high before and a bit after 1;8, decreasing later on. All these characteristics indicate that the mother's active usage of diminutives is a precursor of their spontaneous use by the child.

Graph 2 (below) shows that the percentage of diminutive types and tokens in the speech of Filipp and his mother coincides for the first time at the age of 2;0 when Filipp starts to use them frequently. The number of proper names and hypocoristics in the speech of Filipp's mother is higher than in the speech of the child. She uses from 7 to 18 different proper noun lemmas per session, whereas the maximal number of proper noun tokens per session is 137.

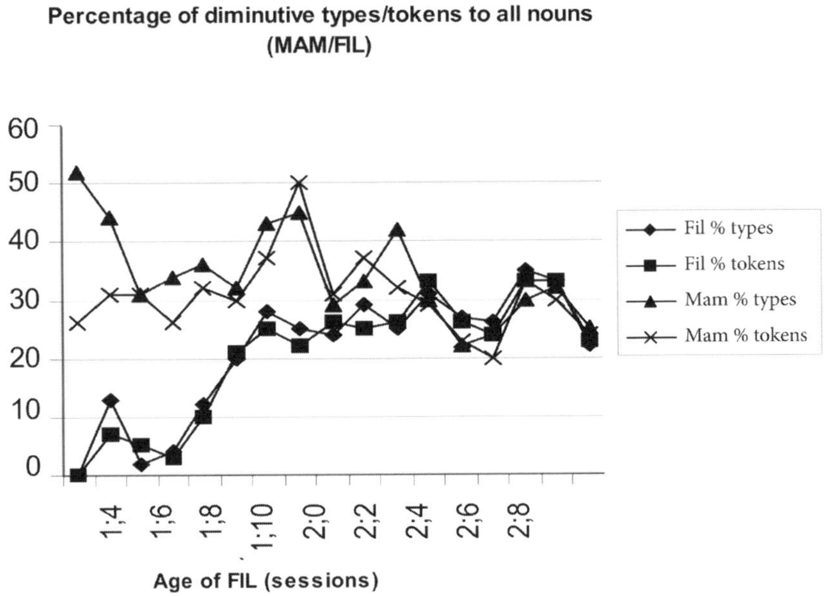

Graph 2. Diminutives in the speech production of Filipp and his mother

Before that, the mother uses more diminutives than afterwards: their percentage in her speech is about 50% at the time when Filipp only starts to speak. These are almost exclusively diminutives formed from common nouns. Interestingly, the percentage of diminutive tokens in the mother's speech is almost always lower than the one for diminutive types (except for the age 1;11). This means that she repeats more simplex tokens and, at the same time, uses many different diminutive lemmas (types). This gives the child an idea of the morphological pattern, which helps him to construct diminutives from different noun stems. This is one more reason to explore the simplifying function of diminutives in the building of the system of declension (cf. Olmsted 1994; Kempe et al. 2003).

2.3.3 *Comparison of the two children*

Filipp's use shows a clear difference from the speech style of Varja, who uses many diminutive tokens from only a few types (e.g. 3 types vs. 50 tokens at 1;7 in Table 3 above). This feature may be explained by several factors: 1) from the earliest sessions onwards Varja is at a more advanced phase of language acquisition than Filipp, who only starts to utter his first words; 2) she is creative in inventing new words and combinations, whereas Filipp repeats a lot after his mother. Comparing the speech production of both children to that of their caregivers, we also notice a striking difference between the two mother-child pairs: the number of diminutives in the speech of Varja may even exceed the corresponding number in her mother's speech, whereas Filipp never approaches the quantity of diminutives used by his mother. In both Filipp and his mother the number of diminutive tokens derived from proper nouns is relatively small in comparison with Varja: especially at the beginning of the recording (1;6–1;7) she may use these diminutives in different forms more than 50 times (see Table 3 above). Both Filipp and his mother never overuse diminutives of proper nouns; actually, they only form them from the name of the boy and his cat. The TTR in mother's speech is almost never significantly influenced by proper nouns. Apparently Varja is at the stage of productive use of diminutives from the very beginning.

Unlike Varja, Filipp does not use his own name or other hypocoristics for a long period after he has already started to use diminutives. After 2;3 the diminutive percentage curves in the speech production of Filipp and his mother demonstrate a close coincidence for both types and tokens.

From the beginning up to the age of 2;0 there is no direct correlation between the mother and the child in the percentage of diminutives among all nouns. When the percentage of diminutives in the speech of the child is low, the mother uses extremely many diminutive types (52%). On the contrary, after Filipp started to use diminutives productively, his mother's use slightly decreases both in types and in tokens. This corresponds to the general instructive style of Filipp's mother: when she feels that the child is ready to acquire some new linguistic skill she increases the number of corresponding word-forms in her speech. The same trend was found in her use of adjectives (Voeikova 2002: 214–228). Although this common fact is true for different syntactic forms in the mother-child interactions for Varja (e.g., for embedded clauses of different types, Protassova 1988), it is not true for diminutives, because Varja's mother does not like this type of noun use and does not stimulate the use of diminutives consciously. For both children, usually, the decreasing frequency of a unit in CDS means that it has been already acquired.

In order to examine the similarities and differences between both caregivers more carefully, we compared the use of diminutives with and without an opposition in their speech (see Graphs 3 and 4). We calculated diminutive lemmas having a corresponding simplex in the same recording, as well as the number of tokens for such lemmas. We counted diminutives (and hypocoristics) of nouns and adjectives for both subjects. However, diminutives of adjectives occurred only in the speech of Varja's mother, and their number was rather low (5 adjective tokens to more than a hundred noun tokens at 1;8, with similar proportions for other ages). Graph 3 shows the results for Varja's mother.

The number of diminutive lemmas used without opposition slightly exceeds the number of those that were used in opposition to their simplicia between 1;7 and 2;4. (Before and after that period they coincide.) However, the number of diminutives used in opposition to their bases is obviously higher than the number of non-opposed tokens. This means that the child hears the names of objects used in both forms much more frequently than other, non-opposed diminutives. This happens partly because of the high frequency of the girl's name used in different diminutivized and specially constructed forms. Other diminutives frequently used together with their simplicia are mostly the names of animals, toys, food and vehicles, whereas many non-opposed forms refer to objects used in everyday activities. Thus, the most important participants of the playing sessions are consistently named both by simplicia and by diminutives. This also supports the importance of pragmatic reasons for using diminutives.

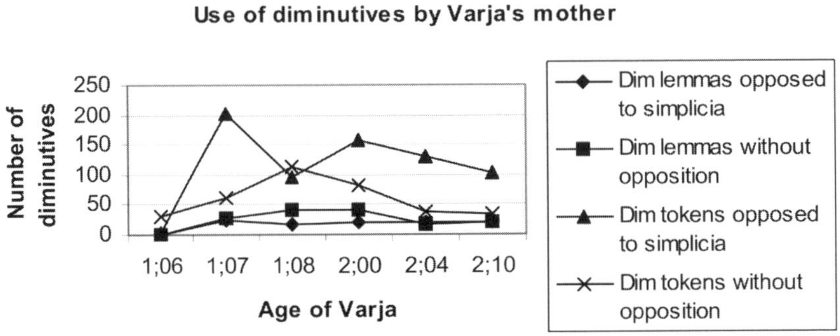

Graph 3. Diminutives used with and without an opposition: Varja's mother

Graph 4 shows the same calculations for Filipp. We took only the corresponding age intervals from Filipp's recordings in order to make both graphs comparable.

The same tendency may be seen in the speech of Filipp's mother. The difference in number between the opposed and non-opposed tokens is even more evident than in the speech of Varja's mother. For both subjects, the frequency of diminutives and their simplicia used in opposition is higher. This shows that both mothers consistently show the difference between diminutives and their simplicia for some nouns and use diminutives of other nouns as the only names of certain objects.

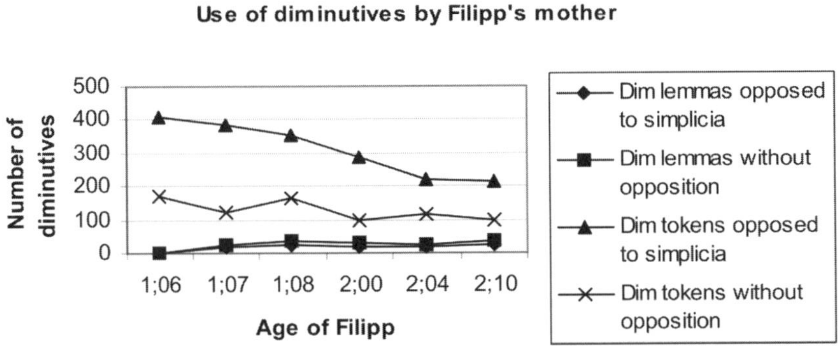

Graph 4. Diminutives used with and without an opposition: Filipp's mother

In the input of both mothers the absolute number of diminutive tokens slightly decreases after the age of two although the mothers have a different style of talking and the children are at a different stage of language acquisition. Several explanations are possible: 1) the older the child, the less emotional conversation is, 2) the mothers stop using too many diminutives after children start to produce them appropriately, or after the first case markers were used correctly.

2.4. Semantic, pragmatic and structural functions of diminutives

In this section we examine the main functions of diminutives in the speech of both children, taking into consideration that they differ in their developmental strategy. The description of Varja's first steps in diminutive use is based upon the diary data of her mother. From the earliest stages onwards, Varja tries to build various lemmas and to form oppositions with various suffixes. Surprisingly, the first oppositions occur at 1;2. This is unusually early in comparison with the mean age of development: according to Čistovič and Šapiro (2000: 47ff.) only 38% of Russian-speaking boys and 44% of girls are able to use 5 different authentic words at the age of 1;3. Filipp is more typical in the speed of his language development. His use of diminutives may presuppose that he rather benefits from their structural properties.

2.4.1 *Semantic and pragmatic role of diminutives (Varja)*

In this subsection, we demonstrate the most typical and atypical situations in which diminutives are used, mostly in chronological order. Varja's first words at the age of about one year were marked by the pseudo-suffixes *-ka,-pa,-ba* that occur in babbling. In the very first diminutive formations like *tjukaka* and *tjutjoki* (from *cvetoček, cvetočki* 'flower-Dim, flower-Dim:Pl') the suffix and the opposition of singular and plural were expressed, however, according to the wrong declension class pattern (2nd declension class instead of the 1st).

The early diminutive forms (between 1;0 and 2;0) were probably memorized, because no corresponding simplex forms were found, but the suffixes drawn out from the input and regularized were absolutely her own: sometimes *apa* instead of *apaka* (in the adult language only *šapka* 'hat' and *šapočka* 'hat-Dim' are used), *kitika* instead of *kika* (*kryška* 'cover', *kryš-ečka* 'cover-Dim') as well as *gazetika* (*gazet-očka* 'newspaper-Dim', in spite of the fact that only other forms like *gazetka, gazetjonka* were produced by adults). All these examples illustrate the productive use of diminutives by Varja in this early period. On the other hand, some formations change gender: *pitik* (masculine, instead of *ptica* 'bird', feminine in adult speech, in colloquial Russian, *ptička* 'bird-Fem-Dim' is common), *kotik* (masculine, instead of feminine *kofta* 'jacket', diminutive *koftočka* can be found in the input), and *pitik* (*butylka* 'bottle', probably derived from *pit'* 'to drink'; diminutive *butyločka* was registered in the input). The unstable (mobile) vowels in suffixes sometimes remain where they should not, as in *na pisotike* for *na pesočke* 'on sand-Masc:Dim: Sg:Gen'. This mistake also shows Varja's creative way of using patterns because the unstressed suffix *-ek-* sounds like *-ik* in the nominative and thus does not undergo a vowel drop. In Varja's speech, some adult diminutives, like *mamaka* for *mamočka* 'mummy-Dim', and *kapuka* for *kapustka* 'cabbage-Dim', appeared at the very beginning as base forms. The self-invented *kanjaka* (Fem. 2nd declension class at 1;1, confused in gender at 1;9, afterwards Masc.) for *karandaš* 'pencil&Masc' shows the use of this pattern. *Kanjaka* was picked up and used by the caregivers in various cases. Later on, *kanjasik* and *kajandasik* occurred, the first reduced and diminutivized, and the second representing a usually diminutivized form *karandašik* from *karandaš*, as well as derived from *kanjaka, kanjakočka* 'pencil-Dim' in various case forms. At 1;11, Varja added an explanation *ja znaju, konjaka – eto kon', lošad', eto karandašik* 'I know, konjaka [from *kon'* 'steed'] is a steed, a horse, this is a pencil'.

As Varja learned to name body parts, she started to use parallel diminutives for each word, such as *uka / ut'ka* for *ruka / ručka* 'hand / hand-Dim'. A bit later (1;2) while trying to repeat the word *platoček* 'handkerchief-Dim' the child uses familiar morphological structures: *pataka, patoc'k, patocika*; however, only the variant *patotik* declined as *patotika, patotiki* persisted in spontaneous speech. Other early diminutives are *kaxetika* or *kasetika* for *konfeta, konfetka, konfetočka* 'sweet-Dim' and the adjective *goiki* for *golen'kij* 'naked-Dim:Masc', used for all genders and numbers, which persisted in that form for some time.

Adult words such as *šar* 'ball', *šarik* 'ball-Dim', although representing the basic word and the derived diminutive respectively, may refer both to a globe, balloon, ball, beads or marbles, and only the context allows us to decide whether we speak about a large or a small thing of the same shape. In Varja's discourse, this difference is maintained; she names large and small things respectively with different words. The word *soska, sosočka* 'dummy', 'dummy-DIM' (1;6) has two realizations in Varja's speech: *sosaka* and *sosika*, with maybe the first variant reflecting the basic form and the second reflecting the diminutive form.

By 1;7 the following phrases illustrate the diminutive use: *dam kam-us-it-ik* 'I'll give the stone-Dim-Dim-Dim', a word that does not occur in CDS, while Varja is asking her mother to give her the stone *kam-us-yk, kuda pitijajsja?* 'stone-Dim-Dim, where are you lost?' (looking for the stone). As is typical of pragmatics, the request coming in a form of suggestion nearly implies a diminutive in such a context. When a four-syllable neuter form *koljosiko* 'wheel-Dim:Neut' was uttered with its word-final phonetic realization [a], which is a typical unstressed feminine ending, Varja reduced it into *kaseka,* yet the suffix was kept. The suffix *-k-* followed by the ending *-a* is the most frequent word-form ending in Russian, thus even erroneous forms follow this pattern.

The majority of acquired words entered the same morphological model, and the ending *-ka* prevailed. The next frequent diminutive type was formed with unstressed *-ik*: *gasjotik* for *goršoček* 'pot-Dim', *kamanik* for *karmančik* 'pocket-Dim' and with the stressed *-ok*: *pisikok* for *pojasok* 'belt-Dim' (at 1;7 also *piisjok, piisjotik)*, and *kisikok* for *košeljok* 'purse-Dim', lexicalized, where the form is adapted to the phonetic abilities of the child. Still, it was followed by *von kukaka izit, kukaka goikaja, i Vaika goikaja* 'there is a doll-Dim, the doll-Dim is naked-Dim, and Varja-Dim is also naked-Dim'. Varja says it, first pointing to the naked doll on the floor, and then uncovering her own belly.

Neuter diminutives with unstressed inflectional endings are understood as feminine. This becomes clear from the fact that children form the illegal feminine accusative ending with *-u* from these nouns, e.g. *sitečku* from *sitečko* 'sieve-Fem*:Acc' instead of the correct *sitečko* 'sieve-Neut:Acc' (2;4,5). The preference for the accusative forms with *-u* can be perceived also in some masculine nouns, e.g. *kusjotiku* 'piece-Fem*-Dim:Acc' instead of *kusoček* 'piece-Masc-Dim:Acc', *takanik-u* 'glass-Fem*-Dim:Acc for the regular *stakančik* 'glas-Masc-Dim:Acc' (1;6). Another candidate for such shift is the genitive ending with *-i* instead of the correct *-a*, e.g. *u sanjonk-i* 'at the elephant-Fem*-Dim:Gen' for *u sanjonka* 'at the elephant-Masc-Dim:Gen'. Even by 1;9 Varja says *sapos'ku* 'boot-Fem*-Dim:Acc' instead of *sapožok* 'boot-Masc-Dim:Acc'. The inverse shift is rare but occurs in the nominative: *kapeik* 'kopeck-Masc*:Nom' instead of feminine *kopejka*.

Another mistake is overgeneralization in plural formation, when some suffixes should be changed, e.g., *cypljonkam* instead of *cypljatam* 'to the chicken-Masc-Dim:Pl:Dat' (1;9). At 2;5 Varja still wants to apply the suffix *-jonok*, regularly deriving the names of small animals directly from the names of adult animals instead of using the different standard lexemes: *barašonok* instead of *barašek* or *jagnjonok* 'lamb' and later *korovjonok* for *teljonok* 'calf' from *korova* 'cow'.

A false accent is present in *lUčik* instead of *lučOk* 'onion-Dim' (1;10).[7] A strange diminutive participle is found in *poxudelen'kij* 'having lost the weight-Dim'. The stacked *tjupan'tin'ki* 'tulip-Dim-Dim-Pl' is not present in CDS. At 2;0 Varja invents the diminutivized adjective *čern-ovat-yj* 'slightly black', but most of the colour diminutivized adjectives have the suffix *-en'k-*. At 2;6 Varja confounds the adult suffixes and says *zel-en-ušk-a* instead of *zel-jonk-a* 'green liniment'.

Two or three diminutive suffixes are combined in the same word to form a double diminutive non-existent in CDS: *tit-ot-in'k-ami* for *cvetočen'kami* 'flower-Dim-Dim:Instr' (at 1;4–1;5), *bant-it-ik* from *bant* 'bow-Dim-Dim', *san-jon-yt-ik* from *slon* 'elephant-Dim-Dim-Dim' (at 1;9), *pit-et'-ki* for *ptičečki* from *ptička* 'bird-Dim-Dim' (1;10), and *kol-eč-ečk-i* from *kol'co* 'ring-Dim-Dim:Pl:Nom' (2;10,5). At 1;9 she engages in a self-invented game of using successive variants of diminutive suffixes, for example *mamat'ka-mamuset'ka* from *mama* 'mummy', and *kamisyk-kamusitik-kamusik-kamik* from *kamen'* 'stone'. An example of a self-made diminutive singulative is *pyl-juš-ečka* with two suffixes, a singulative derived from *pyl'* 'dust', which appeared in CS at 2;4,5. A specific pronominal adverb form is *tutoček* 'here' (2;0), made from a colloquial diminutive in *-i tutočki* (base *tut* 'here'). After the adult proposes a diminutive *xozjajuška* 'host-Fem-Dim', two different base forms *xozjajka, xozjaek* 'host-Fem, host-Masc*' appear (2;4) in the child's speech. Varja produces an innovation *na minut*-Masc*:Acc instead of *na minut(k)u* 'for a minute-Fem:Acc' (2;10,5). This may be a back-formation, like *loga* from *ložka* 'spoon', where the alternation is potentially correct. In family discourse, back-formation or reduction of the suffix *-jonok* to *-jon* is common, and therefore picked up by the child. Thus the child produces a fictive simplex *midvizon* 'bear' (2;10) from the diminutive *medvežonok* 'baby-bear'. Some truncations and back-formations could be understood as de-diminutivization markers, maybe increasing the object in form or meaning, or maybe just putting it to the norm.

At 2;2 Varja suggests that *gus'ka* (non-existent in CDS) is a sort of *gusenica* 'caterpillar' and produces *batatišče* as 'grandmother-Aug' *from batata* (the home name of her granny). Being small, Varja called her bib *nagunik* instead of *nagrudnik* (from *na* 'on'+ *grud'* 'čest' + suffix *-nik*); by the age of 2;6 she tried to make a joke by establishing an etymological connection. She asked whether *nagunik* is a kind of *noga* 'leg' (since the first vowel is unstressed, it is pronounced as *nagA*). Rare in child speech, but common for adults is the augmentative *žarišča* from *žara* 'heat' (at the age of 2;10).

Varja (at 2;5) suddenly uses a diminutivized form of her name that her parents have never heard before, i.e., *Varjunček*. Puzzled, they ask who says it, and Varja answers that it is her nanny (which is, by the way, doubtful). Immediately afterwards she produces the non-existent hypocoristics for the other family members with the same pattern: *mamunček, papunček, batatunček*, and *dedunček*. Although the word should be written with *-ik*, because only *-i-* in *-ik* does not disappear during declension, whereas *-e-* in *-ek* does, we prefer to write it with an *-e-*, because Varja pronounces it here as *-ek* even in its unstressed form. It could be a case of hypercorrection; it did not last.

In all periods of development, Varja rarely reduced and simplified adult forms; she rather used other, innovative diminutives. She overgeneralized non-diminutive and diminutive forms as in *mamuika, papuika, asjat'ka, xaosiki, kajosiki, batatin'ka* (for 'mommy, daddy, horsy, goody, wheels, granny') etc. According to Gavrilova (2002: 85–90), such gender shift in general is one of the favourite strategies in Russian CDS.

The pragmatic/semantic meaning in the use of diminutives can be illustrated by phrases such as: *Eto sumočka moja, vidiš', u menja sumka, ja sumku nadela* (1;9) 'This is my bag-Dim, you see, I have got a bag, I have put the bag on'. The bag is here a belonging; the item taken makes the child grow in her own eyes; she is already wearing an adult's accessory, and the non-diminutive after the diminutive is marking it.

Diminutives were not strongly associated with female speech. In the sessions where her father vs. her mother and grandmother are involved, the male input also offers quite many salient non-standard diminutives.

Augmentatives are probably acquired later than diminutives, yet their function is first fulfilled by back-formations from diminutives. Without the diminutive suffix, the noun becomes the symbol of a bigger object, e.g., *bub* for *bublik* 'donuts' or *jog* for *jožik* instead of *jož* 'hedgehog', confused with 'yoga' (after 2 years).

All in all, the developmental hierarchy seems to be as follows: 1) imitation of a whole word, 2) individual suffixes *-ti, -ka* applied to various words without an opposition to the base noun, 3) a small number of unspecified suffixes with *-k-* as formational element applied to all possible words, 4) multiple suffixation and its productivity in stacking many suffixes in one stem, 5) consideration of gender of the noun before and after diminutivization with all possible semantic and pragmatic implications of gender changes. Various morphophonemic aspects of diminutive formation, such as consonant mutation or dissimilation, were associated with certain steps in general phonological (or even articulatory) development. Considering the fact that in colloquial Russian, gender shifts are common as a special marker of tenderness (for animate and less common for inanimate referents), we might expect that the cases of transition from one gender to another could be classified as a developmental phenomenon. Most of the examples in the corpus conformed to the general use of diminutives, but as we can conclude from the data collection, deviations can be sporadically registered in gender, form, animacy, declension, semantics and pragmatics. Some forms are present in CDS, some are innovative and competing with already existing units.

2.4.2 *The structural role of diminutives (Filipp)*

Unlike Varja, Filipp uses diminutives at first unproductively. Since no diary data is available we cannot give a detailed picture of his acquisition of diminutives step by step. Based on the recordings we may only discuss the data found in his spontaneous speech. The first contrastive instances occur at 1;8. Even after this age many words are used only in the diminutivized form without corresponding simplex forms; for example *zajka* 'hare-Dim', *pupok* 'navel-Dim', and *miška* 'bear-Dim' never occur as simplex until 2;3. The explanation may be that the simplex forms of all these nouns contain rare codas: there are only 29 Russian nouns ending in *-up* like *pup* 'navel', 20 words ending in *-ed'* like *medved'* 'bear', and only 6 words ending in *-jac* like *zajac* 'hare' (Zaliznjak 1977). Rare codas do not allow a child put the word into a phonological connection with other nouns by rhyming it with other words as in nursery rhymes or counting rhymes. The simplex form of these nouns is opaque in declension. Adding vocalic case endings to *medved'* 'bear' thus requires the change of the word-final voiceless [t'] to the voiced [d']. The form *zajac* 'hare' loses the last *-a-* of the stem in most indirect cases, e.g. *zajca* 'hare-GEN'. Diminutive forms make both words rhyme and allow for the learning and declining of them easily and correctly in similar way (cf. *miš-ka* / *miški* 'bear-Dim:Nom / Gen' *zaj-ka* / *zaj-ki* 'hare-Dim:Nom / Gen' instead of having two different morphological patterns for 'bear' and 'hare'). Our suggestion is that using diminutives without oppositions helps mothers to organize the lexicon in such a way that most nouns sound similar and may be united into phonologically homogeneous groups. This helps later to build declension patterns.

For example, the famous Russian tale "Turnip" provides a strong pattern for building the accusative from the nominative. When telling the story every child must repeat the accusative of six different words. All these words are diminutives, or hypocoristics of the 2nd class ending in *-ka*: *Dedka za repku, babka za dedku, vnučka za babku, žučka za vnučku, koška za žučku, myška za košku – vytaščili repku* 'grandfather-Dim:Nom after turnip-Dim:Acc, grandmother-Dim:Nom after grandfather-Dim:Acc, granddaughter-Nom after grandmother-Dim:Acc, žučka-Hyp:Nom after granddaughter-Acc, cat-Dim:Nom after žučka-Hyp:Acc, mouse-Dim:Nom after cat-Dim:Acc – pulled out the turnip'. The tale in this form has a strong rhythmic connection and all the words rhyme, which makes it easy to remember. Most nouns from this tale occur in the first miniparadigms.

If we retell the story using simplex forms, the rhythmic structure and the rhyming of the forms get lost: *Ded za repu, babuška za deda, vnučka za babušku, žučka za vnučku, koška za žučku, myš' za košku.* Therefore, not only the productivity of a pattern is important here but also the rhyming codas of the 2nd class diminutives.

After 2;3 new and rare case forms first occur in diminutives, e.g. the instrumental case that is usually acquired later than other case forms (Gvozdev 1961: 390). Compare example (1) from Filipp's recording at 2;3:

(1) *MAM: A kto eto idet, bol'šoj?
%eng: and who is coming, so big?
*FIL: eto medved' cvetočkom.
%eng: it is a bear (with the) flower-Dim:Instr

Even a rare simplex *medved'* 'bear' that was never used before, occurs in the example (1). However, the lately acquired instrumental case is first formed from the diminutive *cvetoček* 'flower'. More than half of the nouns in Filipp's speech are still used in their base form.

He almost never makes commission errors, except for errors in unstable suffix vowels. Note that the suffixes *-ek* and *-ok* loose the vowel when the inflectional case ending is added (*petuška* 'cock-Dim:Gen', *zamočka* 'lock-Dim:Gen') whereas *-ik* remains unchangeable (*ključika* 'key-Dim:Gen'). Which of these patterns is preferred? The longer but transparent forms in *-ik*, or the shorter but opaque forms in *-ok/-ek*? Graph 5 shows the cumulative distribution of suffixes (measured in tokens from 0 to 1800) in the speech of Filipp and his mother.

The absolute dominance of the feminine *-ka* suffix is characteristic of the speech of both Filipp and his mother. All in all, the mother has used more than 1800 tokens of nouns containing this suffix. The distribution of masculine suffixes is as follows: Filipp used 24 words with the stressed *-ok*, 18 three-syllabic words with the unstressed *-ek* and 45 words with *-ik* (more than both *-ok/-ek* taken together). The unstressed *-ek*, in fact, sounds like *-ik*, so that the child is not aware of the difference in unmarked nominative singular.[8] Diminutives with the *-ik* suffix are also more productive in the speech of Filipp, who uses them for all vehicles (*avtobusik* 'bus-Dim', *vertoletik* 'helicopter-Dim', *korablik* 'ship-Dim', *vagončik* 'vagon-Dim'). In all data of Filipp, only diminutives with *-ik* (*bantik, pal'čik, mjačik, zajčik*) occur in the dative and genitive case, which shows that transparent formation is preferable. We did not register any erroneous formations in which the unstable *-e-* or *-o-* vowel would be conserved. However, the overgeneralization of this rule was observed by Gvozdev (1961: 397) and such examples occur in published data (*kniga bez* epilka* 'a book without epilogue' where the word *epilogue* is erroneously treated by a child as a Russian diminutive with the suffix *-ok*, cf. Voeikova & Eliseeva 1993).

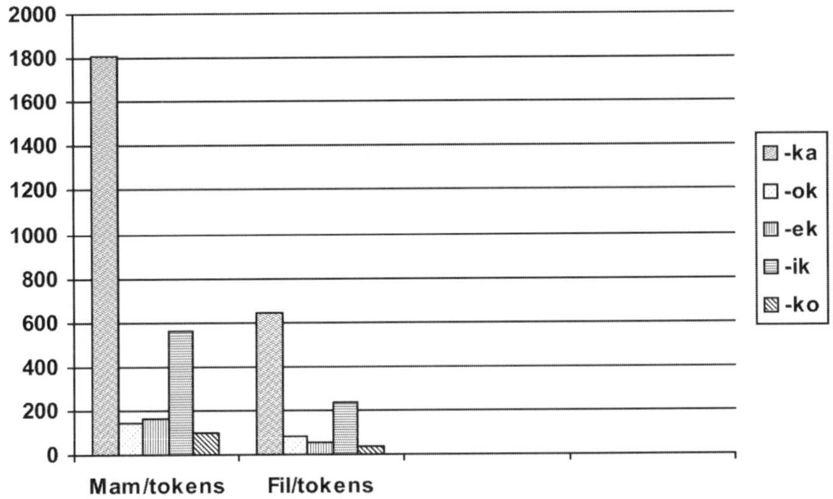

Graph 5. Cumulative distribution of diminutive suffixes in the speech of Filipp and his mother

2.4.3 *Comparison of the two children*

As in many studies on child diminutives, the mothers' and children's imitations of their interlocutors' diminutivized words promoted a similar overall diminutive use. The difference between the two children studied lies in the age of suffix appropriation and in the strategy of acquisition – creative and emotional in Varja but repetitive and not motivated by pragmatic and semantic factors in Filipp. The latter was shown by the low percentage of diminutive-simplex oppositions in the boy's speech and by the fact that he rather uses diminutives from common nouns than from personal names. However, our findings do not support previous studies on gender differences in the parental use of diminutives.

Some nouns never occur as simplex forms until a certain age. The simplex forms of all these nouns contain rare codas. The strategies which children use in the acquisition of the form and pragmatics of diminutives are variable. Consequently, diminutivization is a sphere where individual properties of the person's verbal and cognitive style come to the fore. In particular, children differ in their choice between constructed and ready-made forms.

Table 5 shows how this pattern helps Filipp to acquire the inflectional endings of nouns. Percentage of base forms (PBF) is a measure of nominative-like tokens of all noun forms (Voeikova & Gagarina 2002). Other noun tokens are marked either for case or for number. The decrease of PBF shows the growing mastery of morphology by a child. The PBF for diminutives is constantly lower than for all nouns from 1;8 to 2;3 – before 1;8

there are no inflected forms of nouns – when a child acquires the first mini-paradigms. The situation changes starting from 2;3. From this age on, the PBF in diminutives is always higher than in the simplicia. Since this situation is homogeneous before and after this turning point we may look for the explanation in the system of case oppositions at that time. Starting from 2;2 Filipp is able to produce all possible case forms both in the singular and in the plural (e.g. *v mashinax* 'in car-Pl:Loc', *medvezhat* 'baby-bear-Pl:Gen', *petuxov* 'cock-Pl:Gen') that did not occur in any of the preceding recordings.

Table 5. PBF of all nouns and diminutives in the speech production of Filipp

Age	PBF all Nouns %	PBF Dim %	Total N tokens	Total Dim tokens
1;8	91%	89%	303	37
1;9	86%	72%	363	88
1;10	83%	77%	104	30
1;11	79%	63%	85	22
2;0	63%	38%	204	53
2;1	60%	55%	451	134
2;2	61%	50%	406	105
2;3	64%	49%	420	137
2;4	63%	68%	398	103
2;5	61%	72%	373	90
2;6	59%	64%	208	73
2;7	51%	53%	353	121
2;8	48%	72%	352	87

After 2;3 almost all possible case forms from different stems occur in every recording. This period is, thus, characterizing Filipp's growing mastery in the production of case forms. Therefore, as we assume, he no longer needs the help by diminutive productive pattern, and indirect case forms from diminutives loose their leading role in his system of paradigm formation.

The detailed information from the diary of Varja shows that she uses diminutives even more frequently than her mother. She is aware of the semantic and pragmatic difference between diminutives and corresponding simplicia because she often produces several different diminutives from one and the same word. Also, already in the first recordings Varja is able to use several case or number forms from one and the same noun. Therefore we could expect that the simplifying structural function of diminutives does not play such an important role in her speech. Nevertheless, we examined the PBF value for all noun tokens and for diminutives separately for Varja's speech in the same way as we did for Filipp. The results are given in Table 6 below.

Table 6. PBF of all nouns and diminutives in the speech production of Varja

Age	PBF all Nouns %	PBF Dim %	Total N tokens	Total Dim tokens
1;6	89%	90%	144	121
1;7	72%	60%	505	178
1;9	70%	51%	616	217
1;10	67%	42%	308	104
2;0	60%	15%	478	80
2;4	51%	36%	427	152
2;9	57%	19%	517	74

In spite of the difference between the two children under observation, the decrease of PBF value in all nouns is very similar (from 89% to 57% for Varja compared to 91% to 48% for Filipp). However, with Varja, this process starts earlier: Filipp reaches the value of 79% at 1;11, whereas Varja uses about 30% of nouns in non-base form already at 1;7. This is natural, taking into consideration her earlier language development in general. As for the distribution of PBF in diminutives, it looks different in the data of the two children. With the exception of the first recording, in which the value for all nouns and for diminutives is the same, Varja constantly uses more non-base forms from diminutives than from all nouns together. At 2;0 and 2;9 the PBF value is lower than 20%, which is unusual even for spoken adult Russian, for which the percentage of nominatives is about 30% (according to Krasil'nikova 1990). Most diminutives used by Varja in these recordings are either plurals or indirect case forms. For Filipp, the dominance of diminutives in non-base forms is only obvious until 2;3. In the speech of Varja during the period of observation diminutives are not only of utmost importance for the establishing of psychological contact but also for the expression of case and number marking. The restricted amount of data and the fact that there are some gaps in the corpus of Varja do not allow statistical assessment of these findings. However, they may be seen as a tendency that needs further investigation.

As to emotionality, the diminutive use was accompanied by special intonation and coloured the utterances with endearment, but it also always had a smack of exploration and play.

Our suggestion is that diminutives not only help to avoid the unproductive 3rd feminine declension class but also organize masculine nouns rhythmically, providing them with similar rhyming codas. This helps to learn the 2nd declension patterns. As for the masculine 1st declension, both children use more nouns with the transparent suffix *-ik*, compared to the non-transparent *-ek* and *-ok* suffixes. This tendency is especially clear in the speech of Filipp and his mother. However, overgeneralization errors made by Varja also go in this direction. Conservation of one and the same stem is preferable even when the resulting forms become longer.

3. Discussion and conclusions

Diminutives help generalizing the use of grammatical markers, but this tendency is not absolute and in any case it is much more complex than was previously argued (Kempe et al. 2003). To serve as a trigger of a declension system is not their real purpose; they play other important roles in some semantic and morphological spheres, and this can be demonstrated with the help of abundant longitudinal data. Kempe et al. (2003) examined how diminutives common in Russian child-directed speech affect gender learning. In their study, Russian children aged 2;9–4;8 produced fewer agreement errors for diminutive than for simplex nouns. In general, this is true, except for the fact that not all adults use diminutives, the growing tendency in modern Russian to employ alternative forms on *-ka* may produce an even greater effect on the acquisition of nouns belonging to the 2nd declension class. Diminutive forms are certainly more emotional and more salient, and at the same time more regular than the simplex forms. It is shown and illustrated statistically that in the early stages of development the system of declension develops faster with diminutives than with simplicia, at least with some children. However, our subjects Varja and Filipp do not always use them correctly. Diminutives may be one of the means to generalize the use of grammatical markers.

Children may switch from one productive declension pattern to another, but the words that tend to change their gender belong to the masculine minority in the material. This may trigger agreement errors in hypocoristics of the type **moja Petja* 'my-Fem Petja-Masc' that are especially frequent in the speech of boys. However, our subject Filipp does not make such mistakes, maybe because of his general imitatitive strategy. The comparison of our two subjects shows that Varja produced more non-existent but legal diminutives that did not occur in CDS. This may be shown by the fact that such diminutives occur first without the corresponding simplex forms both in her speech and in CDS.

As to the pragmatics of diminutives, we would suggest an important function for them in adult-child communication, which lasts even after childhood. This is the distinction of the "things for us" versus "things for everyone / the others": diminutives must turn objects (referents) to be good towards the child, to make the child happy, not to be his/her enemies (Protassova 1999, 2001a, 2001b). Our study shows that the pragmatic function of diminutives is complex: on the one hand, the mother uses diminutives to make the world look nice for her child, on the other, diminutives reflect the fact that a child lives in a world of small objects.

The data of the two Russian children show different strategies in the acquisition of diminutives. This is maybe due to their sex (feminine vs. masculine endings become accordingly more frequent in CDS), level of language development (in the early stages, the early-talker Varja has broader phonological possibilities than the later-talker Filipp), the strategy of the caregivers (to use emotional speech or to remain more restrained) and the children themselves (to imitate the way the adults behave verbally or to invent games on their own). This specificity concerns the percentage of proper and common nouns and the general correlation between the number and percentage of diminutives in the speech of the child and his/her caregiver. These percentages correspond in Varja's data (Table 3), whereas the mother of Filipp uses diminutives very frequently in the early period when the child himself does not yet produce them. Only after Filipp starts to use diminutives productively, does the percentage of diminutive types and tokens in the speech production of the child and his mother coincide (Graph 1). However, the frequent use of diminutives in CDS is characteristic of both dyads. Also, in spite of a big difference in the speech style of both caregivers, their use of diminutives is rather similar: there are more diminutive lemmas used without an opposition to their simplicia in the speech of both mothers (Graphs 3, 4). Nevertheless, the opposed forms are much more frequent if measured in tokens rather than diminutives without an opposition.

There are also several structural reasons for using diminutives. They usually move nouns from the unproductive and marginal declension classes to the productive ones, as feminine nouns with the ending *-ka*. Even without the change of a declension class they help to grammatically organize the lexicon in a way that makes unknown words sound like familiar ones. This may be shown by the fact that many Russian diminutives without corresponding simplex forms are produced from words with a phonologically unusual right edge. The repetition of such rhyming words facilitates the acquisition of inflectional patterns. The use of these properties was especially important for Filipp. He did not tend to be very emotional during the recordings; therefore we could not find many examples of a clear pragmatic use of diminutives. However, his system of declension develops faster first with diminutives than with simplicia (Table 5).

One of the most comprehensive considerations for diminutive use in adults comes to us through their developmental history. They are used individually, both in CDS and in child language; they have personal imprints, and they serve as a tool to train and try out grammatical and pragmatic phenomena. In addition, they accumulate culturally loaded emotional contexts.

Notes

1. We thank Ineta Savickienė and Wolfgang U. Dressler for their helpful comments and suggestions on earlier versions of our chapter. We are also grateful to the anonymous reviewers for their proposals that helped to improve the paper.

2. The simplex verb *kušat'* is already pragmatically loaded: it is used by educated people only in the 2nd and 3rd person and is not recommended for use in the 1st person singular referring to an adult speaker.

3. The suffix *-onok* which is regularly used for the derivation of nouns designating baby animals cannot be indeed treated as diminutive *sensu stricto*, but it is used in this sense by children; this can be proved by the use of the suffix for inanimate objects.

4. In parallel, new contracted from phrases and suffixed words have the same structure: *vstrečnaja polosa* – *vstrečka* 'centre strip', *proščal'nye* slova – *proščalka* 'concluding remarks', as well as productive *-nik* for masculine: *platnyj* student – *platnik* 'student who pays for his studies'. The dominance of the feminine declension is strengthened by the non-accentuated endings of the neuter which are understood as *-a*.

5. It is also important for acquisition that there are other possibilities to express intensification of the quality, e.g., augmentative prefix in the adjectives *pre#sladkij* 'Aug#sweet' from *sladkij* 'sweet'. Such augmentatives are usually used in reduplicative form with their simplexes, e.g. *bol'šaja-prebol'šaja* 'big-Aug-big', or simply *bol'šoj-bol'šoj* 'very big', lit. 'big-big'.

6. Filipp was tape-recorded especially for the Cross-linguistic Project on Pre- and Protomorphology in Language Acquisition coordinated by W.U. Dressler on behalf of the Austrian Academy of Sciences.

7. Capital letters indicate a stressed vowel.

8. This may be the explanation also for Varja's form *na pesotike* 'on the sand-Dim', where the unstable vowel remains intact.

References

Andrews, E. 1996. *The Semantics of Suffixation.* München: LINCOM Europa.

Andrews, E. 1999. Gender roles and perception: Russian diminutives in discourse. In *Slavic gender linguistics,* M. H. Mills (ed.), 85–112. Amsterdam/Philadelphia: Benjamins.

Čistovič, I. and Šapiro, J. 2000. *CDRI: Metodičeskie ukazanija po ispol'zovaniju oprosnika dlja russkogo jazyka* [Methodical recommendations for the use of the questionnaire for the Russian language]. St. Petersburg: Institute of Early Intervention.

Clahsen, H., Sonnenstuhl, I. and Blevins, J. P. 2003. Derivational morphology in the German mental lexicon: A dual mechanism account. In *Morphological Structure in Language Processing,* R. H. Baayen and R. Schreuder (eds), 125–155. Berlin: Mouton de Gruyter.

Fentslova, M. 1985. Rol' značenija isxodnogo slova pri obrazovanii značenija deminutiva, issledovannaja na materiale razgovornoj reči russkogo i češskogo jazykov [The role of the meaning of the base word in the formation diminutive meaning, studied on material of the colloquial Russian and Czech languages]. *Czeskoslovenska Rusistika* 30 (5): 221–227.

Gavrilova, T. O. 2002. *Registr obščenija s det'mi: strukturnyj i sociolingvističeskij aspekty* [The register of communication with children: structural and sociolinguistic aspects (based on the Russian language)]. Unpublished PhD dissertation. St. Petersburg: St. Petersburg State University.

Gvozdev, A. N. 1961. *Voprosy izučenija detskoj reči* [Questions of the study of child language]. Moscow: Izdatel'stvo APN RSFSR.

Kempe, V. and Brooks, P. J. 2005. The role of diminutives in the acquisition of Russian gender: can elements of child-directed speech aid in learning morphology? *Language Learning* 55: 139–176.

Kempe, V., Brooks, P. J. and Pirott, L. 2001. How can child-directed speech facilitate the acquisition of morphology? In *Research on Child Language Acquisition. Proceedings of the 8th Conference of the International Association for the Study of Child Language,* M. Almgren et al.(eds), 1234–1244. San-Sebastian.

Kempe, V., Brooks, J. P., Mironova, N. and Fedorova, O. 2003. Diminutivization supports gender acquisition in Russian children. *Journal of Child Language* 30 (2): 471–85.

Krasil'nikova, E. V. 1990. *Imja suščestvitel'noe v russkoj razgovornoj reči* [The noun in spoken Russian]. Moscow: Nauka.

Lepskaja, N. I. 1997. *Jazyk rebjonka (ontogenez rečevoj kommunikacii).* [The language of a child. (Ontogenesis of verbal communication)] Moscow: Lomonosov University.

Olmsted, H. 1994. Diminutive morphology of Russian children: A simplified subset of nominal declension in language acquisition. In *Alexander Lipson: In memoriam,* 165–207. Columbus, Ohio: Slavica Publishers Inc.

Polterauer, I. 1981. Die Deminutiva in der modernen russischen Schriftsprache. Dissertationen der Univ. Wien. Wien: Verband der Wissenschaftlichen Gesellschaften Österreichs.

Protassova, E. 1988. Razvitie semantičeskoj svjaznosti dialoga "mat'-rebjonok" [Development of the semantic connection of the mother-child dialogue]. In *Semantika v rečevoj dejatel'nosti* [Semantics in language activity], R. M. Frumkina (ed.), 55–56. Moscow: Institute of Linguistics, Academy of Sciences of the USSR.

Protassova, E. 1997. Transition from babbling to word structure. *Papers and Studies in Contrastive Linguistics* 33: 153–158.

Protassova, E. 1999. Rol' diminutivov v detskoj reči [The role of diminutives in the child's discourse]. In: *Problemy detskoj reči – 1999* [Problems of child language – 1999], S. N. Ceytlin (ed.), 153–157. St. Petersburg: Herzen Pedagogical University.

Protassova, E. 2001a. Ovladenie kategoriej "svojo – čužoe" v detskoj reči [Acquisition of the category "the own – the else's" in child language]. In *Teoretičeskie problemy funkcional'noj grammatiki* [Theoretical problems of functional grammar], A.V. Bondarko (ed.), 238–246. St. Petersburg: Nauka.

Protassova, E. 2001b. Rol' diminutivov v sovremennom russkom jazyke [The role of diminutives in the modern Russian language]. In *Russkij jazyk: sistema i funkcionirovanie* [The Russian language: system and functionning], I. P. Külmoja (ed.), 72–88. Tartu: Tartu ülikool.

Reuter, J. M. and Wozniak, J. R. 1996. *The Kent Infant Development (KID) Scale. User's Guide and Technical Manual.* Kent, OH: Kent Developmental Metrics, Inc.

Reuter, J. M. and Gruber, Ch. 2000. *Kent Inventory of Developmental Skills (KIDS) Manual.* Los Angeles: Western Psychological Services.

Šaxnarovič, A. M. and Jurieva, N. M. 1990. *Psixolingvističeskij analiz semantiki i grammatiki na materiale ontogeneza reči* [Psycholinguistic analysis of semantics and grammar on data of speech ontogenesis]. Moscow: Nauka.

Švedova, N. J. (ed.) 1980. *Russkaja grammatika.* [Russian grammar] V. 1. Moscow: Nauka.

Vinogradov, V. V. 1947. *Russkij jazyk (grammatičeskoe učenie o slove)* [Russian language: grammatical study of the word]. Moscow-Leningrad: Učpedgiz.

Voeikova, M. D. 1998. Acquisition of diminutives by a Russian child: Preliminary observations in connection with the early adjectives. In: *Studies in the acquisition of number and diminutive marking.* [Antwerp Papers in Linguistics, 95], S. Gillis (ed.), 97–114. Antwerp: Universiteit Antwerpen.

Voeikova, M. D. 2002. The acquisition of case in typologically different languages. In: *Pre- and Protomorphology: Early Phases of Morphological development in Nouns and Verbs*, M. D. Voeikova and W. U. Dressler (eds), 25–45. LINCOM Studies in Theoretical Linguistics, 29. München: LINCOM Europa.

Voeikova, M. D. and Eliseeva, M. B. (eds.). 1993. *Detskaja reč': Teksty, dnevniki, nabljudenija.* [Child speech. Texts, Diaries, Observations.]. St. Petersburg: Obrazovanie.

Voeikova, M. D. and Gagarina, N. 2002. Early syntax, first lexicon and the acquisition of case forms by two Russian children. In: *Pre- and Protomorphology: Early Phases of Morphological development in Nouns and Verbs*, M. D. Voeikova and W. U. Dressler (eds), 115–133. LINCOM Studies in Theoretical Linguistics, 29. München: LINCOM Europa.

Volek, B. 1987. *Emotive signs in language and semantic functioning of derived nouns in Russian.* Amsterdam: Benjamins.

Wierzbicka, A. 1980. *Lingua Mentalis: The Semantics of Natural Language.* Sydney: Academic Press.

Wierzbicka, A. 1984. Diminutives and depreciatives: semantic representations for derivational categories. *Quaderni di Semantica* 5: 123–130.

Worth, D. S. 1987. Formal and aesthetic functions of diminutives in the Russian lament. *New Studies in Russian Language and Literature*, A. L. Crone and C. V. Chvany (eds), 279–290. Columbus, Ohio: Slavica Publishers Inc.

Zaliznjak, A. A. 1977. *Grammatičeskij slovar' russkogo jazyka.* [Grammatical dictionary of the Russian language]. Moscow: Russkij jazyk.

CHAPTER 3

The acquisition of diminutives in Croatian

Marijan Palmović

Diminutives are very frequent in Croatian child language; children acquire them before they master many other elements of morphology. A great majority of diminutives used by the child are nouns. Although diminutives phonologically are more difficult than the simplex forms, diminutives make paradigms more transparent and reduce the number of noun classes. In this study the data of one Croatian girl were analyzed. The analysis includes frequencies, oppositions of diminutives and simplex forms, mini-paradigms and a comparison of child's production and parental input.

Introduction

Frequent use of diminutives is one of the things that an observer could notice when watching a Croat mother with her child and paying attention to the language she uses when talking to him or her. To see whether this impression is correct, a systematic investigation into child language should be done. It is not enough to say that, indeed, there is a child's preference for diminutives. This preference is not a self-evident fact. Diminutives are longer, in Croatian they require some derivational morphology rules and are phonologically more complex than simplex nouns. Therefore, an account of the acquisition of diminutives in Croatian should include an explanation for the early emergence of this category in child's language. This explanation should show how diminutives facilitate the acquisition of other grammatical categories that Croatian children acquire around their second birthday.

In Croatian, nouns, verbs and adjectives can be diminutivized. For each of these word categories there are many affixes (both suffixes and prefixes) for diminutive derivation, but only a few are productive. In the recorded material of our child, the material that will be used in this study, only a few adjective and verb diminutives were recorded, thus the analysis will concentrate on noun diminutives. Also, only suffix types of noun diminutive derivation were found. Therefore, in the second part of the chapter only this type of diminutive derivation will be discussed.

Diminutive formation in Croatian is a productive model of derivational morphology. The range of diminutive meanings is wide, from expressing smallness to pejorative meaning and irony, depending on the word that is diminutivized or on the context.

Diminutives are frequent in child-directed speech. Parents use them mainly to create a child-centered atmosphere (Jurafsky 1996). With only a few examples of opposition between diminutives and simplex forms it is difficult to talk about the meaning of early child diminutives. It may be that they do not have any meaning other than the simplex form. Later on, as the number of oppositions between diminutives and simplex forms grows, the diminutives in Antonija's speech have a pragmatic value. Together with the appropriate intonation, whether used by Antonija or her parents, diminutives contribute to the child-oriented atmosphere, the feeling of closeness and endearment.

1. A short description of the adult target system

There exists a morphologically marked category of diminutives in Croatian. Diminutives are used to express smallness, endearment, irony or pejorative meaning. There are also other lexical means to express smallness, endearment, irony or pejorative meaning (ADJ+N, e.g. *mali*+N 'small+N', *slatki*+N 'sweet+N', *dragi*+N 'dear+N').

As mentioned in the Introduction, in Croatian, nouns, adjectives and verbs can be diminutivized. Noun diminutives are formed mainly by adding a suffix to a stem. The suffixes are gender-dependent, i.e. masculine diminutives are derived from masculine simplex nouns adding gender specific suffix (*m. nož* → *m. nož-ić* 'knife' → 'knife-DIM', *f. lađa* → *f. lađ-ica* 'ship' → 'ship-DIM'). The gender of the diminutivized noun changes only exceptionally (e.g. *f. cura* → *m. curetak* 'girl', *f. soba* → *m. sobičak*, 'room'). The formation of diminutives is morphologically productive, i.e. it is possible to form a diminutive practically from any noun, including mass or abstract nouns, e.g. *voda* → *vodica* 'water-DIM' or *posao* → *poslić* 'job-DIM'. Diminutives are not formed only from collective nouns. Feminine nouns formed with the suffix *-ost* '-ness' also form no diminutives, but since they are derived from adjectives, the diminutive meaning is expressed with the adjective in diminutive (e.g. *ćelav* → *roćelav* 'bald' → 'bald (DIM)', *ćelavost* → *roćelavost* 'baldness' → 'baldness (DIM)'. Usually it is possible to use different suffixes to form diminutives of the same noun (e.g. *cvijet* → *cvijetak* and *cvjetić* 'flower-DIM'). Although Croatian grammars (e.g. Barić & al. 1995) list fourteen suffixes for the derivation of diminutives, only a few are productive. The most productive diminutive suffixes are:

1.1 Masculine

-ić is used with most stems ending in *-dž, -đ, -č, -ć, -c*; this suffix turns root-final *k, g, h* into *č, ž, š*, e.g. *rak* → *račić* (palatalization) 'crab-DIM'. An exception is the noun *dečkić* (*dečko*, 'boy-DIM');

-čić *čamac* → *čamčić* 'boat-DIM', *golub* → *golupčić* 'pigeon-DIM'; with root-final *g, h, z, s* → *š*, e.g. *rog* → *roščić* 'horn-DIM';

1.2 Feminine

-ica the default suffix for feminine nouns and masculines belonging to the inflectional class *e**; (*žlica* → *žličica*, 'spoon-DIM'); note the change of *k, g, h* → *č, ž, š* in front of *i* (palatalization), e.g. *ruka* → *ručica* 'hand-DIM'. Feminine nouns formed from masculines with the suffix *-ica* do not have the diminutive meaning, e.g. *jelen* → *jelenica* ('m. deer'→ 'f. deer'), *majmun* → *majmunica* ('m. monkey' → 'f. monkey');

-čica a few feminine nouns of the *i* and *e* inflectional classes, e.g. *grana* → *grančica* 'branch-DIM', *stvar* → *stvarčica* 'thing-DIM'.

(*There are three noun classes in Croatian, **a**, **e** and **i**. The division is based on the case marking in the Genitive Singular. Briefly, masculine and neuter nouns belong mostly to the class **a** (e.g. *čovjek* 'man', *čovjek-a* 'man-GEN:SG'. Feminine nouns belong to the class **e** (e.g. *žena* 'woman', *žen-e* 'woman-GEN:SG', while feminine nouns that end in a consonant belong to the class **i** (e.g. *radost* 'joy', *radost-i* 'joy-GEN:SG').

1.3 Palatalized and nonpalatalized forms

It should be noted that palatalization as mentioned above, depends on the arbitrary decision or the dialect of the speaker, e.g. *biljčica* = *biljkica*, 'plant-DIM'. Sometimes, palatalized and nonpalatalized forms differ in meaning or style, e.g. *kvaka* 'knob' → *kvakica* ~ *kvačica* 'little knob' ~ 'clip', *muha* 'fly' → *muhica* ~ *mušica* 'little fly' ~ 'caprice' or *ruka* 'hand'→ *rukica* ~ *ručica* 'little hand' ~ 'handle'.

The distribution of *-ić* and *-čić* is partly based on phonological constraints. Babić (1986) gives a table showing the distribution of the suffix *-čić* according to the final phoneme of the stem:

Table 1. Distribution of the diminutive suffix -čić (Babić 1986)

	No. of derived diminutives	Percentage
Suffix *-čić*	205	
Final sonorant	160	73
Other phonemes	55	27

1.4 Dialectal suffixes

Dialectal suffixes should be added since they are quite frequent in our child-language data. The Croatian standard is Štokavian, whereas the capital Zagreb, where Antonija lives, is in the Kajkavian dialect area. Kajkavian suffixes for masculine and neuter, that are present in Antonija's speech, are listed below:

-ek (masc.) e.g. *pes*→ *pesek* 'doggy', *zec* → *zeček* 'rabbit-DIM'
-ec (masc.) e.g. *dečko* → *dečec* 'boy-DIM'
-eko (neuter) e.g. *sunce* → *sunčeko* 'sun-DIM'
-eco (neuter) e.g. *mlijeko* → *mlekeco* 'milk-DIM'

1.5 Homophonous suffixes

The most productive diminutive suffixes *-ica, -ić* are homophonous with other word-formation suffixes. Some diminutives formed with these suffixes have lost their diminutive meaning and became 'frozen diminutives' e.g. *čaša* 'glass' → *čašica* 'calyx', *jagoda* 'strawberry' → *jagodica* 'fingertip'. These words can sometimes be diminutivized again (e.g. *glavica* → *glavičica* 'head-DIM-DIM', *iglica* → *igličica* 'needle-DIM-DIM', *kapljica* → *kapljičica* 'drop-DIM-DIM', *dječarac* → *dječarčić* 'boy-DIM-DIM'), especially when the original diminutives have become at least partially lexicalized.

At this point it can also be noted that some of the diminutives make paradigms more transparent, e.g. a very common noun in child language *ruka* ('hand', 'arm') does not have a transparent paradigm due to the palatalization (*k, g, h* changes to *c, z, s* in front of *i*): Gen. *ruke*, Dat. *ruci*, Acc. *ruku*, Loc. *ruci*, Inst. *rukom*. The diminutive of *ruka*, i.e. *rukica* has a transparent paradigm: Gen. *rukice*, Dat. *rukici*, Acc. *rukicu*, etc. A similar simplification of the paradigm can be noted with masculines that have mobile vowel *a* in the Nominative, e.g. *vrabac* 'sparrow', but not in the oblique cases: Gen. *vrapca*, Dat. *vrapcu*, etc. When the word is diminutivized, the mobile vowel is avoided: *vrapčić* 'sparrow-DIM' in Nom., Gen. *vrapčića*, Dat. *vrapčiću*, etc. Masculine nouns with the ending *-o* in Nom. with a moving vowel before it, e.g. *posao* 'job', Gen. Sg. *posl-a*, have also a more transparent paradigm when they are diminutivized: *posao* → *poslić* 'job-DIM'. Since the diminutive is built from the stem (*posl-*), there is no insertion of the moving vowel and no change of the final *-l* into *-o*.

A reduction in the number of inflectional classes also takes place. Nouns that belong to a weakly productive class ***i*** of feminine nouns (feminine nouns that end in a consonant) derive diminutives with the suffix *-ica* and have a paradigm according to the productive class ***e***. For example, *kost* 'bone', Gen. *kosti* 'bone-GEN', but *koščica* 'bone-DIM', *koščice* 'bone-DIM-GEN'.

1.6 Augmentatives

In Croatian there exists a morphologically marked category of augmentatives, as well. There are four productive augmentative suffixes (Barić et al. 1995):
-ina *rep* → *repina* 'tail-AUG', *junak* → *junačina* 'hero-AUG' (with palatalization);
-čina *lažov* → *lažovčina* 'liar-AUG'
-etina *jama* → *jametina* 'hole-AUG'
-urina *kosa* → *kosurina* 'hair-AUG'

Augmentatives are used to express the meaning of bigness. Sometimes, they can also express pejorative meaning.

It is often mentioned that the distribution of diminutives and augmentatives is not equal in all Croatian dialects. The Kajkavian dialect is characterized by more frequent usage of diminutives (Lončarić 1996), while augmentatives are more common in the Lika region. However, quantitative data on this are not available.

1.7 Adjective and verbal diminutives

Adjective diminutives are formed either by adding suffixes or prefixes to the stem. They mean that the nouns they describe have some property only partially or to a smaller extent. Roughly, their meaning corresponds to the English suffix *-ish*.

There are more than 20 suffixes for deriving verbal diminutives, but only two are productive. They are *-uljiti*: *smijati* → *smijuljiti* 'laugh-DIM' and *-kati*: *gristi* → *grickati* 'bite-DIM'.

1.8 Hypocoristics

Derivation of hypocoristics is less predictable than the derivation of diminutives. Usually, they are formed from a truncated stem (only the first syllable with one or two consonants of the second syllable) and suffixes *-a, -e, -o, -ica* and *-ko*. However, sometimes the first syllable is missing: *Antonija* often becomes *Toni*, *Tončica* or *Tonija*. It is also possible to form hypocoristics by adding the suffixes to adjectives (with truncation or without it), e.g. *pospan* → *pospan-ko* 'sleepy-HYP' or *nestašan* → *nestaš-ko* 'playful-HYP' to form a nickname, for example. Sometimes, hypocoristics are formed just like any other diminutive, e.g. *Renata* → *Renatica* or *Helena* → *Helenica*.

2. The data

The Croatian data consist of Antonija's spontaneous speech recordings from the age of 1;3 to 2;8. Usually, recordings were made three times in a month with each recording session lasting about 45 minutes. The recordings were made at Antonija's home, during everyday activities, such as playing, cooking, talking about friends and family, commenting TV and radio shows etc. There were 42 sessions in 18 months of recording. In that period 5.157 utterances of Antonija were collected. The total size of the corpus is 13.718 utterances and 47.846 word tokens. The total number of Antonija's word tokens is 12.878. The transcripts were morphologically coded according to CHILDES (MacWhinney 1997). Antonija's parents are middle class urban dwellers and speak Zagreb Štokavian dialect with some elements of Zagreb Kajkavian dialect. A period of about one month – when Antonija was 1;8 – is missing due to family reasons.

3. Antonija's acquisition of diminutives

Extended usage of noun diminutives is a prominent feature of child-directed speech in Croatian. In Antonija's files the vast majority of diminutives were nouns. During the recording period of nearly 18 months only two adjective diminutives were recorded (*malički* 'smallish' and *crvenkast* 'reddish'). Only the first one was used by the child. Four verbal diminutives were recorded (*kašljucati* 'cough-DIM', *piškiti* 'pee-DIM', *šaputati* 'whisper-DIM', *smijuljiti se* 'laugh-DIM'). Antonija used two of them (*piškiti* and *smijuljiti se*). In short, there were only two adjective diminutives and four verbal diminutives in the input language and Antonija's production is even smaller.

Antonija used her first diminutive when she was 1;5 and it was the word *mamica* 'mummy' alongside with *mama*. The more extended usage of diminutives started at 1;9, when she used 9 different diminutives on 13 occasions in a single recorded session. From that moment on the number of diminutives in the recorded sessions grows. The number of diminutives varies throughout the recoding period (see Table 1). The input also varies in both types and tokens (see Table 2). Although there are not many examples of diminutives used together with their simplex forms, it is obvious that Antonija recognizes the semantic connection between the simplex form and the diminutive since she uses them interchangeably in the same situation. For example, at age 1;6 she recognized that *Helenica* was the same person as *Helena*, that *naranđica* and *naranča* 'orange' were the same fruit or that *olovčica* and *olovka* represented the same thing (a pencil).

Although only the most productive suffixes are used to form diminutives, Antonija's parents use different suffixes to form diminutives of the same stem, e.g. *brežuljak* can be found together with *brijegić* 'hill-DIM'. This trait is noticeable especially when dialectal forms are used together with the standard ones, e.g. *pesek* (dial.) – *psić* 'dog-DIM', *zeček* (dial.) – *zečić* 'rabbit-DIM', *sunčeko* (dial.) – *sunašce* 'sun-DIM', etc.

3.1 The quantitative analysis

Table 2 and Figure 1 give the total number of diminutives (in types and tokens) and in percentages for Antonija. Table 3 shows the number of diminutives in Antonija's parents' speech and gives the percentages of diminutives

Table 2. The number of diminutives in Antonija's speech

Antonija	No. of dim. (types)	% of dim. (types)	No. of dim. (tokens)	% of dim. (tokens)
1;3	0	0	0	0
1;4	0	0	0	0
1;5	1	14,29	2	14,29
1;6	0	0	0	0
1;7	3	6,00	4	3,42
1;8	,	,	,	,
1;9	11	26,83	18	22,78
1;10	16	20,25	24	20,87
1;11	10	20,83	10	15,15
2;0	3	8,82	3	6,25
2;1	19	32,76	21	22,83
2;2	22	25,00	43	23,89
2;3	18	19,15	30	16,22
2;4	13	15,12	21	14,58
2;5	20	25,32	26	19,12
2;6	11	17,46	14	15,56
2;7	24	25,53	32	22,07
2;8	13	29,55	17	27,87

The number of diminutives was small during the first months of the recordings. Only after 1;9 the number of diminutives increased, both in types and tokens. The number of simplex forms used by Antonija in the same period varied from 7 to 81, but it was usually around 60. The recordings comprise both the pre- and the protomorphological period. Antonija reached the period of protomorphology around her second birthday (Katičić 2003) and this is the period in which diminutives start to occur more regularly. The absolute number of diminutives varies, but the percentage of diminutives stabilizes at about 1/5th of all nouns after Antonija's second birthday. Note that the percentage of diminutive types is higher than the percentage of diminutive tokens.

The oscillation in the number of diminutives is generally parallel in Antonija's speech and the parental input. This fact reflects the usual adaptation between speakers in conversation.

Table 3. The number of diminutives in input

Input	No. of dim. (types)	% of dim. (types)	No. of dim. (tokens)	% of dim. (tokens)
1;3	9	27,27	23	31,94
1;4	23	30,26	36	19,78
1;5	16	37,21	22	26,51
1;6	4	19,05	4	9,30
1;7	23	19,17	39	13,22
1;8	,	,	,	,
1;9	16	20,25	24	15,09
1;10	43	27,04	61	19,18
1;11	13	15,48	18	11,46
2;0	15	15,63	17	10,56
2;1	56	36,84	77	26,28
2;2	58	30,37	102	26,02
2;3	57	23,75	91	19,91
2;4	54	21,43	93	19,42
2;5	73	35,78	104	24,88
2;6	42	26,92	59	19,87
2;7	59	29,50	89	24,12
2;8	58	35,80	87	31,41

3.2 Diminutives – simplex contrasts

Only a few diminutives were found in contrast to their simplex bases, i.e. there were only a few occasions when Antonija used the same lemma as a diminutive and as a simplex form (see Table 4.). Diminutives are often the only words for some objects. However, more oppositions between diminutives and simplex forms were found in Antonija's speech after she reached the age of 2;2. Interpretation of these oppositions is difficult due to their small number oppositions in the data. It is at least partially a consequence of a low probability of capturing this opposition in a 45' to 1-hour recording session.

However, one must note that in the given period there were not many noun lemmas with an opposition in inflection or lemmas in mini-paradigms in Antonija's speech. In conversations in which Antonija used between 40 and 80 different noun lemmas and 70 to 200 noun tokens only a few of them occur in two or more case forms. A table showing the distribution of Antonija's diminutives according to case forms is given in Figure 1a. For a comparison a figure showing the distribution of Antonija's simplex nouns is given in Figure 1b.

Table 4. The diminutives in contrast to all nouns

Age	No. of lemmas with an opposition	Total No. of dim. lemmas	Total No. of noun lemmas	Total No. of dim. tokens	Total No. of noun tokens
1;3	0	0	7	0	33
1;4	1	1	9	0	27
1;5	0	1	7	2	18
1;6	0	0	5	0	10
1;7	1	7	47	4	127
1;8	,	,	,	,	,
1;9	0	8	40	18	88
1;10	2	16	69	24	121
1;11	1	9	79	10	123
2;0	1	1	43	3	73
2;1	0	16	54	24	110
2;2	3	17	69	45	226
2;3	2	14	72	30	212
2;4	3	13	81	21	148
2;5	2	13	60	28	210
2;6	2	12	68	14	131
2;7	5	21	85	32	190
2;8	2	8	44	17	80

Figures 1a and 1b show that the plural forms of both simplex forms and diminutives are rare even after 2. However, they show greater diversity in cases (both in singular and plural) after the age of 2;0. Finally, Figures 1a and 1b suggest that Antonija was more inclined to use diminutives in oblique cases than one would expect from the ratio of oblique/nominative cases in simplex nouns, presumably due to the differences in productivity and transparency of oblique case formation in diminutives (§ 1). This is not surprising since pre-school children and even children in the first grades of the elementary school often use diminutives in oblique cases although they use simplex forms in the Nominative (e.g. Nom. *leptir* 'butterfly', but Gen. *leptir-ić-a* 'butterfly-DIM-GEN' or *konj* 'horse', Gen. *konj-ić-a* 'horse-DIM-GEN').

Table 5 lists all lemmas that occur in the opposition between simplex form and diminutive in chronological order. The first three-member mini-paradigm occurred at the age of 2;2:

(1) Nom. Sg. *beba* 'doll' *bebica* 'doll-DIM'
Acc. Sg. *bebicu*
Nom. Pl. *bebice*

1a. Diminutives

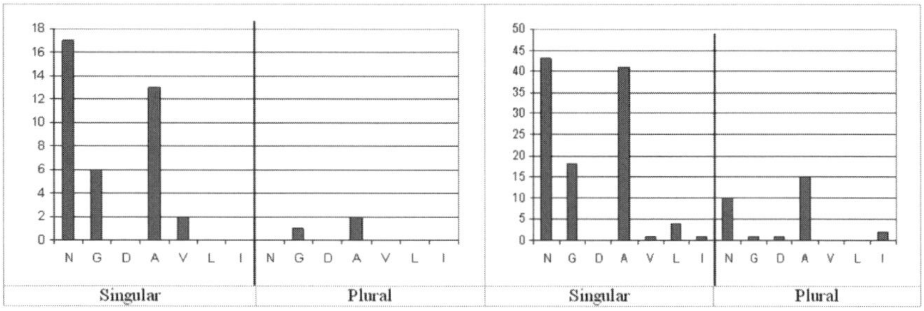

1b. Simplex nouns

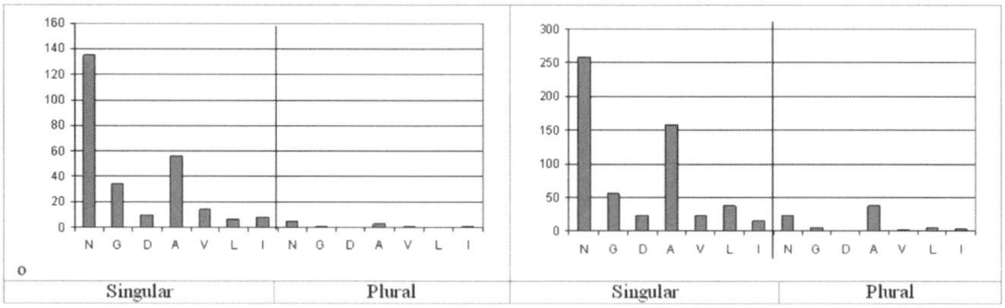

Figure 1. The distribution of case forms before the age of 2;0 (left) and after (right)

A month later the first mini-paradigm with a simplex form of the same noun can be found in the data (although the first oppositions occur earlier, the first at the age of 1;6: *tat-a* ~ *tat-i* 'daddy-NOM' ~ 'daddy-DAT'):

(2) Nom. Sg. *beba* 'doll'
Acc. Sg. *bebu*
Inst. Sg. *bebom*
Nom. Pl. *bebe*
Acc. Pl. (=Nom.) *bebe*

In the recorded data there are several diminutives that have more transparent paradigms than their simplex forms and Antonija uses diminutives rather than the simplex forms. The first to occur was *štapić* 'stick-DIM' with short plural *stapići*. The simplex form has the long plural *stap-ov-i*. There are several feminine diminutives with a more transparent paradigm than their simplex forms, e.g. *rukica* 'hand-DIM' and *nogica* 'leg-DIM' or *knjigica* 'book-DIM'; Dat./Loc. *rukici* ~ *ruci*, *nogici* ~ *nozi* and *knjigici* ~ *knjizi*.

A closer inspection of the plural forms reveals that the plural forms are restricted to only a few words – words for things that usually come in pairs (arms, legs, shoes, etc.). The accusative plural turns out to be the most frequent oblique case for syntactic reasons – usually, the mentioned words that occur in plural are direct objects of the sentences (e.g. 'I put on the shoes'). Genitives are usually instances of a partitive genitive in sentences where Antonija is either offered some food or drink or she wants some food or drink (*Hoću čajeka*, and *Hoćeš čajeka?* – 'I want some tea-DIM.' and 'Do you want some tea-DIM?' – are the most common examples.).

Table 5. Lemmas with oppositions in diminutives

Age	Lemma	Simplex type	Case	DIM-type	Case
1;7	masquer	**maškara**	Nom.Sg-	**maškarica**	Nom.Sg.
1;10	dot	**točka**	Nom.Sg	**točkica**	Nom.Sg.
1;10	cat	**mače**	Nom.Sg	**mačića**	Acc.Sg.
1;10	dog	(pas, pes)		**pesek, psić**	Nom.Sg.
1;11	horse	**konj**	Nom.Sg.	**konjić**	Voc.Sg.
2;0	hedgehog	**jež**	Nom.Sg.	**ježeko**	Nom.Sg.
2;2	Renata	Renata, Renate	Nom.Sg., Gen.Sg.	**Renatica**	Nom.Sg.
2;2	Anita	**Anita**	Nom.Sg	**Anitica**	Nom.Sg.
2;2 2;3	baby	**beba** **bebu**	Nom.Sg., Acc. Sg.	**bebica, bebicu** **bebice**	Nom.Sg., Acc. Sg., Nom. Pl.
2;3	orange	**naranča**	Nom.Sg.	**narančica**	Nom.Sg.
2;4	ball	**loptu**	Acc.Sg.	**loptica**	Nom.Sg.
2;4	Anita	**Anita** **Anite**	Nom.Sg., Gen.Sg.	**Anitica**	Nom.Sg.
2;4	milk	**mlijeko**	Acc.Sg.	**mljekeco**	Acc.Sg.
2;5	horse	**konj**	Nom.Sg.	**konjić**	Nom.Sg.
2;5	eye	**oko**	Acc.Sg.	**okeco**	Acc.Sg.
2;6	Renata	**Renatu, Renate**	Acc.Sg., Gen.Sg.	**Renatice**	Gen.Sg.
2;6	aunt	**ujni**	Dat.Sg.	**ujnicu**	Acc.Sg.
2;7	arm	**ruka**	Nom.Sg.	**rukicu** **ruke**	Acc.Sg. Acc.Pl.
2;7	mommy	**mama, mama**	Nom.Sg., Voc.Sg.	**mamice**	Voc.Sg.
2;7	cat	**maci**	Dat.Sg.	**mačićima**	Dat.Pl.
2;7	boot	**čizma**	Acc.Sg.	**čizmicu**	Acc.Sg.
2;7	stick	**štapom**	Inst.Sg.	**Štapić** **štapiće**	Loc.Sg. Acc.Pl.
2;8	hat	**šešir**	Acc.Sg.	**šeširić**	Nom.Sg.
2;8	dog	**pes** **pas**		**peseka** **psića** **psiću**	Acc.Sg. Acc.Sg. Dat.Sg.

3.3 The distribution of the diminutive suffixes

In order to verify the statement that only the most productive suffixes were found in the speech of Antonija and her parents, the distribution of the diminutive suffixes is given in Figure 2.

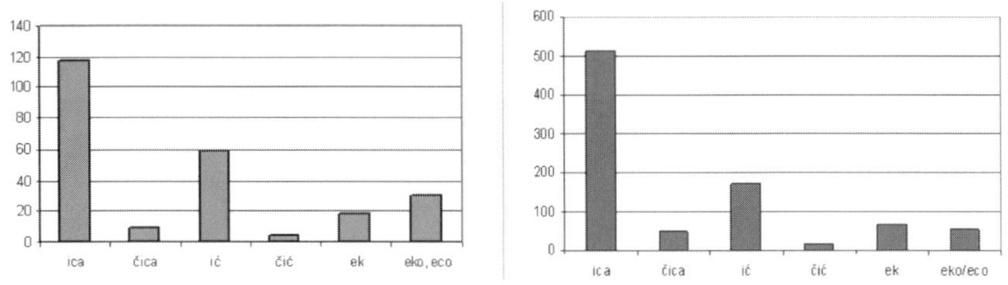

e

Figure 2. The distribution of the diminutive suffixes: left – Antonija, right – parents

One can notice that, first, in Antonija's output there are more feminine (55%) than masculine (37%) diminutives and the percentage of neuter diminutives is around 8%. There were no masculine diminutives until 1;9.

Second, the distribution of the suffixes in Antonija's speech generally reflects the distribution of the same suffixes in the parental input. Furthermore, it reflects the system of diminutive derivation in Croatian, in general. It consists of two default suffixes (*-ica* and *-ić* for feminine and masculine nouns, respectively) and two phonologically constrained suffixes (*-čica* and *-čić*). There is a productive neuter diminutive suffix *-ce*, but it was not recorded in our data. Instead, Antonija uses two dialectal neuter suffixes (*-eko* and *-eco*). In addition, Antonija uses the masculine dialectal suffix *-ek*.

However, the dialectal neuter suffixes are restricted to the only two neuter diminutives, *sunčeko* 'sun-DIM' and *mljekeco* 'milk-DIM'. The masculine dialectal suffix is restricted to *striček* 'uncle-DIM' and *pesek* 'dog-DIM' and *čajek* 'tea-DIM'. Therefore, Antonija's system reflects the target system well.

3.4 Errors

Antonija made very few errors in the derivation of diminutives. In fact, only one such mistake was recorded at 2;5, and even this error can be understood as a sign of productivity. Namely, Antonija sometimes used both the dialectal and the standard variant of the same lemma. But sometimes she used the standard suffix *-ić* for a dialectal simplex form *pes* 'dog' producing **pesić* where either standard *psić* or dialectal *pesek* were expected.

Other mistakes are related to inflection and are typical for all nouns, not only diminutives. She had problems with the plural, especially with pluralia tantum. She produced the non-existing oblique cases of these nouns in the singular, e.g. **gaćicu* instead of *gaćice* 'panties'. She committed similar errors with *kolica* 'baby buggies' and

Sesvete (a proper name). Other inflectional errors can be found, as well. The majority of them are masculine inanimate nouns in the Genitive, where Accusative is expected, e.g. *sapun-a* 'soap-GEN:SG' instead of *sapun*. In total, there are about twenty such errors in the corpus. Only once Antonija made this kind of error with a diminutive saying *šos-ić-a* 'dress-DIM-GEN:SG' instead of *šosić*.

3.5 The meaning of Antonija's diminutives

The most frequent diminutives are words for body parts, toys, animals and clothes. Food is also diminutivized frequently, especially in child-directed speech, probably in order to make it more acceptable as a meal. Food, toys, family members and animals are central figures and objects in Antonija's life and it is not unusual that words for these things are used more frequently and are to be more likely diminutivized than other words, e.g. *posao* or *škola* ('job' or 'school') which are never diminutivized.

As shown in Table 6 the most frequent diminutives are nouns for animals. They make up around 1/3 of the Antonija's diminutives. Diminutives for toys, food and body parts can also be found among the most frequent diminutives. Comparing the two parts of the table one can easily see that half of Antonija's diminutives are very frequently used by her parents, too.

Among the most frequent diminutives there are many that are found only in Antonija's data and not in the input. Usually, the reason is the nature of the conversation between the child and her mother: in many occasions it is some sort of elicitation of the target word, a direct question or an incomplete sentence. Therefore, Antonija's choice of diminutives in these contexts can be a good sign of her productive use of diminutives.

The rules for deriving diminutives were the first rules of derivational morphology, but Antonija did not use diminutives to express smallness. This is in accordance with the predictions of the theory of natural morphology (Dressler & Karpf 1995). Parents' diminutives have pragmatic value. A good example of the pragmatic value of diminutives is the use of diminutives in the feeding routine. When Antonija's mother wants Antonija to eat some meat, for example, she uses a diminutive *mesić* 'meat-DIM', a word that would hardly be used in any other situation being a mass neuter noun having a diminutive only in Kajkavian dialect: *meseko*.

(3) *MOT: Evo izvoli **mesića**.
%eng: Here is some **meat-DIM**.
*MOT: Ham.

This example (3) illustrates well the basic function of diminutives in child directed speech: to create a child-oriented situation or the specific atmosphere of endearment and love.

The child starts to use diminutives imitating the adults, but the function of the first child's diminutives is just referring to the objects: in one situation Antonija's mother and grandmother talk about cuddling using a diminutive together with the appropriate intonation and Antonija wants some tea. She used a diminutive, as she always did when she refers to that drink. She does not know another word for this drink or, at least, the word *čaj* 'tea' cannot be found in her data (see Table 4.). It is difficult to give a proof that at some point Antonija started to use diminutives knowing that their usage would make her get what she wanted due to the endearment, emotions and the sense of closeness they imply.

Table 6. The most frequent diminutives in the speech of Antonija and her parents

Antonija			**Adults**	
konjić	'horse'	12	konjić	18
čajek	'tea'	7		
cipelica	'shoe'	6	cipelica	6
knjigica	'book'	6		
bančica	'bank'	5		
psić	'dog'	4	psić	6
bombončić	'candy'	3		
medić	'bear'	3		
pesek	'dog' (dial.)	3	pesek	12
rukica	'hand'	3	rukica	10
vrećica	'bag'	3	vrećica	10
bombica	'bomb'	2		
crkvica	'church'	2	crkvica	4
flašica	'bottle'	2	flašica	5
gazica	'gauze'	2		
košarica	'basket'	2	košarica	5
loptica	'ball'	2		
mačić	'kitty'	2		
maškarica	'masquer'	2		
pjetlić	'rooster'	2		
ribica	'fish'	2		
tutica	'potty'	2	tutica	4
zvečkica	'rattle'	2		

As for hypocoristics, both Antonija and her parents used them when they refer to family members, friends and their dog. *Antonija* was often *Tonija*, *Tončica*, *Toni* or even *Antica*. Uncle *Darko* became *Darac*, *Zvonko* became *Zvonac*. Of course, hypocoristics for 'brother', 'sister', 'mother', 'father', 'grandmother' and 'grandfather' can be found in the data, as well. Generally, their number (in tokens) is bigger than the number of diminutives, but the picture is blurred with numerous imitations and repetitions. In the first months of the recording sessions there were about 20 hypocoristic tokens in input and usually a dozen of hypocoristics in Antonija's speech per month. Later on this ratio was around 50 (input) to 20 (Antonija) which makes up to 25% of noun tokens. However, the number of lemmas that occur as hypocoristics is relatively small – total of 18 noun lemmas and two adjective lemmas in the input (*zloćko* 'bad-HYP' and *ljutko* 'angry-HYP'). In both cases Antonija's mother used them when talking to uncooperative Antonija (1;6 and 1;10).

4. Conclusion

Diminutives are a prominent feature of child-directed speech in Croatian. They express endearment and closeness rather than smallness as in adult speech. They emerge during the premorphological period, but their productive use starts with protomorphology (in Antonija's case around second birthday).

First diminutives in Antonija's speech are words for animals, toys, body parts and toys. Whether used side by side with their simplex forms or not, diminutives do not show any tangible difference in meaning. They have a pragmatic value, contributing to the child-centered atmosphere and endearment. There is no example of Antonija's using diminutives for expressing smallness.

The number of diminutives in the input is high. There is an obvious parallelism between Antonija's speech and the parental input, not only in the tokens, but also in lemmas.

Generally, diminutives facilitate the acquisition of Croatian noun morphology by increasing the transparency of paradigms, as, for example, in Finnish (Laalo, 1998). The most frequent mechanism is avoidance of morphonological changes, among which palatalization in front of *-i* and *-e* is the most frequent change that is avoided when diminutives are used. For this reason even older pre-school children use diminutives in oblique cases although they use simplex forms in the Nominative. The reduction of noun classes from three to two also adds to the paradigm transparency, as in Lithuanian where this feature is more prominent reducing 12 declinations to only three (Savickienė 1998). However, the available data is scarce with only a few examples in the entire corpus.

References

Babić, S. 1986. *Tvorba riječi u hrvatskom književnom jeziku*. Zagreb: Globus.

Barić, E., Lončarić, M. et al. 1995. *Hrvatska gramatika*. Zagreb: Školska knjiga.

Dressler, W. and Karpf, A. 1994 (1995). The theoretical relevance of pre- and protomorphology in language acquisition. In *Yearbook of morphology 1994*, G. Booij and J. Van Marle (eds), 99–122. Dordrecht: Kluwer Academic Publishers.

Jurafsky, D. 1996. Universal tendencies in the semantics of the diminutive. *Language* 72: 533–578.

Katičić, A. 2003. Early verb development in one Croatian-speaking child. In *Development of Verb Inflection in First Language Acquisition*, D. Bittner, W. U. Dressler, M. Kilani-Schoch (eds), 239–267. Berlin: Mouton de Gruyter.

Laalo, K. 1998. Diminutives in Finnish child-directed and child speech. In: *Studies in the Acquisition of Number and Diminutive Marking* [Antwerp Papers in Linguistics 95], S. Gillis (ed.), 137–148. Antwerp: Universiteit Antwerpen.

Lončarić, M. 1996. *Kajkavsko narječje*. Zagreb: Školska knjiga.

MacWhinney, B. 1997. *The CHILDES Project Tools for Analysing Talk*. Hillsdale: Erlbaum.

Savickienė, I. 1998. The acquisition of diminutives in Lithuanian. In *Studies in the Acquisition of Number and Diminutive Marking* [Antwerp Papers in Linguistics 95], S. Gillis (ed.), 115–135. Antwerp: Universiteit Antwerpen.

CHAPTER 4

Diminutives in Greek child language

Evangelia Thomadaki and Ursula Stephany

In this chapter, the emergence and use of the forms and functions of the most frequent diminutive suffixes occurring in the longitudinal data of a Greek monolingual child from age 1;8 to 3;0 are studied and compared to child-directed speech, which is rich in diminutives and hypocoristics. Furthermore, the distinction between pragmatic and semantic functions of diminutives as compared to simple nouns is explored, focussing on the innovative use of a non-standard suffix in this particular mother-child dyad. Since diminutives occur in a high number of singular and plural forms both type- and tokenwise from 1;9 on, the relation between derivational and inflectional morphology in early child Greek is discussed.

1. Introduction*

In spite of the fact that diminutives are among the first structures to be encountered in the speech of Greek children, their development and that of derivational formations more generally is a poorly investigated area in the acquisition of Modern Greek (henceforth MG) (Stephany 1997a, 1997b).

In this chapter, we present a detailed analysis of the development of diminutives in the speech of a Greek girl from 1;8 to 3;0 years. Formal as well as semantic and pragmatic aspects of diminutives and hypocoristics will be taken into account. We begin with an overview of the derivational and inflectional morphology as well as the semantics of diminutives, hypocoristics and augmentatives in standard MG (sect. 2). Next, the data will be presented (sect. 3). The two main sections 4 and 5 are devoted to diminutives and hypocoristics in child speech and child-directed speech (henceforth CS and CDS). Finally, our results will be summarized and compared to those of other languages (sect. 6).

2. Diminutives, hypocoristics and augmentatives in MG

2.1 Morphology

2.1.1 *Derivational aspects of diminutives*

Suffixation is the most productive process of diminutive formation in MG and the only kind of diminutive formation occurring in CS and CDS. As can be seen in Table 1 the system of MG diminutive suffixes is rather extensive.[1] These suffixes are mainly attached to nouns although some may also be used with adjectival (and occasionally adverbial) bases while others, such as *-útsikos*, are restricted to adjectives. Most of the suffixes shown in the table are productive, with *-áki* and *-úlis* exceeding the others in frequency. The learned suffixes *-ískos* and *-ídhio* and the dialectal ones *-éli* and *-údhi* have a more limited use.

Table 1. Diminutive suffixes of MG

SUFFIXES	EXAMPLES	GLOSSES
-áki	pedhaki	'little child'
	lighaki	'a little bit'
-úlis	Xristulis (N) – mikrulis (ADJ)	'little Christ' – 'little one' (M)
-úla	adherfula (N) – mikrula (ADJ)	'little sister' – 'little one' (F)
-úli/-úliko	Anuli (N) – mikruli/mikruliko (ADJ)	'little Ann' – 'little one'(NE)
-ítsa	kuklitsa	'little doll'
-ákos	kipakos	'little garden'
-ákis	Dhimitrakis	'little Dimitris'
-útsikos	ftinutsikos/i/o (ADJ)	'rather cheap' M/F/NE
-ískos	ipaliliskos	'unimportant employee'
-ídhio	amaksidhio	'small carriage'
-éli (dial.)	morudheli	'little baby'
-údhi (dial.)	kor(i)tsudhi	'little girl'
	kalimerudhja (coll.)	'a very good day' (greeting)

All MG diminutive suffixes carry inflectional markers and are stressed on their initial syllable. The main suffixes are disyllabic creating a trochaic foot which remains stable throughout the inflectional paradigm (see sect. 2.1.3 below). The most productive suffix is *-aki* (Babiniotis 1970: 214, Daltas 1985: 69–70, Mackridge 1985: 158, Stephany 1997b: 149) attributing neuter gender to diminutives. It is usually attached to neuter bases (example 1a) but may be used with bases of any gender (1b, c). By contrast, the feminine suffixes *-ula*, *-itsa* and masculine *-ulis*, *-akos*, which also occur quite frequently, require bases of the same gender (examples 2).

(1)	a.	luludhi (NEUT)	luludh-aki (NEUT)	'flower'
	b.	naftis (MASC)	naft-aki (NEUT)	'sailor'
	c.	kaliva (FEM)	kaliv-aki (NEUT)	'hut'
(2)	a.	eklisia (FEM)	eklis-ula	'church'
		skala (FEM)	skal-itsa	'ladder'
	b.	papus (MASC)	pap-ulis	'grandpa'
		naftis (MASC)	naft-akos	'sailor'

Different diminutives formed from the same base tend to evolve major or minor semantic distinctions. Thus, the meaning of example (3a) is more strongly lexicalized since it may have a pejorative nuance absent from (3b).

(3)	a.	anthrop-aki	'little man, unimportant man'
	b.	anthrop-akos	'little man'

Chaining of different diminutive suffixes is also attested, but is rather unusual, mainly because of restrictions on the order of suffixes imposed by gender. While both *misth-ul-akos* 'salary-DIM-DIM:MASC' and *misth-ul-aki* 'salary-DIM-DIM:NEUT' are possible, the form **misth-ak-ula* is not because the final diminutive suffix *-ula* would attribute feminine gender to the masculine noun *misthos* 'salary'.[2] The function of suffix chaining is to 'enhance the endearing aspect of what is being-talked about' (Sifianou 1992: 157).

Lexicalized diminutives are of two types. They may end in formatives homophonous with productive diminutive suffixes but are no longer considered as diminutives on semantic grounds (examples 4a – c) or they can be traced back to diminutives whose ending has lost its diminutive meaning (example 4d).

(4)	a.	avl-aki	'ditch'
	b.	sak-ula	'bag'
	c.	majir-itsa	'Easter soup'
	d.	tir-i	'cheese'

The fact that lexicalized diminutives ending in *-aki* have to be considered as simple nouns ending in *-i* is made obvious by their non-defective inflectional paradigm. It includes a genitive case form in contrast to that of non-lexicalized diminutives which does not (examples 5a vs. 5b) (see also sect. 2.1.3 below).

(5)	a.	avlaki ditch:NOM/ACC:SG	avlakj-u ditch-GEN:SG	avlakj-on ditch-GEN:PL
	b.	pedh-aki child-DIM:NOM/ACC:SG	*pedhakj-u	*pedhakj-on

2.1.2 *Hypocoristics and augmentatives*

Hypocoristics and diminutives are not clearly distinguished either formally or functionally. For the purposes of the present paper, we consider terms referring to persons and expressing an affectionate attitude, more particularly endearment, as hypocoristics. Although some of the most frequently used diminutive suffixes also appear in hypocoristics formed from proper nouns (examples 6), other types of hypocoristics are derived by different processes. These include abbreviation or truncation (examples 7a, b), reduplication (7c), or a combination of suffixation and abbreviation/truncation (7d, e).[3] In the latter case, the base of the hypocoristic form cannot be recovered. These hypocoristics do not necessarily convey an endearing meaning and may even replace the full forms of the respective first names in informal discourse.

(6) a. Dhimitr-akis < Dhimitris
b. Dhimitr-ula < Dhimitra

(7) a. Dhimitris < Dhimitrios
b. Dhimos/Mitros < Dhimitrios
c. Fofi/Fofo/Fifi < Fotini
d. Akis < Dhimitrakis/Xristakis and others
e. Rula < Dhimitrula/Xarula and others

Hypocoristics of kinship terms are also common in everyday speech, especially in exchanges between adults and young children (examples 8). Forms derived by suffixation carry an especially endearing meaning.

(8) a. mama 'Mummy', mam-aka, man-ula (< mana 'mother'), man-ul-itsa
b. babas 'daddy', bab-akas, bab-ak-ulis
c. pap-ulis (< papus 'grandfather'), pap-ul-akos
d. jaj-aka (< jaja 'grandmother'), jaj-ula

In child-centered contexts, affection is also quite often expressed by diminutives based on common nouns used to address a person (e.g. *kardh-ula* 'heart-DIM').

Diminutives and augmentatives are generally considered to be semantically opposed, both of them belonging to the category of 'evaluatives' (Dressler & Merlini Barbaresi 1994, 2001; see also Corbin et al. 1999). MG augmentatives are derived by suffixation (*komáti* 'piece' > *komat-ára* 'big piece', *míti* 'nose' > *mít-aros* 'big nose') often accompanied by gender shift since augmentatives can only be masculine or feminine (*kefáli* (NEUT) 'head' > *kefála* (FEM) 'big head'). In addition, the derivational process may be marked by stress shift (*komáti* (NEUT) 'piece' > *kómatos* (MASC) (lit.) 'big piece', 'very beautiful woman').[4] Augmentatives have been found to emerge later than diminutives in child language (for Italian see Ceccherini et al. 1997: 159). Since they do not appear to play any role in the Greek data analyzed in the present paper, they will not be further discussed.

2.1.3 *The inflection of diminutives*

In order to compare the declension of MG diminutives to that of simple nouns the inflection of the latter must be briefly sketched. It follows two basic patterns, one of which is based on a binary opposition of case forms (pattern A) while the other one shows a ternary opposition (pattern B) (see Table 2).[5] Masculine nouns following pattern A distinguish the nominative from an oblique case in the singular, while feminine and neuter ones contrast the genitive with a common nominative/accusative form (see Table 3a). In the plural, nouns of the three genders inflecting according to pattern A contrast the genitive with the nominative/accusative (see Tables 3a and 3b). Nouns following pattern B, most of which are masculine (with a few being feminine) distinguish the nominative, accusative, and genitive case in the singular as well as the plural. Most of them also have a special vocative form (see Table 2). In the written and spoken language, pattern A is the most frequent tokenwise (81%) while pattern B constitutes only 16% of tokens, the rest representing some unproductive classes (Kavoukopoulos 1996: 10). A similar distribution has been found in the speech of a Greek mother to her two-year-old son, i.e. 83% for pattern A and 12% for pattern B (Christofidou & Stephany 1997: 129).

Table 2. Declension classes of simple nouns: Pattern A vs. Pattern B

	PATTERN A	PATTERN B
	'man'	'angel'
	SINGULAR	
NOM	ándras	ángelos
VOC	ándra	ángele
ACC		ángelo
GEN		angélu
	PLURAL	
NOM/VOC	ándres	ángeli
ACC		angélus
GEN	andrón	angélon

Diminutive nouns generally follow the most productive patterns of simple nouns. This may occasionally result in their shifting to a different declension class as compared to their base. More particularly, masculine diminutives derived by *-ulis* or *-akis* as well as feminine ones ending in *-ula* or *-itsa* inflect according to pattern A, while masculine diminutives ending in *-akos* belong to pattern B. However, there are no masculine diminutives conforming to subpattern AI of plural formation but only to subpattern AII, which comprises an extra syllable in the plural (*papulis/papulidhes* 'grandfather:DIM' SG/PL) (compare Table 3a with Table 4). Diminutives derived by *-ula*, *-itsa* or *-akos* are defective in not showing a genitive plural. In addition, with diminutives in *-akos*, the nominative plural is either not commonly used or is completely unacceptable. The most frequent diminutives, namely those ending in *-aki*, do not distinguish any case forms. They show no genitive.

Table 3a. Declension classes of simple nouns following Pattern A

	I				II	
	MASC		FEM		MASC	FEM
	'man'	'sailor'	'cream'	'soul'	'grandfather'	'fox'
			SINGULAR			
NOM	ándras	náftis	kréma	psixí	papús	alepú
VOC	ándra	náfti			papú	
ACC						
GEN			krémas	psixís		alepús
			PLURAL			
NOM	ándres	náftes	krémes	psixés	papúdhes	alepúdhes
VOC						
ACC						
GEN	andrón	naftón	kremón	psixón	papúdhon	alepúdhon

Table 3b. Declension classes of simple nouns following Pattern A

	NEUTER				
	I		II		III
	'mountain'	'dog'	'step'	'meat'	'ground'
			SINGULAR		
N/V/A	vunó	skilí	víma	kréas	édhafos
GEN	vunú	skiljú	vímatos	kréatos	edháfus
			PLURAL		
N/V/A	vuná	skiljá	vímata	kréata	edháfi
GEN	vunón	skiljón	vimáton	kreáton	edhafón

Table 4. Declension classes of diminutives

	PATTERN A					PATTERN B
	I		II		III	
	FEM		MASC		NEUT	MASC
	'hour-DIM'	'soul-DIM'	'grandfather-DIM'	Jorghos-DIM	'dog-DIM'	'sailor-DIM'
			SINGULAR			
NOM	orítsa	psixúla	papúlis	Jorghákis	skiláki	naftákos
VOC			papúli	Jorgháki		naftáko
ACC						
GEN	orítsas	psixúlas			–	naftáku
			PLURAL			
N/V	orítses	psixúles	papúlidhes	Jorghákidhes	skilákja	?naftáki/ ?naftákidhes
ACC						naftákus
GEN	–	–	papúlidhon	Jorghákidhon	–	?naftákon

As shown above, the derivation of diminutives on the one hand diminishes the number of declensional types overall and on the other converts nouns belonging to less productive classes such as *kreas* (NEUT) 'meat' to more productive ones (*kreat-aki* 'meat-DIM:NEUT'). Diminutives never follow the neuter classes II and III, which comprise only a limited number of members.[6] In contrast to simple nouns, the inflection of diminutives does not involve stress shift since word stress invariably falls on the diminutive suffix. The plural of diminutives may, however, involve stem alternation (*papulis/papulidhes* 'grandfather-DIM' SG/PL). Due to the frequent use of diminutives in CDS, the declensional patterns followed by diminutives gain more importance than they have with simple nouns.

2.2 Semantic and pragmatic aspects of MG diminutives and hypocoristics

Both diminutives and hypocoristics occur very frequently in MG informal discourse. In spite of the fact that the semantic feature of smallness does play a role in diminutives, Dressler and Merlini Barbaresi's (2001: 43–44) observation that the superordinate pragmatic feature 'fictive' is basic in the use of diminutives is also valid for MG (Stephany 1997b: 148). The use of diminutives for attenuating or downgrading the speaker's imposition on the addressee or for diminishing formality, "thus reducing psychological distance" (Stephany 1997b: 148) can be more adequately explained in this framework.

MG diminutives may express the semantic notion of 'smallness' in a literal or metaphorical sense (examples 9b and 10). In other contexts, the pragmatic meanings of intimacy and attachment may predominate to the exclusion of the notion of smallness (example 11).

(9) a. ta fot-a tu dhromu
the light-NOM/ACC:PL of.the street
'the street lights'

b. ta fot-akj-a tu xristujenjatiku dhendru
the light-DIM:NEUT-NOM/ACC:PL of.the Christmas- tree
'the Christmas-tree lights'

(10) sikose vorjadh-aki
raised north.wind-DIM:NEUT:ACC:SG
'a north wind has begun to blow'

(11) ine fil-ar-aki mu
is friend-EXT-DIM:NEUT:NOM:SG of.me
'he/she is my pal'

In spite of the fact that diminutives are characteristic of more informal styles of spoken MG language (Daltas 1985: 63),[7] they are not restricted to such styles since they "serve a wide variety of politeness needs" (Sifianou 1992: 159). One reason for choosing a diminutive when offering something to somebody is that it is considered more polite not to keep a distance from the addressee (example 12).

(12) na sas fero ena potir-aki nero?
MOD.PTL you (2P) bring:1S one glass-DIM:ACC:SG water
'Shall I bring you a glass of water?'

In the context of child-centered speech, the most important pragmatic meaning of diminutives and hypocoristics is endearment. Thus, in example (13), both mother and child refer to body parts of the mother by diminutives.

(13) Anna at 1;11
MOT: ne, matja mu, ponai ligh-aki to mat-aki
yes eyes of.me hurts little-DIM the eye-DIM
tis mamas.
of.the mummy
'Yes, my darling, Mummy's eye is hurting a bit.'
ANN: k(e) i kil-itsa?
and the belly-DIM
'And the belly?'

Hypocoristics are distinguished from diminutives pragmatically rather than semantically. What seems to be central to their use is an affective attitude of the speaker toward a human being or an animal referred to directly or indirectly. While the hypocoristic function is primarily served by proper nouns (*Anulina* 'dear little Anna'), it is also possible to use diminutives derived from common nouns (*aghap-ula* 'love-DIM') or even simple common nouns (*matja mu* 'my eyes') in this way (example 14). Hypocoristics will be more extensively discussed in section 5.

(14) Anna at 1;11
MOT: to idhes to fegar-aki an-ul-ina?
it saw.2S the moon-DIM Anna-DIM-DIM
'Did you see the little moon, dear little Ann?'
MOT: to idhes to fegar-aki matja mu?
it saw.2S the moon-DIM eyes of.me
'Did you see the little moon, the apple of my eye?'
MOT: to idhes aghap-ula?
it saw.2S love-DIM
'Did you see it, my love?'

3. The data

The present analysis is based on part of the audiotaped speech of the monolingual Greek girl Anna growing up in Athens.[8] The data analyzed for the present paper comprise a total of 37 hours of spontaneous interaction between the child and mainly her mother in various everyday situations and cover the period from 1;8 to 3;0. As shown in Table 5, the amount of data collected during each month varies significantly and by consequence so does the number of diminutives.

In sum, it amounts to an average of 3 hours per month until 1;11, dropping to 2.5 hours for the period 2;0 to 2;6 and to 1.5 hours for the last half of the third year.

Table 5. Recorded data analyzed

age	minutes	age	minutes
1;8	60	2;5	180
1;9	150	2;6	90
1;10	180	2;7	60
1;11	300	2;8	120
2;0	180	2;9	60
2;1	180	2;10	30
2;2	210	2;11	150
2;3	90	3;0	60
2;4	120		

4. The development of diminutives in child language

4.1 Quantitative aspects

Since approximately 25% of the total number of 1,078 nouns (lexemes) in the child data studied in the present paper are diminutives, they have an important role to play in the child's language. The total number of diminutives encountered in the child's speech during the period studied amounts to 343 in terms of grammatical types and to 1,664 in terms of tokens. Lexicalized diminutives (such as *xeruli* 'handle', *mustaki* 'moustache'), as well as nontransparent hypocoristics derived from proper nouns such as *Kula* and *Taki(s)* have been excluded (see sect. 2.1.2 above and 5.1 below). Diminutives ending in the non-standard suffix *-ina* were also set aside (see sect. 5.2 below).

Diminutives occurring between 1;8 and 3;0 in Anna's speech carry six different suffixes. As is apparent from Fig. 1, these suffixes neither emerge at the same time nor do they develop at the same pace (see Table 6a for the raw scores of types and tokens). There are also important differences between the three suffixes *-aki*, *-ula*, and *-itsa* on the one hand, and the suffixes *-akos*, *-ulis*, and *-uli* on the other as far as type frequency is concerned, i.e. as regards their use with different lexical bases. The same difference holds for the type frequency between *-aki* on the one hand and the suffixes *-ula* and *-itsa* on the other. Furthermore, the diminutive suffix *-aki* seems to be quite well established from 1;8 on, while the suffix *-ula* occurs with an important number of types only at 1;11. Although the data at age 1;11 is more extensive than in the preceding three months, this does not seem to influence the number of diminutives ending in *-aki*, so that the larger number of types formed with *-ula* cannot be attributed only to corpus size.

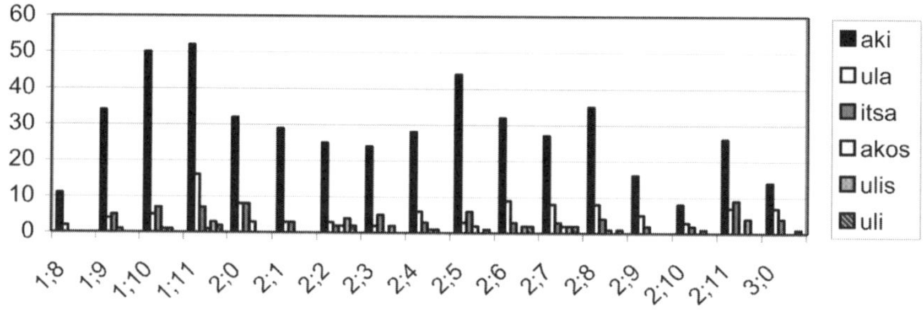

Figure 1. Diminutives occurring in Anna's speech (type frequency)

Table 6a. Diminutives occurring in Anna's speech (types/tokens)

Age	Diminutives						*N*
	-aki	-ula	-itsa	-akos	-ulis	-uli	
1;8	11/23	2/11	–	–	–	–	13/34
1;9	34/115	4/8	5/12	1/1	–	–	44/136
1;10	50/92	5/20	7/22	1/4	1/6	–	64/144
1;11	52/134	16/70	7/26	1/1	3/29	2/2	80/262
2;0	31/67	8/36	8/13	3/3	–	–	50/119
2;1	29/49	3/9	3/13	–	–	–	35/72
2;2	25/54	3/28	2/7	2/7	4/11	2/2	38/109
2;3	24/36	2/15	5/6	–	2/3	–	33/60
2;4	28/48	6/28	3/9	1/2	1/2	–	39/89
2;5	44/93	3/12	6/16	2/5	–	1/2	56/128
2;6	32/60	9/20	3/5	–	2/7	2/3	48/95
2;7	27/50	8/26	3/7	2/6	2/2	2/2	44/93
2;8	35/75	8/21	4/8	1/1	–	1/1	49/106
2;9	16/21	5/11	2/25	–	–	–	23/57
2;10	8/17	3/9	2/2	–	1/1	–	14/29
2;11	26/47	7/17	9/15	–	4/6	–	46/85
3;0	14/29	7/11	4/6	–	–	1/3	26/49

The important differences in type and token frequency between the three diminutive suffixes *-aki, -ula, -itsa* on the one hand and *-akos, -ulis, -uli* on the other observed in the child's speech reflect those of CDS (see Fig. 2 for type frequency and Table 6b for types and tokens). In fact, among the first three, the preference for *-aki* in comparison to *-ula* and *-itsa* is even stronger in CS than in CDS (cf. Tables 6a and 6b).

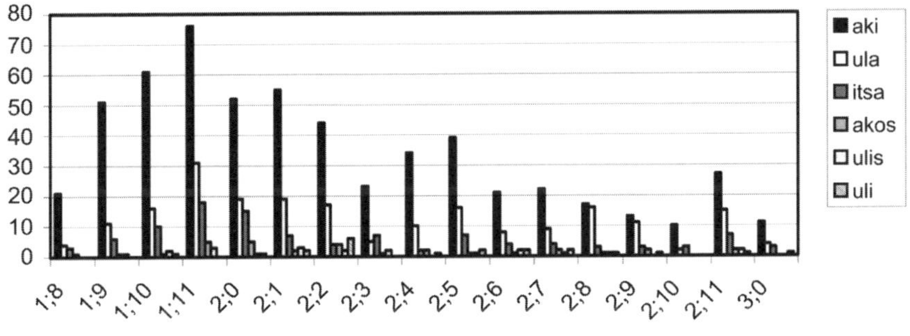

Figure 2. Diminutives occurring in CDS (type frequency)

Table 6b. Diminutives occurring in CDS (types/tokens)

Age	Diminutives							*N*	
	-aki	-ula	Anula	-itsa	-akos	-ulis	-uli	a*	b**
1;8	21/58	4/15	174	3/8	1/4	–		29/85	30/259
1;9	51/192	11/34	382	6/40	1/2	1/25		70/293	71/675
1;10	61/246	16/100	398	10/49	1/1	2/6	1/3	90/405	91/803
1;11	76/348	31/472	438	18/95	5/14	3/36		133/965	134/1403
2;0	52/160	19/171	280	15/51	5/18	1/3	1/1	93/404	94/684
2;1	55/134	19/137	336	7/65	2/10	3/3	2/2	88/351	89/687
2;2	44/116	17/132	249	4/30	4/9	2/4	6/8	77/299	78/548
2;3	23/51	5/36	130	7/18	1/4	2/9		38/118	39/248
2;4	34/76	10/53	103	2/8	2/6	–	1/5	49/148	50/252
2;5	39/132	16/49	156	7/27	1/7	1/1	2/14	66/230	67/386
2;6	21/46	8/26	64	4/4	1/1	2/2	2/13	38/92	39/156
2;7	22/43	9/12	2	4/9	2/7	1/1	2/3	40/75	41/77
2;8	17/33	16/40	100	3/8	1/1	1/1	1/20	39/103	40/203
2;9	13/22	11/15	73	3/7	2/3	–	1/6	30/53	31/126
2;10	10/23	2/2	34	3/4	–	–	–	15/29	16/63
2;11	27/55	15/46	234	7/17	2/2	2/3	1/11	54/134	55/368
3;0	11/17	4/7	67	3/5	–	–	1/1	19/30	20/97

* excluding *Anula*, ** including *Anula*

Until the age 2;2, the number of diminutives used by the caretakers (mainly the mother) exceeds those found in Anna's speech both type- and tokenwise (Figs. 3a and 3b). However, from 2;3 on, diminutives produced by Anna approach the number found in CDS both in terms of types and tokens.

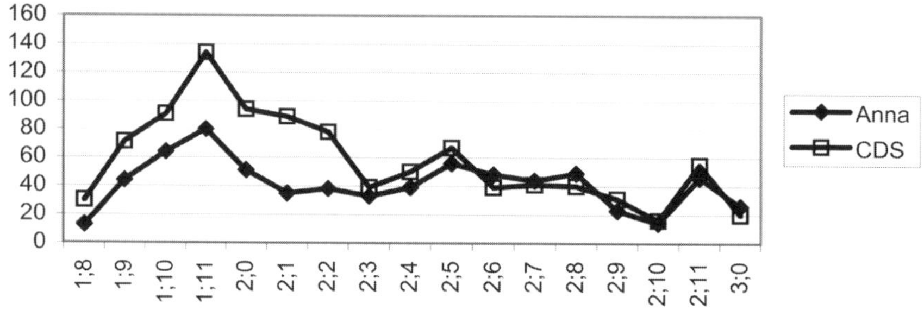

Figure 3a. Diminutives in Anna's speech and in CDS (types)

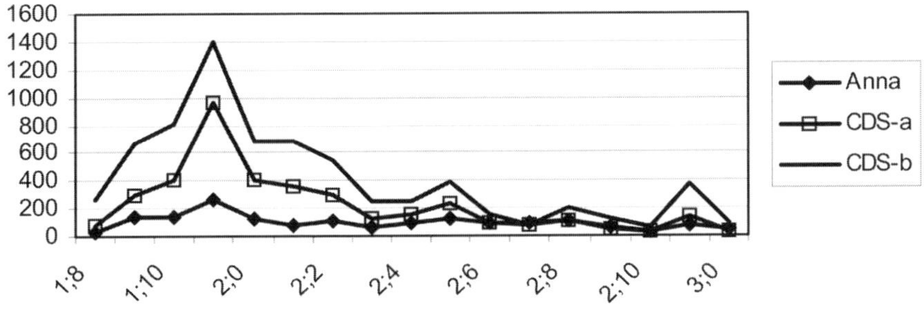

Figure 3b. Diminutive tokens in Anna's speech and in CDS (CDS-a excluding, CDS-b including the hypocoristic *Anula*)

The question is which role the frequency distributions of the different diminutives in CDS may play in the development of the derivation of diminutives in the child. As it is held by proponents of usage-based approaches to language acquisition, token frequency of an expression tends to "entrench" it while type frequency is a necessary prerequisite for productivity and the abstraction of linguistic patterns (Bybee 1995: 428, 434; Tomasello 2000: 72, 76–77). Thus, the extremely high token frequency of the hypocoristic form of the girl's name (*Anula*) as well as the occasional high frequency of the form *man-ula* 'Mummy-DIM' lead to an imbalance of the occurrence of tokens with the diminutive suffix *-ula*. According to the aforementioned theory, this will not, however, play an important role in the development of the productivity of this suffix. As becomes apparent from a comparison of Fig. 5b with Figs. 5a and 4a the high token frequency of *-ula* in CDS does not indeed lead to a high productivity in Anna's speech if compared to the suffix *-aki*.[9] We will return to issues of type frequency and pattern abstraction below (see sect. 4.2).

We now move on to a detailed analysis of the three most frequently used diminutive suffixes. After 2;3, Anna uses nearly as many different types of diminutives as her caretakers and, from 2;6 to 2;8, she even produces a slightly wider range of diminutive types than they do.[10] This is to be mainly attributed to the child's use of diminutives in *-aki* and does not hold for either *-ula* or *-itsa* (compare Fig. 4a to Figs. 5a and 6a). It may be concluded that it is the high type frequency of the diminutive suffix *-aki* in CDS that leads to the productivity of diminutives in the child's language.

In order to understand the role played by diminutives in Anna's speech overall, their number was compared to that of simple nouns at those ages for which a comparable amount of data exists. There is an increase in the percentage of diminutive types from 1;8 through 1;10, while it drops sharply at 2;2 with little further fluctuation until 2;11 (Table 7).

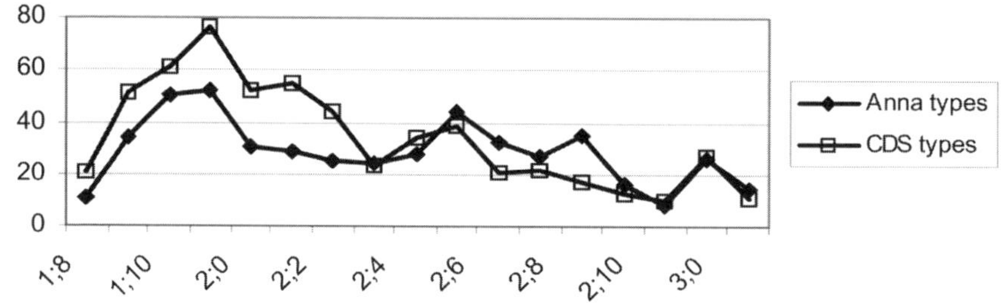

Figure 4a. Diminutives ending in *-aki* in Anna's speech and in CDS (types)

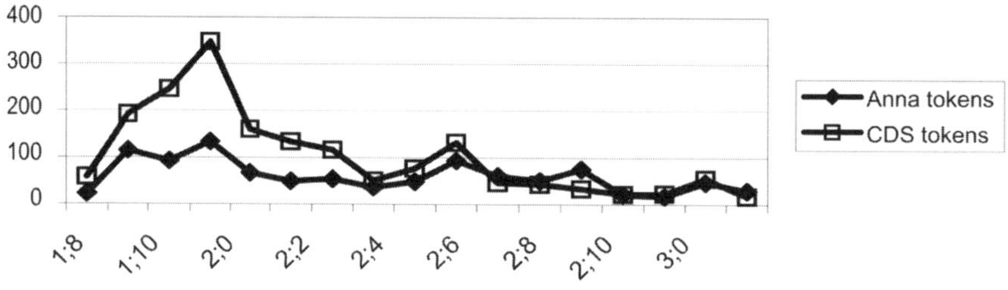

Figure 4b. Diminutives ending in *-ula* in Anna's speech and in CDS (tokens)

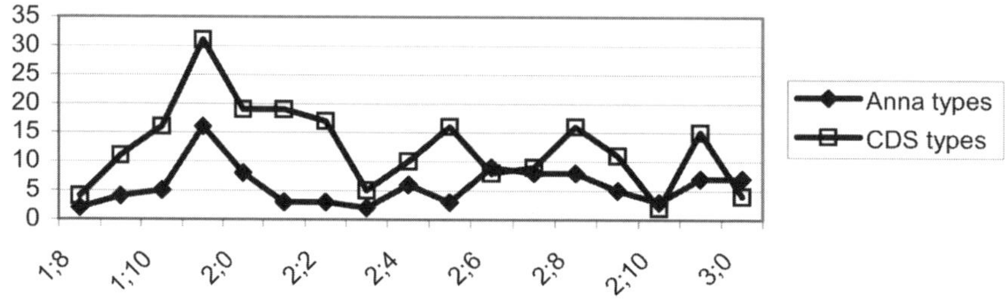

Figure 5a. Diminutives ending in *-aki* in Anna's speech and in CDS (types)

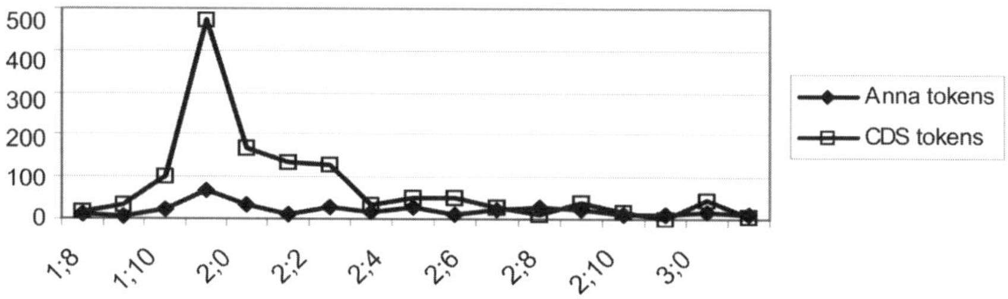

Figure 5b. Diminutives ending in *-ula* in Anna's speech and in CDS (tokens)

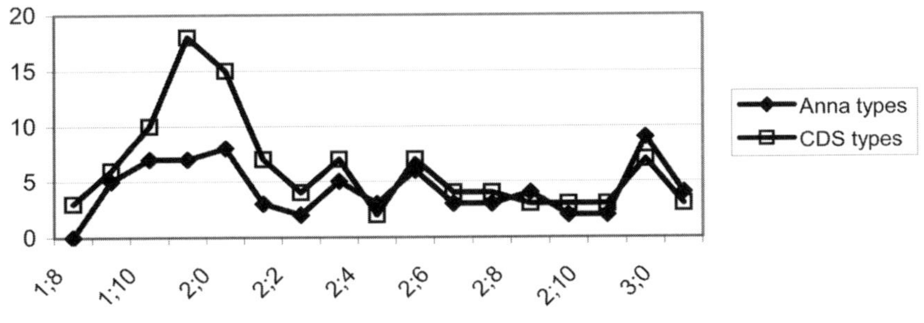

Figure 6a. Diminutives ending in *-itsa* in Anna's speech and in CDS (types)

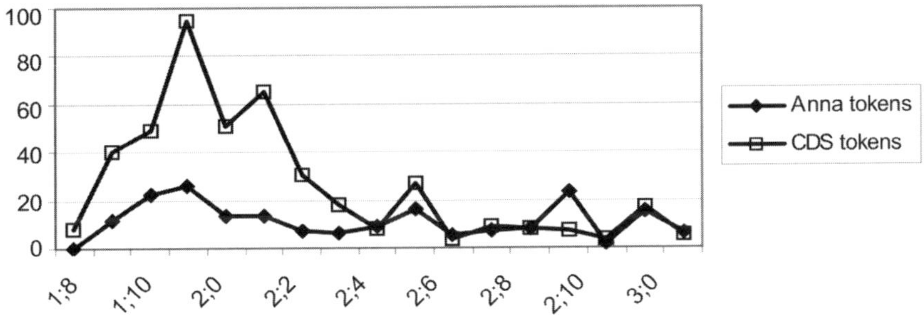

Figure 6b. Diminutives ending in *-itsa* in Anna's speech and in CDS (tokens)

Table 7. Diminutives/simple nouns in Anna's speech (types)

Age	1;8	1;9	1;10	2;2	2;5	2;11
DIM (%)	14.6	22.2	20.8	11.5	13.2	12.6
N (DIM)	13	44	64	38	56	46

As far as CDS is concerned, a cursory inspection of the data suggests that the percentages of diminutive types scarcely vary during the entire age range studied. Ratios of diminutives and simple nouns in CDS have only been established for the ages 1;10 and 2;2. They roughly coincide with those of the child in the very beginning of data collection at 1;8 and after the drop at 2;2. Thus, the ratio in CDS is 16.5% at 1;10 (N = 91) and 14.4% at 2;2 (N = 78).

A comparison of the percentages of diminutives used by the mother-child dyad studied in the present paper with two other dyads studied by Stephany (1997b: 151) reveals that there may be important differences between specific dyads in this respect. The percentage of diminutive types used by Anna's mother at 1;10 is much lower than that used by the mothers of both Spiros and Mairi at 1;9, the children studied by Stephany. Most importantly, the values found with the mothers parallel those established for the three children (Table 8). Thus, the children seem to be tuned to the type of speech they are exposed to.

Table 8. Diminutives/simple nouns in CDS and child speech at 1;9 (types)

	Child speech			CDS		
	Anna	Spiros	Mairi	Anna	Spiros	Mairi
%	22.2	30	43	16.5	35	52
N (DIM)	44	71	67	91	41	117

As shown by Daltas (1985: 83), the use of diminutives (and augmentatives[11]) in Greek adult-adult conversation depends on the degree of formality of the topics discussed.[12] Thus, for more informal topics, he found 11.8% of all noun types to be diminutives (N (DIM) = 176) while with more formal topics this percentage dropped to 4.9% (N (DIM) = 34). While Anna has reached the level of diminutive types characteristic of informal adult-adult conversation in her third year (see Table 7), the other two children studied at 1;9 still use diminutives more frequently.

4.2 Derivational development of diminutives

As mentioned in sect. 2.1.1, many Greek derivational formations carrying a diminutive ending are lexicalized and not semantically transparent. Examples occurring in Anna's speech are common nouns such as *bratsaki* 'life preserver (children's armbands)' (base: *bratso* 'arm') and *kalamaki* 'straw' (base: *kalami* 'reed') as well as exocentric compounds used for naming fairy tale characters such as *kokin-o-skuf-itsa* (red-CONN-cap-DIM:FEM:NOM/ACC:SG) 'Little Red Riding Hood' and *kod-o-revith-ulis* (short-CONN-chickpea-DIM:MASC:NOM:SG) 'Tom Thumb'. Such lexemes, which occur exclusively as diminutives, are found in the girl's data throughout the period studied but do not exceed a total of 31. According to usage-based models of language acquisition, they may nevertheless play a role in the development of the derivation of diminutives since, due to their phonological (and even partly semantic) connections with pairs of diminutives and simple nouns, they may be fitted into the product-oriented schemas of diminutives (see Bybee 1995: 430).

As far as diminutives bearing a more or less semantically transparent relation to their bases are concerned, there are 13 types (74 tokens) formed productively according to the standards of MG grammar which occur only as diminutives in Anna's data (examples 15).[13] These may also be thought to contribute to creating emergent generalizations describable as (product-oriented) schemas both because of their phonological and semantic interconnections (Bybee 1995:430). This can be supposed even if product-oriented schemas do not specify how a category is derived from some other since they generalize over forms of a specific category (Bybee 2001: 126).

(15) arnaki/arnakja 'lamb/lambs:DIM' (7 tokens)
ghurunaki/ghurunakja 'piggy/piggies' (26 tokens)
kuluraki/kulurakja 'pretzel:DIM' (15 tokens)
siropaki 'syrup:DIM' (5 tokens)

Since some of these diminutives occur quite frequently, the non-occurrence of their bases cannot be ascribed solely to data limitations. It is interesting to note that some of them are embedded in a fixed pragmatic context. Thus, in early phases, the plural form *kulurakja* 'pretzel-DIM:PL' is almost always used in connection with a well-known baby rhyme both by the child and her mother.[14] In all such instances, the rhyme never occurs in its entirety but only partially (examples 16). It is only at 2;0, when Anna asks her parents to give her a pretzel that we first find the form *kuluraki* outside the baby rhyme context.

(16) Anna 1;10
a. ANN: kano kulurakja tora. xxx ti akus?
I.make pretzel-DIM:ACC:PL now. xxx what you.hear?
MOT: dhen akuo tipota. tin anula akuo
not I.hear anything the Ann-DIM I.hear
pu kani kulurakja. ti kani i anula?
who makes pretzel-DIM:ACC:PL. what makes the Ann-DIM?
MOT: plathi kulurakja?
forms pretzel:DIM:ACC:PL?
ANN: plathi kulurakja [=! singing] +...
MOT: me ta dhio <xerakja> [>] [=! singing] +...
with the two hands-DIM
ANN: <xerakja> [<] [=! singing].
b. ANN: ti troi?
what (he) eats?
MOT: ti vlepis esi na troi o babas? ...
what see you that eats the Daddy?
ANN: t(r)oi ta kulurakja a psisi [=! singing].
eats the pretzel-DIM:PL PTL bakes

Baby rhymes may nonetheless play a role in the acquisition of diminutives in so far as fixed constructions (or their parts) occurring in them are later used by the child in her spontaneous utterances (example 17a). Interestingly, the "baby rhyme strategy" is also exploited by the child's mother (17b).

(17) Anna 1;11

a. MOT: ti lei to koritsi mas?
what says the girl of.us?
ANN: edho (dh)en echi *fagaraki* [: fegar-aki] *lalabro* [: labro].
here not has moon-DIM shining.
'There is no shining moon here.'

b. ANN: pu pije to fagaraki [: fegaraki]?
where went the moon-DIM?
MOT: *to fegaraki to labro?*
the moon-DIM the shining (one)?

In contrast to nouns occurring only as diminutives, others are exclusively found as simple nouns in the child's speech. Some belong to semantic classes which are anyhow commonly used as simple nouns in standard MG, such as toponyms (e.g. *kriti* 'Crete', *ajiamarina*, a summer resort in Attica), names of days and months (e.g. *kirjaki* 'Sunday', *avghustos* 'August') and proper names, whether foreign or Greek (e.g. *mikis* 'Mickey mouse', *pinokios* 'Pinochio', *pitepan* 'Peter Pan', *aleksandros* 'Alexander', *ajiovasilis* 'Saint Basil', *adighoni* 'Antigone').

What is of course most interesting for the development of the derivational aspect of diminutives is the contrastive use of diminutives with their respective simple nouns. Although four of the thirteen diminutive types found at 1;8 also occur as simple nouns, contextual cues do not allow us to infer a semantic or pragmatic difference between them (examples 18).

(18) Anna 1;8

a. ANN: baba tu efije <ti (s)piti tis> [: sto spiti tu].
daddy of.him went the house of.her
MOT: efije o babas tu sto spiti tu?
went the daddy of.him to.the house of.him?
'Did his daddy go to his house?'

b. ANN: pai. 'Gone'
MOT: pu? 'Where?'
ANN: peraki [:? spitaki] tu ta [: tha] to pai.
house-DIM of.him FUT.PTL takes it
'He will take him to his house.'

There are also some examples at various ages in which reference to smallness is emphasized by the adjective *mikros* 'small' in combination with a diminutive noun (examples 19). These examples do not involve redundancy since the diminutive refers to the offspring of an animal. Nonetheless, the diminutive at the same time expresses endearment (example 19a) (see Stephany 1997b: 153 for similar examples). In other cases, use of the adjective *mikros* along with a diminutive seems to emphasize its core meaning, i.e. smallness (examples 19b, c).

(19) a. Anna 1;10
MOT: ti ta exi ta arkudhakja?
what them has the bears-DIM
'What are the little bears to her (= mother bear)?'
ANN: ke a(r)kudhaki mi [/] mikro.
and bear-DIM small
MOT: mikro? afta ine pjo mikra akomi,
small these are more small still
pjo mikrulika in(e) afta, poli mikra.
more small-DIM are these very small
b. Anna 3;0
ANN: ine tu pedhju tu niku.
is of.the child of.the Nikos
'This belongs to the child Nikos.'
ANN: ena mikro pedhaki pu to lene niko.
a small child-DIM who him they.call Nikos
'A small child called Nikos.'

No significant development in the semantics and pragmatics of diminutives seems to take place in Anna's language during her third year. However, toward the end of this year, the child distinguishes between the meaning of smallness and that of endearment by expressing the former with simple nouns combined with size adjectives and the latter with diminutives (example 20a vs. 20b).

(20) Anna 2;11
a. ANN: esi xxx meghalo xeri.
you xxx big hand
'You have a big hand.'
MOT: poli meghalo xeri.
very big hand
'A very big hand.'
ANN: esi exis mikro mikro.
you have:2S small small
'You have a very small one.'
b. MOT: anula mu ti ton thelis to baba?
Ann-DIM of.me what him want:2S the father?
'Anna dear, why do you want daddy?'
ANN: thelo [/] thelo na ton kratiso xeraki xeraki
I.want that him hold hand-DIM hand-DIM
'I want to hold him hand in hand.'

From 1;11 on, a principled choice of the simple noun seems to occur in cases where the inflectional paradigm of the diminutive is defective (see sect. 2.1.3 above). Thus, in examples (21), the simple noun *moro* 'baby' is preferred since the genitive of the diminutive *mor-aki* 'baby-DIM' does not exist. By contrast, diminutives ending in *-ula* may form a genitive (example 21b).

(21) Anna 1;11
a. MOT: ti? 'What?'
ANN: aft(i) ine tu moru.
this is of.the baby:GEN
'This belongs to the baby.'
MOT: dhen ine tu moru, anulina mu.
not is of.the baby:GEN Ann-DIM of.me
ine tis anulinas.
it.is of.the Ann-DIM:GEN
'It does not belong to the baby, my little Ann. It is little Ann's.
b. ANN: afto ine tu moru,
this is of.the baby:GEN
afto ine <tis rin> [//] tis anulas.
this is of.the Ann-DIM:GEN
'This is the baby's (and) this is little Ann's.'

Anna's speech also provides evidence of a given base combining with different diminutive suffixes.[15] Some of this variation is conditioned by the gender of the referent (examples 22a) while other examples differentiate between the young and adult members of a species (examples 22b). Some variants may have no clear meaning difference (examples 22c).[16] In cases where a given base is combined both with the diminutive suffix *-aki* and some other such suffix, the first always emerges earlier. This suffix may be considered as the most productive in terms of lexical types. All the examples found in CS in which a given base is combined with more than one diminutive suffix are modeled by the input.

(22)	a.	1;10	ghat-ula	'cat-DIM:FEM:SG'	(cat generally or female cat)
		2;7	ghat-ulis	'cat-DIM:MASC:SG'	(tom-cat)
		1;11	mikr-ula	'small-DIM:FEM:SG'	'small one'
		2;2	mikr-uli	'small-DIM:NEUT:SG'	'small one'
	b.	1;9	ghat-aki	'cat-DIM:NEUT:SG'	'kitten'
		1;10	ghat-ula	'cat-DIM:FEM:SG'	'kitty cat' (generic or female)
		1;9	pap-aki	'duck-DIM:NEUT:SG'	'duckling/little duck'
		2;2	papj-ules	'duck-DIM:FEM:PL'	'little ducks' (generic or female)
	c.	1;8	an-ula	'Ann-DIM:FEM'	'dear little Ann'
		2;8	an-ul-itsa	'Ann-DIM:FEM-DIM:FEM'	'dear little Ann'
		1;10	bal-aki	'ball-DIM:NEUT:SG'	'little ball'
		1;11	bal-itsa	'ball-DIM:FEM:SG'	'little ball'

The possibility of one base combining with various diminutive suffixes is not generally exploited in MG (e.g. *dhul-itsa* 'work-DIM' but not **dhul-aki*[17] or **dhul-ula*). Nonetheless, it occurs more often in CDS than in CS. Yet, almost 80% of the bases of diminutives derived by *-itsa* or *-ula* are restricted to either one of these suffixes, this percentage being even higher with the suffix *-aki* (92.5%). When different diminutives formed from a given base occur in the same speech situation, they tend to involve semantic or pragmatic distinctions. Thus, in example (23), the mother exploits the different degrees of affective connotation by coining two non-standard diminutives from the base *beba* 'baby:FEM'.

(23) Anna 1;11

MOT:	jati	ekleje	i	beba,	i	beb-una?
	why	cried	the	baby:FEM	the	baby-DIM:FEM?
	jati	ekleje	afti	i	beb-ina?	
	why	cried	this	the	baby-DIM:FEM?	

'Why did the baby cry, the little baby? Why did this little baby cry?'

ANN: i bebina.
'The little baby.'

In order to reach adult competence in diminutives, the child must on the one hand move beyond item-based diminutive constructions while on the other hand respecting the various restrictions placed on generalizations, many of which are lexically based. As has been observed in the domain of inflection, especially that of verbs, Greek children are conservative learners, so that overgeneralizations, reflecting creative use of patterns, are rare before the age of three (Stephany 1985, 1997a). The same seems to hold for the development of derivational formations, i.e. diminutives, at least as far as the two Greek children studied by Stephany (1997b) and the girl examined in the present paper are concerned. Until 3;0, the age at which the present study ends, Anna does not produce any deviant diminutives, a fact suggesting that she does not form them creatively. This does not, however, necessarily mean that she restricts herself to memorizing single diminutive forms.

According to Usage-Based Theories of language acquisition, such as Bybee's Network Model, morphological patterns "emerge from associations made among related words in lexical representation" (Bybee 1995: 428; see also Bybee 1998, 2001). Such connections between words stored in the lexicon are based on "identical and similar phonological and semantic features" (Bybee 1995: 428). "Sets of words having similar patterns of semantic and phonological connections reinforce one another and create emergent generalizations describable as schemas" (Bybee 1995: 430). They are less abstract than the rules of structuralist models of language in that they "have no existence independent of the lexical units from which they emerge" (Bybee 2001: 27). It is the actual usage "in terms of both type and token frequency" which "plays an important role in establishing and maintaining representation" (Bybee 1995: 428). Schemas can be applied to new combinations of elements. Both the number of restrictions placed on a schema and its strength determine its productivity. The strength of a schema is largely based on type frequency (Bybee 1995: 430, 2001: 13).

In the child data studied here, it is the schema of diminutives ending in *-aki* which is strongest. This explains why its use may at a certain point exceed that of CDS (see sect. 4.1). Furthermore, the *-aki* diminutive pattern places the least restrictions on bases (see sect. 2.1.1). Productivity is therefore higher with this pattern than with others.[18] "Productivity is the extent to which a pattern is likely to apply to new forms" (Bybee 2001: 12–13; see also Kilani-Schoch & Dressler 2005: 129). High token frequency of a given diminutive expression in the input will on the one hand serve to "entrench" it (Tomasello 2003: 178–182) but may on the other hand lead to greater lexical autonomy and weaker connections with other items (Bybee 1995: 429; see also Tomasello 2003: 126). The diminutive *Anula* 'little Anna' in our data seems to be a case in point, since its extremely high token frequency in CDS does not lead to a greater productivity of diminutives ending in *-ula* in CS (see sect. 4.1).

4.3 Inflectional development of diminutives

We will restrict our study of the development of diminutive inflection to types carrying the three most frequently occurring suffixes, namely *-aki*, *-ula*, and *-itsa*. The inflectional contrasts attested with these suffixes concern number as well as case distinctions (nominative/accusative vs. genitive in the singular) (Table 9). These distinctions do not, however, develop in unison, as case emerges later than number. In addition, both categories develop differently with each of these suffixes.[19]

While in the earliest period of the child's development, diminutives ending in *-ula* and *-itsa* occur in a single inflectional form (corresponding to the NOM/ACC:SG of MG), we note both the singular ending in *-aki* as well as the plural ending in *-akja* (corresponding to MG SG and PL forms). This does not, however, mean that at 1;8 or 1;9 the number distinction has been generally acquired for this particular type of nouns. In fact, some nouns are exclusively used in their singular form (e.g. *tiraki* 'cheese', *ghataki* 'cat') while others are used only in the plural (e.g. *morakja* 'babies', *matakja* 'eyes'). Certain nouns do nevertheless occur in the singular as well as in the plural from the very beginning (e.g. *pedhaki* 'child', *skilaki* 'dog'). Although it is difficult to find clear evidence for a semantic distinction between the respective forms at this point, their use seems to be systematic and adequate. Thus, the singular form *pedhaki* refers to individual children such as a playmate or the infant Jesus, while the plural form *pedhakja* is used in reference to the children killed by Herod (see Table 10).[20]

As far as number distinctions are concerned, notable variation is found in the emergence of the singular and plural form of a given diminutive noun ending in *-aki* (Table 10). A plural form emerges earlier with some nouns, while the reverse holds for others. Moreover, with some lexemes, singular and plural forms emerge simultaneously. With frequently used lexemes the distance between the emergence of singular and plural tends to be only one or two months (e.g. *moraki* 'baby', *mataki* 'eye', *fotaki* 'light, lamp', *arkudhaki* 'bear') while with more rarely used ones it tends to be greater. This shows that the acquisition of number distinctions develops slowly and in an item-based way.

Table 9. Inflectional forms of diminutives in Anna's speech (types/tokens)

Age	-aki		-ula			-itsa		
	SG	PL	SG (N/A)	PL	SG (G)	SG (N/A)	PL	SG (G)
1;8	5/13	8/10	2/11	–	–	–	–	–
1;9	26/81	15/34	4/8	–	–	5/11	1/1	–
1;10	32/66	17/26	5/20	–	–	7/19	2/3	–
1;11	37/88	21/46	15/57	2/3	1/10	7/24	2/2	–
2;0	24/54	11/13	6/27	4/6	1/3	8/11	1/2	–
2;1	21/30	12/19	3/9	–	–	3/13	–	–
2;2	13/27	13/27	3/27	1/1	–	2/7	–	–
2;3	19/23	6/13	2/14	–	1/1	1/1	4/5	–
2;4	20/36	9/12	5/24	1/1	2/3	2/8	1/1	–
2;5	36/65	16/28	3/10	–	1/2	5/11	2/5	–
2;6	24/46	11/14	6/17	3/3	–	3/5	–	–
2;7	18/38	11/12	8/24	2/2	–	2/6	1/1	–
2;8	23/43	16/32	5/13	4/5	1/3	4/7	1/1	–
2;9	12/16	5/5	5/11	–	–	2/23	–	1/2
2;10	5/13	4/4	1/7	2/2	–	2/2	–	–
2;11	21/36	9/11	6/13	2/4	–	8/13	2/2	–
3;0	9/22	5/7	3/7	4/4	–	4/6	–	–

Table 10. Emergence of singular and plural forms of some diminutives in *-aki*

Age	moraki	mataki	psaraki	arnaki	arkudhaki	banaki	parathiraki	pedhaki
	'baby'	'eye'	'fish'	'lamb'	'bear'	'bath'	'window'	'child'
1;8	PL					SG		SG/PL
1;9	SG	PL	PL	SG	PL			
1;10				PL	SG		PL	
1;11		SG						
2;1			SG					
2;6						PL		
3;0							SG	

As already noted, some diminutives only occur in the plural, seemingly because their singular forms are not commonly used (examples 24a) or they are avoided by this specific mother-child dyad (examples 24b). Other diminutives are exclusively used in the singular either for pragmatic reasons (including occurrence in nursery rhymes) (examples 25a, b) or for semantic ones (mass nouns) (examples 25c).

(24) Diminutives occurring only in the plural
  a. palamakja 'clapping (of hands)', kakakja 'poopoo'
  b. (a)ghalakja 'hug', patatakja 'potato chips'

(25) Diminutives occurring only in the singular
  a. fegaraki 'moon', kefalaki 'head'
  b. jaurtaki 'joghurt', lukumaki 'Turkish delight', maghnitofonaki 'tape recorder'
  c. ghalataki 'milk', kreataki 'meat', rizaki 'rice', neraki 'water'

The relatively limited productivity of the number distinction with *-aki* diminutives can be seen if the percentages of lexemes attested in either number or in both of them are calculated for the entire period studied. 37.5% appear in both forms, 45% only in the singular and 17.5% only in the plural (N = 160).

If we compare the emergence of number distinctions in the *-aki* diminutives to that of their respective simple nouns, the same picture of item-based development seems to emerge. Although we have not been able to examine the data in a detailed way, Table 11 presents number development in three randomly chosen nouns. The question is whether the contrasting number forms of a given simple noun and the diminutive derived from its stem may be considered as early child mini-paradigms (see Bittner et. al 2003).

Table 11. Emergence of number distinctions in simple nouns and diminutives ending in *-aki*

Age	mati	fos	traghudhi
1;8		SIMP:SG, DIM:PL	
1;9	SIMP:SG, DIM:PL	DIM:SG	
1;10		SIMP:PL	DIM:PL
1;11	SIMP:PL, DIM:SG		
2;2			SIMP:SG
2;6			SIMP:PL

5. The semantics and pragmatics of affectivity: hypocoristics

5.1 Hypocoristics vs. diminutives in child speech and child-directed speech

As mentioned in sect. 2.1.2, the set of hypocoristics does not completely coincide with that of diminutives. The hypocoristics found in the data studied here are of various types: first names derived by diminutive suffixes (example 26a), truncated forms of first names (26b), and simple or derived nouns referring to family members (26c, d).[21] Both in the child's speech and in CDS, hypocoristics of first names derived by diminutive suffixes are the most numerous in terms of types. In terms of tokens, the highest frequencies are found with simple nouns referring to family members. Derived hypocoristic terms for family members score higher in CDS than in the child's speech, both type- and tokenwise.

(26) a. Dhafn-ula 'Daphne-DIM'
b. Kula (girl's name)
c. mama, babas 'Mummy', 'Daddy'
d. man-ula 'mother-DIM'

A hypocoristic function is also served by diminutives derived from common nouns. For example, Anna's parents refer to the child by using the form *arn-aki* 'lamb-DIM' as a hypocoristic. Other diminutives frequently used in this way are *kardh-ula* 'heart-DIM' and *aghap-ula* 'love-DIM'.[22]

In both CS and CDS, hypocoristics appear in a restricted number of types relative to other diminutives. Moreover, the child's hypocoristic types are more restricted than those of CDS and their overall token frequency is notably lower than that of other diminutives.[23] The latter more particularly is in sharp contrast to CDS, where hypocoristics occur abundantly (figs. 7a and 7b).[24]

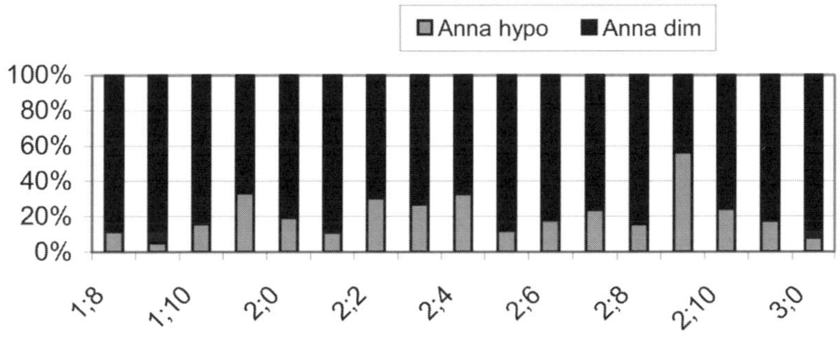

Figure 7a. Diminutives and hypocoristics occurring in Anna's speech (tokens)

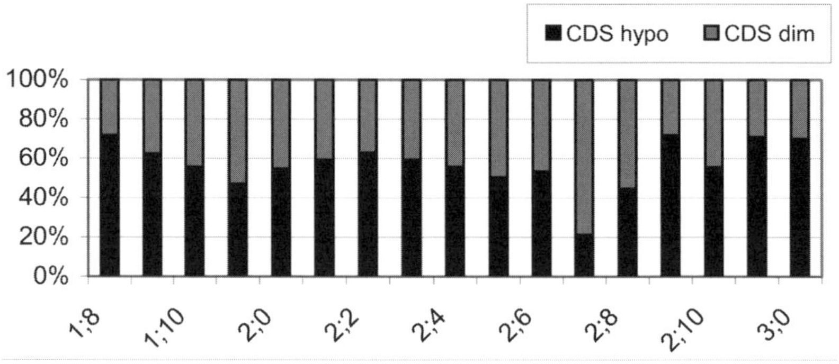

Figure 7b. Diminutives and hypocoristics occurring in CDS (tokens)

However, the high token frequency of hypocoristics in CDS is mainly caused by forms for the child's name (mainly *Anula*) created by Anna's mother (and sometimes by other adults). At 2;2, for instance, the hypocoristics referring to Anna carry different suffixes (examples 27a, b); some of them are occasional formations (27b) and others involve suffix chaining (27c).

(27) a. An-úla, An-úli
b. An-úka, An-uljó, An-ulú
c. An-ul-áki, An-ul-ína, An-ul-íni, An-ul-in-íska, An-ul-in-íski

The richness of hypocoristic forms based on the child's name may be special to this particular mother-child dyad. Stephany (1997b: 155) did not find similar evidence with the two children she studied at 1;9, since their mothers mostly relied on simple nouns when addressing the children.[25]

For obvious reasons, self-referring hypocoristics are found less often in Anna's speech than in CDS, both type- and tokenwise. The child only occasionally refers to herself by the hypocoristic *Anula*, with the exception of the doubly suffixed *An-ul-itsa* occurring once at 2;8. She also sometimes uses hypocoristics for the names of her twin sisters Eva and Jorjia (*Ev-ula*, *Jorj-itsa*) as well as for names of neighbors, friends, relatives, fairy tale figures and religious figures derived by different suffixes (e.g. *koki-noskuf-itsa* 'Little Red Riding Hood', *Xrist-ulis* 'dear little Christ'). We also find a few truncated forms of first names (*Takis*, *Kula*).[26] Finally, common nouns denoting family members occur both with and without diminutive suffixes (examples 28a vs. 28b).

(28) a. mama 'Mummy', babas 'Daddy'
b. man-ula 'Mummy-DIM', jaj-ula 'Granny-DIM', pap-ulis 'Grandfather-DIM', pap-ul-aki(s) 'Grandfather-DIM-DIM', pap-ul-inos 'Grandfather-DIM-DIM'

It is also important to note that all hypocoristic terms in Anna's speech are also attested in CDS. In other words, the child does not introduce any innovative hypocoristics.

5.2 A suffix for creating one's personal affectionate world: the case of *-ina*

Anna's mother not only makes extensive use of hypocoristic forms but also uses other derivational suffixes such as *-ina*, *-una*, *-udha*, *-eli* in a non-standard way for marking the affectionate character of mother-child interactions. Of these, *-ina* represents the most prominent means for accomplishing pragmatic functions normally fulfilled by standard diminutive suffixes.

In standard MG, the suffix *-ina* derives feminine nouns denoting females from masculine or neuter ones serving as generic terms or denoting males (e.g. *papaghalos* (parrot:MASC) > *papaghal-ina* (parrot-FEM), *jatros* (physician:MASC) > *jatr-ina* (physician-FEM).[27] In both CS and CDS, this function is extended to animals for which gender distinctions are normally unimportant, such as snakes and mice (examples 29). When the 'motion' suffix *-ina* is added to feminine nouns it explicitly marks feminine gender (e.g. *papja* 'duck:FEM' > *papj-ina*).[28]

(29) a. Anna 2;5
ANN: na (v)lepi ti mama tu ti fidh-ina...
that sees the mummy his the snake-FEM
'to watch its mother, the female snake...'

b. Anna 1;11
MOT: natos edho me tin agheladh-itsa
there.he.is here with the cow-DIM
ke tin podik-ina.
and the mouse-FEM
'There he is with the dear little cow and the mother-mouse.'

In addition, Anna's mother very frequently draws on this suffix for deriving non-standard diminutives. In examples (30), the alternative form *patatines* carrying the suffix *-ina* is used in the same speech situation as the standard diminutive *patatules* derived by *-ula*.

(30) Anna 1;11
a. MOT: An-ul-ina eftjakses sti mama
Anna-DIM-DIM you.prepared for.the mummy
patat-ul-es na fai?
potato-DIM-PL that she.eat
'Anna, did you prepare potatoes for mummy to eat?'

b. MOT: eftjakses sti man-ul-ina patat-in-es?
you.prepared for.the mother-DIM-DIM potato-DIM-PL
'Did you prepare potatoes for mummy?'

Although the non-standard form *patat-in-es* 'potato-DIM-PL' is synonymous with the more commonly used standard form *patat-ul-es* 'potato-DIM-PL', from a pragmatic point of view, the former carries an affective potential surpassing that of the latter. This explains why the suffix *-ina* may even be added to derivations containing the diminutive suffix *-ula*, such as *an-ul-ina* < *an-ula* 'little Anna' or *man-ul-ina* < *man-ula* 'little Mummy'.

In comparison with the other diminutives occurring in CDS, words derived by *-ina*[29] are quite substantial both type- and tokenwise. They are much more important in CDS than in Anna's speech, however. The most frequent ones used by the girl's mother are hypocoristics referring to the child (mainly *an-ul-ina* 'Ann-DIM-DIM:FEM', but also *aghap-ina* 'love-DIM:FEM', *aghap-ul-ina* 'love-DIM-DIM:FEM' or other doubly suffixed forms such as *aghap-in-ula* 'love-DIM-DIM:FEM', *an-ul-ini* 'Ann-DIM-DIM:NEUT'). The high token scores observed in CDS between 1;11 and 2;2 are mainly due to such forms (Fig. 8). In comparison to the child, the mother also has a much larger repertoire of bases at her disposal, which she combines with one of the variants of this suffix.

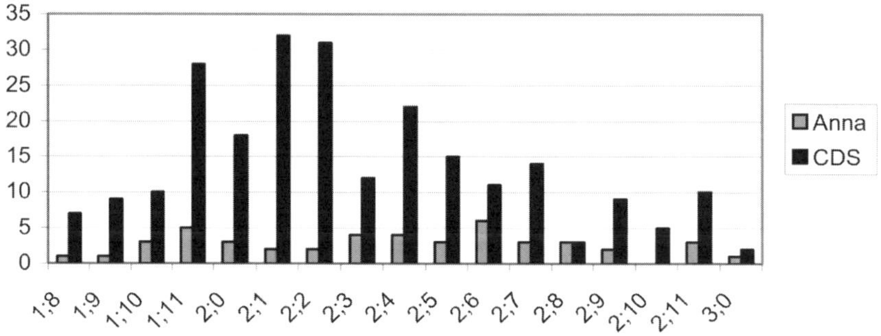

Figure 8. Forms derived by *-ina/i/os* in Anna's speech and in CDS (types)

Overall, there are 62 types of nouns derived by *-ina* (or one of its variants) in CDS as opposed to 15 such types in Anna's speech. In both CDS and CS, these are mostly used as diminutives and much less often for referring to female members of a species (Table 12). The fact that the suffix is also employed in cases where the generic term for a species carries feminine gender proves that feminine gender is not considered a sufficient marker of reference to females. Table 12 shows that the main function of the extensive and innovative use of the suffix *-ina* by Anna's mother is that of establishing intimacy as the keynote of mother-child exchanges.

Table 12. Derived words in *-ina* with diminutive and non-diminutive meaning (types)

Subjects	Diminutives	'motion' nouns	'motion' N < FEM	*N*
Mother	77.4 %	13 %	9.6 %	62
Anna	73.4 %	6.6 %	20 %	15

Since most *-ina* forms in Anna's speech also occur in CDS, one may conclude that the child's speech mirrors that of her mother in this respect as it does in the use of diminutives more generally. However, the high token frequency of particular forms in CDS, such as that of the hypocoristic *anulina*, does not influence Anna's speech. This form does not occur in her data at all, while the mere diminutive *anula* does. This may suggest that the child has grasped the special pragmatic meaning of the form *anulina*, which renders it inappropriate for self-reference. Similarly, while using the terms *babulinos* and *papulinos* for referring to her father and grandfather, respectively, just as her mother does, Anna restricts the form *aghapina* (PL *aghapines*) to her twin sisters, never using it for self-reference. Another reason why Anna does not use many *-ina* forms in spite of their extensive occurrence in child-directed speech may be the semantic complexity of this suffix alternating between standard 'motion' on the one hand and non-standard diminutive meanings on the other.

6. Conclusions: Form and function of diminutives in Greek as compared to other languages

To conclude this chapter on the development of diminutives and their role in the development of morphology in the language of a Greek monolingual girl from 1;8 to 3;0, we will summarize our main findings and compare them to Stephany's (1997b) results on Greek as well as to those found in other languages.

In child Greek, as in other languages, diminutive morphology develops early (see Dressler & Karpf 1995 on German, Russian, Czech, Polish, and Hebrew). From 1;8 on, *-aki*, the most productive of six diminutive suffixes, gradually emerging from 1;8 to 1;11 in the speech of the Greek girl studied in the present paper, is well documented both type- and tokenwise. With the two other Greek children investigated by Stephany (1997b) this same suffix is also much more amply documented than the other two diminutive suffixes they use at 1;9. The richness of diminutive endings characteristic of the Greek language and their ample use, especially in child-centered situations, is thus reflected in the array and frequency of diminutives found in early child Greek.

A theoretically interesting question is the chronological relation between the development of derivational and inflectional morphology in first language acquisition (Dressler & Karpf 1995). As far as Greek is concerned, there is no evidence that the development of diminutives, and thus derivational morphology, sets in earlier than the development of inflection. The two children studied by Stephany (1997b) not only give evidence of a considerable type frequency of the most productive diminutive suffix of MG (*-aki*) but also distinguish number and case forms of nouns as well as tense-aspect-mood forms of verbs at 1;9 when they were first observed (Stephany 1997a). The development of inflection of the girl studied in the present paper has not yet been investigated. However, singular and plural forms of diminutives ending in *-aki* are adequately used from 1;8 on with high numbers of types as well as tokens appearing from 1;9 on. Greek diminutives cannot provide evidence for early case distinctions since these are absent from the large class of diminutives ending in *-aki*. With the other diminutives, case distinctions emerge later and remain rare. Therefore, quite in contrast to Lithuanian (Savickienė 1998: 122), diminutives are unlikely to facilitate the acquisition of case in early Greek language acquisition. Since the inflectional patterns of diminutives are generally less complex than those of simple nouns and diminutives exhibit a stable stress pattern (see sect. 2.1.3 above), they may nevertheless contribute to the acquisition of nominal inflection once a wider array of diminutive suffixes has become available to the child. It is evident from the data studied in the present paper that, initially, the inflection of diminutives develops in an item-based way.

In child Greek as well as in all other languages studied so far, the pragmatic function of diminutives expressing affection and intimacy develops earlier than the semantic notion of smallness. These pragmatic functions of diminutives and hypocoristics are also prominent in child-directed speech, especially so in the Greek mother-child dyad studied in the present paper, where even innovative uses of a non-standard suffix are attested on a par with standard diminutive suffixes. The semantic core notion of 'smallness' attributed to diminutives does not seem to develop during the period studied in the present paper. A clear semantic contrast between diminutives and the respective simple nouns can only be established for those diminutives which refer to the young ones of animals. In this case, diminutives formed from a single base by different suffixes may also be semantically distinguished. Otherwise, explicit reference to smallness is expressed by lexical means, namely the adjective for 'small' in combination with a simple noun or even a diminutive. It is only by the end of her third year that the Greek girl studied here distinguishes between the meaning of smallness and that of endearment, expressing the former with simple nouns combined with size adjectives and the latter with diminutives. These findings on Greek are similar to what has been reported for other languages such as Italian (Ceccherini et al. 1997; de Marco 1998, 2002), Dutch (Gillis 1997), Lithuanian (Savickienė 1998), and Russian (Voeikova 1998).

Another finding on Greek which confirms observations made on many other languages is that the inventory and frequency distribution of diminutives in CS parallel those in CDS. In our data, the child's frequency becomes comparable to that of CDS both type- and tokenwise from 2;3 onward. However, this mainly results from the use of the most common diminutive suffix (for a similar result on Dutch see Gillis 1997: 172). While, in CDS, the proportion of diminutive lexemes to simple nouns slightly exceeds that found in informal adult-adult interaction and seems to remain stable throughout the period studied, in the girl's speech this ratio drops to that characterizing informal adult-adult interaction by 2;2. From about 2;3 onward, the rate of diminutive tokens decreases both in CDS and the child's speech. Such a tendency has also been observed for the Spanish speech addressed to 3-year-old as compared to 5-year-old children (Melzi & King 2003: 300). A comparison of three Greek mother-child dyads shows nonetheless important individual differences between the proportion of diminutives to simple nouns found in CDS. It is interesting to note that the children seem to closely follow the type of speech they are exposed to.

As is evidenced by the frequent use of the hypocoristic *Anula* 'little Ann' by Anna's mother in reference to her child, high token frequency does not affect the child's productivity of this suffix. Also, the high rate of tokens of other hypocoristics occurring in the mother's speech, especially in reference to the child, does not induce their frequent use by the child. This result differs from what Savickienė (1998: 129) found in Lithuanian, where a girl very frequently used a diminutive form of her name for self-reference.

In contrast to what has been reported for other languages, the child studied in the present paper seems to be a conservative learner, at least during the period of 1;8 through 3;0, since she neither produces innovative 'juvenile' diminutives such as those found in the speech of children acquiring Hebrew and Italian (Ravid 1998; de Marco 1998: 187) nor gives evidence of backformation, i.e. the derivation of (non-standard) simple nouns from diminutives (see Gillis 1997: 178 for Dutch and de Marco 1998: 187–188 for Italian).

By separating the stressed suffix *-aki* from diminutives and using it as an all-purpose common noun to demand different objects she desired, another two-year-old Greek girl not only drove several adult caretakers to the verge of despair during a summer afternoon spent on an Attic beach but demonstrated to linguists her ability to pay attention to the structural patterns occurring at the end of words.

Notes

* We would like to thank Demetra Katis and Anastasia Christofidou for valuable comments on an earlier draft of this paper. Furthermore, Demetra Katis kindly brushed up our English. All remaining inadequacies are our own responsibility.

1. The table is not exhaustive as we have excluded derivational endings such as *-adhio* or *-itsi*, which, although characterized as diminutives by Daltas (1985: 68–71), only occur in lexicalized examples such as *filadhio* 'leaflet' and *koritsi* 'girl'.

2. Gender restrictions of the distribution of diminutive suffixes are discussed by Babiniotis (1970: 205–214).

3. On phonological constraints of these processes in diminutive formation see Malikouti-Drachman (1999) and Topintzi (2004).

4. For MG augmentatives see Minas (1978) and Thomadaki (1988: 53–55).

5. For different approaches to Greek nominal inflection see Triantafyllidis (1941/1978), Holton et al. (1997), Ralli (2000), Christofidou (2003).

6. This kind of simplification seems to hold for other languages as well (see Savickienė 1998: 122 on Lithuanian).

7. See also Triantafyllidis (1941/1978: 124), Mackridge (1985: 158), Joseph & Philippaki-Warburton (1987: 217), Sifianou (1992: 157).

8. We would like to thank Demetra Katis for giving us access to the transcripts of the rich data of her daughter Anna computerized by Vicky Kantzou within the CHILDES Project.

9. We have so far not been able to investigate the productivity of the respective diminutive endings in Anna's speech in terms of "rate of additions" as suggested by Bauer (2001:156), according to whom productivity of a morphological process can be measured in terms of the number of coinages "that occur created by that morphological process in a given time period."

10. It should be mentioned that as the child becomes more fluent, the mother's conversational turns tend to decrease in both size and number (Demetra Katis, p.c.).

11. Augmentatives amount to less than 2% of tokens in Daltas' data (Daltas 1985: 69).

12. Frequency of diminutives has also been found to correlate with text type in MG (Thomadaki 1996: 80).

13. The bases of these diminutives are mostly absent from CDS as well. Those which do occur, such as the simple noun *arni* 'lamb', exhibit a lower token frequency than the corresponding diminutive.

14. The entire rhyme goes as follows: *platho kulurakja me ta dhio xerakja, o furnos tha ta psisi, to spiti tha mirisi* 'I.form biscuits-DIM with both of (my) hands-DIM, the oven will bake them, the house will smell.'

15. Such examples rarely occur within the same speech situation, however. An example found at 2;4 is *portula, portitsa* 'door-DIM'.

16. In the standard language, *balaki* refers to a small ball, e.g. a tennis ball, while *balitsa* carries an affective meaning. It seems doubtful, however, whether this meaning difference has been grasped by the child. On the other hand, affective differences between forms such as *anula* and *anulitsa* (ex. 25c) cannot be excluded.

17. The diminutive *dhulaki* derives from the base *dhulos* 'slave', not from *dhulja* 'work'.

18. Due to the high type frequency of diminutives derived by *-aki* as well as the high token frequency of some of these, it seems likely that the child has grasped their structural built-up and has at the same time stored the most frequent of these diminutives as full-form representations (see Clahsen, Sonnenstuhl and Blevins 2003 for a refinement of the Dual Mechanism Model to account for findings on German derivational morphology).

19. Since no analysis of the development of nominal inflection in Anna's speech is available, we cannot presently discuss the hypothesis that the use of diminutives may facilitate the acquisition of case and number inflection in MG (see Savickienė 1998: 122 for Lithuanian).

20. Christofidou (1998: 50, 54–55) found that, although her son Christos used plural forms of simple nouns as standard reactions to certain pictures already at 1;10, there was evidence for a semantic distinction between singular and plural forms of a given noun only at 2;5.

21. Since the hypocoristic terms *babakas* 'Daddy' and *mamaka* 'Mummy' derived by the diminutive suffix *-aka(s)* are attested only once in CDS they were not included among derived diminutives in the preceding analyses. They will, however, be taken into consideration in this section.

22. Since the context plays a decisive role for determining the hypocoristic function of diminutives derived from common nouns, the present section will be limited to those hypocoristics which are formally distinguished from diminutives.

23. A single exception is to be noted at 2;9, when the child narrates a fairy tale in which the hypocoristic *kokinoskufitsa* 'Little Red Riding Hood' appears quite often.

24. This is also true for the Mother's use of the derivational suffix *-ina*, which has not been taken into consideration in the present counts, but will be discussed in sect. 5.2 below.

25. It could be hypothesized that one reason for this difference is that the interaction between Anna 's mother and her daughter is more private.

26. Since the relation of such hypocoristics to their bases is not quite clear they may function as simple nouns for the child.

27. Pavlidou (2003: 186–187 et passim) notes that the "prestige differential" between derived forms *i jatr-ina* and non-derived "two-gendered" nouns *i jatros* 'the:FEM physician' vs. *o jatros* 'the:MASC physician' persists in the standard language until the present day.

28. Corroborating evidence comes from a Greek boy aged 6;0, who uses such derivations in a quasi-experimental task explicitly attributing the meaning 'female' to *vodh-ina* 'OX:FEM' (from *vodhi* 'OX:NEUT') or *ghat-ina* 'cat:FEM' (from *ghata* 'cat:FEM'), contrasting the latter with the endearing diminutive *ghat-ula* (Thomadaki 1986; see also Stephany 1997a: 256).

29. There are also some examples derived by the cognate suffixes *-ini* (NEUT) and *-inos* (MASC), such as *aghap-ini* (love-DIM) and *papul-inos* (grandfather-DIM).

References

Babiniotis, G.D. 1970. Pleurai tu 'met' epithimatos' ypokorismu tis ellinikis [Aspects of Greek hypocoristics derived by suffixes]. *Athena* 71: 194–235.

Bauer, L. 2001. *Morphological productivity*. Cambridge: Cambridge University Press.

Bittner, D., Dressler, W.U. and Kilani-Schoch, M. (eds). 2003. *Development of verb inflection in first language acquisition*. Berlin/New York: Mouton de Gruyter.

Bybee, J. 1995. Regular morphology and the lexicon. *Language and Cognitive Processes* 10: 425–455.

Bybee, J. 1998. The emergent lexicon. *Chicago Linguistic Society* 34 [Part 2, Papers from the Panels]: 421–435.

Bybee, J. 2001. *Phonology and language use*. Cambridge: Cambridge University Press.

Ceccherini, M., Bonifacio, S. and Zocconi, E. 1997. Acquisition of diminutives in Italian (Sara). In *Studies in Pre- and Protomorphology*, W.U. Dressler (ed.), 157–163. [Veröffentlichungen der Kommission für Linguistik und Kommunikationsforschung Nr. 26]. Wien: Verlag der Österreichischen Akademie der Wissenschaften.

Christofidou, A. 1998. Number or Case first? Evidence from Modern Greek. In *Perspectives on Language Acquisition, Selected Papers from the VIIth International Congress for the Study of Child Language*, A. Aksu-Koç, E. Erguvanlı-Taylan, A. Sumru Özsoy and A. Küntay (eds), 46–59. Istanbul: Boğaziçi University.

Christofidou, A. 2003. Genos ke klisi stin elliniki: mia fisiki prosegisi [Gender and inflection in Greek: a natural approach]. In *To genos* [Gender], A. Anastassiadi-Symeonidi, A. Ralli and D. Chila-Markopoulou (eds), 100–131. Athens: Patakis.

Christofidou, A., Stephany, U. 1997. The early development of case forms in the speech of a Greek boy: A preliminary investigation. In *Pre- and Protomorphology in Language Acquisition* [Papers and Studies in Contrastive Linguistics, vol. 33], K. Dziubalska-Kolaczyk (ed.), 127–139. Poznan: Adam Mickiewicz University.

Clahsen, H., Sonnenstuhl, I. and Blevins J.P. 2003. Derivational morphology in the German mental lexicon: A dual mechanism account. In *Morphological Structure in Language Processing*, R. H. Baayen and R. Schreuder (eds), 124–155. Berlin/New York: Mouton de Gruyter.

Corbin, D., Dal, G., Fradin, B., Habert, B., Kerleroux, F., Plénat, M. and Roché, M. (eds). 1999. La morphologie des dérivés évaluatifs [Forum de morphologie (2e rencontre), Toulouse 29–30 avril 1999. Special issue]. *Silexicales 2.*

Daltas, P. 1985. Some patterns of variability in the use of diminutive and augmentative suffixes in spoken Modern Greek koine (MGK). *Glossologia* 4: 63–88.

de Marco, A. 1998. The acquisition of diminutives in Italian. In *Studies in the acquisition of number and diminutive marking* [Antwerp Papers in Linguistics, 95], S. Gillis (ed), 175–192. Antwerp: University of Antwerp.

de Marco, A. 2002. The development of diminutives in Italian: input and acquisition. In *Pre- and protomorphology: Early phases of morphological development in nouns and verbs*, M.D. Voeikova and W.U. Dressler (eds), 133–151. Munich: Lincom Europa.

Dressler, W.U. and Karpf A. 1995. The theoretical relevance of pre- and protomorphology in language acquisition. In *Yearbook of Morphology 1994*, G. Booij and J. van Marle (eds), 99–122. Dordrecht/Boston/London: Kluwer Academic Publishers.

Dressler, W.U. and Merlini Barbaresi, L. 1994. *Morphopragmatics: diminutives and intensifiers in Italian, German, and other languages*. Berlin/New York: Mouton de Gruyter.

Dressler, W.U. and Merlini Barbaresi, L. 2001. Morphopragmatics of diminutives and augmentatives: On the priority of pragmatics over semantics. In *Perspectives on Semantics, Pragmatics and Discourse: A Festschrift for Ferenc Kiefer*, I. Kenesei and R.M. Harnish (eds), 43–58. Amsterdam/Philadelphia: John Benjamins Publishing Company.

Gillis, S. 1997. The acquisition of diminutives in Dutch. In *Studies in Pre- and Protomorphology* [Veröffentlichungen der Kommission für Linguistik und Kommunikationsforschung Nr. 26], W.U. Dressler (ed.), 165–179. Wien: Verlag der Österreichischen Akademie der Wissenschaften.

Holton, D., Mackridge, P. and Philippaki-Warburton, I. 1997. *Greek Grammar. A Comprehensive Grammar of the Modern Language*. London: Routledge.

Joseph, B. and Philippaki-Warburton, I. 1987. *Modern Greek*. London: Croom Helm.

Kavoukopoulos, F. 1996. Ousiastika, epitheta kai rimata: Statistikes kai alles episimansis [Nouns, adjectives, and verbs: Statistics and other remarks]. In *Zitimata ellinikis glossas* [Questions of Greek language], G. Katsimali and F. Kavoukopoulos (eds), 7–16. University of Crete: Rethymnon.

Kilani-Schoch, M. and Dressler W.U. 2005. *Morphologie naturelle et flexion du verbe français*. Tübingen: Gunter Narr.

Mackridge, P. 1985. *The Modern Greek language: A descriptive analysis of Standard Modern Greek*. Oxford: Clarendon Press.

Malikouti-Drachman, A. 1999. Constraints on Greek hypocoristics. In *Greek Linguistics '97* [Proceedings of the 3rd International Conference on Greek Linguistics], A. Moser (ed.), 391–399. Athens: Ellinika Grammata.

Melzi, G. and King, K.A. 2003. Spanish diminutives in mother-child conversations. *Journal of Child Language* 30: 281–304.

Minas, K. 1978. *I morfologia tis megethinseos stin elliniki glossa* [The morphology of augmentation in Greek]. Ioanina: Epistimoniki epetiris Filosofikis Sxolis, University of Ioanina.

Pavlidou, Th.-S. 2003. Women, gender and Modern Greek. In *Gender Across Languages. The linguistic representation of women and men,* M. Hellinger and H. Bußmann (eds), 175–199. Amsterdam/Philadelphia: John Benjamins.

Ralli, A. 2000. A feature-based analysis of Greek nominal inflection. *Glossologia* 11–12: 201–228.

Ravid, D. 1998. Diminutive -i in early child Hebrew: An initial analysis. In *Studies in the acquisition of number and diminutive marking* [Antwerp Papers in Linguistics, 95], S. Gillis (ed.), 149–173. Antwerp: University of Antwerp.

Savickienė, I. 1998. The acquisition of diminutives in Lithuanian. In *Studies in the acquisition of number and diminutive marking* [Antwerp Papers in Linguistics, 95], S. Gillis (ed.), 115–135. Antwerp: University of Antwerp.

Sifianou, M. 1992. The use of diminutives in expressing politeness: Modern Greek versus English. *Journal of Pragmatics* 17: 155–173.

Stephany, U. 1985. *Aspekt, Tempus und Modalität: Zur Entwicklung der Verbalgrammatik in der neugriechischen Kindersprache.* [Language Universals Series 4]. Tübingen: Gunter Narr.

Stephany, U. 1997a. The acquisition of Greek. In *The crosslinguistic study of language acquisition,* Vol. 4, D.I. Slobin (ed.), 183–333. Mahwah, NJ/London: Lawrence Erlbaum.

Stephany, U. 1997b. Diminutives in early child Greek, a preliminary investigation. In *Studies in Pre- and Protomorphology* [Veröffentlichungen der Kommission für Linguistik und Kommunikationsforschung Nr. 26], W.U. Dressler (ed.), 147–156. Wien: Verlag der Österreichischen Akademie der Wissenschaften.

Thomadaki, E. 1986. Wortbildungsstrategien und Mutterspracherwerb. Institut für Sprachwissenschaft, Universität zu Köln. Unpubl. ms.

Thomadaki, E. 1988. *Neugriechische Wortbildung.* [Arbeitspapier No 8 (neue Folge)]. Institut für Sprachwissenschaft – Universität zu Köln.

Thomadaki, E. 1996. Paragoga sti nea elliniki [Derivation in Modern Greek]. In *Zitimata ellinikis glossas* [Questions of Greek language], G. Katsimali and F. Kavoukopoulos (eds), 69–96. University of Crete: Rethymnon.

Tomasello, M. 2000. First steps toward a usage-based theory of language acquisition. *Cognitive Linguistics* 11: 61–82.

Tomasello, M. 2003. *Constructing a language, a usage-based theory of language acquisition.* Cambridge, MA/London: Harvard Univ. Press.

Topintzi, N. 2004. Prosodic patterns and the minimal word in the domain of Greek truncated nickname. In *Proceedings of the 6th International Conference of Greek Linguistics* (18–21 September 2003). Rethymnon: Laboratory of Linguistics, University of Crete [multi-media CD-ROM].

Triantafyllidis, M. 1941/1978. *Neoelliniki grammatiki (tis dimotikis)* [Modern Greek grammar (dhemotiki)]. Thessaloniki: Aristotle University.

Voeikova, M.D. 1998. Acquisition of diminutives by a Russian child: Preliminary observations in connection with the early adjectives. In *Studies in the acquisition of number and diminutive marking* [Antwerp Papers in Linguistics, 95], S. Gillis (ed.), 97–113. Antwerp: University of Antwerp.

CHAPTER 5

The role of diminutives in the acquisition of Italian morphology

Sabrina Noccetti, Anna De Marco, Livia Tonelli, Wolfgang U. Dressler[1]

The paper deals with the acquisition of diminutives by four Italian children with three objectives: to highlight parallelisms and differences in input and output data; to contrast the mechanism of item-based learning (cf. Tomasello 2003) to the dual-route model (Clahsen et al. 2003) as regards the acquisition of diminutives; to investigate whether the productive use of diminutives is a simplifying strategy for acquiring the morphology of non-productive, opaque inflectional classes.

The analysis of data reveals a common developmental pattern in the children and that the acquisition of diminutive suffixes (especially *-ino*) can be ascribed to children's rule extraction. The children, more markedly two of them, use the regular inflection of the diminutives as a strategy to simplify the input data.

1. Introduction

One reason for the interest in the acquisition of diminutives is their presence in the earliest stages of child speech, when hardly any other morphological operations are present. This is also true of Italian, a language which, for a long time, has had the reputation of being diminutive-rich (cf. Dressler and Merlini Barbaresi 1994: 410ff).

The very first empirical investigation on the acquisition of Italian diminutives has been the classical study by Bates and Rankin (1979). It consists of a longitudinal study of two children and of transversal experiments with nonsense words supplied to two- to six-year-old children. In their linguistic framework they assign Italian diminutives, augmentatives and pejoratives to inflection (which would be good for Bantu languages but not for Italian) and differentiate their meanings as referring denotatively to size and connotatively to value judgements, a line of thought continued in Grandi (2002). Their main results are that the longitudinal corpora up to the age of 1;8 contain "no evidence of either understanding or an attempt to encode size or value concepts" (Bates and Rankin 1979: 35). Next these concepts are expressed by adjectives, afterwards size concepts, and very rarely value concepts, are expressed by diminutive (and later also by augmentative) suffixes. This also holds throughout the experimental results. They conclude (1979: 51) with the interpretation: "It is possible that the use of size inflections to encode value is in fact a sort of metaphorical usage, and that children below six are restricted in their ability to comprehend or produce metaphors". Translated into our framework, this amounts to the claim that pragmatic usage is secondary and later acquired than primary semantic usage.

All the following empirical studies have been carried out within the Crosslinguistic Project in Pre- and Protomorphology, the first by Ceccherini, Bonifacio and Zocconi (1997). They observe that diminutives represent the very first morphological operation acquired by Sara, the child they analyzed, and that they are very productive in her early speech, as they are extended to bases which would usually take other DIM suffixes in the target language (e.g. *pesc-etto* instead of *pesci-olino* 'fish-DIM'). The pragmatic meaning of endearment is the first meaning to emerge whereas the semantic meaning clearly emerges later when the child is older and when there is a contrast with the augmentative. Similar facts have been established by De Marco (1998, 2002), where a close correspondence between input and output with respect to the frequency of diminutivized words was found, a correspondence which is not possible to observe in Sara, since no child-directed speech (CDS) is available for her. An analogous development of the semantic and pragmatic meaning of child diminutives has been reported by Noccetti (2002). She also notices that after close lexical correspondences between CDS and child speech (CS) in pre- and protomorphology, diminutives start to be less input-dependent in the modularized phase and, at the same time, the first examples of diminutives with some adult-like pragmatic meaning emerge in requests.

So far studies on the acquisition of Italian diminutives have not investigated whether or how DIM can facilitate the acquisition of grammatical categories but interestingly a study on Italian as a second language shows evidence that some learners use the feminine diminutives *-ina*, *-etta* when they acquire means for deriving feminine gender from masculine, e.g. f. *spettator-ina* < m. *spettatore*, instead of *spettatrice*, *Fabi-etta* < *Fabio* instead of *Fabia*, *Fabiana* (Chini and Ferraris 2003).

In this paper we will study the diminutive production of four Italian children Camillo, Marco, Matteo, and Rosa with three main objectives: 1) to describe and compare their use of diminutives and contrast CS diminutives with input data both quantitatively and qualitatively; 2) to understand whether the acquisition of diminutives (or at least of some diminutive suffixes) can be assigned to the morphological rule component (cf. Clahsen et al. 2003) or is rather item-based (Tomasello 2003); 3) to investigate whether some features of their production might be interpreted as a strategy for simplifying the target-language morphology.

2. Description of Italian diminutives

Italian diminutives form a rich paradigm of alteratives together with the augmentatives (AUG) *-one* (e.g. *lett-one* 'bed-AUG') and the pejoratives (PEJ) *-accio, -ucolo, -astro* (e.g. *ragazz-accio* 'boy-PEJ'). [2] In the adult language, diminutives are often strongly lexicalized, e.g. *cucchiaio* 'spoon', *cucchiaino* 'tea spoon' (cf. Mutz 2000: 73f; Merlini Bararesi 2004).

In contrast to other alteratives, at least some diminutives are very frequent in child-directed speech (CDS) and, from an early age onwards, also in child speech (CS).

The Italian language shows a great number of DIM suffixes (see Table 1, more in Alberti et al. 1991; Mutz 2000; and Merlini Barbaresi 2004), simple (SD), compound (CD) and interfixed (ID) ones.

Table 1. Diminutive suffixes in Italian

SD	CD	ID
-ino	-in-etto	-er-ozzo
-etto	-in-ino	-er-ello
-ello	-in-otto	-ar-ino
-otto	-in-olo	-ic-ello
-olo/uolo	-ell-ino	-ic-ino
-acchiotto	-ett-ino	
-uccio/uzzo	-erell-ino	
-iccio/icchio	-ott-olo	
-occio	-ucc/icc-ino	
-iciattolo	-acchiott-ino	
-onzolo	-ell-etto	
-u(n)colo	-ol-ino	

As a default, they directly attach to the root of the base, e.g. *tanto* 'so much' → *tant-ino* (sd) → *tant-in-ino* (CD). The only exception are bases ending in *-one* (homophonous with the augmentative suffix), e.g. *leone* 'lion', which form the DIM through the allomorphic rule of inserting the unvoiced palato-alveolar affricate [č] between base and suffix: *leon-[č]-ino* 'lion-DIM' (the same holds for AUG: *leon-[č]-one* and PEJ: *leon-[č]-accio*). [3] The last column (id) of table 1 shows the types with the insertion of an interfix (or "empty" linking morph) between the base and the diminutive suffix.

Diminutives are derivatives, though not prototypical ones (Dressler 1994; Dressler and Merlini 1994) in so far as they hardly ever change the category of the base: e.g. [*maiale*]N → [*maial-ino*] N, 'pig-DIM', i.e. diminutive suffixes are not prototypical heads. However, as Scalise (1994) maintains, they still have some head properties, considering that (a) they can change the inflectional class of the base and (b) the gender of the base:

(a) the DIM suffixes of nouns and adjectives belonging to unproductive inflectional microclasses, change the class of the base into the most stable and most productive microclasses, namely those of Sg. *-o* and Pl. *-i* for the masculine, and Sg. *-a* and Pl. *-e* for the feminine, as in Sg. m. *il duc-a* 'the duke' → *il duch-in-o*, Sg. m. *l' elefant-e* 'the elephant' → *l' elefant-in-o*, Sg. f. *la man-o* 'the hand', Pl. *le man-i* → Sg. *la man-in-a*, Pl. *man-in-e*, Sg. f. *la lepr-e* 'the hare' → *la lepr-in-a*, Sg. m. *il ginocchi-o* 'the knee', Pl. f. *le ginocchi-a* → Sg. DIM *il ginocch-ino*, Pl. *i ginocch-in-i*. Moreover, opaque and prosodically non-uniform plurals become transparent and uniform in the diminutive. For example, bisyllabic singular *uomo* 'man' has a trisyllabic plural *uomini*, whereas its trisyllabic diminutives have regular trisyllabic plurals: Sg. *om-ino, om-etto, Pl. om-ini, om-etti*. Loan words such as *bar*, with zero suffix in the plural, follow the most productive inflection of masculine nouns in *-o/-i*, when diminutivized, Sg. *bar-ett-ino* Pl. *bar-ett-ini* (CD).

Class shifts also eliminate opacifying morphonological palatalizations, as in: Sg. *ami[k]o* 'friend', Pl. *ami[č]i* → DIM Sg. *ami[k]-etto*, Pl. *ami*[k]*-etti*, Sg. *atti[k]o* 'attic', Pl. *atti[č]i* → DIM Sg. *atti[k]-etto*, Pl. *atti[k]etti*. (b) although DIM suffixes, in the default case, maintain the gender of the base, they may sometimes modify it. This change generally affects the marked gender category of feminines by changing them into the unmarked category of masculines (cf. Rohlfs 1968: 64; Merlini Barbaresi 2004: 273f), as in Sg. f. *l' aquila* > m. *l' aquil-otto* 'eagle-DIM', in the lexicalized DIM Sg. m. *il camer-ino* 'dressing room' < f. *la camera* 'bedroom', Sg. m. *lo spazzol-ino* 'tooth brush'< f. *la spazzola* 'brush'. Counterexamples are f. *la pettin-ina* 'curved comb'< m. *il pettine* 'comb' and f. *la vel-etta* 'hat-veil' < m. *il velo* 'veil', f. *la sigar-etta* < m. *il sigaro* 'cigar' (cf. Mutz 2000: 84f).

DIM suffixes can have the status of a word as shown by the following example reported in Dressler and Merlini (1994): un *boccon-c-ino, proprio -ino* 'a mouthful-DIM, really -DIM' (cf. also AUG *-one* and PEJ *-accio*).

The denotative meaning is SMALL for DIM and BIG for AUG, the connotative meaning (if any) is positive for DIM and generally negative for PEJ and AUG.[4] The pragmatic meanings of diminutives are vast and range from speech-act mitigations to indication of child-centred speech situations, emotion, sympathy and empathy (cf. Dressler and Merlini Barbaresi 1994).

Diminutives differ from other suffixes in admitting recursivity either in the strict sense (e.g. *-in-ino*) or in the loose sense of the combination of different DIM suffixes (e.g. *-in-etto*, cf. the column CD in Table 1). In their position, they are external to the other derivational suffixes, e.g. *cucchiaio* 'spoon' + derivational suffix → *cucchiai-ata* + DIM → *cucchiai-at-ina*, but they are internal to the inflectional suffixes, *cucchiaio* + inflectional plural suffix → *cucchia-i* + DIM → *cucchia-in-i*.

Italian DIM suffixes prefer the category of noun as a base. Nouns have fewer restrictions for the application of DIM rules and more freedom in the choice of DIM suffixes than, for instance, adverbs, adjectives or numerals (cf. Merlini Barbaresi 2004). Thus in the L.I.P., the lexicon of spoken Italian (De Mauro et al. 1993), within a corpus of 500,000 words, 69.8% of DIM has a noun as a base, 17.8% an adverb and 12.4% an adjective. Diminutives represent 0.13% of the total word tokens, but within nouns 3.5%, within adjectives 7.7%, and within adverbs 2.85%. Whereas all count nouns and nearly all adjectives can be diminutivized, many adverbs and numerals cannot. Prepositions, pronouns, demonstratives and interjections (with some rare exceptions) are excluded. Diminutivization of verbs differs in form and meaning.[5]

Proper nouns usually take up DIM suffixes in order to form hypocoristics. These hypocoristics are mostly trochaic, e.g. *Francesco → Francesch-ino, Giovanni → Giovann-ino, Maria → Mari-etta, Mari-uccia*. An alternative hypocoristic strategy is truncation as in *Francesco → Cecco, Checco, Franci, Giovanni → Nanni, Gianni, Anton-ino → Nino, Tommaso → Tommi*. These hypocoristics are usually trochaic. In *Gianni ← Giovanni, Mizio ← Maurizio, Rolfo/Roffo ← Rodolfo*, only the word-initial consonant is maintained in pre-tonic position, in *Massa ← MariaLuisa, Dade ← Davide* only the word-initial syllable. Proper nouns are sometimes truncated after the first two syllables, e.g. *France ← Francesco, Nicco ← Niccolò, Silva ← Silvana*, and can also be realized with a final [i], e.g. *Franci, Tommi, Silvi* (cf. Thornton 2004: 605f).

Diminutives of kinship terms, even if used like hypocoristics, are formally identical with other diminutives: *mamm-ina, mamm-etta ← mamma* 'mum', *babb-ino, babb-etto ← babbo* 'dad', *nonn-ino, nonn-etto ← nonno* 'grandfather'.

Within the great variety of competing DIM suffixes, actual choice appears to depend most often on idiosyncratic lexical choice. This is true of unproductive suffixes, such as *-acchiotto*, which is only used with the nouns *lupo* 'wolf' > *lupacchiotto, orso* 'bear' > *orsacchiotto, volpe* 'fox' > *volpacchiotto* referring to cubs, and the adj. *fesso* 'dimwit' > *fessacchiotto*.

The most productive of the DIM suffixes is *-ino* (55.8% tokens in L.I.P. vs. 30.2% of *-etto*), which is also the most frequent one with loans, e.g. *roulott-ina, computer-ino* and admits root-based and word based recursivity e.g. *-in-ino* in *poch-in-ino* 'little-DIM-DIM' and *ino-ino* in *poch-ino ino-ino*.

3. Methodology

The present paper is based on the data of four children, Camillo, Rosa, Matteo, and Marco (cf. note 1) collected in the period from the one-element stage to when the children demonstrate morphological operations and more elaboration in syntactic structures (see table 2). All the children were audio-recorded twice a month, Rosa was also video-recorded; the recordings of Matteo were taken once a week for the first month, diary notes compensated for the months lacking audio-recordings (1;5 1;7, 1;9, 2;0, 3;0). The recording sessions, during spontaneous interactions with the mother and sometimes in the presence of other caretakers (usually the father and the grandmothers), and mainly consisted of daily routines: breakfast, play situations, and book-reading activities.

Transcripts were made in Chat format (MacWhinney 1997) and data were analyzed with Clan.[6] Transcripts were checked by the authors of this paper, both manually and using the Clan program.

Data are assembled in four different phases: pre-morphology, protomorphology (1st period and 2nd period), and modularized morphology, which mark different evolutionary steps in language development (see Dressler 1997; Dressler and Karpf 1995; Kilani-Schoch and Dressler 2002).

The table below shows the period of recording for each child, which starts when all the children were in their pre-morphological phase.

Table 2. Children studied

Children	Camillo	Rosa	Matteo	Marco
Place of birth	Pisa Central Italy	Pisa Central Italy	Cosenza Southern Italy	Udine Northern Italy
Period of recording	2;0-3;6	1;7–3;3	1;3–3;8	1;5–2;5
Pre-morph.	2;00.10–2;03.05	1;07.13–1;10.08	1;03.13–2;01.19	up to 1;05.04
Proto 1st p.	2;03.15–2;04.04	1;11.24–2;00.04	2;01.19–2;02.16	1;05.18–1;09.01
Proto 2nd p.	2;04.19–2;08.24	2;01.14–2;11.12	2;03.15–2;07.23	1;09.15–2;03.29
modular	2;10.05–	2;11.30–	2;08.08–	2;04.13–

4. Emergence and evolution of diminutives

The first diminutives appear in pre-morphology (with Marco only in protomorphology at 1;05.18). In Matteo they signify in particular animal names, such as *uccell-ino* 'bird-DIM' and *cavall-uccio* 'horse-DIM'. Camillo's diminutives increase in the earliest period of protomorphology both in types and tokens, whereas Rosa's and Matteo's data are initially higher than Camillo's and show no such increase in early protomorphology. For later developments of types and tokens (with many fluctuations, except for Rosa in the modularized phase) see table 3.

Table 3. Percentages of types and tokens of Dim of total no. of word types and tokens in cs and cds

PRE-MORPHOLOGY

Camillo	CHI	MOT	**Rosa**	CHI	MOT
age	ty/to	ty/to	age	ty/to	ty/to
2;00.10	0/0	0/0	1;7.13	0/0	**11.46/6.92**
2;01.07	1.38/0.58	0/0	1;9.11	3.44/1.76	5.71/3.74
2;01.22	0/0	1.74/3.70	1;10.08	**5.18/3.78**	**7.94/5.28**
2;02.05	0/0	0/0			
2;02.14	**2.81/2.31**	**4.40/3.73**			
2;03.05	1.56/1.57	0/0			

Matteo	CHI	MOT	**Marco**	CHI	MOT
age	ty/to	ty/to	age	ty/to	ty/to
1;03.13	13.3/12.5	**21.3/16.1**	1;05.04	0/0	**4.56/2.53**
1;04.13	**40/60**	**20/10**			
1;05.17	6.3/4.7	**20.7/14.5**			
1;07.23	**19.7/21.3**	**21.7/22.1**			
2;00.04	0/0	16.7/17.6			

PROTOMORPHOLOGY 1st PERIOD

Camillo	CHI	MOT	**Rosa**	CHI	MOT
age	ty/to	ty/to	age	ty/to	ty/to
2;03.15	**4.25/3.33**	2.94/1.30	1;11.24	3.76/3.81	**6.25/3.74**
2;04.04	0/0	3.52/2.84	2;0.04	**4.32/3.76**	**6.02/2.33**

Matteo	CHI	MOT	**Marco**	CHI	MOT
age	ty/to	ty/to	age	ty/to	ty/to
2;01.19	11.8/10.8	33.3/25	1;05.18	2.5/1.2	**5.34/2.83**
2;02.16	29.7/16	23.6/16.1	1;06.02	2.7/2.6	**6.54/3.31**
			1;06.22	1.4/0.5	4.49/1.98
			1;07.06	3.6/1.5	4.90/2.12
			1;07.19	**5.4/3.6**	3.61/1.41
			1;08.03	**4.1/1.9**	3.65/2.52
			1;08.17	3.9/2.9	3.35/2.58
			1;09.01	3/1.2	3.54/1.73

PROTOMORPHOLOGY 2nd PERIOD

Camillo	CHI	MOT
age	ty/to	ty/to
2;04.19	0/0	2.15/2.21
2;05.02	1.85/3.12	2.45/1.48
2;05.10	2.87/2.11	3.57/1.42
2;05.28	**5.6/2.73**	**6.82/3.57**
2;06.30	0.54/0.20	**4.93/2.77**
2;07.13	1.42/0.93	3.60/1.59
2;07.27	2.17/0.84	**4.60/1.99**
2;08.10	**6.25/4**	**4.56/2.27**
2;08.24	4.80/2.66	**5/3.38**

Rosa	CHI	MOT
age	ty/to	ty/to
2;01.14	2.81/3.29	5.55/3.08
2;1.27	0.60/1.83	**13.14/4.77**
2;2.11	3.07/2.22	4.98/2.25
2;04.07	2.10/2.13	**10.35/4.55**
2;4.21	**5.53/2.85**	**10.39/4.38**
2;5.25	2.95/1.14	**11.57/4.43**
2;6.24	**4.72/2.36**	8.89/4.40
2;7.26	4.60/2.62	7.78/3.55
2;9.04	1.77/0.78	7.54/3.86
2;09.24	1.61/3.02	–
2;10.14	2.06/0.91	**9.87/4.18**
2;11.12	5.26/3.75	11.16/5.51

Matteo	CHI	MOT
age	ty/to	ty/to
2;03.15	**25.7/25.8**	27.1/46.3
2;04.13	10.5/20	20.8/17.7
2;05.06	**13.4/11.5**	12.3/7.7
2;06.10	11.1/9.2	13.9/9.7
2;07.23	7.1/17.9	8.3/12.7

Marco	CHI	MOT
age	ty/to	ty/to
1;09.15	0.7/0.6	2.09/1.37
1;09.29	**6.3/5.8**	**4.32/3**
1;10.12	2/1.1	3.93/1.59
1;10.26	1.7/0.9	2.54/1.16
1;11.16	**5.7/4.8**	**4.08/2.41**
2;00.00	1.8/1.2	2.8/1.1
2;00.14	**5.7/4.1**	4.3/2.8
2;00.27	**4.7/2.7**	4.1/1.7
2;01.11	2.3/0.9	4.0/2.0
2;01.27	1.4/2.2	3.5/2.1
2;01.27	1.4/2.2	3.5/2.1
2;02.11	**3.5/2**	**5.3/2.4**
2;03.02	6.8/3.7	5.7/2.8
2;03.15	3.2/2.3	4.3/2.3
2;03.29	**4/2.5**	**3.7/1.8**

MODULARIZED MORPHOLOGY

Camillo	CHI	MOT
age	ty/to	ty/to
2;10.05	1.87/2.35	2.44/0.85
2;10.23	0/0	2.83/1.97
3;00.23	2.09/0.83	1.73/0.81
3;01.09	2.95/1.32	3.32/1.33
3;02.04	2.36/1.40	2.92/1.23
3;02.20	**6.66/3.73**	1.63/0.76
3;03.05	0/0	**4.89/2.83**
3;03.19	**5.76/4.91**	**5.10/2.99**
3;05.22	1.94/1.31	3.13/1.45
3;06.09	3.67/2.13	3.50/2.03

Rosa	CHI	MOT
age	ty/to	ty/to
2;11.30	3.50/1.83	**9.91/3.44**
3;0.24	**4.61/2.70**	**8.37/3.72**
3;1.29	4.77/2.84	6.70/3.14
3;3.23	3.11/1.08	6.40/2.48

Matteo	CHI	MOT
age	ty/to	ty/to
2;08.08	2.56/1.3	16.63/3.8
2;09.10	4/3.6	5.71/6.9
3;00.23	7.50/4.1	12.9/4.3
3;02.28	2.56/1.5	2.56/0.7
3;03.06	5/2.6	5.47/2.4
3;04.23	13.9/10.3	8.33/10.1
3;05.20	12.15/9.1	8.15/8.4
3;06.14	5.56/7.9	9.09/11.06
3;07.22	10.71/8.2	4.76/10.1
3;08.04	5.94/3.9	7.32/7.7

Marco	CHI	MOT
age	ty/to	ty/to
2;04.13	**4.4/2.7**	**4.7/2.1**
2;04.26	**4.5/2.9**	**4.1/2.1**
2;05.10	1.9/1	2.9/1.4
2;05.24	2.7/1.3	**5.4/2.4**

The comparison between CS and CDS yields four main facts: a) the mothers generally produce more DIM types and tokens than the child, but in protomorphology the children sometimes produce more diminutives than the mothers, otherwise there are very similar percentages; b) CS and CDS show a parallel development of diminutive types and tokens, i.e. the recordings which have peaks of diminutive types and tokens are almost always approximately the same in mother and child. Thus diminutive use appears to be context-bound; c) maternal peaks are often longer than child peaks, i.e. they precede and follow child peaks, which points to the interactive relation between CS and CDS: the mother appears both to stimulate and to echo the child's increasing use of diminutives; d) the input frequency of diminutives decreases in modularized morphology (less so with Marco). In other words, CDS use develops towards ADS, as if children were no longer prototypical small children who have to be addressed with an excessive amount of diminutives.

Hypocoristics are in general extremely rare both in CDS and CS, for example in Marco's data we found 3 tokens of *mamm-ina* 'mum-DIM' and 4 of *Ros-ina* 'Rose-DIM' (in protomorphology).

In premorphology (and in most of protomorphology) nouns may be phonologically reduced to trochees of the syllable shapes VCV, CVCV and CVCCV. When the first diminutives emerge in pre-morphology, they present the same reduced phonological structure: e.g. CAM: *pilla* (for *pall-ina* 'ball-DIM', 3 tokens in one and a half months, thus a frozen form), *pino* (for *bac-ino* 'kiss-DIM'), *pinna* (for *panc-ina* 'belly-DIM'), ROS: *lina* (for *pallina*), *nino* (for *camion-ino*, without the morphonological change of the adult language *camion-c-ino* 'truck-DIM'), MAR: *lino* (for *uccell-ino* 'bird-DIM'), *pete* (for *scarp-ette* 'shoes-DIM'), *lina* (for *farfall-ina* 'butterfly-DIM'), *cini* (for *pallon-c-ini* 'soccer ball-DIM', cf. *cini* for *mic-ini* 'cat-DIM' in Bates and Rankin 1979: 35). The only reductions which are neither trochaic nor take the word initial consonant are Matteo's trisyllabic *cilii* < *uccell-ini* 'birds-DIM' and *chiia* < *macchin-ina* 'car-DIM' (premorphology, cf. *ellino* for *vitell-ino* 'calf' in Bates and Rankin 1979: 36).

During the first phase of protomorphology not only do different inflectional forms of verbs and adjective-noun plural agreement emerge, but base forms also start to co-occur with their diminutive form, initially with articulatory inaccuracy, e.g. CAM: *acchiotto/otto* 'bear-DIM' (cf. Noccetti 2002: 36, 38), ROS: *biba/bib-ina* 'little girl-DIM' < *ors-acchiotto, orso, bimba, bimb-ina*. In Matteo *formica/formich-ina* 'ant-DIM'. The last reduced forms are ROS: *nina* < *bambol-ina* 'doll-DIM' and CAM: *tina* < *tartarugh-ina* 'turtle-DIM', *mina* < *man-ina* 'hand-DIM'; thus adult hypocoristics such as *Gianni* < *Giovanni*, (cf. § 2) appear to be frozen pre-morphological forms. In Marco four three-member paradigms occur, e.g. *scarpa* 'shoe', Pl. *scarpe*, DIM *scarp-ette* (cf. Tonelli and Fabris 2004 for details on Marco's linguistic development).

In later protomorphology, diminutive noun types and base form/diminutive oppositions increase in the corpora, the first diminutive adjectives (CAM: *bello/bell-ino* 'beautiful-DIM'), and adverbs (ROS: *pian-ino* 'slowly-DIM') and even three-member noun paradigms appear (e.g. *fiore* 'flower', Pl. *fiori*, DIM *fior-ell-ini* in Matteo), see Table 4. In Marco three-member paradigms expand to 13, and three four-member paradigms occur, e.g. *palla* 'ball', Pl. *palle*, DIM *pall-ina*, Pl. *pall-ine*. Camillo produces just one three-member paradigm: *pesce* 'fish', Pl. *pesci*, interfixed DIM Pl. *pesci-ol-ini*.

This supports the view that in protomorphology children detect morphological suffixes (cf. for verbs and nouns Noccetti 2002; 2003) and start to expand paradigms during this period (cf. Kilani-Schoch and Dressler 2002).

Camillo still has problems with the production of palatals and glides, which may explain why he produces *conigl-ino* 'rabbit-DIM' as *linno* and *fillini* instead of *figliol-ini* 'sons-DIM'. At 2;5.10 in CAM there is the first allomorphic insertion: *leone* > *leon-c-ino* 'lion-DIM' (further spontaneous examples occur in the modularised phase). In Marco *pallon-c-ino* 'ball-DIM' emerges already at 1;07.19.

Compound diminutives, as important evidence of productivity, emerge in CAM, ROS and MAR in the second phase of protomorphology, CAM: *ors-ett-ino* 'bear-DIM-

DIM' (as an allomorphic variant of *ors-etto*), ROS: *pezz-ett-ino* 'piece-DIM-DIM:Sg:m.', MAR: *scarp-ett-ine* 'shoes-DIM-DIM', *pezz-ett-ino* 'piece-DIM-DIM'.

Table 4. Main changes in CS through the four periods

	Pre-morph.	Proto 1st	Proto 2nd	Modular
Frozen/formulaic	Camillo Matteo Rosa			
DIM nouns	Camillo Matteo Rosa	Marco		
Base form/DIM	Matteo	Camillo Marco Rosa		
AUG		Marco	Camillo	Matteo Rosa
DIM Adj.		Rosa	Camillo Marco Matteo	
3-member Paradigm			Marco Matteo Rosa	Camillo
DIM Adv.		Matteo	Rosa	Camillo Marco
Allomorphic variants		Rosa	Camillo Matteo	Marco

Except for the early truncated forms (e.g. *pilla, tina,* see above) there are no diminutives in the output which would be ungrammatical or unacceptable in adult speech. Thus Matteo's *tutt-ino* 'all-DIM' and *molt-ino* 'much-DIM' appeared strange to his family but exist in Italian (cf. Merlini Barbaresi 2004: 267). However incorrect gender occurs in Rosa's *lus-ini* and *pecor-ini* (at 3;0.24, in the modularized phase), masculine plurals of f. *luc-ina* 'light-DIM' and *pecor-ina* 'sheep-DIM'. These might be analogies after many other masculine diminutives of feminine base forms (cf. § 2), the first form also influenced by *lum-ini* 'lights-DIM' (both in CS and CDS). Only *ov-in-ett-e* 'eggs-DIM-DIM:f' has a strange sequence of suffixes, because in adult Italian normally the most productive suffix *-ino* is normally the most peripheral, and X-*in-etto* seems to be restricted to derivations of lexicalized X-*ino* (cf. Merlini Barbaresi 2004: 276, 281). A strange sequence of diminutives occurs in Matteo's *un attim-ino soltant-ino* 'a moment-DIM only-DIM' (cf. also § 6).

Only Matteo forms potential diminutives which do not occur in ADS and CDS, *guant-etto* 'glove-DIM' (instead of *guant-ino*) and *penn-ell-ina* 'pen-DIM-DIM'. The only backformations, another sign of productivity, occur in Matteo during protomorphology: *violo* < *violino* 'violin', *cagno* < *cagn-ol-ino*, opaque interfixed diminutive of *cane* 'dog'. Note also his substitution of lexicalised *cappotto* 'coat' with *capp-uccio*, which in adult language occurs only with the lexicalised meaning of 'hood'.

Interfixed forms emerge in modularised morphology (*-ic-ino*), e.g. *cuor-ic-ino* 'heart-DIM' (Rosa), *pesci-ol-ini* alongside *pesc-ini* 'fish-DIM' (Camillo). For augmentatives see § 6.

Table 5 shows the prominence of nouns among bases of diminutives both in the output and in the input, as well as in the adult speech (as documented in L.I.P.). The highest percentages are in the inputs of Rosa and Matteo and in the outputs of Camillo and Marco: these asymmetries weaken the correspondence between inputs and outputs. Diminutivized adverbs are more frequent in ADS than in CDS.

Table 5. Types/tokens of the bases of DIM suffixes of total number of DIM

	CAMILLO	MOT	ROSA	MOT	
NOUNS	**90.4/77.8**	**88.3/75**	**81.6/79.4**	**91.9/76.4**	
ADJECTIVES	7.7/19.2	9.2/8.6	14.9/18.8	6.7/18.2	
ADVERBS	1.9/3	2.5/16.4	3.5/1.8	1.4/5.4	
	MATTEO	MOT	MARCO	MOT	LIP (tok.)
NOUNS	**85.4/88.7**	**91.8/93.5**	**86.9/92.2**	**82/90.6**	**69.8**
ADJECTIVES	10.2/7.7	7.6/5.5	12.3/7.3	17.4/8	12.4
ADVERBS	4.4/3.6	0.6/1.0	0.8/0. 5	0.6/1.4	17.8

Table 6 compares diminutivized noun, adjective and adverb tokens with the tokens of the bases. Despite interindividual differences among children, nouns are again the most prominent among diminutives. CDS is always richer in diminutives than CS (with the exception of adjectives in Matteo). ADS (both of L.I.P. and Camillo's mother) has less diminutivized nouns than CDS and CS, but this difference decreases in modularized morphology (cf. above). The fluctuation in adverb tokens depends on the amount of usage of *poch-ino* 'a bit-DIM'.

Table 6. DIM tokens of the total no. of nouns, adjectives, adverbs (whole corpus and per phases)

	NOUN	ADJ	ADV			NOUN	ADJ	ADV
CAM	6.73	5	0.60	**CAM**	Proto 1st	**10.71**	0	0
MOT	13.40	5.50	3.90		Proto 2nd	8.84	4.22	0
ADS	3.20	1.20	3.30		Modular	7.24	8.02	0.50
ROS	12.43	2.94	0.29	**ROS**	Proto 1st	**12.72**	5.88	0
MOT	23.13	5.51	1.64		Proto 2nd	11.39	14.95	0.87
					Modular	14.53	3.11	0
MAR	6.74	0.53	0.04	**MAR**	Proto 1st	**4.44**	0	0
MOT	8.41	0.74	0.13		Proto 2nd	7.90	0.25	0
					Modular	6.67	2.37	0.22
MAT	13.1	1.15	0.85	**MAT**	Proto 1st	**13.07**	0.42	0.22
MOT	14.9	0.88	0.13		Proto 2nd	12.45	1.23	0.54
					Modular	9.23	1.02	0.34
LIP	3.50	7.70	2.85					

5. Suffix allomorphy

The suffix *-ino* emerges first, either in premorphology (Camillo and Rosa) or at the beginning of protomorphology (Marco, Matteo). The other diminutive suffixes emerge in protomorphology, e.g. CAM: *-ello* (*campanella* 'bell-DIM'), *-etto* (*orsetto*) mat: *-acchiotto* (*lupacchiotto* 'wolf-DIM'), cf. frozen *orsacchiotto* in the first period of protomorphology.

The only other type and token of the suffix *-acchiotto* occurs in Matteo's *lup-acchiotti* 'wolves-DIM' (protomorphology), (more details in table 7).
The overall distribution of suffixes (see table 8) also shows the prominence of the suffix *-ino*.

Table 7. Emergence of DIM suffixes and Augmentative -ONE

	Pre-morph.	Proto 1st	Proto 2nd	modular
ino	CAM, ROS	MAR, MAT		
adj-ino		ROS	CAM, MAR	MAT
adv-ino			ROS	CAM, MAR, MAT
etto	MAT	MAR, ROS		CAM
ello		MAR	CAM, MAT	ROS
acchiotto		CAM, ROS	MAT	
ol-ino			CAM, ROS, MAR, MAT	
ett-ino		MAR	CAM, ROS, MAT	
in-etto				CAM
ic-ino				ROS
ONE		MAR	CAM	MAT, ROS

In all corpora *-ino* is the most used suffix. It is the only diminutive suffix employed with adjectives and adverbs in these data. The suffix *-etto* comes second, whereas *-ello* is marginal, the others often even non-existent. However in the inputs of the Tuscan children Camillo and Rosa, *-ino* appears to have a default status: in all its combinations 88.28/90.9% (CAM) and 93.8/94.4% (ROS). Moreover, it is the only diminutive suffix employed with adjectives and adverbs and – with the exception of idiosyncratic *ov-in-ette* 'eggs-DIM-DIM'– it is the only suffix which occurs after other diminutive suffixes, a further sign of being the most productive one (cf. Dressler 2004). Finally, potential variants in *-ino* of diminutives with other suffixes are the most acceptable ones. Thus default status and highest productivity explain why *-ino* emerges first in Camillo and Rosa, earlier than the other most frequent diminutives and with even higher frequencies than in their inputs. However *-ino* emerges first and is the most productive suffix even with Matteo and Marco, in whose inputs it does not have default status, but where it is still the most productive suffix. In fact, type and token frequencies are much higher in their CS than in their CDS. A further factor might be that the suffix *-ino* with its stressed phoneme [*i*] is more iconic than the other diminutive suffixes.

Table 8. Distribution of DIM suffixes in CS and CDS

	CAM	MOT	ROS	MOT	MAT	MOT
ino	**82.4/85.9**	77.5/81.7	**87.7/91.5**	81.6/91.4	**74.1/82.5**	59.6/63.7
etto	**7.8/6.1**	11.7/9.3	**3.5/4.2**	5.8/2.4	**18/11.2**	24.7/23.8
ello	1.96/1	4.2/1.8	1.8/1.1	1.4/0.4	7.4/5.7	9.2/7.8
acchiotto	1.96/2	0.8/0.4	0.9/0.3	0.5/0.4	0	3.5/2.7
ol-ino	1.96/2	1.7/1.1	2.6/1.1	2.7/1	0	1.1/1.0
ett-ino	1.96/2	1.7/0.7	2.6/1.3	5.4/2.7	0.2/0.4	1.5/0.8
in-etto	1.96/1	0	0	0	0	0
icino	0	0.8/0.4	0.9/0.5	0.9/0.3	0.2/0.2	0.4/0.2
in-ino	0	0.8/3.9	0	0	0	0
acchiott-ino	0	0.8/0.7	0	0	0	0
olo	0	**0**	0	0.4/0.1	0	0
ell-ino	0	**0**	0	1.3/1.3	0	0
otto	0	**0**	0	0	0	0
uccio	0	**0**	0	0	0	0
er-ino	0	**0**	0	0	0	0

	MAR	MOT	LIP (tok)	AS (CAM's MOT)
ino	**57.5/60.6**	55.3/59.7	**55.8**	85.7
etto	**30/30.3**	33.2/34.5	**30.2**	14.3
ello	4.2/5.1	4.5/2.9	2.3	0
acchiotto	0	0	0	0
ol-ino	0	0	2.3	0
ett-ino	2.5/1.5	1.2/0.9	3	0
in-etto	0	0	0	0
icino	0.8/0.5	0.3/0.1	0	0
in-ino	0.8/0.2	0.3/0.1	0	0
acchiott-ino	0	0	0	0
olo	0	0.3/0.1	0	0
ell-ino	0	0	2.3	0
otto	3.4/1.0	4.2/1.6	1.5	0
uccio	0.8/0.8	0.6/0.2	2.3	0
er-ino	0	0	0.3	0

One may be inclined to interpret this prominence of *-ino* in the light of Clahsen et al.'s (2003) dual-route model of subjecting only a part of word formation to rule mechanism. Thus we might assign only *-ino* suffixation to the morphological rule component. However *-etto* suffixation is extremely frequent both in the input and output of Marco and Matteo, and for Camillo we can observe that in protomorphology the only examples are *ors-etto* and *ov-in-ette* 'bear-DIM', 'eggs-DIM-DIM', but in the few recorded months of modularised morphology also *camp-etti* 'fields-DIM', *nan-etti* 'dwarfs-DIM' and *stell-ette* 'stars-DIM' appear. Thus in his protomorphological phase we might claim that only *-ino* suffixation is rule-derived. The same holds for the whole corpus of Rosa.

On the whole, there is no overall direct relation between frequency distribution of the input and the output other than the tendency for frequent input DIM to be still more frequent in the output and for infrequent DIM to be still more infrequent in CS.

In order to evaluate the model of item-based acquisition (Tomasello 2003), let us compare the most frequent diminutive forms in CS and CDS:

Table 9. Comparison of the most frequent DIM tokens in CS and CDS

CAM	CDS (CAM)	ROS	CDS (ROS)
5 campino	**21 librino**	**28 canino**	**47 bambolina**
4 coniglino	15 canzoncina	18 omino	**31 mucchina**
4 lettino	**12 orsetto**	**15 mucchina**	31 cavallino
4 librino	7 bimbino	**14 maialino**	**30 maialino**
4 pallina	6 novellina	13 macchinina	**27 manina**
3 agnellino	5 canino	**10 pallina**	**26 canino**
3 casina	5 topino	9 vecchietto	**23 pallina**
3 orsetto	5 uccellino	6 farfallina	23 gattino
2 bacino	4 pratino	**6 manina**	23 cucchiaino
2 maialino	3 cavallino	**4 bambolina**	21 pecorina
MAR	CDS (MAR)	MAT	CDS (MAT)
37 palloncino	**137 libretto**	20 porcellino	25 cavalluccio
34 pallina	**85 pallina**	18 piccolino	20 cagnolino
22 libretto	**72 palloncino**	12 topolino	15 fratellino
17 orsetto	**68 palline**	12 gattino	15 piedino
13 capretti	**63 cestino**	12 pochino	13 porcellino
13 palloncini	**40 orsetto**	11 forbicetta	**12 piccolino**
12 lettino	**38 palloncini**	9 uccellino	12 gallinella
11 porcellini	31 topolino	9 pallina	12 fiorellini
10 palline	**27 porcellini**	8 paperelle	**11 gattino**
9 cestino		8 gallinella	**9 topolino**

In Marco, where we find the closest correspondences, the frequency ranks of the three first types coincide but in reverse order, the next six types of CS correspond only partially to CDS. Thus the coincidence is modest. More importantly, the most frequent lemmas of CDS do not emerge as the first ones in CS, with the exception of *libr-etto* 'book-DIM', which occurs in early protomorphology, whereas the other most frequent types of CDS emerge only later. The coincidences are still more modest for the other children. And of the ten most frequent input diminutives of Camillo, none emerges early in CS, whereas in the corpus of Rosa, *pall-ina, bambol-ina, man-ina* and *mucch-ina* emerge early. Therefore, at least for Marco, one could argue that item-based learning might be linked to the early emergence of *libr-etto*, which is very frequent both in input and output and is accompanied during the protomorphological period by very few other diminutives ending in *-etto*.

In contrast, for *-ino* diminutives there are very modest correspondences between input and output, they emerge in great variety (note also that only this diminutive pattern emerges with adjectives and adverbs), they represent the final suffix in combined and interfixed diminutives, and are subtracted in back formations. This supports the assumption of a productive use of the diminutive-formation rule and of across-the-board learning rather than item-based learning.

6. Semantic and pragmatic aspects

During premorphology, when the few spontaneous diminutives of the corpora appear without the corresponding base forms, it is impossible to identify either their pragmatic or semantic meaning.

In the first period of protomorphology, when base forms start to co-occur with the diminutive derivatives, the semantic meaning has not yet been acquired, as shown by diminutives and base forms employed to refer to the same object in the same microcontext, e.g. CAM (2;03.18): *orso, ors-acchiotto* 'bear', ROS (1;11.24): *bambola, bambol-ina* 'doll', MAR (second period of protomorphology (1;08.17)): *palla, pall-ina* 'ball', (1;03.02) *bastone, baston-c-ino* 'club', (1;06.22) *scarpe, scarp-ette* 'shoes', (1;07.06) *cigni, cign-etti* 'swans'. This also results from the following dialogue between mat (2;01.27) and his mother:

(1) MOT: *Matteo, come fa il cane grande?*
'Matteo, what does the big dog do?'
MAT: *Bau!* (making a very harsh noise)
MOT: *E come fa il cagn-ol-ino?*
'and what does the dog-DIM do?'
MAT: 0 (silence).
MOT: *E il cane piccol-ino?*
'and the dog little-DIM?'
MAT: *Bau!* (in very sweet and acute tone). [8]

This example shows that the child recognizes the meaning 'small' only when it is expressed with the analytic form.[9] During the second period of protomorphology, the semantic meaning of 'smallness' is still conveyed analytically through the adjective *piccolo* 'little', which is very often confronted with *grande* 'big', e.g.:

(2) CAM (2;05.10): *lole lole, plima è piccino e poi glosso.*
'lion, lion first it is small and then big.'

(3) ROS (2;04.23): *(p)iccino*
'little.'
MOT: *piccino quel sapone*
'little, that soap.'
ROS: *mio, (gr)ande*
'mine, big.'
MOT: *il tuo è grande.*
'yours is big.'
ROS: *pe' (=questo) piccin-ino.*
'this little-DIM'

(4) MAT (2;06.10): *ma questo domme, domme anche i gatt-ino.*
'but this sleeps, also the cat-DIM sleeps'
MOT: *ce n'è uno grande e uno piccolo vero? Questo chi è?*
'there is one big and one small, isn't there? Who is this?'
MAT: *è grande.*
'he is big'
MOT: *e come si chiama?*
'and what is his name?'
MAT: *si chiama gatto.*
'He is a cat'
MOT: *e questo?*
'and this one?'
MAT: *gatto piccolo che domme.*
'small cat that sleeps.'

Other examples of the second period of protomorphology confirm that diminutives are not used semantically, e.g. MAT (2;04.13): *man-ina* 'hand-DIM', ROS (2;02.11): *man-ine* 'hands-DIM', referred to the hands of an adult, ROS (2;09.04): *mamm-ina* 'mum-DIM', (2;09.24) *babb-ino* 'dad-DIM', when addressing her parents, (2;11.12) *panier-ino grande* 'basket-DIM big'.

Early diminutives of CDS and CS seem to have a primitive pragmatic meaning which indicates child-centred speech situations and involves 'emotion' and 'endearment', while the base forms are never characterized by some sort of pragmatic meaning. This is even more evident when mini-paradigms of base forms and their diminutive derivations occur. De Marco (2002) also observes that diminutives are often accompanied by prosodic traits that indicate 'tenderness' and 'empathy' both in CS and CDS.

In child-adult interactions, the most common semantic groups selected belong to the child's world, such as the child's belongings, animals/pets, toys. With these semantic groups the prevailing meaning tends to be more pragmatic (again tenderness, love, sympathy) than semantic. The four children and their inputs show homogeneity when, for diminutive use, they preferentially select the lexico-semantic groups of animals, toys, clothes and, among inanimates, usually familiar concrete objects used by the child (see table 10). The different use of DIM in inputs with kinship terms and proper names depends on idiosyncratic as well as regional choices. Here diminutives of proper names, more in Rosa and in Matteo than in the other children, are generally 'family-frozen' forms, i.e. forms used only within the family to refer to siblings or other close relatives, e.g. ROS (from 1;09.11): *Nino < Antonio,* MAT (3;07.22): *Cri < Cristina.*

Table 10. Lexico-semantic groups selected as bases for diminutivization in CS and CDS

	CAM	MOT	ROSA	MOT
food	4.4/2.6	5.7/3.8	2.8/0.8	2/1
body parts	4.4/5.2	8.5/7.1	5.6/3.3	9.8/9.4
animals	**17.8/20.8**	**19.8/18.1**	**19.4/25.8**	**15.2/27.1**
inanimate	**20/28.6**	**17.9/23.8**	**27.8/13.3**	**27.9/17**
toys	**35.6/31.2**	**16/16.2**	**15.3/15.1**	**18.1/20.4**
abstract	0	4.7/2.9	0	1.5/1.5
clothes	**13.3/7.8**	11.3/6.7	8.3/5.2	12.7/9
other	2.3/2.5	5.7/11.9	2.8/1.5	2.5/1.9
humans/proper N	2.2/1.3	10.4/9.5	**18/35**	**10.3/12.7**
	MAT	MOT	MAR	MOT
food	0	4.59/2.5	3.4/3.3	3.8/2.5
body parts	3.4/0.6	8.2/6.2	5.2/2.8	9.5/4.8
animals	**46.6/50**	**30.2/40.06**	**33.6/24.2**	**22.2/21.4**
inanimate	**24.7/14.1**	**27.5/21.4**	**28.5/23.7**	**32.8/34.8**
toys	**10.4/6**	5.7/5.9	14.7/36.2	9.6/24.7
abstract	2.9/18.5	14.6/14.9	3.4/1.8	8.8/5.0
clothes	0	0	6.0/2.6	6.1/3.4
other	3.4/1.9	1.01/0.54	0	0
humans/proper N	8.6/8.9	8.2/8.5	5.2/5.4	7.2/3.4

In addition to the limits imposed by the semantic groups selected in interactive contexts, in Rosa's and Matteo's CS and CDS, during the first and second period of protomorphology, the adjective *piccino* 'small' and its variants are very often employed together with the diminutive noun, e.g. mat (2;07): *una lumach-ina piccol-ina,* 'a snail-DIM little-DIM', ROS (2;05.25): *capr-ett-ina piccina* 'goat-DIM-DIM little-DIM', (2;06.29) *bell-ino piccin-ino* 'nice-DIM little-DIM', (2;07.26) *gatt-ino piccino* 'cat-DIM little-DIM', *mucch-ine piccine* 'cow-DIM little', (2;11.12) *maial-ino piccin-ino* 'pig-DIM little-DIM'. In these examples, the pragmatic meaning of endearment emerges within the diminutivized words while the semantic meaning of 'smallness' is highlighted by the adjective. The pragmatic meaning of DIM is reinforced by the adjective *piccino* 'little', which also often carries a connotative meaning when it is diminutivized to *piccin-ino* 'little-DIM', e.g. ROS (2;11.12): *maial-ino piccin-ino* 'pig-DIM little-DIM', mat (1;07.23): *un gatt-ino piccol-ino* 'a cat-DIM little-DIM'. In MAT and ROS, the pattern 'noun-DIM + little (-DIM)', particularly frequent in Rosa's CS and CDS, seems to delay the acquisition of the denotative meaning of DIM until the last recordings of the modularized and the end of the protomorphological phase respectively. MAR (at 1;09.29) has instances of augmentatives already in the second phase of protomorphology, alongside the base forms and sometimes even alongside the respective diminutives, e.g. *lett-one* 'bed-AUG' and *lett-ino, scatol-one* 'box-AUG', and *scatol-ino, libr-one* 'book-AUG' and *libr-ino* (cf. *tor-one* 'bull-AUG' at 2;03.29). Such oppositions between augmentatives and diminutives derived from the same bases have been identified by Ceccherini et al. (1997) as a constellation which stimulates the detection of the semantic opposition between smallness (DIM) and bigness (AUG). [10]

CAM (at 2;08.10) seems to acquire the denotative meaning of DIM as well:

(5) SAB: *questo è il re leon-c-ino.*
'This is the king lion-DIM.'
CAM: *(leon)c-ino.*
'lion-DIM.'
SAB: *è piccino eh, non è un leon-ci-one*!
'it is small eh, it is not a lion-AUG!'
MOT: *invece quando è grande come diventa*?
'instead when he grows up how will he become?'
CAM: *glosso, one*!
'big, -AUG suffix!'

It is in modularized morphology, though, that examples of augmentatives are more frequent and present in all corpora, often together with their base forms, e.g. CAM (3;02.20): *alberi, alber-oni* 'trees-AUG', MAR (2;04.26) *una grossa formic-ona* 'a big ant', ROS: (at 3;01.29) *palla, pall-ona* 'ball-AUG, (at 3;03.23) *buc-one* 'hole-AUG', MAT (3;03.06): *denti, dent-one* 'tooth-AUG' (3;03.06).

MAR (2;04.13) uses the DIM semantically, e.g., *nonn-ina* 'grandmother-DIM' referring to a little woman in a book, ROS explains why she has used a diminutive:

(6) ROS (2;11.12): *un can-ino un can-ino.*
'a dog-DIM a dog-DIM.'

MOT: *come un can-ino?*
'why a dog-DIM?'
ROS: *un can-ino eh!*
'a dog-DIM eh!'
MOT: *è un can-ino.*
'it is a dog-DIM.'
ROS: *piccin-ino!*
'little-DIM!'

There are also some examples where the augmentative and the diminutive oppose their semantic meanings, e.g. ROS (3;01.29): *pall-ina* 'ball-DIM', *pall-ona* 'ball-AUG', *maial-ino* 'pig-DIM', *maial-one* 'pig-AUG'.

Also notice the explanation given by MAT (2;08.08) of a false back-formed augmentative that he uses in interaction with his mother:

(7) MAT: *mamma quello è un barbone*
'mummy that is a poodle'
MOT: *perché dici che è un barbone?*
'why do you say it is a poodle?'
MAT: *perché è un barbon-c-ino grande*
'because it is a big poodle-false-DIM.'[11]

A similar example occurs in CAM (3;06.09):

(8) CAM: *nonna è una pasticciona!*
'grandmother is a messer (lit. cake)-AUG!'
MOT: *perché?*
'why?'
CAM: *perchè mangia tanti pasticcini!*
'because she eats so many cakes!'

where the word *pasticcino* 'cake' is a false DIM, which is analysed by Camillo as *pasticcio*-DIM.[12]

In modularized morphology, DIM are still used with the pragmatic meanings of tenderness and sympathy, but CAM (3;01.09) and MAT (3;07.22) also show examples where the DIM is used strategically to soften a request, like in ADS:

(9) MOT: *di regalo c'era quella signorina, quella donn-ina.*
'as a present there was that young lady, that woman-DIM.'
CAM: *mi fai vedere mamma quella donn-ina?*
'can you show me mum that woman-DIM?'
MOT: *c' era questa se ti ricordi, no dov' era? Questa era?*
'there was this one if you remember, no where was it? Was it this one?'
CAM: *sì mamma, no, mi dai il regal-ino?*
'yes Mummy, no, will you give me the present-DIM?'

(10) MAT: *puoi darmi quella pall-ina un attim-ino soltant-ino?*
'can you give me that ball-DIM just-DIM a moment-DIM to ask for a ball.' [13]

MAT begins to produce diminutives in a wider range of situations very close to those of the adult, such as in child-centred speech situations (with the younger brother). For pragmatic effects he starts to diminutivize categories that are impossible to diminutivize in the adult language, such as the adverbs *tutt-ino* 'all-DIM', *molt-ino* 'much-DIM', *sempr-ino* 'always DIM'. He also starts to reiterate the suffixes: *buon-in-ino* 'good-DIM-DIM', *piccol-ett-in-ino* 'little-DIM-DIM-DIM'.

7. Do diminutives facilitate the acquisition of inflection?

Diminutive formation emerges early, first for pragmatic reasons, second because of its productivity (and iconicity of *-ino* see above § 5), third possibly because nearly all diminutive suffixes are salient word-final trochees. Now the question arises, whether this has some impact on the acquisition of plurals.

First of all let us look at the opposition of base forms and diminutive derivation. With the first period of protomorphology, base forms start to co-occur with their diminutive forms: CAM: *orso, ors-acchiotto* 'bear-DIM', ROS: *bimba, bimb-ina* 'little girl-DIM', *mani, man-ina* 'hand-DIM', MAT: *formica, formich-ina* 'ant-DIM', MAR: *cigni, cign-etti* 'swans-DIM', *ricci, ricc-ini* 'hedgehogs-DIM'. First there is no more than one diminutive type for each lemma (either singular or plural). The base forms and diminutive forms of these emergent (extended) mini-paradigms are used to refer to the same objects. In this phase Rosa has the first diminutive plurals: *(fiorel)lini* 'flowers-DIM'.

In the second phase of protomorphology more such mini-paradigms are produced: CAM *coniglio, conigl-ino* 'rabbit-DIM'; *bicicletta, biciciclett-ina* 'bike-DIM'; *treno, tren-ino* 'train-DIM'; *letto, lett-ino* 'bed-DIM'; ROS (at 2;04.29): *omo, om-ino* 'man-DIM'. Now also three-member paradigms emerge, ROS (at 2;4.29 and 2;11.12) *omo, om-ino, om-ini* 'man'; *albero, alberi, alber-ino* 'tree', *cavallo, cavalli, cavall-ini* 'horse', (2;4.07): *mucca, (muc)ch-ina, (muc)ch-ine* 'cow', (2;04.29) *mano, mani, man-ina* 'hand'; *bella, bell-ina, bell-ine* ' beautiful', (2;07.26) *bimbo, bimbi, bimb-ino* 'little boy'; MAT: *fiore, fiori, fior-ell-ini* 'flower', MAR: *palle, pall-ina, pall-ine* 'balls'; *pallone, pallon-c-ino, pallon-c-ini* 'soccer ball'.

Towards the end of the protomorphological phase CAM (2;08.10) has the first three-term paradigm, *pesce, pesci, pesci-ol-ini* 'fish' (cf. also § 4).

Table 11 shows how the percentage of base forms co-occurring with their diminutives rises in time and approaches input amounts.

Table 11. DIM, base forms, paradigm tokens and lemmas of the total No. of nouns in the corpora (and per phases)

Tokens	Base	DIM	Base & DIM	**Lemmas**	Base	DIM	Base & DIM
CAM	**73.5**	4.2	22.3	**CAM**	**85**	5.9	9.1
MOT	66.3	3.3	30.4	MOT	81.4	6.1	12.5
ROS	**82**	7	11	**ROS**	**81.7**	7.4	10.9
MOT	48.4	4.4	47.2	MOT	69.9	11.5	18.6
MAT	**81.9**	12.09	6.0	**MAT**	**80.2**	15.4	4.4
MOT	72.1	23.28	4.62	MOT	78.2	11.3	10.5
MAR	**81.4**	8.7	9.9	**MAR**	**81.9**	7.6	10.5
MOT	76.7	7.8	15.5	MOT	76.2	7.7	16.1

Lemmas	Proto 1st		Proto 2nd		Modular	
	CAM	MOT	CAM	MOT	CAM	MOT
Base	90	79.5	82.8	79.5	84.6	84.4
DIM	10	15.4	9.7	8.6	9.2	6.6
Base+DIM	0	5.1	7.5	11.9	6.2	9
	ROS	MOT	ROS	MOT	ROS	MOT
Base	84.3	79.2	78.4	70	77.7	69.8
DIM	9.8	10.4	7	13.8	10.2	11.8
Base + DIM	5.9	10.4	14.6	16.2	12.1	18.4
	MAT	MOT	MAT	MOT	MAT	MOT
Base	80.21	79.5	81.55	76.49	79.25	78.7
DIM	13.42	12.62	10.23	14.26	9.23	7.1
Base+DIM	6.37	7.88	8.22	9.25	11.52	14.2
	MAR	MOT	MAR	MOT	MAR	MOT
Base	86.1	73	79.7	78.5	77.2	77
DIM	5.2	7.2	10.1	8	10.7	7.9
Base + DIM	8.7	19.8	10.2	13.5	12.1	15.1

In each period the base forms are much more frequent than DIM, and the singular forms are more frequent than the plural ones. The difference between plural and singular forms also holds for their DIM derivatives.

Mini-paradigms of base forms and DIM emerge at the same time in ROS: (1;11.24) *bimb-o, bimb-i* 'boy', *caprett-in-a, caprett-in-e* 'goat-DIM', (2;2.11) unproductive *bicchier-e, bicchier-i* 'glass', *man-o, man-i* 'hand', (2;4.07) *scarp-a, scarp-e* 'shoe', *mucch-in-a, mucch-in-e* 'cow-DIM'. In CAM there are only paradigms of plural and singular base forms: (2;05.10) *Elis-a, Elis-e,* (2;08.10) *giorn-o, giorn-i* 'day', (3;01.09) unproductive *pesc-e, pesc-i* 'fish', (3;03.05) *fior-e, fior-i* 'flower', certainly due to a lack of data since there are instances of DIM plural and singular with base forms, e.g. (2;05.28) *biciclett-in-a, biciclett-a* 'bike', (2;08.10) *lett-in-o, lett-o* 'bed', (2;05.28) *pesci-ol-in-o, pesc-e*.

Since the diminutives of unproductive and opaque classes are productive and transparent, the question arises whether children's preference for inflections which are highly productive and transparent influences their production of diminutives vs. base forms. Thus children should produce relatively more often the productive and transparent diminutives *om-ino* and Pl. *om-ini*, from unproductive and opaque *uomo*, Pl. *uomini* 'man', than the diminutives *bimb-ino, bimb-ini* derived from already productive and transparent *bimbo, bimbi*. Positive evidence for the productivity preference comes from Marco. The distribution of tokens of diminutives and their base forms (where only lemmas which have at least one base form and one diminutive token are included) is during his protomorphological period:

	Base form tokens	Derived diminutive tokens
Prod. base forms	73	30
Unprod. base forms	9	13

Thus the ratio DIM/Base form is 0.41 for productive base forms and 1.44 for unproductive ones. This demonstrates a clear preference for the shift from the base form to DIM if the base form belongs to an unproductive class. There is a significant main effect (χ^2 =7.21, $p < 0.01$). Rosa also shows a significant main effect (χ^2 =6.11, $p < 0.05$). For Camillo and Matteo, the token numbers are too small to be of statistical weight, but they show a trend in the same direction. The same holds for all children for the variable of transparency, because too few base forms belong to an opaque inflection class.

The above distribution of base forms and of their derived diminutives gives evidence for the sensitivity of at least two children to inflectional productivity. They are inclined to avoid base forms which belong to an unproductive inflection class (notably of the type *pesce*, Pl. *pesci* 'fish') and prefer, instead, derived diminutives (such as *pesci-ol-ino, pesci-ol-ini*), apparently because they belong to a productive inflection class. This facilitates the development of diminutives and strengthens the acquisition of the two productive inflection classes, masc. Sg. *-o*, Pl. *-i*, fem. Sg. *-a*, Pl. *-e*.

8. Concluding Remarks

Our initial objectives were to compare the use of DIM in the four children and their respective CDS, to investigate whether DIM are rule-derived and whether or not DIM could facilitate the acquisition of noun morphology, i.e. plural formation.

As for the first aim, data show that the four children investigated have a common DIM acquisition pattern. What emerges is that DIM are productive from protomorphology onwards when parents and caretakers also show a wider use of diminutivized words. The productivity of DIM suffixes in CS is evident in the four children both in the quantitative analysis, which shows an increasing number of types and tokens, and qualitatively via signs of creativity of the DIM suffixes, i.e. in backformation, the use of compound diminutives, allomorphic variants of DIM and the creation of grammatically correct diminutivized words close to the limits of acceptability (in the adult language).

Data also show a similar behaviour in the selection of the landing sites for DIM and the semantic classes, which are usually those more suitable to child-centred speech situations. Even the semantic development of DIM follows an analogous pattern in the four children. What emerges is that initially the children use diminutives as pragmatic variants of the respective base forms. The acquisition of the semantic meaning takes place later, towards the end of protomorphology or at the beginning of modularized morphology (against contrasting claims by Bates & Rankin 1979).

The comparison between CS and CDS, in addition to similarities, also reveals some important differences. Quantitatively speaking, the parental input is usually richer in DIM at least in the two first periods, i.e. premorphology and protomorphology, as if CDS promoted the production of DIM in CS. However, when the child approaches the modularized period the percentages are similar. This could be interpreted as a sign of a change in mother-child interaction, which gradually modifies its features in parallelism to the child's cognitive maturation (maternal fine-tuning).

Moreover it emerges that the most frequent diminutives of the input do not emerge first in CS. This result suggests that the acquisition of diminutives is not item-based but basically rule-governed, at least for the suffix *-ino*. All the children studied, in fact, form DIM in *-ino*, which is the most productive suffix in the target language and which is more widely used in CS than in CDS. In protomorphology only *-ino* diminutives appear to be rule-derived, but later, in the modularised period, there also appear to be instances of rule-derived *-etto* diminutives. This is demonstrated by their productivity (see above).

As for the other aim of this paper, i.e. to see whether diminutives facilitate the acquisition of plural formation, the results can be interpreted in favour of this hypothesis at least for two of the children, Rosa and Marco, whose data were quantitatively the most significant. The distribution of base forms and diminutives of productive and unproductive classes and their ratio show a preference for diminutives when the base forms belong to an unproductive class (e.g. Sg. *-e*, Pl. *-i*), i.e. at least two children find the diminutive suffix more reliable because it always belongs to the productive inflectional classes. This preference for diminutivization is present from protomorphology onwards and indicates that the children select the most stable rules of grammar, overextending those already acquired across the board. As for the other two children, Camillo and Matteo, the preference for diminutives in case of unproductive base form inflection is not significant, but goes in the same direction.

Abbreviations

AS	Adult speech
AUG	Augmentative
C	Consonant
CAM	Camillo
CD	Compound Diminutive
CHI	Child
ID	Interfixed Diminutive
L.I.P.	*Lessico dell'Italiano Parlato* 'Italian Spoken Lexicon'
MAR	Marco
MAT	Matteo
Modular	Modularised morphology
PEJ	Pejorative
Premorph.	Premorphology
Proto 1st	Protomorphology 1st period
Proto 2nd	Protomorphology 2nd period
ROS	Rosa
sd	Simple Diminutive
To/tok	Tokens
Ty	Types
V	Vowel

Notes

1. The data of Camillo have been collected and analyzed by Noccetti, who also elaborated Rosa's data (available on the CHILDES database), which are part of a corpus of data of the Institute Stella Maris of Pisa. Matteo's data have been collected and analyzed by De Marco, and Marco's data by Tonelli and Fabris. We would like to thank the Institute Stella Maris for allowing the use of Rosa's data and Fabris for his contribution to the analysis of Marco's data. Although the paper is the result of the joint work of the authors, Noccetti has been the main responsible for the elaboration of §§ 1, 6, 8 and the first part of § 4, De Marco for §§ 2, 3 and the second part of § 4, Tonelli for § 5, Dressler for § 7.

2. Our description adopts the framework of Dressler & Merlini Barbaresi (1994, 1997) and Merlini Barbaresi (2004) with its distinction of morphosemantics (basic meaning SMALL) and morphopragmatics (basic meaning NON-SERIOUS).

3. If the suffix is the PEJ *-accio* [ač:o], the suffix may be directly attached to the base without the insertion of the palato alveolar (i.e. variant *leon-accio*) in order to avoid repetition, i.e. there is a preventive dissimilation.

4. There are however regional differences which determine the evaluation of the alterative. For example in the Tuscan variety the PEJ *-accio* has an affective connotation that diminishes its

negative force, especially when it is used with children, pets or lovers. Thus it may be no coincidence that *-accio* emerges only in the Tuscan corpus of Camillo (2;7). For the case of pejoratives see also Bates and Rankin (1979: 39).

5. Diminutivized verbs take other suffixes: *-ucchi-are, icchi-are*, e.g. *mangi-ucchi-are* 'eat-DIM' whose meaning corresponds more or less to 'to nibble, to pick at'. They occur neither in our data nor in the respective inputs.

6. Matteo's data were also partially analyzed with the help of the Morph program elaborated by Giuseppe Cappelli of CNR (National Centre of Research) of Pisa (cf. Tonelli et al. 1997).

7. Here and elsewhere in the tables boldface shows the highest percentages and numbers for each child.

8. Cf. Bates and Rankin (1979: 31) for high-pitched voice signaling smallness.

9. Cf. Bates and Rankin (1979: 35, 37f). Although the form *cagn-ol-ino* is morphotactically opaque due to the palatal instead of the dental nasal of the base form *cane* 'dog', the child knows and uses this form to refer to the dog. Therefore, it is to exclude that he might not recognize the identity of the base and of the interfix *-ol-*.

10. The earliest example in Bates and Rankin (1979: 39) is at 2;3.

11. Actually the word *barboncino* 'poodle' is a false diminutive and *barbone* means 'a beggar' or 'a long bearded man' (although it is seldom used with this meaning derived from *barba* 'beard'). The word, also used in Italian with the meaning of 'poodle', but never used with this meaning in Matteo's parental speech, is here analysed as if *barbone* were the base of *barbon-c-ino* and reanalyzed in MAT's second turn as an AUG.

12. The word *pasticciona* does exist in adult language with the meaning of 'botcher', but the child forms the AUG from the wrong base form *pasticcio*, which exists in Italian and means 'jumble'.

13. Cf. Bates and Rankin (1979: 36) for an early (1;9) pragmatic use of *man-ine* vs. *mano* 'hand' in a request.

References

Alberti, C., Ruimy, N., Turrini, G. and Zanchi, G. 1991. *La Donzelletta Vien dalla Donzella: Dizionario delle Forme Alterate della Lingua Italiana*. Bologna: Zanichelli.

Bates, E. and Rankin, J. 1979. Morphological development in Italian: conotation and denotation. In *Journal of Child Language* 6: 29–52.

Ceccherini, M., Bonifacio, S. and Zocconi, E. 1997. Acquisition of diminutives in Italian (Sara). In *Studies in Pre- and Protomorphology*, W. U. Dressler (ed.), 157–164. Vienna: Verlag der Österreichischen Akademie der Wissenschaften.

Chini, M. and Ferraris, S. 2003. Morfologia del nome. In *Verso l' Italiano,* A. Giacalone Ramat (ed.), 37–69. Roma: Carocci Editore.

Clahsen, H., Sonnenstuhl, I. and Blevins, J. P. 2003. Derivational morphology in the German mental lexicon: A dual mechanism account. In *Morphological Structure in Language Processing*, H. R. Baayen and R. Schreuder (eds), 125–155. Berlin: Mouton de Gruyter.

De Marco, A. 1998. The acquisition of diminutives in Italian. In *Studies in the Acquisition of Number and Diminutive Marking* [Antwerp Papers in Linguistics 95], S. Gillis (ed.), 175–192. Antwerpen: Universiteit Antwerpen.

De Marco, A. 2002. The development of diminutives in Italian: input and acquisition. In *Pre- and Protomorphology: Early Phases of Morphological Development in Nouns and Verbs,* M. D. Voeikova and W. U. Dressler (eds), 133–151. München: Lincom Europa.

De Mauro, T., Mancini, F., Vedovelli, M. and Voghera, M. 1993. *Lessico di Frequenza dell'Italiano Parlato*. Milano: Etas libri.

Dressler, W. U. 1994. Evidence from the first stages of morphology acquisition for linguistic theory: extragrammatic morphology and diminutives. *Acta Linguistica Hafniensia* XXVII (1): 91–108.

Dressler, W. U. (ed.). 1997. *Studies in Pre- and Protomorphology*. Vienna: Verlag der Österreichischen Akademie der Wissenschaften.

Dressler, W. U. 2004. Hypercharacterisation and Productivity in Inflectional Morphology. In *Analecta Homini Universali Dicata*, T. Kriesch, T. Lindner and U. Müller (eds), 514–524. Stuttgart: Heinz.

Dressler, W. U. and Karpf, A. 1995. The theoretical relevance of pre- and protomorphology in language acquisition. In *Yearbook of Morphology,* G. E. Booij and J. Van Marle (eds), 99–122. Dordrecht: Kluwer Academic Publishers.

Dressler, W. U. and Merlini Barbaresi, L. 1994. *Morphopragmatics. Diminutives and Intensifiers in Italian, German, and Other Languages*. Berlin: Mouton de Gruyter.

Dressler, W. U. and Merlini Barbaresi, L. 1997. Morphopragmatics. In *Handbook of Pragmatics,* J. Verschueren, J. O. Östman, J. Blommaert and C. E. Bulcaen (eds). Amsterdam: Benjamins.

Gillis, S. (ed.). 1998. *Studies in the Acquisition of Number and Diminutive Marking* [Antwerp Papers in Linguistics 95]. Antwerpen: Universiteit Antwerpen.

Grandi, N. 2002. *Morfologie in Contatto: Le Costruzioni Valutative nelle Lingue del Mediterraneo*. Milano: FrancoAngeli.

Kilani-Schoch, M. and Dressler, W. U. 2002. The emergence of inflectional paradigms in two French corpora: an illustration of general problems of pre- and protomorphology. In *Pre- and Protomorphology: Early Phases of Morphological Development in Nouns and Verbs,* M. D. Voeikova and W. U. Dressler, (eds), 45–59. München: Lincom Europa.

MacWhinney, B. 1997. *The CHILDES Project: Tools for Analyzing Talk.* Hillsdale, NJ: Erlbaum.

Merlini Barbaresi, L. 2004. Alterazione. In *La Formazione delle Parole in Italiano,* M. Grossmann and F. Rainer (eds), 264–292. Tübingen: Niemeyer.

Mutz, K. 2000. Die italienischen Modifikationssuffixe. Synchronie und Diacronie. Frankfurt: Peter Lang.

Noccetti, S. 2002. *Pre- and Protomorphology in Language Acquisition: an Italian Case Study*. Pisa: Edizioni PLUS, Università di Pisa.

Noccetti, S. 2003. Acquisition of verb morphology in Italian: a case study. In *Development of Verb Inflection in First Language Acquisition. A Crosslinguistic Perspective,* D. Bittner, W. U. Dressler and M. Kilani-Schoch (eds), 351–378. Berlin: Mouton de Gruyter.

Rohlfs, G. 1968. *Grammatica Storica della Lingua Italiana e dei suoi Dialetti. Morfologia*. Torino: Einaudi.

Scalise, S. 1994. *Morfologia*. Bologna: Il Mulino.

Thornton, A. M. 2004. Formazione delle parole nell'onomastica. In *La Formazione delle Parole in Italiano,* M. Grossmann and F. Rainer (eds), 599–610. Tübingen: Niemeyer.

Tomasello, M. 2003. *Constructing a Language: a Usage-Based Theory of Language Acquisition*. Harvard: Harvard University Press.

Tonelli, L., Cappelli, G., Lanzetta, E., Bonifacio, S., Dressler, W. U. and Thornton, A. M. 1997. The application of MORPH to the study of the development of Italian verb morphology. In *Papers and Studies in Contrastive Linguistics* 33: 103–116.

Tonelli, L. and Fabris, M. 2004. L'acquisizione della flessione verbale. Esemplificazione di un Metodo di Ricerca. In *Annali della Facoltà di Lingue e Letterature Straniere dell'Università di Sassari* 1, (to appear).

CHAPTER 6

The acquisition of diminutives in Spanish

A useful device

Victoria Marrero, Carmen Aguirre and María José Albalá

The acquisition of diminutives in Spanish, facilitated by phonoprosodical, morphological and pragmatic means, becomes more than a simple morphopragmatic device to be acquired. We propose that it provides the child with essential cues for grammatical segmentation, which proves very useful in later stages of language development.

To test this hypothesis, an analysis of two longitudinal corpora of Spanish L1 has been carried out. Quantitative considerations included type/token ratio in children and CDS across ages and word classes; qualitative considerations included a search for the emergence of the first contrast (mini-paradigms). Both perspectives confirm a pattern of a very rapid development and mastery of diminutive formation.

Some other aspects, such as morphophonology, suffix selection and spontaneity versus imitation, are also considered. We round up with some considerations regarding the semantics and pragmatics of diminutives in Spanish.

Introduction

Diminutives in Spanish are formed by suffixation in a highly productive manner. The use of diminutives between adults is scarce in standard Spanish, but increases considerably in child-directed speech, and children themselves begin to use them at a very early stage.[1] This early productivity is facilitated by morphological and phonoprosodical factors. On the one hand, diminutive morphemes recover the prototypical gender markers (*-o* for the masculine and *-a* for the feminine form) and number markers (zero for singular and *-s* for plural) when these are not expressed in the base (e.g. *árbol* 'tree' > *arbolito* 'tree-DIM', *arbolitos* 'trees-DIM'). And on the other, they shift the stress on any word to the penultimate syllable, the simplest and most common pattern of accentuation in Spanish. Besides these factors, the pragmatic functions of the diminutive also contribute to the frequent appearance of this device in children speech.

Our overall hypothesis suggests that competence in the use of the diminutive form, facilitated phonoprosodically, morphologically and pragmatically, eventually allows the child to gain awareness of the morphological mechanisms (segmentation to separate root from suffix) necessary for the acquisition and subsequent development of gender, number and person morphemes.

1. The diminutives in Spanish

In Spanish, diminutives are formed by means of suffixation,[2] with several allomorphs (*-it-*, *-ill-*, *-ín-*, *-ino-*, *-iñ-*, *-ic-*, *-et-*, *-uel-*, *-ej-*), but the most frequent and widely applicable form is *-ito*. The use of the other allomorphs depends on preferences within the sociolect, or on personal preferences, but not on the characteristics of the simplex form.

There is also the possibility of concatenative double suffixation, by adding two suffixes to the simplex form (*poco* 'little' > *poquito* 'little-DIM' > *poquitito* 'little-DIM-DIM'). In some areas its use is widespread and adds a superlative meaning. However there is no sharing of functions (semantic/pragmatic) as it can be found in Russian (Voeikova 1998).

Diminutives are a part of the evaluative derivation system, which also includes the formation of augmentatives (*casa* 'house' > *casona* 'house-AUG') and pejoratives (*casucha* 'house-PEJ').

Diminutive suffixes show gender and number information. The gender inflection, as already mentioned, is recovered even when the marker is not expressed in the simple form (*árbol* 'tree' (masc.) > *arbolito* 'tree-DIM'; *señal* 'signal' (fem.) > *señalita* 'signal-DIM'; *teniente* 'lieutenant' (invariant) > *tenientillo* 'lieutenant-DIM-MAS', *tenientilla* 'lieutenant-DIM-FEM'). The same is true of augmentatives and pejoratives (*arbolazo* 'tree-AUG', *señalucha* 'signal-PEJ', *tenientucho* 'lieutenant-PEJ-MAS', *tenientona* 'lieutenant-AUG:FEM').[3]

Turning to morphophonological aspects, a *-c-/-ec-* segment occasionally appears between root and suffix (again, depending on dialectal and individual preferences). This is regarded by some authors (including the Real Academia Española de la Lengua 1931, as well as Malkiel 1958; Dressler 1986; Lázaro Mora 1999) as an interfix, and by others (Jaeggli 1980; Crowhurst 1992; Prieto 1992) as another allomorph: *padre* 'father' > *padrecito* 'father-DIM'; *flor* 'flower' > *florecita* 'flower-DIM'. There are also situations where the final vowel of the simplex form is dropped when the diminutive suffix is added: *papá* 'dad'> *papito* 'dad-DIM' or alternatively *papaíto* 'dad-DIM', and the truncated form *papi*.

The grammatical categories that appear in their diminutive form without restrictions are substantives (*casa* 'house' > *casita* 'house-DIM'), proper nouns with their hypocoristics (*Fernando* > *Fernandito*, *Pepe* > *Pepito*) and adjectives or some determiners (*poco* 'little' > *poquito* 'little-DIM'; *todo* 'all' > *todito* 'all-DIM'). The appearance of diminutive forms of other word-classes is far more limited and dialectal / sociolectal depending: adverbs (*cerca* 'near' > *cerquita* 'near-DIM'; *pronto* 'soon' > *prontito* 'soon-DIM'; *ahora* 'now' > *ahorita* 'now-DIM'); gerunds (*corriendo* 'running' > *corriendito* 'running-DIM'), or participles (*terminado* 'finished' > *terminadito* 'finished-DIM') and even an occasional interjection (*aúpa* 'up' > *aupita* 'up-DIM').[4]

As far as content is concerned, the denotative meaning traditionally assigned to these suffixes is that of a reduction in size. But recent theories propose that pragmatic values such as the affective, moderating, attenuative, courteous etc. are more relevant (Dressler & Merlini Barbaresi 1994). These usages are widespread in familiar, intimate situations, such as in conversations with children. In these conversations, the substantive bases most commonly found in diminutive form belong to semantic groups such as body parts, everyday objects, the family, toys, animals, food, clothing, etc. The adjective stems almost invariably refer to size, quality or quantity, state, etc.

The frequency of usage for the evaluatives (diminutives, augmentatives and pejoratives) is not very high in Standard Spanish.[5] Children, however, use 13 times more diminutives than adults, and adults addressing children use them as much, if not more, than the children themselves (Marrero, Albalá & Moreno 2002: 155).[6] This is a well-known phenomenon (Ferguson 1977), that has been observed in many languages (Wójcik 1994; Savickienė 1998, 2003 for Lithuanian; Voeikova 1998 for Russian etc.) and also in Spanish (Melzi & King 2003).

2. Objectives

The role of diminutives in language acquisition can be regarded as more than a simple derivational mechanism that must be acquired. It is the first morphological device mastered by children in Spanish and in many other languages. Furthermore, in accordance with our hypothesis, diminutive formation facilitates the acquisition of other morphological aspects, allowing the child to discover and use many other features, such as gender, number and verbal inflection.

Many studies have demonstrated that certain input features act as activation mechanisms during first language acquisition processes: phonological bootstrapping (Gleitman & Wanner 1982; Morgan & Demuth 1996), semantic bootstrapping (Pinker 1984) and syntactic bootstrapping (Gleitman 1990). The role of the diminutive as a morphological facilitator has been pointed out in previous studies (for Russian gender: Olmsted 1994; Kempe et al. 2003; Kempe & Brooks 2005). In Spanish, there are several features which help to explain this role: full productivity, regularity and transparency.

The structure of our paper is as follows: after a brief description of the corpus (one that is commonly-used in Spanish L1 studies), we will present a quantitative analysis of diminutive type/tokens in child language and CDS using monthly samples taken over one year. In the second part we qualitatively analyze the initial contrasts (mini-paradigms) between diminutive and simplex, morpho-phonology and suffix selection, spontaneity versus imitation, and the manner in which the morphological system begins to emerge. We finish with some considerations of the semantics and pragmatics of diminutives.

3. Description of the corpus

The results of our research are based on the analysis of data drawn from two longitudinal corpora, which contain a record of spontaneous conversations of two children with their parents: María (López Ornat et al. 1994) and Magín (Aguirre 1995). Both children are members of middle-class professional families, and both are natives of Madrid.

Both corpora begin at age 1;7. The first continues until 3;11, and the second ends at age 2;7 (at this point the number of utterances was similar for both children).

The data are transcribed and encoded in CHAT,[7] and can be found in the CHILDES data bank (MacWhinney 2000). Morphological analysis was carried out using the AyDA *(Automatic Analyzer and Disambiguator)* computer system, developed jointly with the CNR's Istituto di Linguistica Computazionale (Cappelli & Moreno 2001; Albalá & Marrero 2001).[8]

4. Quantitative Descriptive Overview

The whole corpus constitutes more than 51,030 child tokens (all words, divided almost equally between the two children) and nearly 82,000 adult tokens from interactions with the children. Our sample contains almost one thousand diminutives in children's speech, and nearly 1,500 in child-directed speech. This amount corresponds to 10% of the total productiones of nouns, proper nouns and adjectives, that is, the nominal categories with a greater tendency to appear in diminutive form in Spanish. This rate is notably higher than previous results (7% in Melzi & King 2003), probably due to differences in the sample (our children were younger). However, languages such as Lithuanian, Russian, Dutch and Italian, show higher frequencies for diminutive forms (Gillis 1998).

General results are very similar in both corpora, the two children begin with a very limited or inexistent usage of diminutives (premorphology stage, 1;7 to 1;9), but in only two or three months contrasts appear with a very high frequency (start of protomorphology, 2;0).

Percentages of diminutives used, considering only types (different words, represented by the line graph) are higher in both subjects than percentages of tokens (all forms produced, represented by the bar chart). This implies that diminutivization can be considered a highly productive mechanism, applicable to a wide range of different units.

Table 1. Sample's tokens

	María's corpus	Magín's corpus
Children's tokens	25,650	25,380
Child-directed tokens	38,307	43,620
Children's nominal tokens	4,941	5,669
Child-directed nominal tokens	6,230	6,971
Children's diminutive tokens	406 (8.21%)	577 (10.17%)
Child-directed diminutive tokens	566 (9.08%)	899 (12.89%)

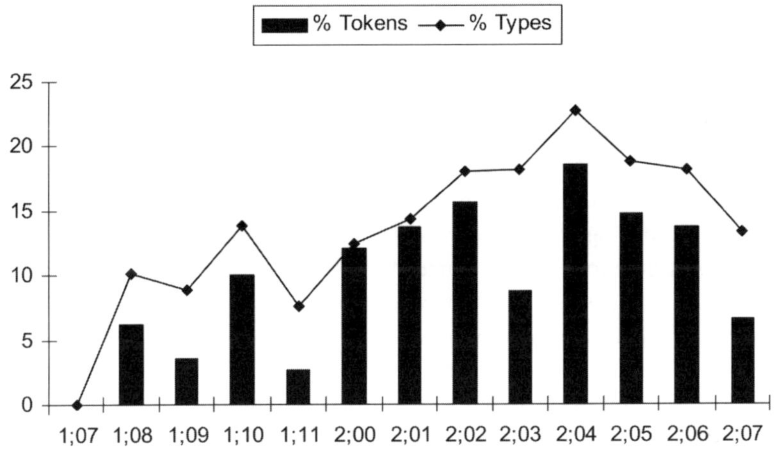

Graph 1. Magín's diminutives types and tokens. Percentages

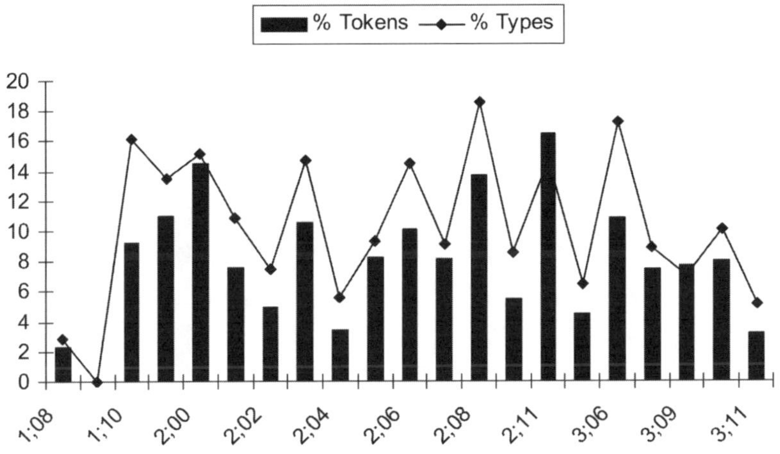

Graph 2. María's diminutive types and tokens. Percentages

Nevertheless, from the moment that contrasts stabilize and are extended, including number and sometimes gender variations, the use of diminutives shows an irregular pattern, with peaks and troughs in usage as shown in the graphs. In our opinion, once the diminutive device is acquired, its frequency in discourse depends on factors closely related to the development of each conversational exchange (topics, style, affective situation, etc.). This is consistent with the findings of Melzi and King (2003: 299): three years old children use diminutives in similar ways as five years old and mothers, varying "along many factors, including the caregiver's particular discourse patterns".

4.1 Child-directed speech

When analyzing the relationship between children's speech and received input, in general we observe the same 'saw-tooth' pattern. The most noticeable difference is that, in CDS, percentages of types (line graph) are lower than that of tokens (bar chart), indicating more repetitions of the same diminutive in adults than in children.

Comparing token data (represented as bars) of CDS (Graphs 3 and 4) and children (Graphs 1 and 2), we can observe that Magín follows very closely the peaks and troughs of his mother, according to the findings of Melzi and King: "imitation of diminutive forms by one interlocutor is highly correlated and serves as a strong predictor of total frequency of diminutives use by their interlocutor" (2003: 302). Nevertheless, María shows a more independent pattern, using more diminutives than adults in a third of the monthly samples. In this sense, the girl shows a more mature behaviour, gaining conversational independence with fewer tendencies to imitate.

However, our 11% of diminutives in adults is lower than results for Russian (Voeikova 1998), and very much lower than those obtained for Lithuanian (Savickienė 1998).

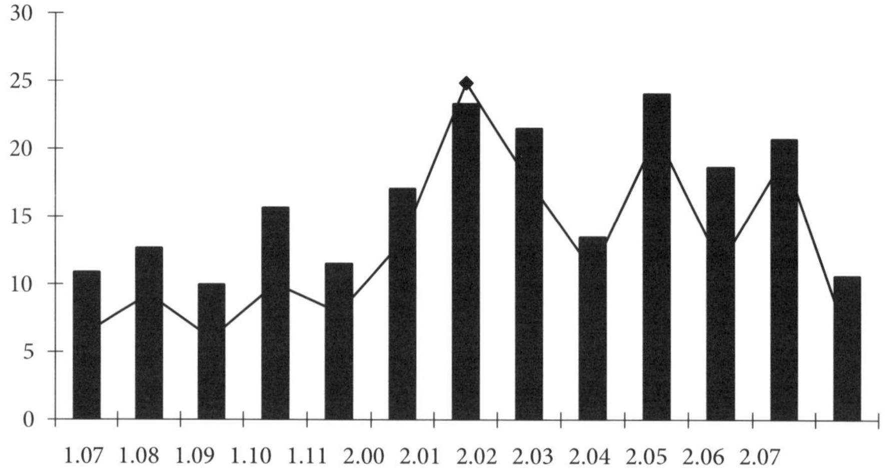

Graph 3. Magín's corpus. Child-directed speech. Percentage of types (lines) and tokens (bars)

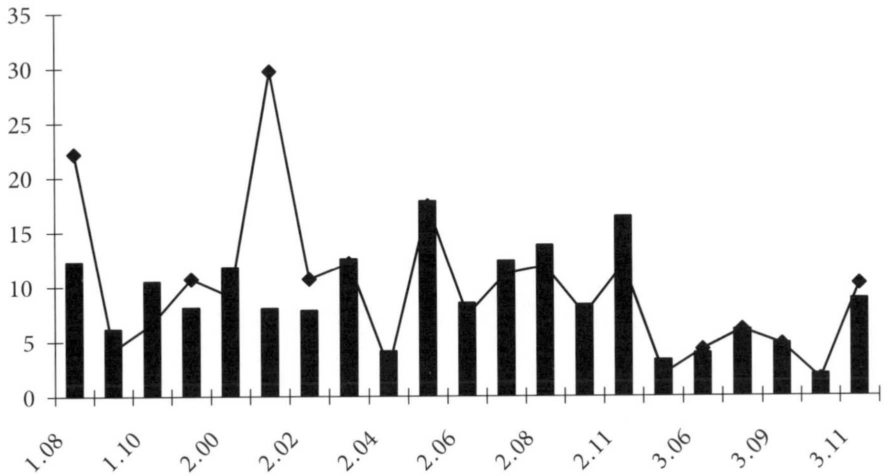

Graph 4. María's corpus. Child-directed speech. Percentage of types (lines) and tokens (bars)

Comparing both CDS data, we see that Magín's mother uses more diminutives than her son, whilst María's parents do not always do so. In the latter corpus the adult speaker is sometimes the father, and this may explain the difference observed, as female speech is strongly associated with diminutives (Berko Gleason & Ely 2002).

In any case, as shown in 5.3, there is a close relationship between CDS and child speech in both quantitative and qualitative terms, with many samples showing imitation in both directions (parents imitate child diminutives; child imitates parent diminutives)

4.2 Distribution across Word classes

With regard to the most diminutivized morphological categories, once again very similar results are shown in both corpora (Graphs 5 and 6). Nouns are clearly predominant (about 70% of the total), adjectives total 18–19%, and proper nouns (hypocoristics) range between 5% and 10%. Adverbs and pronouns are found very rarely (e.g. *poquito*, 'very little'), and very isolated incidences of interjections (*aupita*, 'up-DIM').

Nevertheless, when obtaining the relative frequency of diminutivization within each class of words, the situation changes dramatically (Graph 7). The most frequently diminutivized category is adjective: 20% of units were uttered in diminutive forms by Magín, and 12% by María (while no more than 5–10% of common and proper nouns were in their diminutive form).

The first two bars represent the percentage of diminutive nouns out of the total amount of common nouns. The second two show the percentage of proper nouns diminutivized with respect to global use of proper nouns. And in the last two we see the rate of diminutive adjectives as a percentage of global adjective use.

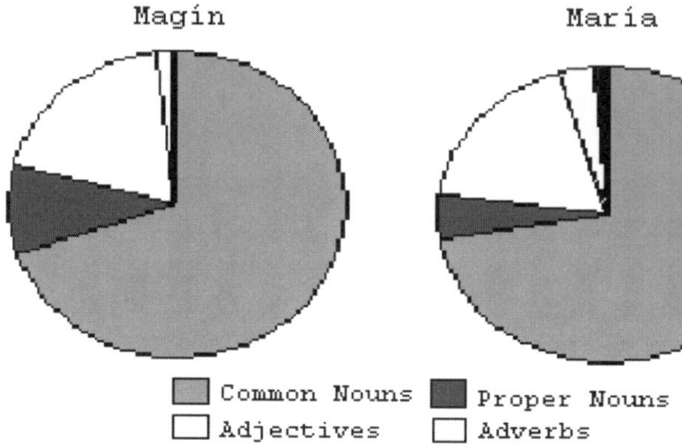

Graphs 5 and 6. Distribution of diminutives across word classes in children

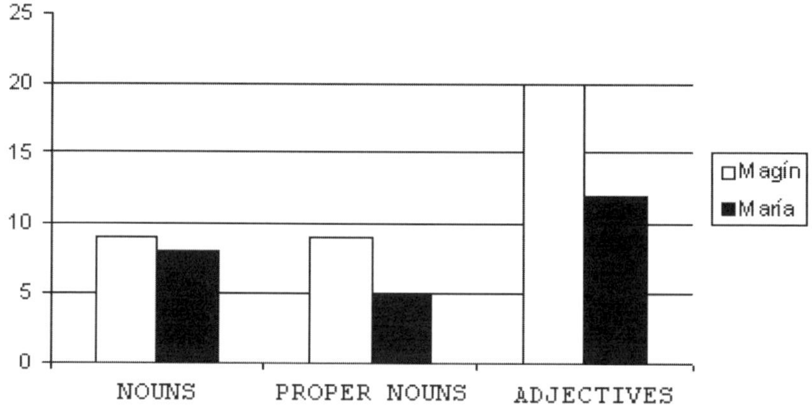

Graph 7. Percentages of total emissions in each category

4.3 Summary

In a sample of almost 133,000 tokens, 38% belonging to child speech and 62% to CDS, the frequency of diminutives amounted to 1.8% of the entire sample, although this rose to 10.2% of nominal categories.

Our two children initially show very limited or inexistent use of this morphopragmatic device (between 1;7 and 1;9 we find no diminutive forms, or no contrastive use with the corresponding simplex form). However (see 5.1) within a very short timeframe these contrasts begin to occur with notable frequency: around 1;10 there is a turning point, as the number of contrasts reaches 10–12 utterances (see the following Tables 2, 3, 4 and 5).

Comparing this data with results for other languages, we are reminded that in Russian the first (imitated) diminutive appears at 1;6, but major changes are registered between 1;7 and 1;8 years, when many diminutives are used together with their simplex form. Also in Lithuanian "the usage of diminutives strongly increases in a month's time" (Savickienė 1998: 120), between ages 1;7 and 1;8.

In CDS the frequency of diminutives is also much lower than in other languages, but slightly higher than in Spanish children's speech.

Once diminutivization has been mastered, the rate of use of this morpheme seems to depend on discourse topics, and there is a strong link between children and the adults interacting with them (same peaks and troughs).

As for the distribution across word classes, even though nouns are the most frequent category in our sample (three quarters), adjectives tend to be diminutivized twice as often as nouns.

We will now go on to consider how these processes take place.

5. Qualitative analysis

5.1 The first contrasts

The beginnings of developing morphology, during the protomorphological phase, are signaled by the emergence of the first mini-paradigms at the end of the second year (Bittner, Dressler & Kilani-Schoch 2003). Both in María's and in Magín's corpus, the earliest contrast between a diminutive and its corresponding simple form appears at 20 months of age (1;8), but during this period contrasts are scarce and no productivity is demonstrated. They are, in fact, imitations (María's first contrast) or lexicalized diminutive forms that do not follow the most common *-ito* pattern (Magín's *mami, papi* forms 'mum-DIM, dad-DIM'). As for the hypocoristics, the first contrast between a proper noun and its corresponding diminutive form appears at age 1;9 in Magín and age 1;10 in María (see Tables 4 and 5 below).

It is not until two months later that the data show productivity. At 1;10 the number of contrasts increases dramatically and mini-paradigms with a triple contrast appear (see Tables 2 and 3 below).

Table 2. Mini-paradigms (contrasts between diminutives and hypocoristics with simple forms) in María's speech

Age	2 member mini-paradigms	3 or more member mini paradigms	Total	Total lemmas (nouns and adjectives)	Total tokens (nouns and adjectives)
1;8	1	-	1	35	176
1;9	-	-	0	65	390
1;10	7	2	9	142	403
1;11	3	1	4	74	173
2;0	4	-	4	86	241
2;1	3	3	6	129	318
2;2	5	1	6	133	285
2;3	8	1	9	149	304
2;4	1	3	4	72	178
2;5	7	-	7	160	399
2;6	3	3	6	69	187
2;7	2	-	2	44	86
2;8	8	-	8	70	160
2;9	6	1	7	105	253
2;11	4	-	4	122	212
3;1	2	-	2	77	134
3;6	8	2	10	116	286
3;7	5	2	7	180	348
3;9	4	-	4	99	181
3;10	4	-	4	69	100
3;11	2	-	2	78	127

The forms that appear in these early contrasts correspond to substantive lemmas (the prevailing category throughout the sample, see 4.2.), although there are also some proper nouns, and they belong to semantic groups appropriate to the infant lexicon.

Table 3. Mini-paradigms in Magín's speech

Age	2 member mini-paradigms	3 or more member mini-paradigms	Total	Total lemmas (nouns and adjectives)	Total tokens (nouns and adjectives)
1;7	-	-	-	13	65
1;8	3	-	3	59	291
1;9	3	-	3	90	561
1;10	6	3	9	181	1113
1;11	2	-	2	92	447
2;0	6	3	9	144	391
2;1	-	1	1	63	109
2;2	9	2	11	155	506
2;3	15	5	20	165	466
2;4	15	4	19	203	615
2;5	5	4	9	101	238
2;6	8	6	14	210	534
2;7	1	3	4	128	333

Table 4. Mini-paradigms between 1;8 and 1;10 in María's speech

Age	lemma	simplex	diminutive	category
1;8	oso 'bear'	oso 'bear'	osito 'bear-DIM'	Noun m. sg.
1;9	-	-	-	-
1;10	galleta 'cookie'	galleta 'cookie'	Galletita 'cookie-DIM'	Noun f. sg.
	pato 'duck'	pato 'duck'	patito 'duck-DIM'	Noun m. sg.
	papá 'dad'	papá 'dad'	papi 'dad-DIM'	Noun m. sg.
	silla 'chair'	silla 'chair'	sillita 'chair-DIM'	Noun f. sg.
	culo 'backside'	culo 'backside'	culito 'backside-DIM'	Noun m. sg.
	zapato 'shoe'	zapato 'shoe'	zapatito 'shoe-DIM'	Noun m. sg.
			zapatitos 'shoes-DIM'	Noun m. pl.
	cosa 'thing'	cosa 'thing'		
		cosas 'things'	cositas 'things-DIM'	Noun f. pl.
	Ana	Ana	Anita	Name f. sg.

Table 5. Mini-paradigms between 1;8 and 1;10 in Magín's speech

Age	lemma	simplex	diminutive	category
1;8	mamá 'mum'	mamá 'mum'	mami 'mum-DIM'	Noun f. sg.
	papá 'dad'	papá 'dad'	papi 'dad-DIM'	Noun m. sg.
	nene 'boy'	nene 'boy'	neni 'boy-DIM'	Noun m. sg.
1;9	Clara	Clara	Clarita	Name f. sg.
	mamá 'mum'	mamá 'mum'	mami 'mum-DIM'	Noun f. sg.
	tata 'nanny'	tata 'nanny'	tatita 'nanny-DIM'	Noun f. sg.
1;10	mamá 'mum'	mamá 'mum'	mami 'mum-DIM'	Noun f. sg.
			mamita 'mum-DIM'	
	papá 'dad'	papá 'dad'	papi 'dad-DIM'	Noun m. sg.
			papaíto 'dad-DIM'	
	zapato 'shoe'	zapato 'shoe'	zapatilla* 'slipper'	Noun m./f. sg.
		zapatos 'shoes'		Noun m. pl.
	Clara	Clara	Clarita	Name f. sg.
	caca 'poo'	caca 'poo'	caquita 'poo-DIM'	Noun f. sg.
	cola 'tail'	cola 'tail'	colilla 'tail-DIM'	Noun f. sg.
	cuna 'crib'	cuna 'crib'	cunita 'crib-DIM'	Noun f. sg.
	pollo 'chicken'	pollo 'chicken'	pollito 'chicken-DIM'	Noun m. sg.
	pata 'leg'	pata 'leg'	patita 'leg-DIM'	Noun f. sg.

* Magín used *zapatilla* (an ancient diminutive, currently lexicalized, meaning 'slipper') instead of *zapatito*, as the diminutive for *zapato*

5.2 Morphophonology and selection of suffixes

The derivation of diminutive forms in both corpora follows the norms of standard Spanish, both in the selection of interfixes (*jaboncito* 'soap-DIM', *piececito* 'foot-DIM'), and in cases where the diminutive operates as an infix (*azuquítar* 'sugar-DIM'). As to the selection of suffixes, almost invariably *-ito* was chosen, but there are some occurrences of *-ín*, *-ino* (with stems meaning 'smallness': *chiquitín* 'small-DIM', *chiquinín* 'small-DIM', *pequeñino* 'small-DIM', *chiquitino* 'small-DIM'; or 'brevity': *momentín* 'moment-DIM'). Also there were cases of *-illo* and *-ete* observed in the boy, a dialectal influence (*pajarillo* 'bird-DIM', *enanilla* 'tiny-DIM', *tartilla* 'cake-DIM', *bollete* 'bun-DIM', *bañete* 'bath-DIM', *agujerete* 'hole-DIM').

As for alternation between two suffixes with the same root, Magín showed a first example at a very early stage (*papi* 'dad-DIM' and *papaíto* 'dad-DIM' at 1;10), while in María the first example does not appear until 3;1 (*poquito* 'little-DIM' and *poquitín* 'little-DIM'). In Lithuanian examples of alternation between three different suffixes with the same root occurs even earlier, at 1;7 (Savickienė 2003).

There are also standard examples of double suffixation, such as *chiquitito* 'small-DIM-DIM' (as well as those already mentioned: *chiquitín* 'small-DIM', *chiquitino* 'small-DIM', *chiquinín* 'small-DIM', etc.) and *poquitito* 'little-DIM-DIM'. In María, the first contrast between single and double suffixation of the same root comes at 2;3 (*poquito* 'little-DIM' and *poquitito* 'little-DIM-DIM').

5.3 Spontaneity and imitation in use of diminutives

One of the characteristics of our conversational exchanges is that a speaker often repeats the other's utterance, as seen in this extract from María's corpus:

(1) MOTHER: *María. ¿Y papá cómo se llama?*
'María. So what's dad's name?'
CHILD: *Teo.*
'Teo.'
MOTHER: *Teo.*
'Teo.'
CHILD: *Teíto.*
'Teo-DIM.'
MOTHER: *Teíto.*
'Teo-DIM.'
(López Ornat et al. 1994: 266)

In this example, in addition to repeating the hypocoristic *Teo*, both speakers play with the contrast between the simple form and the diminutive and imitate reciprocally. Melzi and King (2003: 298) observe that phenomenon: "children and mothers encourage the use of diminutives by imitating each other's use". The frequency of imitation shows a direct relationship: "the greater the percentage of diminutives the child used, the more the mother imitated her child. Conversely, the more the mother mimicked her child, the more diminutives the child used" (Melzi & King 2003: 297). This relationship "highlights the sensitivity of both interlocutors to each other's speech. As the mother picks up her child's diminutives and imitates them back to him or her, she appears to reinforce the child's use of diminutivized forms and thereby to facilitate greater use of diminutives" (*ibid.*: 301). Such relationships play a role in mother-child conversation: "the imitation of diminutives by interlocutors serves to establish – or possibly reflect – the intimate, playful, warm, or loving nature of the interaction, which ultimately results in greater total use of diminutive forms" (*ibid.*: 301). As we have seen, quantitative analysis also showed a pattern of considerable similarity between CDS and child emission data (4.1.).

The first diminutives to appear in María's corpus (the substantive *osito* 'bear-DIM', at 1;8, and the adjective *solita* 'alone-DIM' at 1;9) are in fact imitations of adult forms:

(2) FATHER: *oye, ¿qué es, un osito o una osito?*
'Hey, what is it, a [masculine article] bear-DIM or a [feminine article] bear-DIM?'
CHILD: *osito, a bi* [=*el muñeco*]
'bear-DIM, a bi [=*the doll*]'
aquí bibis [=*muñecos*]
'here bibis [=*dolls*]'
as to... [=?]
MOTHER: *¿Dónde están los osos?*
'Where are the bears?'
CHILD: *A soso* [=*el oso*] *otá* [=*no está*], *a soso* [=*el oso*] *otá* [=*no está*].
'The bear isn't here, the bear isn't here.'
(López Ornat et al. 1994: 214)

(3) FATHER: *¿Te vas a la calle?*
'Are you going outside?'
CHILD: *Sí.*
'Yes.'
FATHER: *¿Vas solita?*
'Are you going alone-DIM?'
CHILD: *Sí, sí, opita* [=*solita*].
'Yes, yes, alone-DIM.'
FATHER: *No puede ser.*
'You can't.'
(López Ornat et al. 1994: 248)

Nonetheless, Magín starts to produce spontaneous diminutives at age 1;8, and imitated diminutive forms do not appear until 1;9.

Occasionally, as in the *Teo* and *Teíto* examples(1), the repetition also demonstrates the contrast of pragmatic significance between the simple and diminutive forms. Similarly, in the following examples, the mother repeats her daughter's simple utterance in diminutive form:

(4) CHILD: *¡Ay, caballo, caballo!* [*poniendo la muñeca en las rodillas de mamá*].
'Oh, horse, horse! [*putting the doll on mother's knees*]'
MOTHER: *¡Arre, caballito!*
'Gee-up, horse-DIM.'
(López Ornat et al. 1994: 333).

(5) MOTHER: *¿Y cómo se llama éste?*
'And what's this one called?'
CHILD: *Un Pitufo. ¿A que sí?*
'A smurf. Isn't it?'
MOTHER: *Claro. ¿Cómo es ese pitufito?*
'Of course. What's that smurf-DIM like?'
(López Ornat et al. 1994: 399–400)

On other occasions, from the early stages, the girl converts the parents' diminutives to simple forms, like in this example from 1;8, where mother also imitates the child simple form:

(6) MOTHER: *¿Quién los tiene los ositos?*
'Who has the bears-DIM?'
CHILD: *A yaya* [*=la abuela*] *a soso* [*=el oso*].
'Grandmother the bear.'
MOTHER: *¿La yaya tiene los osos?*
'Grand mother has the bears?'
CHILD: *Ah* [*afirma*].
'Ah [*she affirms*].'
(López Ornat et al. 1994: 214)

This case shows a loss of affective significance in child simplex, in contrast to the adult's initial diminutive. These alterations are also found in Lithuanian (Savickienė 2003) and demonstrate that from a very early age children are aware of the pragmatic meaning of diminutives.

5.4 Constructing a morphological system

We consider diminutive use in Spanish to be a highly productive device, mastered extremely early (the first morphological process, in fact) and very quickly compared with nouns (development of the plural) or verbs (verbal inflection).

At 1;10 María and Magín use 16% and 14% of nominal items in diminutive form, and contrasts between simplex and diminutive forms are frequent (9 contrasts for each child).

This dramatic increase in the use and number of contrasts is a symptom of productivity: at this early stage, children have already acquired diminutivization. In other words, given any concrete noun or adjective, they are able to construct its diminutive form in a creative way, without having heard this form modelled previously by an adult.

At this same stage, plural morphology and verbal morphology acquisition are just emerging. The first plurals in nouns and articles appear, but most of the required plural markers are still absent as Marrero and Aguirre (2003) explain. As for verbs, the child enters the protomorphological stage and the first mini-paradigms appear. Nevertheless, the verbal morphological system is too complex and many more verb items are required in order to construct a morphological system with rules that enable the child to be productive.[9]

The acquisition data analyzed in this study for diminutives, in Marrero and Aguirre (2003) for plurals and in Aguirre (2003, 2006) for verbs, show that all of these morphological markers are first detected and analyzed as meaningful elements at the same stage – around 1;10 in Magín and María. Nevertheless, while diminutive acquisition as a morphological mechanism is mastered within a very short period of time (around a single month) plural and verb morphology takes longer to become truly productive.

These facts are coherent with the structure of the model language. In the morphological system of Spanish, the diminutive is the strongest candidate for early acquisition because of its full productivity, its regularity and its transparency, among other reasons (see Introduction):

- The saliency of its suffix (*-ito, -ita*), which is disyllabic, with two vowels, and with the first of these always stressed.
- Its total productivity in concrete nouns and adjectives, and its high frequency of use in child-directed speech for pragmatic reasons.
- No competing morphological classes. All nouns and adjectives add the same suffixes (*-ito*, and *-illo* in some dialects).
- Almost total biuniqueness between form and meaning (transparency). *-ito* is the only corresponding productive suffix (with the exception of dialectal variations) and this suffix form corresponds only to diminutive meaning.
- The fact that diminutive forms are reinforcing affection in most situations.

Are rules necessary during morphological acquisition processes? We consider that our data are much better explained if we consider the existence of a developing rule system. The first rule should be the possibility of transforming any simplex and concrete noun or adjective into a diminutive by adding a suffix (*-ito*) for semantic or pragmatic reasons.

In our opinion neither a simple model of acquisition (Bybee 1995; Tomasello 2003) nor a connectionist one (Marchman et al. 1997; McClelland & Plaut 1999; McClelland & Patterson 2002), where all inflected forms are considered as rote-learned and productivity a consequence of analogy and statistical learning procedures, cannot explain an acquisition process which results in such high productivity in such a short period of time.

Overregularizations lend further support to our proposal, since they involve the analysis of words considered erroneously to be diminutives. In Magin's data, *mosquito* 'mosquito', *mariquita* 'ladybird', and *anillo* 'ring', simplicia but nonetheless ending in *-ito*, and *-illo*, are erroneously conceived as being derived from *mosco* (uttered at 2;0), *marica* (at 2;7) and *ano* (at 2;7).

Our findings are perfectly compatible with a rule-based model, i.e. with rapid rule extraction. A morphological acquisition device based on rules, as proposed by Marcus et al. (1992), Clahsen (1999), Clahsen et al. (2002), Pinker (1999), Dressler (1999, 2002), would much better explain the potentiality of the system, and also offers explanations for early acquisition, the high degree of productivity and the erroneous analysis involved in overregularization.

In other words, rules are a theoretical necessity if we aim to understand this potential behaviour of morphology, even if there is not an empirical need for morphological acquisition, as the simple acquisition model proposes.

Our claim is that morphological rules are first detected and mastered in diminutive morphology in Spanish. Once these morphological rules have been identified in diminutive morphology, they act as bootstrapping elements in the development of remaining morphological domains, such as plural markers and verb inflection.

6. Semantics and pragmatics of diminutives

6.1 The hipocoristics and diminutives: semantics and pragmatics

Diminutives have two different meanings in Spanish: a semantic meaning, to denote smallness, and a pragmatic meaning. The use of diminutives creates a range of connotative aspects such as tenderness and affection and also serves to attenuate negative aspects and to help diminish responsibility (Dressler & Merlini Barbaresi 1994).

The pervasiveness of diminutives in CDS, in contrast with adults' interactions, is pragmatically motivated. Parents and caregivers use the diminutive to be "closer" to the child, to enter the children's world and to make the child feel more comfortable. He creates a warm, affectionate environment that is not directly linked with the "smallness" meaning.

This explains the fact that very often in our transcriptions we find diminutives without any denotative value. The following examples show how diminutives and simplicia are used by the adult in the same situation to refer to the same object or aspect.

(7) MOTHER: *Así el tapón, el taponcito.*
'Like this – the stopper, the stopper-DIM.'
(Aguirre 1995. Magín's age 1;8)

(8) MOTHER: *Toma, que te he echado azuquítar.*
'Here, I've put sugar-DIM on for you.'
MOTHER: *No llores, ya verás como ahora está muy bueno [dándole un zumo].*
'Don't cry, you'll see it tastes really good now [giving him juice].'
MOTHER: *Que le he echado azúcar.*
'Because I've put sugar in it.'
(Aguirre 1995; Magín's age 1;8)

(9) FATHER: *María, está aquí el hipopótamo muy solito, no puede hacer la peli él solo.*
'María, the hippopotamus is very lonely-DIM here, it can't make the film alone.'
(López Ornat et al. 1994)

This affective function can be very well understood when adjectives and adverbs are in their diminutive form, as it is impossible to assign a smallness meaning to the diminutive in these circumstances. This is illustrated by an example from Magín's corpus.

(10) MOTHER: *Oye, quietecito.*
'Hey, steady-DIM.'
MOTHER: *Ven aquí.*
'Come here.'
MOTHER: *Está hechita la cama y la deshaces.*
'The bed is made -DIM and you unmake it.'
(Aguirre 1995; Magín's age 1;10)

The pragmatic value most frequently found in our data is affection (60%). We also find diminutives in which the play situation predominates (25%) and the remainder helps to attenuate negative characteristics. This latter pragmatic meaning can have a euphemistic quality, as we can appreciate in this example from María's corpus.

(11) CHILD: *[señalando a su padre] Ete [= éste] e [= es] calvo.*
[Pointing at his father] 'He's bald.'
MOTHER: *No es calvo, es calvito.*
'He's not bald, he is bald-DIM.'
(López Ornat et al. 1994: 339)

We can find some cases where the diminutive performs a subtle intensifying function.

(12) MOTHER: *¡Una porra, hija! Están limpitas, están recién lavadas.*
'Rubbish! They're clean-DIM-PLU, they've just been washed.'
(López Ornat et al. 1994: 446)

(13) FATHER: *Venga, ahora ponemos otra al ladito de la roja, venga.*
'Come on, now we're going to put another one [right] beside-DIM the red one, come on.'

(López Ornat et al. 1994: 443)

We find another interesting value widely used by the adult aiming to convince the child that something is better. This value is linked to the affective and attenuative function.

The strategy utilized to persuade the child to do something is affective, reinforcing the pleasantness and desirability of the activity, and the diminutive strongly contributes to creating this environment in Spanish CDS. In the following examples we can see Magín's father trying to convince his son to stay at home rather than go outside. The diminutive helps to make being at home sound far more desirable and attractive.

(14) FATHER: *Que hace mucho calor fuera.*
'It's very hot outside.'
FATHER: *Aquí estás muy fresquito.*
'Here you are very [nice and] cool-DIM.'
FATHER: *Que hace calor.*
'It's hot.'
FATHER: *¿Te hago una casita?*
'Shall I make you a house-DIM?'
(Aguirre 1995; Magín's age 1;10)

In the example bellow the mother tries to convince her child to accept food.

(15) MOTHER: *¿Te vas a comer un yogurcito?*
'Are you going to eat a yogurt-DIM.'
(Aguirre 1995; Magín's age 1;10)

The child decodes all these pragmatic meanings, understanding and employing them with ease. We can find many utterances in which the simplex and the diminutive are both used to refer to the same object, without any contrastive semantic value.

(16) CHILD: *Es por [= para] que pasen los niños, los niñitos.*
'That's for the children to go in, the children-DIM.'
(López Ornat et al. 1994: 482)

(17) CHILD: *Ya se van a casa, a casita* [*los mueve*].
'They're going home now, home-DIM [*moves them*].'
(López Ornat et al. 1994: 484)

The following utterance is a clear example of how María uses the diminutive to attenuate negative qualities.

(18) CHILD: *Bueno, que así como es tontito, tontito, tontito.*
'Well, then he is silly-DIM, silly-DIM, silly-DIM.'
(López Ornat et al. 1994: 541–542)

The pragmatic value where the speaker seeks to create an endearing environment to help convince the other and achieve an aim is understood and used by the child from very early on, as we can see in the following examples from Magín.

(19) CHILD: *Mamá.*
'Mum.'
CHILD: *Por favo* [= *por favor*], *mamá.*
'Please mum.'
CHILD: *Por favo* [= *por favor*], *mami.*
'Please mum-DIM.'
CHILD: *Mami, mami, mami, mami, mami.*
'Mum-DIM, mum-DIM, mum-DIM, mum-DIM, mum-DIM.'
CHILD: *Ven aquí, mami.*
'Come here, mum-DIM.'
(Aguirre 1995; Magín's age 1;10)

In this example, Magín's mother just left him in his bed for an afternoon nap; the boy, not wanting to be alone, calls his mother. He begins using the simplex, but when he sees that he cannot does achieve his aim he starts to use the hypocoristic, to appeal more directly to his mother's emotions and make her come.

In the following sample we can see this pragmatic use clearly in both mother and child. In this case, the mother's aims are opposed to the child's, and each uses the diminutive to convince the other.

(20) MOT: *¿Quieres un poquito a la cama?*
'Do you want to go to bed a little-DIM.'
CHILD: *No.*
'No.'
MOT: *¿Por qué?*
'Why.'
CHILD: *No quiero.*
'I don't want it.'
MOT: *No quieres dormir?*
'Don't you want to sleep?'
CHILD: *Abajito.*
'Downstairs-DIM.'
MOT: *¿Abajito?*
'Downstairs-DIM.'
CHILD: *Sí.*
'Yes.'
(Aguirre 1995; Magín's age 2;0)

Now, we will see how Magín refuses to obey an adult's order and this refusal leads her also to avoid the diminutive form. The father uses the diminutive to soften and to make the order more acceptable, but the child declines to accept it and uses the simplex.

(21) FATHER: *Oye, no te quites la batita que se enfada mamá.*
'Hey, don't take your apron-DIM off, or mum'll get angry.'
CHILD: *No quiero la bata.*
'I don't want the apron.'
(Aguirre 1995; Magín's age 2;2)

The semantic value of the diminutive to denote something small is much less evident. Both child and adult use adjectives like *pequeño* 'little' or *chiquito* 'small', that appear frequently in their diminutive forms, to denote smallness.

As suggested by Dressler and Merlini Barbaresi (1994), we assume that the pragmatic meaning is essential, or exclusive in many situations, in the use of diminutive in Spanish. This is the case in children's language and in child-directed speech. The precedence of the pragmatic meaning over semantic meaning is also identified by Voeikova (1998) for Russian, de Marco (1998) for Italian, and Savickienė (2003) for Lithuanian.

6.2 Nouns' semantic groups and diminutive

Nouns that relate to the child and his or her environment are the most prone to appear in diminutive form. The fact that the diminutive is used to reinforce the affectivity explains that one of the largest groups of words that appear in diminutive form are words for humans: common nouns (*papaíto* 'daddy', *hermanito* 'brother-DIM') or hypocoristics. For the same reason, another large group of diminutives is that which refers to animals and toys. It is difficult to come upon an animal noun (toy or real) whose diminutive form is not used. Body parts for child and animals also usually appear in the diminutive form. As well as these groups, nouns referring to objects that the child normally uses, to clothing and to food are all often used in their diminutive form. These same semantic groups are also reported to appear frequently in diminutive form in other languages like Greek (Stephany 1997), Italian (de Marco 1998) and Lithuanian (Savickienė 2003).

We have already seen that the adjective is proportionally the most diminutivized category. Adjectives normally refer to qualities and the qualities that normally appear in diminutive form are those that refer to persons, animals and objects around the child.

Table 6. María. Often diminutivized semantic categories

Parts of body	26	13%
Games/toys	26	13%
Relationships	19	10%
Inanimate objects	14	7%
Animals	13	7%
Quantity	12	6%
Size	12	6%
Quality	11	6%
Humans	8	4%
State	7	4%
Food	9	5%
Health	6	3%
Clothing	6	3%
Weather	5	3%
Others	22	11%

Table 7. Magín. Often diminutivized semantic categories

Quality	40	19%
Animals	37	17%
Humans	30	14%
Body parts	24	11%
Objects	18	8%
Inanimate	12	6%
Toys	12	6%
Food	10	5%
Accion	9	4%
Quantity	7	3%
Clothing	6	3%
Others	10	5%

7. Conclusions

The diminutive is a highly productive morphological device, mastered very quickly at a very early stage. It emerges in the protomorphological stage (the first stage in morphological acquisition), coinciding with the first contrasts in verbal inflection, though the acquisition of these verbal paradigms takes place far more slowly and with greater difficulty. Children initially show a very limited or even inexistent usage of this morpho-pragmatic instrument (between 1;7 and 1;9). However, within the space of a month (between 1;9 and 1;10) a significant number of alternations between simplex and diminutive forms occur for a given lemma in both children. The first two-member mini-paradigm consists of a diminutive and a simplex form for the same lemma (1;8 in María and Magín); three-member mini-paradigms (diminutive/simplex/number or gender) appear two to three months later. The hypocoristic forms in alternation with the corresponding proper noun appear in Magín at 1;9 and in María at 1;10.

This dramatic increase in diminutive productivity within such a short period of time is better explained, in our opinion, by considering the existence of a developing rule system in child language acquisition. The first rule should be the change of a simplex noun into a diminutive by adding the *-ito* suffix, where the pragmatic situation is appropriate. Once the rule is detected and mastered, it acts as a bootstrapping factor to help develop the remaining nominal and verbal morphology.

Spanish diminutive characteristics reinforce this interpretation, because they are phonologically salient, totally productive in nouns and adjectives, highly regular (same suffix for all word classes) and transparent (form-meaning biuniqueness). Logically, nouns are the predominant category in our sample, (more than two thirds of the children's diminutives belong to this category), followed by adjectives, with a higher tendency for diminutivization. Additionally our most frequent suffix has been *-ito*, also the most frequent in adult speech, which is always stressed, and very easy for the child to perceive and produce.

The use of diminutives in child-directed speech is very similar to children's usage. The only difference is a higher lexical productivity in children, because they use it with more lemmas than parents (the percentages of types is higher than the percentage of tokens). But once the child is able to produce diminutives the device is used in a rather irregular way. There are moments when we find abundant diminutive rates, and others when they are scarce, depending on the context and the topic of conversation. The most frequent diminutives are words for body parts, toys, animals and names referring to persons: proper nouns and nouns to denominate types of relatives.

Most diminutives have an exclusively pragmatic value. These pragmatic values are affective, playful or attenuative (in this frequency order). The semantic value of 'smallness' is very scarce in our data, with more examples showing simplex and diminutives in the same context, and to refer to the same object. To denote smallness children and adults normally utilize some other adjectives, such as *pequeño* or *chiquito* both meaning 'little' or 'small'. These adjectives can also appear in diminutive. For this reason we consider that in a first stage of child language acquisition the diminutive is a pragmatic device.

Notes

1. Many studies in several languages notice early acquisition of diminutives in the speech of even very young children (Dressler and Merlini Barbaresi 1994; Ferguson 1977; Cecherini, Bonifacio and Zocconi 1997; De Marco 1998, 2002; Voeikova 1998; Marrero, Albalá and Moreno 2002; Savickienė 1998, 2003 etc.).

2. In some cases the diminutive operates as an infix (*azúcar* 'sugar' > *azuquítar* 'sugar-DIM', *Victor* > *Victítor*, *paraguas* 'umbrella' > *paragüitas* 'umbrella-DIM').

3. Nonetheless, when the stem ending is *-o* or *-a* but these segments are not gender markers, the diminutive copies the final vowel (*tema* 'theme' (masc.) > *temita* 'theme-DIM', *moto* 'motorbike' (fem.) > *motito* 'motorbike-DIM', *hipócrita* 'hypocrite' (invariant) > *hipocritilla* 'hypocrite-DIM'). In contrast, augmentatives and pejoratives recover the gender mark (*temazo* 'theme-AUG', *motaza* 'motorbike-AUG', *hipocritón* 'hypocrite-AUG-MAS', *hipocritona* 'hypocrite-AUG-FEM').

4. Bauer (1997) proposes a cross-linguistic or universal hierarchy for word-classes that can be diminutized: Noun, Adjective/Verb, Adverb/Numeral/Pronoun/, Interjection, and Determiner. Melzi and King (2003) confirm their existence for Spanish.

5. Corresponding, in Hispanic sociolinguistics, to the Castilian variety, with an average sociocultural level.

6. In a sample of 14,051 words pertaining to inter-adults standard exchanges, diminutives represent 0.14% of the words. In child-directed-speech, it rises to 2.52% of 19,235 words.

7. The work of Margin's corpus has been supported by the Austrian Academy of Sciences and the Spanish Ministerio de Educación y Ciencia.

8. This tool was presented at the *3rd International summit on the acquisition of the languages of Spain*, held in Malaga in September 2001. The system allows us to carry out a precise morphological analysis of more than 95% of the words in any text, but was specifically developed to work with CHAT format and with the CLAN set of programs.

9. See Aguirre (2003) for a detailed study of verbal morphology acquisition.

References

Aguirre, C. 1995. *La adquisición de las categorías gramaticales en español*. Madrid: Ediciones de la Universidad Autónoma de Madrid.

Aguirre, C. 2003. Early verb development in one Spanish-speaking child. In *Development of verb inflection in first language acquisition: A cross-linguistic perspective*, D. Bittner, W. U. Dressler and M. Kilani-Schoch (eds), 1–25. Berlin: Mouton de Gruyter.

Aguirre, C. 2006. What do overregularizations tell us about morphological knowledge? *Círculo de lingüística aplicada a la comunicación*. Madrid: Facultad de Ciencias de la Información, Universidad Complutense de Madrid.

Albalá, M. J. and Marrero, V. 2001. Las características lingüísticas de AyDA un analizador morfológico del español. *III Encuentro internacional sobre la adquisición de las lenguas del Estado*. Málaga (Spain).

Bauer, L. 1997. Evaluative morphology: in search of universals. *Studies in Language* 21: 533–575.

Berko Gleason, J. and Ely, R. 2002. Gender differences in language development. In *Biology, Society, and behavior: The development of sex differences in cognition*, A.V. McGillicuddy-De Lisi and R. De Lisi (eds), 127–154. Greenwich, CT: Ablex.

Bittner, D., Dressler, W. U. and Kilani-Schoch, M. (eds.). 2003. *Development of verb inflection in first language acquisition: A cross-linguistic perspective*. Berlin: Mouton de Gruyter.

Bybee, J. 1995. Regular morphology and the lexicon. *Language and Cognitive Processes* 10: 425–455.

Cappelli, G. and Moreno, I. 2001. Las características informáticas de AyDA. *III Encuentro internacional sobre la adquisición de las lenguas del Estado*. Málaga (Spain).

Ceccherini, M., Bonifacio, S. and Zocconi, E. 1997. Acquisition of diminutives in Italian. In *Studies in pre- and protomorphology*, W. U. Dressler (ed.), 157–163. Wien: Österreichischen Akademie der Wissenschaften.

Clahsen, H. 1999. Lexical entries and rules of language: A multidisciplinary study of German inflection. *Behavioral and Brain Sciences* 22: 991–1060.

Clahsen, H., Aveledo, F. and Roca, I. 2002. The development of regular and irregular verb inflection in Spanish child language. *Journal of Child Language* 29: 127–136.

Crowhurst, M. J. 1992. Diminutives and augmentatives in Mexican Spanish: a prosodic analysis. *Phonology* 9: 221–253.

Dressler, W. U. 1986. Forma y función de los interfijos españoles. *Revista Española de Lingüística* 16(2): 381–391.

Dressler, W. U. and Merlini Barbaresi, L. 1994. *Morphopragmatics. Diminutives and intensifiers in Italian, German and other languages*. Berlin: Mouton de Gruyter.

Dressler, W. U. 1999. What is the core of morphology. In *Language Contact, Variation, and Change* [Studies in Language 32], J. Niemi, T. Odlin and J. Heikkinen (eds), 15–32. Joensu: University of Joensu.

Dressler, W. U. 2002. Latin inflection classes. In *Selected Papers from the XIth International Colloquium on Latin Linguistics*, A.M. Bolkenstein, C.H.M. Kroon, H. Pinkster, H.W. Remmelink and R. Risselada (eds), 91–110. Amsterdam: J. C. Gieben.

Ferguson, C.A. 1977. Baby talk as simplified register. In *Talking to children: language input and acquisition*, C. E. Snow and C.A. Ferguson (eds), 209–235. Cambridge: Cambridge University Press.

Gillis, S. (ed.). 1998. *Studies in the acquisition of number and diminutive marking* [Antwerp papers in Linguistics 95]. Antwerp: Universiteit Antwerpen.

Gleitman, L. 1990. The structural sources of verb learnings. *Language acquisition* 1: 3–55.

Gleitman, L. and Wanner, E. 1982. Language acquisition: The state of the art. In *Language acquisition: The state of the art*, E. Wanner and L. R. Gleitman (eds), 3–48. Cambridge: Cambridge University Press.

Jaeggli, O. A. 1980. Spanish diminutives. In *Contemporary studies in romance languages*, F. H. Nuessel (ed.), 142–158. Bloomington: IULC.

Kempe, V., Brooks, J.P., Mironova, N. and Fedorova, O. 2003. Diminutivization supports gender acquisition in Russian children. *Journal of Child Language* 30 (2): 471–485.

Kempe, V. and Brooks, P. J. 2005. The role of diminutives in the acquisition of Russian gender: can elements of Child-Directed Speech aid in learning morphology? *Language Learning* 55: 139–176.

Lázaro Mora, F. 1999. La derivación apreciativa. In *Gramática descriptiva de la lengua española*. Madrid: Espasa Calpe.

López Ornat, S., Fernández, A., Gallo, P. and Mariscal, S. 1994. *La adquisición de la lengua española*. Madrid: Siglo XXI.

Malkiel, Y. 1958. Los interfijos hispánicos. Problemas de lingüística histórica y estructural. In *Miscelánea homenaje a André Martinet*, vol. II, 107–199. Madrid: Gredos.

MacWhinney, B. 2000. *The* CHILDES *project: tools for analysing talk*. Mahwah, New Jersey: Erlbaum.

Marchman, V., Plunkett, K., Goodman, J. 1997. Overregularization in English plural and past tense inflectional morphology: a response to Marcus. *Journal of Child Language* 24: 767–779.

Marco, A. de. 1998. The acquisition of diminutives in Italian. In *Studies in the acquisition of number and diminutive marking* [Antwerp papers in Linguistics 95], S. Gillis, (ed.), 175–192. Antwerp: Universiteit Antwerpen.

Marco, A. de. 2002. The development of diminutives in Italian: input and acquisition. In *Pre- and protomorphology: early phases of morphological development in nouns and verbs*, M. Voeikova and W. U. Dressler (eds), 133–153. Munich: Lincom.

Marcus, G. F., Pinker, S., Ullman, M., Hollander, M., Rosen, T. J. and Xu, F. 1992. Overregularization in Language Acquisition. *Monographs of the Society for Research in Child Development* 57 (4. Serial No. 228).

Marrero, V. and Aguirre, C. 2003. Plural acquisition and development in Spanish. In *Linguistic Theory and Language Development in Hispanic Languages*, S. Montrul and F. Ordóñez (eds), 275–296. Somerville: Cascadilla Press.

Marrero, V., Albalá, M. J. and Moreno, I. 2002. Use of diminutives by children and adults in Spanish. A preliminary analysis. In *Pre- and protomorphology: early phases of morphological development in nouns and verbs*, M. Voeikova and W. U. Dressler (eds), 153–162. Munich: Lincom.

Melzi, G. and King, K. A. 2003. Spanish diminutives in mother-child conversations. *Journal of Child Language* 30 (2): 281–304.

McClelland, J.L and Patterson, K. 2002. Rules or connections in past tense inflections: what does the evidence rule out? *Trends in cognitive Sciences* 6 (11): 465–472.

McClelland, J. L. and Plaut, D. C. 1999. Does generalization in infant learning implicate abstract algebra-like rules? *Trends in cognitive Sciences* 3: 166–168.

Morgan, J. L. and Demuth, K. (eds.). 1996. *Signal to syntax: Bootstrapping from speech to grammar in early acquisition.* Mahwah, NJ: Lawrence Erlbaum.
Olmsted, H. M. 1994. Diminutive morphology of Russian children: a simplified subset of nominal declension in language acquisition. In *Alexander Lipson: In memoriam*, 165–209. Columbus, Ohio: Slavica Publishers Inc.
Pinker, S. 1984. *Language learnability and language development.* Cambridge MA: Harvard University Press.
Pinker, S. 1999. *Words and rules: the ingredients of language.* New York: Basic Books.
Prieto, P. 1992. Morphophonology of Spanish Diminutive Formation: A Case for Prosodic Sensitivity. *Hispanic Linguistics* 5 (1–2): 169–205.
Real Academia Española de la Lengua. 1931. *Gramática de la lengua española.* Madrid: Espasa Calpe.
Savickienė, I. 1998. The acquisition of diminutives in Lithuanian. In *Studies in the acquisition of number and diminutive marking* [Antwerp papers in Linguistics 95], S. Gillis, (ed.), 115–135. Antwerp: Universiteit Antwerpen.
Savickienė, I. 2003. *The acquisition of Lithuanian noun morphology.* Wien: Verlag der Österreichischen Akademie der Wissenschaften.
Stephany, U. 1997. Diminutives in early child Greek, a preliminary investigation. In *Studies in Pre- and Protomorphology*, W.U. Dressler (ed.), 147–156. Wien: Verlag der Österreichischen Akademie der Wissenschaften.
Tomasello, M. 2003. *Constructing a Language.* Cambridge: Harvard University Press.
Voeikova, M. 1998. Acquisition of diminutives by a Russian child: Preliminary observations in connection with the early adjectives. In *Studies in the acquisition of number and diminutive marking* [Antwerp papers in Linguistics 95], S. Gillis (ed.), 97–113. Antwerp: Universiteit Antwerpen.
Wojcik, P. 1994. Some characteristic features of Lithuanian baby-talk. *Linguistica Baltica* 3: 71–86.

CHAPTER 7

A longitudinal study of the acquisition of diminutives in Dutch[1]

Agnita Souman and Steven Gillis

The acquisition of diminutives in the language of three Dutch-speaking children from the Netherlands is described on the basis of longitudinal observational data between the age of 21 and 36 months. It is shown that diminutives occur early, i.e. in the first stage of vocabulary development, and that the frequency of diminutives is high and increases over time. The language of the parents does not shown such a development, but they seem to provide more diminutive lemmas in the first stages of diminutive acquisition. Furthermore, a higher occurrence of diminutives is found in child directed speech than in adult speech. The allomorphs that occur in child directed speech are used with relative similar frequency in child speech, except for certain low frequent ones.

Introduction

In this chapter we will describe the development of diminutives in Netherlandic Dutch. Dutch, in general, is a pluricentric language (Clyne 1992) which is spoken mainly in the Netherlands and in the northern part of Belgium, which is called Flanders. In both countries Dutch is used as the standard language and promoted by an institute called the "Taalunie" which is funded by the Flemish and Netherlandic government. The institute takes care of (among others) a standard spelling, grammar, dictionary etc. Differences between the two varieties of Dutch are mainly phonetic and lexical, although phonological and morphological differences also exist, for instance with respect to diminutive allomorphs. For reasons of clarity, we will call Dutch as spoken in the Netherlands "Netherlandic Dutch" and Dutch as spoken in Belgium "Belgian Dutch".

Only a few studies on the acquisition of nominal morphology in Dutch have been performed and on the acquisition of diminutives even less. The experimental study (wug-test) by Snow et al. (1979) on some morphological rules in Netherlandic Dutch analyzes the acquisition of diminutives by children in the ages of 7 and 12. They show that the phonological rules for diminutive allomorphs are not fully acquired yet by the

7 year olds but fully acquired by the 12 year olds. Den Os and Harder (1987) find in their experimental study with 4 to 12 year olds that the range of diminutive allomorphs is not even fully acquired by the adults and they conclude that the order of acquisition is influenced by the frequency of occurrence. In a longitudinal study of the Belgian Dutch speaking girl Jolien (Gillis 1997) is shown that diminutives emerge from the age of 19 months on i.e. in the first stage of her vocabulary development, and over the total period of data collection (13–29 months) a maximum frequency of 27.7% of diminutives over the total number of noun forms is found. Hence, diminutives in the language of Jolien emerge from early on and occur frequently in her speech. Early and frequent occurrence in child language acquisition is also found in Italian (Ceccherini, Bonifacio & Zocconi 1997) as well as in Greek (Stephany 1997).

Here we will describe the acquisition of diminutives in the language of three Netherlandic Dutch speaking children, called Abel, Laura, and Matthijs over the period of 21 to 36 months.

The structure of the chapter is as follows: first the morphophonology of diminutive formation in Dutch is presented. Then we will proceed to the analysis of the empirical data: we will show that diminutives emerge early and that they are used frequently in the speech of three children. Diminutive frequency in child directed speech (CDS) is compared to the frequency in the language of the children. Secondly, we will analyze whether diminutive formation is a productive process in the age period studied here. Thirdly, the order of acquisition of the allomorphs and their distribution over diminutive forms is calculated and compared to what is found in CDS. In the final section a comparison between adult speech and CDS will be made. For analysis of adult speech we will use the Spoken Dutch Corpus: a large corpus of spoken adult Dutch with Belgian Dutch and Netherlandic Dutch component. These data enable us to make a comparison between adult speech and CDS.

1. Adult diminutive system

In Dutch diminutives are formed by attaching the diminutive morpheme to the stem. The diminutive morpheme in Dutch is /tjə/[2,3] (Booij & van Santen 1995; Kooij & van Oostendorp 2003; Trommelen 1983). The morpheme /tjə/ has several allomorphs, namely: /pjə/, /kjə/, /ətjə/ and /jə/. The exact choice between these allomorphs is determined by the phonology of the base's ending (final rhyme) as well as by the base's stress pattern.

In table 1 the diminutive allomorphs are shown. The table is followed by the phonological restrictions on attachment of each allomorph to the stem.

Table 1. Diminutive allomorphs in Dutch. Phonemic transcriptions are made in SAMPA (http://www.phon.ucl.ac.uk/home/sampa)

Variant	Example	SAMPA transcription*	Gloss
-tje (/tjə/)	kikker-tje	/k'Ikərtjə/	'frog-DIM'
	banana-tje	/ba'nantjə/	'banana-DIM'
	sokkel-the	/'sOkəltjə/	'socle-DIM'
	exemplaar-tje	/EksEm'plartjə/	'exemplar-DIM'
	pasta-tje	/'pAstatjə/	'pasta-DIM'
	vallei-tje	/vA'lIEitjə/	'valley-DIM'
	tube-tje	/'tybətjə/	'tube-DIM'
	spreeuw-tje	/'sprewtjə/	'starling-DIM'
	gaai-tje	/'xajtjə/	'jay-DIM'
-etje (/ətjə/)	roman-etje	/rom'Anətjə/	'novel-DIM'
	bal-etje	/'bAlətjə/	'ball-DIM'
	bar-etje	/'bArətjə/	'bar-DIM'
	ring-etje	/'rINətjə/	'ring-DIM'
-pje (/pjə/)	lichaam-pje	/'lIxampjə/	'body-DIM'
	pluim-pje	/'plœYmpjə/	'feather-DIM'
	bezem-pje	/'bezəmpjə/	'broom-DIM'
	olm-pje	/'Ol(ə)mpjə/	'elm-DIM'
-kje (/kjə/)	koning-kje	/'konINkjə/	'king-DIM'
-je (/jə/)	wereld-je	/'werəltjə/	'world-DIM'
	kop-je	/'kOpjə/	'cup-DIM'

The rules can be described as follows:[4]

-tje (/tjə/) is the default which applies in those conditions not stipulated below. This means that the allomorph */tjə/* is used as the diminutive allomorph when one of the following conditions is met:

- the word ends in a coronal sonorant (/n/, /l/, /r/) preceded by a long vowel, diphthong or schwa (e.g., *banana* 'banana', *sokkel* 'socle', *exemplaar* 'exemplar');
- the word is polysyllabic and ends in a short vowel plus /r/ (e.g., *radar* 'radar');
- the word ends in a vowel, diphthong or schwa (e.g., *pasta* 'pasta', *vallei* 'valley', *tube* 'tube');
- the word ends in a glide (e.g., *spreeuw* 'starling', *gaai* 'jay')

-etje (/ətjə/) is used after a nasal (/m/, /n/) or the liquid /l/ preceded by a short vowel (*roman* 'novel', *bal* 'ball'). The allomorph *-etje* is also used when the penultimate syllable is unstressed, as in *zoldering* (/'zOldərIN/, 'ceiling') – di-

minutive *zoldering-etje* (/'zOldərINətjə/) (compare *soldering* (/sOld'erIN/, 'soldering') – which takes the allomorph */kjə/*).
In addition, /ətjə/) is used with monosyllabic words ending in /r/ and proceeded by a short vowel (*bar* 'bar'). The latter restriction distinguishes monosyllabic words from polysyllabic words such as *radar* (/radar/, 'radar') which take the allomorph */tjə/*.

-pje (/pjə/) is used after a long vowel, a diphthong or a schwa followed by /m/ (*lichaam* 'body', *pluim* 'plume/compliment', *bezem* 'broom'), and after a short vowel followed by a liquid (/r/ or /l/) plus /m/ (*olm* 'elm').[5]

-kje (/kjə/) is used in multisyllabic words ending in *-ing* (/IN/) that carry main stress on the penultimate syllable. This is the case of *koning-kje* ('konIN-kjə) 'king-DIM', which is to be distinguished from monosyllabic words such as *ring* (/rIN/, 'ring') which take the allomorph *-etje*.

-je (/jə/) is used after an obstruent as in *wereld-je* (/'werəltjə/) 'world-DIM'.

The diminutive allomorphs mentioned so far are the ones that occur in standard Dutch, however, other allomorphs appear in spoken Dutch as well: the allomorphs *-ke* (/kə/), *-ske* (/əskə/), *-eke* (/əkə/), and *-ie* (/i/). According to the ANS (Haeseryn et al. 1997)[6], the allomorph */i/* occurs in the western part of the Netherlands and also occurs in non-high register speech. The allomorphs */kə/*, */skə/*, and */əkə/* occur in the north and the south of the Netherlands, and in the Dutch speaking part of Belgium. The use of these three allomorphs in Standard Dutch as it is spoken in the Netherlands, is mainly restricted to girls' names (such as *Anneke*, An-DIM, *Marieke*, Marie-ke), though they also occur in affective and literary language (for instance: *een dapper manneke* 'a brave man-DIM' or *een kindeke klein* 'a child-DIM small'). We will not describe the phonological rules for the use of the allomorphs /kə/, /skə/, and /əkə/ here, since their occurrence in our Netherlandic Dutch material is very restricted. The allomorph /i/ occurs in the following context:

-ie (/i/) The ending */i/* may replace */jə/* when the word ends in an obstruent (except when /t/ precedes), for instance, *aap* > *apie* 'ape-DIM', *boom* > *boompie* 'tree-DIM', *koning* > *koninkie* 'king-DIM', but not *plaat* > **plaatie* 'plate-DIM') (Kooij & van Oostendorp 2003). Thus, /i/ can occur in the same phonological contexts as the allomorphs /jə/, /pjə/, and /kjə/, resulting in /i/, /pi/, and /ki/.

The diminutive allomorphs /tjə/, /ətjə/, /pjə/, /kjə/, and /jə/ are in complementary distribution, with the exception of a few words to which (two) different allomorphs can be attached (De Haas & Trommelen 1993; Bakema 1998). Examples of words that may take more than one diminutive allomorph are given in (1). Some monosyllabic lemmas ending in an obstruent take the allomorph /jə/ but also allow the allomorph /ətjə/ (1a). Particular words that take /tjə/, /pjə/ or /kjə/, also allow /ətjə/ depending on the last consonant (1b). Note that this latter alternation may entail a difference in meaning. For example, in 1b, *bloemetje* means a ‘small flower’ or a ‘bunch of flowers’, while *bloempje* can only mean ‘a small flower’.

(1) a. kip / kip-je / kip-etje
N / N-DIM / N-DIM
chicken / chicken-DIM / chicken-DIM

b. bloem / bloem-pje / bloem-etje
N / N-DIM / N-DIM
flower / flower-DIM / flower-DIM

Quite a few lexical categories can be diminutivized:

a. **Nouns:** The process of diminutive formation applies to morphologically simple nouns, but also to compound nouns as well as derived nouns. These adhere to the same regularities as their morphologically simple counterparts. In principle every count noun can be diminutivized. Certain collective nouns, abstract, material nouns and other non-count nouns can be diminutivized given particular restrictions. In those cases the diminutive adds an ‘individualizing’ meaning component to the morphologically simple form. For these cases, no formal constraints can be formulated. Examples are *bier-/tjə/* (‘beer-DIM’, ‘a beer’), *krijt-/jə/* (‘chalk-DIM’, ‘a piece of chalk’), *eten-/tjə/* (‘food-DIM’, ‘a dinner-party’), etc.
b. **Proper nouns:** proper nouns exhibit the same diminutivization patterns as common nouns. Examples are: *Peter-/tjə/* (Peter-DIM), *Hans-/jə/* (Hans-DIM).
It may be the case that hypocoristics[7] in Dutch are formed by the allomorph /i/, but it is not possible to formally discern this allomorph from the more regional diminutive allomorph /i/ (Hinskens 2001).
c. **Adjectives**: de-adjectival diminutivized nouns only occur as such, i.e., the form without the diminutive allomorph does not occur (thus diminutivization in these cases is a prerequisite for nominalization). Forms such as *zoet-/jə/* (‘sweet-DIM’, ‘something sweet’), *blauw-/tjə/* (‘blue-DIM’, ‘(get) the mitten’) tend to have a lexicalized meaning. These are examples of *diminutiva tantum*.[8] Person names derived from adjectives share this feature, but their meaning is not (always) lexicalized: *sloom-/pjə/* (‘lazy-DIM’, ‘a stick-in-the-mud’), *groen-/tjə/* (‘green-DIM’, ‘freshman’).
d. **Verbs**: those verb stems that can be used as nouns without any alternation (derivation through a zero morpheme) allow diminitivization. Examples are *duw-/tjə/* (‘push-DIM’, ‘a little push’), *prik-/jə/* (‘prick-DIM’), *zeg-jə* (‘say-DIM’), etc. But also certain other verb stems allow diminutivization, as for instance *bedank-/jə/* (‘thank-DIM’, ‘acknowledgement’)
e. **Numerals**: numerals can be diminutivized. In most cases the diminutives refer to banknotes or coins (e.g., *tien-/tjə/* ‘ten-DIM’, *duizend-jə* ‘thousand-DIM’), though not necessarily so (e.g., *een-/tjə/* ‘one-DIM’).

f. **Pronouns**: diminutivization of pronouns is rather restricted. Examples: *iets-je* ('something-DIM') and the collocation *dit-/jəs/ en dat-/jəs/* ('this-DIM' and 'that-DIM', i.e., 'all sort of things'), *ik-/jə/* ('I-DIM').
g. **Prepositions**: The meaning of diminutivized prepositions is lexicalized. Examples: *uit-/jə/* ('out-DIM', 'outing'), *om(m)-/ətjə/* ('around-DIM', 'turn').
h. **Adverbs**: some adverbs allow diminutivization such as *allegaar-/tjə/* ('hotchpotch-DIM'), *apart-/jə/* ('separate-DIM'). A related case is de-adjectival adverbs. They take the allomorph *-/tjəs/* with precisely the same allomorphy as the diminutive allomorph, so that the allomorph may well be analyzed as consisting of *-/tjə/* plus *-s*. Examples are: *zacht-/jə/-s* ('soft-DIM-s'), *warm-/pjə/-s* ('warm-DIM-s'), *gewoon-/tjə/-s* ('ordinary-DIM-s'), etc.
i. **Phrases**: Certain phrases can be diminutivized as a whole, for instance, *onderons-/jə/* ('among us-DIM, a select few'), *bijdehand-/jə/* ('sharp-DIM'), *vieruur-/tjə/* ('four o'clock-DIM'), *tussendoor-/tjə/* ('inbetween-DIM'), etc.

Diminutives assign neuter gender to the nouns they form, independent of the gender of the base (noun) category. Furthermore, category shift takes place when a base is diminutivized: all categories become nouns. Diminutives are considered to be lexicalized or frozen when they do not have a base counterpart, i.e. with a similar non-diminutive meaning. Examples are shown in (2).

(2) a. meis-/jə/   *meis
N-DIM   N
girl

b. beet-/jə/   *beet
N-DIM   N
little bit

2. Data

Spontaneous longitudinal data of three children – Abel, Laura, and Matthijs – are analyzed in this study. The transcriptions are available through CHILDES (MacWhinney 2000). The data from Abel and Matthijs are from the Groningen corpus, Laura from the Van Kampen corpus. We analyzed one recording per month from the start of the recordings until the age of three. Table 2 provides details about the precise age range for each child and number of recordings. The transcriptions of the recordings were lemmatized, part-of-speech tagged and morphologically coded using a lexicon based version of the CLAN tool MOR (MacWhinney 2000). MLU's were calculated in words and in morphemes for the first and last recordings analyzed here. In addition, table 2 also stipulates the total number of child utterances as well as the number of utterances addressed to the child (CDS). The last two columns of the table provide the number of tokens of diminutives in the children's speech as well as in the language addressed to them (CDS). Frozen or lexicalized diminutives were excluded from our analyses.

Table 2. Range of age, MLU in words of first and last recording, MLU in morphemes of first and last recording, number of recordings per child, total number of utterances, and total number of diminutive tokens

	Age months	*MLU words*	*MLU morphemes*	*No. Recordings*	*Total no child utterances*	*Total no utterances CDS*	*Total no of dim. Tokens Child*	*Total no of dim. Tokens CDS*
Abel	23–35	1.2–3.1	1.4–3.7	13	5299	10172	224	383
Laura	21–36	1.2–2.4	1.3–2.7	16	5551	7644	278	642
Matthijs	22–35	1.5–3.0	1.8–3.4	14	5884	13570	512	1376

3. Development

In this section we describe the development of diminutives in the language of the three children: the onset of diminutive usage, and the frequencies of diminutives in the children's language as well as in the ambient language.

3.1 Early emergence

Diminutives are found in the very first available transcript of the three children: for Laura at the age of 21 months and for Matthijs and Abel at the age of 22 and 23 months. Comparing these ages to the first emergence of diminutives by the Belgian Dutch speaking girl Jolien, it appears that she starts producing diminutives at the age of 21 months. Inspection of the data from two Belgian Dutch speaking triplets reveals the following as to the first occurrence of diminutivized forms[9]: Arnold at 24 months, Diederik at 22 (or earlier), Maria at 24, for the first triplet, and Gijs at 21, Joost at 22, and Katelijne at 22, for the second triplet. This means that diminutives emerge early, possibly at an earlier age than the first available recording of the three children studied here.

What is the size of the children's vocabularies when the first diminutives appear? The total vocabulary size in the first recordings of the children is 56, 47, and 71 lemmas for Abel, Laura, and Matthijs respectively. Vocabulary size in noun lemmas is 25 for Abel, 14 for Laura, and 52 for Matthijs. The number of noun lemmas that occur in the data of the children is comparable to the vocabulary size in noun lemmas of the Belgian Dutch speaking children (Jolien and two triplets): Jolien 54, Arnold 45, Diederik 13, Maria 32, Gijs 34, Joost 60, Katelijne 62. It can be concluded that both the Netherlandic Dutch speaking children as well as the Belgian Dutch speaking children have a vocabulary size in nouns of less than 100 lemmas and in most cases less than 50 lemmas. In other words, diminutives occur already in the very first stages of vocabulary development.

3.2 Frequencies in child speech

So far we have shown that diminutives emerge form early on in lexical acquisition. When we have a further look at the frequency of occurrence, a relatively high token frequency appears: the ratio of diminutive tokens over the total number of noun tokens is 16% for Abel (median, range 2%–33%), 11% for Laura (median, range 2%–34%) and 19% for Matthijs (median, range 4%–33%). In all three children, the relative number of diminutive tokens increases over the period studied, in other words, the number of diminutivized nouns relative to the total number of nouns produced, increases significantly, except for Matthijs (Abel: $F(1,12) = 11.6$, $p< 0.01$; Matthijs: $F(1, 13) = 0.0$, $p > 0.05$; Laura: $F(1, 15) = 10.5$, $p < 0.01$).

Token frequency only shows the number of diminutives a child produces; it does not elucidate whether diminutives are restricted to a fairly limited set of lemmas or whether there is a wide diversity of lemmas that occur in diminutivized form. In order to attain an insight into the dispersion of diminutives over lemmas in the data, the cumulative frequency of lemmas that actually occur with a diminutive allomorph is calculated. The percentage of the noun lemmas with a diminutive form over the total number of noun lemmas is displayed in Figure 1. Figure 1 shows that the ratio of diminutivized noun lemmas over the total number of noun lemmas steadily increases for all children. In all three children the ratio stabilizes towards the end of the recordings analyzed here. Note that the frequency of lemmas with a diminutive is low at the very beginning of the recordings, which causes the instable looking shape of the curve.

All three children show a significant increase of the ratio over the total period (Abel: $F(1,11) = 80.4$, $p < 0.01$, Laura: $F(1,15)=20.9$, $p < 0{,}01$; Matthijs: $F(1,13) = 29.5$, $p < 0.01$). Closer inspection of Figure 1 reveals that there is a steep increase in the ratio of diminutives for Abel and Matthijs, while Laura shows a more "hesitant" start of the use of diminutives. The two former children's developmental curve seems to attain a ceiling ratio at around 30 months of age. For Laura it is not quite clear whether she has reached a plateau at the end of the period studied.

So far, we have shown an early emergence of diminutive tokens and lemmas in the three children acquiring Dutch. Furthermore, diminutive tokens are relatively frequent as compared to the frequency of noun tokens, and the usage of diminutives increases during the period studied. We also found a high dispersion of diminutivized lemmas over noun lemmas.

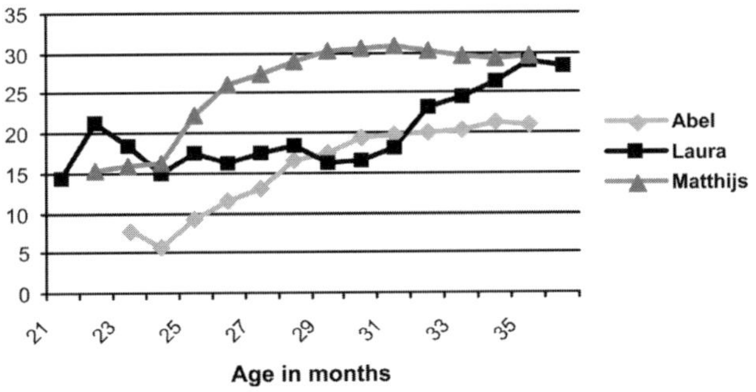

Figure 1. Ratios of diminutive lemma frequency over noun lemma frequency of Abel, Laura, and Matthijs calculated cumulatively

3.3 Frequencies in CDS

With respect to the frequency of diminutives in the input, we expect that as the children start using diminutives, and as their usage grows markedly, the parental input will also show an increase: we expect parents to use more diminutivized nouns (tokens) and we expect them to use a broader range of nouns (lemmas) in their diminutive form. Contrary to our expectations, the parental input frequencies of diminutives show an interesting characteristic in terms of tokens and types. As to token frequency, the input of the three children does not undergo a significant quantitative change over the period studied (Abel: $F(1,12) = 0.0$, $p > 0.05$; Matthijs: $F(1, 13) = 0.6$, $p > 0.05$; Laura: $F(1,15) = 2.4$, $p > 0.05$). Hence, in terms of the relative amount of diminutivized tokens, there is no significant development in the adults' language use. Although the children are producing progressively more diminutives, the parents' output does not follow this trend.

In order to complete the picture of the input, Figure 2 shows the cumulative development of the diminutivized lemmas. For the sake of comparison, also the cumulative data of the children are added. The curves depicting the cumulative number of diminutivized lemmas in the input increase significantly for all three children (Abel: $F(1,12) = 5.6$, $p < 0.05$; Laura: $F(1,15)= 76.4$, $p < 0.01$; Matthijs: $F(1,13) = 6.0$, $p < 0.05$). Thus, in the parental language, there is an increasing number of different lemmas that occurs as a diminutive over time. It is not the case that the parents restrict their use of diminutives to a particular set of words: the number of different lemmas that are diminutivized increases significantly over time, providing the children with a growing set of examples of diminutives.

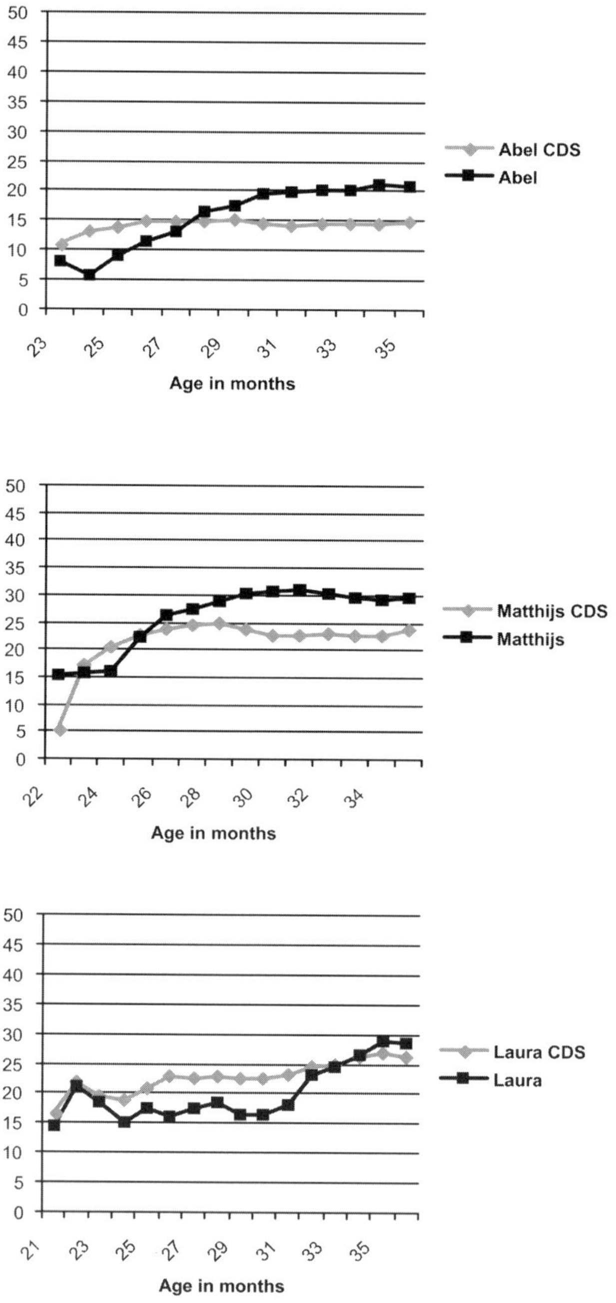

Figure 2. Cumulative frequency of diminutives in both input and output per child, represented as a ratio of diminutivized lemmas over noun lemmas

Examining more closely the graph depicting Abel's data in Figure 2, it is remarkable that initially the input contains more diminutivized lemmas than the child's output, and the number of lemmas in the input increases. It reaches its ceiling at around 30 months, after which the rate of diminutivized lemmas remains more or less stable at around 15%. A similar profile appears from the graphs depicting Matthijs' and Laura's data: at the beginning input frequency outnumbers the frequency in the output, the ratio of diminutivized lemmas increases, and reaches a ceiling (at around 25% for Laura and Matthijs at the age of about 30 months). Interestingly, the children end up with a ratio of diminutivized lemmas that is higher than that of their parents: this is especially apparent in the case of Abel and Matthijs.

4. Form oppositions

Oppositions between forms of the same lemma may indicate that a morphological process is active in the language of the children. (Gillis 1997; Kilani-Schoch & Dressler 2002). We expect that a high frequency of oppositions between a base noun form and a diminutive form of the same lemma, will tell us something about the productive use of diminutives in the language of the children.

As noted in section 3.1, the first diminutives appear right at the start of the recordings. The first oppositions between diminutives and their base noun forms also occur in the very first observation session of the three children. For example, in Abel's data we find an opposition between *koek* 'cake' and *koek-/jə/* 'cake-DIM'. In Laura's data we find two oppositions i.e. between *boek* and *boek-/i/* 'book / book-DIM' and between *paard* and *paard-/jə/* 'hors / hors-DIM'. In the data of Matthijs we find even three oppositions i.e. *ijs* – *ijs-/jə/* 'ice cream / ice cream-DIM', *poes* – *poes-/jə/* 'cat / cat-DIM' and also *paard* / *paard-/jə/*. Both base nouns and diminutives occur in the same contexts, except for Laura's opposition between *paard* and *paard-/jə/*. She uses the base noun *paard* when she is reading a book with her mother and produces the diminutive form when she wants to play a game called "*paard-/jə/ rijden*" (*to hors-*DIM *ride*: she wants to sit on her mother's knee), which is a kind of 'standing expression'. Abel uses one out of the two diminutivized lemmas in opposition with the base noun in the first recording, Laura two out of two and Matthijs three out of five. In other words, oppositions appear as soon as there are diminutives. But since our data presumably do not cover the very beginning of the use of diminutives, we cannot make any firm statement about the emergence of the opposition between base nouns and diminutivized nouns.

In Table 3 the relative frequency of lemmas that occur exclusively in their base form is calculated for each child over the entire period of study. In addition the table also indicates the proportion of lemmas that occur only as a diminutive, and the proportion for which both forms are attested in the corpora. It appears that the incidence of diminutives that occur in opposition with their base noun, is similar to the incidence of lemmas that occur in the diminutive form only. There are much more lemmas, though, that occur only in their base form.

Table 3. Number of noun lemmas, lemmas that occur as Base Nouns only, as Diminutive only, and as Base Noun as well as Diminutive, calculated over the total period of recordings

	Base only	*Diminutive only*	*Base +Diminutive*
Abel	83%	8%	9%
Laura	80%	7%	12%
Matthijs	70%	16%	14%

In Figure 3 the development of oppositions is shown as the median of the three children.[10] It is compared to the development of lemmas that occur in the diminutive form only and lemmas that occur in the base noun form only. In addition, the cumulative number of noun lemmas is shown.

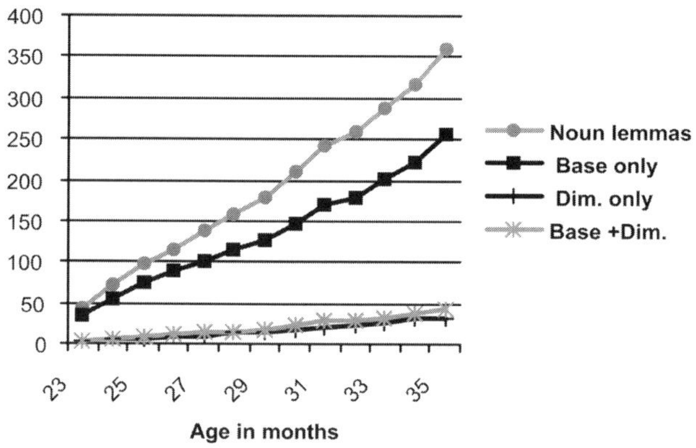

Figure 3. Cumulative development in lemmas of vocabulary, base forms only, diminutive forms only and lemmas that occur in both forms: represented as median values of the three children

As shown in Table 3 and Figure 3, relatively few oppositions between diminutive and base noun form of the same lemmas occur. As pointed out before, the frequency of lemmas that occur in the diminutive form only is just slightly lower. Gillis (1997) found similar results in the data of the Belgian Dutch speaking girl Jolien. Between 25 and 29 months of age, she uses a percentage of 74% for the category base noun only, 15% for diminutive only and 12% for word forms that show opposition between these two forms. The relatively low percentage of oppositions (base noun and diminutive) of the same lemma indicates at least that the child does not produce automatically several forms of a particular lemma. Whether this points at a lack of productivity of diminutive formation remains to be seen: according to Laaha et al. (2006) morphological productivity is "the ability to form new potential words". But when do longitudinal observational data such as the ones analyzed here show the existence of this ability? Especially in the case of diminutives this is a very difficult question, since unlike obligatory grammatical processes such as congruence, morphological marking of plural referents, and the like, diminutives do not have a clear semantic or pragmatic domain in which they are obligatorily marked. Hence, the relatively low incidence of diminutivized lemmas does not permit us to make any definite statements about the children's ability to productively form diminutives. A more thorough analysis of the appropriate contexts in which the base noun and its diminutivized counterpart might be properly used in opposition (e.g., a big cat versus a small one), could give us an insight into children's ability to productively form diminutives. Note, however, that the latter analysis might be contaminated by the fact that the child may have encountered the appropriate diminutive form in the ambient language so that our analysis would reveal only a contextually appropriate use of a diminutive (driven by semantic or pragmatic considerations), so that our analysis would not uncover the child's ability to form a diminutive from a bare noun. Given these notes of caution, correlations were computed between the increase of new noun lemmas per month and the increase of oppositions between base nouns and diminutive forms per month. For neither of the children a significant correlation was found between these measures (Abel: Spearman Rho = 0.4, $p > 0.05$; Laura: Spearman Rho = 0.3, $p > 0.05$; Matthijs: Spearman Rho = 0.1, $p > 0.05$), which means that there is no significant correlation between vocabulary growth (the number of new lemmas entering the child's lexicon) and the number of formal oppositions between base nouns and diminutives.

5. Diminutive distribution

In this section, we will analyze the distribution of diminutive allomorphs. We will look at the order of emergence and the ages at which the children acquire the various allomorphs. In addition, the frequency of each allomorph in the data of both the children and their input will be analyzed.

5.1 First emergence

In Table 4 the first occurrence of the various diminutive allomorphs is indicated for each child and also the first attested occurrence in the input the child receives. In all three children's speech the first diminutive allomorphs to appear are /jə/ and /tjə/. They either occur during the same month or in consecutive months. In Abel's data one instance of /jə/ occurs and one instance of /tjə/, i.e. *koek-/jə/* 'cook-DIM' and *schoen-/tjə/* 'shoe-DIM'. In Matthijs' data diminutivized lemmas with /jə/ and /tjə/ occur in the first recording, including *eend-/jə/* 'duck-DIM', *ijs-/jə/* 'ice cream-DIM', and *cadeau-/tjə/* 'present-DIM'. In the first recording of Laura *paard-/jə/* 'hors-DIM' and *boek-/i/* 'book-DIM' are found. Thus, the first allomorphs to appear are /jə/ and /tjə/, moreover, /i/ also appears relatively soon in Abel's and Laura's data, though this allomorph shows up later in Matthijs' data. The allomorphs /ətjə/ and /pjə/ – in that order – are the last to appear in all children's data. Finally, /kjə/ does not appear in the children's data, and neither do /kə/ and /əkə/. The order of emergence is similar for all three children, though the allomorph /i/ shows some variation in the exact order of appearance: it occurs right form the start in the Laura's data, while in the data of Matthijs this allomorph emerges for the first time after /ətjə/ and in the data of Abel, we find this allomorph before /ətjə/ occurs.

In the next section the order of appearance will be related to the frequency of the allomorphs in the ambient language. Closer inspection of Table 4 reveals that the first diminutive allomorphs to appear in the children's speech are also the ones that show up in the parental language from the very first observation sessions onwards. A difference with the output concerns the allomorphs /kjə/ and /əkə/ in the input of Matthijs and the allomorph /kə/ in the input of Abel. These allomorphs do not occur in the data of the children. The allomorph /kjə/ in the input of Matthijs occurs once with one lemma, viz. *ketting-/kjə/* 'necklace-DIM' at 24 months. At 26 months the allomorph /əkə/ is found in the input, occurring 5 times with the lemma *man* 'man' which becomes *man-/əkə/* 'man-DIM' in the diminutive form. The allomorph /kə/ in the input of Abel appears once with one lemma *moeder-/kə/* 'mother-DIM' at 29 months. The fact that these allomorphs only occur in the parental language with a very low frequency may explain why they are lacking in the children's repertories.

In summary, the order of appearance of the allomorphs is /jə/ = < tjə < ətje < pjə. The first appearance of the allomorph /i/ is less predictable: it is among the first in Abel's and Laura's data but emerges much later in Matthijs' data. In addition to these allomorphs, we also find the allomorphs /kjə/, /kə/, and /əkə/ in the input, but they do not show up in the children's data.

Table 4. First emergence per allomorph of Abel, Laura, and Matthijs and their input ('X' stands for no recordings available for that age)

	Abel		Laura		Matthijs	
Age in months	input	output	input	output	input	output
21	X	X	/jə/ /tjə/ /ətjə/	/i/ /jə/	X	X
22	X	X		/tjə/	/jə/ /tjə/ /ətjə/	/jə/ /tjə/
23	/jə/ /tjə/ /ətjə/	/jə/ /tjə/	/i/		/i/	
24	/i/ /pjə/	/i/			/kjə/	/ətjə/
25					/pjə/	/i/
26					/əkə/	
27		/ətjə/ /pjə/	/pjə/			
28						
29	/kə/					
30				/ətjə/		
31						
32						
33						
34						/pjə/
35				/pjə/		
36	X	X			X	X
Not occurring in the data/ Not yet acquired	/kjə/ /əkə/ /skə/	/kjə/ /kə/ /əkə/ /skə/	/kjə/ /kə/ /əkə/ /skə/	/kjə/ /kə/ /əkə/ /skə/	/kə/ /skə/	/kjə/ /kə/ /əkə/ /skə/

5.2 The frequency of allomorphs

As to the distribution of allomorphs over diminutives, displayed in Table 5, it appears that the most frequent allomorphs are /jə/ (median: 59% of the lemmas and 66% of the tokens) and /tjə/ (median: 20% of the lemmas and 22% of the tokens), followed by

/ətjə/ (median: 7% of the lemmas and 5% of the tokens), /i/ (median: 6% of the lemmas and 6% of the tokens), and /pjə/ (median: 1% of the lemmas and 0.4% of the tokens). None of the children uses the allomorphs /kjə/, /kə/ and /əkə/. The distribution of the allomorphs is not significantly different among the three children: neither for the lemmas ($\chi^2(8) = 3.1$, $p > 0.05$), nor for the tokens ($\chi^2(8) = 10.7$, $p > 0.05$), and it shows a striking agreement between lemmas and tokens: a comparison of the distributions of the allomorphs yields non-significant results, meaning that the three children use the allomorphs in highly comparable proportions of tokens and with a highly comparable distribution with respect to the types of words. Taken together with the highly similar order in which the allomorphs appear in the children's language, the highly similar frequency distributions in the children's speech suggest the hypothesis that the input the children receive shows very few differences: parents use roughly the same amounts of diminutives and use these in approximately the same distributions.

The distributional characteristics of the parental use of the diminutive allomorphs can be seen in Table 5 (viz. the rows headed by the children's names followed by CDS). It is indeed the case that the same distributional pattern emerges from the parental data: /jə/ is the most frequent allomorph (median: 56% of the lemmas and 60% of the tokens), followed by /tjə/ (median: 28% of the lemmas and 29% of the tokens), /ətjə/ (median 11% of the lemmas and 9% of the tokens), /i/ (median: 5% of the lemmas and 4% of the tokens), and /pjə/ (median: 4% of the lemmas and 2% of the tokens). Strikingly, the median values for the other allomorphs (i.e., /kjə/, /əkə/, /kə/) equals 0.4% of the lemmas and 0.3% of the tokens, which probably explains why these do not occur in the children's language. Over the entire period studied, the parental input that the three children receive has the same distributional characteristics: there is no significant difference between the relative frequencies of the various allomorphs neither for the tokens ($\chi^2(10) = 10.5$, $p > 0.05$) nor for the lemmas ($\chi^2(10) = 8.1$, $p > 0.05$).

Lining up these findings: we found that the distributional characteristics of the children's use of diminutive allomorphs do not differ significantly and that their parents' use also shows the same characteristics. When we statistically compare the parents' use with their children's use of the various allomorphs, it turns out quite expectedly that there are no significant differences neither in terms of lemmas nor in terms of tokens (all $\chi2$-test yield $p > 0.05$). Hence our findings indicate that the order in which the allomorphs emerge in the children's language, reflects the frequency of the allomorphs in the parental input, and in addition also the children's frequency of usage reflects the frequency distribution found in their parents' language. Note that these findings are well in agreement with those of Gillis (1997). He found in the speech of the Belgian Dutch speaking girl Jolien the following distribution of allomorphs over diminutive word forms: /jə/ takes 59%, /tjə/ 30% and /pjə/, /ətjə/, /kə/, and /əkə/ together show a use of 11%. The girl's mother distributes the allomorphs over diminutive word forms as follows: 57% for /jə/, 34% for /tjə/ and 8% for the other variants.

Table 5. Distribution of allomorphs as a percentage of the total number of allomorphs (lemmas and tokens) in the children's speech and in the child directed speech (CDS)

	/tjə/		/ətjə/		/pjə/		/kjə/		/jə/		/i/		/kə/		/əkə/		Total number of allomorphs	
	lem	tok	lem	tok	lem	tok	lem	tok	lem	tok	lem	tok	lem	tok	lem	tok	lem	tok
Abel CDS	21.8	16.4	11	10.4	4.2	2.6	0	0	58.2	66.3	4.6	3.9	0.3	0.4	0	0	239	383
Abel	22.4	15.6	9.3	12.1	0.9	0.4	0	0	58.9	66.1	8.4	5.8	0	0	0	0	107	224
Laura CDS	31.4	31.2	10.5	9.2	1.5	1.6	0	0	55	56.5	1.5	0.8	0	0	0	0	389	642
Laura	24.2	25.9	7.2	4.7	1.3	0.7	0	0	61.4	65.5	5.9	3.2	0	0	0	0	153	278
Matthijs CDS	28	28.6	9.1	6.6	0.7	0.5	0.3	0.1	56.2	59.9	5.6	4	0	0	0.2	0.4	607	1376
Matthijs	18.5	20.1	6.6	4.1	0.4	0.2	0	0	68.3	67.6	6.2	8	0	0	0	0	227	512

An important remark needs to be made with respect to the actual distribution of the diminutive allomorphs in child directed speech, and their emergence in the children's language (see Table 4 for the order of emergence of the allomorphs in the data). As a matter of course, the emergence of particular allomorphs is crucially dependent on the availability of examples in the input. An obvious case is the allomorph /kjə/, which does not occur in the language of the three children. The reason for the non-emergence is probably very few instances of the allomorph in the input (one lemma and one token only). A second consideration is a sufficiently high pattern incidence. Following a lead given by Dressler et al. (2006), it may well be that child directed speech offers a 'simplified' or 'impoverished' selection of the rich patterns of the adult language. For instance, Dressler et al. (2006) show for plural formation in Dutch, that although the system of plurals in Dutch is quite intricate, complicated and characterized by regularities, sub-regularities, and plain exceptions, the plurals that appear in CDS, are highly transparent and almost completely predictable. Thus, the complicated adult system is simplified in CDS through a drastic reduction of the possible patterns.

Translated to the case of diminutives: it may be that particular allomorphs are not, or only late acquired by a child, because in CDS the potentiality of diminutive formation is reduced. For instance, particular patterns may only scarcely be presented in the language that children hear, which may explain their lack or late emergence in the child's speech. More specifically, if in CDS all possible patterns of diminutive formation are represented, we can compute for each allomorph which potential share it has given the complete set of nouns in CDS. In other words, suppose all nouns that occur in CDS are diminutivized, what would be the relative share of each diminutive allomorph? But if not every potential landing spot for a diminutive is also actually diminutivized in CDS (not all nouns actually occur as a diminutive), we can compute the actual share of each allomorph in the actual CDS. In other words, we can calculate the actual number of nouns that take each diminutive allomorph in order to arrive at the actual share of each allomorph. A comparison of the potential share with the actual share of each allomorph, will elucidate if that allomorph occurs with more or less frequency than what is potentially possible given the words in CDS. Thus, as a null hypothesis, we expect that the potential share of each allomorph equals its actual share. But if that is not the case, we have good reasons to believe that diminutive allomorphs follow the pattern described for plurals by Dressler et al. (2006): the potentiality of the system is reduced in actual CDS.

In order to operationalize this line of thinking the following procedure was implemented. In the case of diminutives, the allomorph that is actually realized is dependent on the phonological pattern of the lexical item. As elaborated on in section 1, the diminutive allomorphy is governed by the final rhyme of the base noun and by the item's stress pattern. For instance, words ending in a short vowel followed by a liquid (/r/ or /l/) plus /m/ (*olm* 'elm'), take the allomorph /pjə/. In order for the child to learn this pattern, there need to be sufficient examples in the input. As an approximation of what can be considered 'sufficient presence in the input', this concept was operationalized as follows. For each noun lemma in the input the diminutive allomorph was determined over the entire corpus.[11] In this way the potential number of lemmas that take a particular allomorph was determined. This number is called 'the expected frequency'. Thus, candidates for each diminutive allomorph were computed by predicting the allomorph on the basis of the phonological form of the lemma, and the number of lemmas that potentially take that allomorph is designated as 'the expected frequency'. For each allomorph 'the expected proportion' was computed, based on the proportional share of each allomorph in the total 'expected frequency'. For example, all noun lemmas that potentially take the allomorph /pjə/ were identified, and the proportion of those lemmas on the total number of noun lemmas was computed. This computation was repeated for the actual corpus of diminutivized nouns: 'the observed frequencies'. That is, for each allomorph the actual number of lemmas taking that allomorph was determined in the corpus, and its relative share in the total number of diminutivized nouns was determined, i.e., 'the observed proportion'. Next, the ratio of observed proportions over expected proportions was computed. It can readily be seen that if the ratio of the expected proportion over the observed proportion is one, this means that the actually observed proportion is exactly equal to the expected proportion. If the ratio is greater than one, this means that the observed proportion is greater than what was expected. In terms of allomorphy, if the ratio is greater than one, then the number of lemmas taking a particular allomorph (e.g., /pjə/) in the corpus is superior to the number of lemmas that was expected to take the allomorph.

The ratios were subsequently entered into a binomial statistic in order to verify if the ratios differed significantly from one. For each specific allomorph the ratio is indicated in Table 6, and the statistical significance of the ratio is shown.

Table 6. Ratios of observed over expected frequencies of diminutive allomorphs (** = $p < 0.01$, * = $p < 0.05$, NS = $p > 0.05$, / = allomorph does not occur in the data)

	/tjə/	/ətjə/	/pjə/	/kjə/	/jə/
Abel	0.78	0.88	1.70	0.01	1.22
	NS	NS	NS	*	*
Laura	0.80	1.02	1.11	/	1.18
	*	NS	NS		*
Matthijs	0.79	1.09	0.45	0.20	1.21
	**	NS	NS	NS	**

The gist of the results in Table 6 is that for all children, the actual input significantly contains more than expected lemmas that take the diminutive allomorph /jə/. Interestingly, the allomorph /tjə/ occurs less than expected in all three children: the ratio of observed and expected frequencies is less than one. In Laura's and Matthijs' input the difference is significant. The allomorphs /ətjə/ and /pjə/ occur with an expected frequency. /kjə/ occurs less than expected in the three data sets. In all three children's input, there are potentially a number of lemmas that could have occurred with a /kjə/ diminutive, but in the actual data, no lemma with a /kjə/ allomorph occurs or it occurs with a frequency less than expected.

From this analysis, we can conclude that one allomorph, viz. /jə/ is used more frequently than expected, and one less than expected, viz. /tjə/. The reason for this discrepancy is not clear at present. In the next section we will indicate more contradictory findings regarding the frequency of /jə/ versus /tjə/ that await further explanation. The allomorph /kjə/ occurs less than expected in the input. None of the children use this allomorph, which leads us to hypothesize that this lack of input is causally related to the lack of emergence in the language of the children.

6. Comparing CDS with ADS

It is often argued that a high diminutive frequency is characteristic of CDS. In order to obtain support for this claim, the parental speech analyzed here will be compared with a large corpus of spoken Dutch. More specifically in this section we will analyze the frequency of diminutives and their distribution in the Spoken Dutch Corpus. The Spoken Dutch Corpus is a large corpus – approximately 10 million word forms – collected around the turn of the century. It consists of recordings of contemporary spoken Belgian and Netherlandic Dutch. The analyses presented in this section are based on Netherlandic Dutch spontaneous speech, since the acquisition data are also spontaneous data of children who are living in the Netherlands. Frozen diminutives are included here, since these are not separately coded in the Spoken Dutch Corpus. In Table 7 frequencies of lemmas and tokens in our sample are shown. The ratio of noun lemmas with a diminutive allomorph over the total number of nouns is: 10.7% for lemmas and 6.2% for tokens in ADS.

Table 7. Frequencies in Spoken Dutch Corpus

CGN frequency	*lemmas*	*tokens*
Total number of words	53,853	4,579,426
Total number of diminutives	3,593	31,280
Total number of nouns	33,068	497,250
Total number of diminutivized nouns	3,552	30,788
% diminutivized nouns	10.7%	6.2%

A comparison of the number of diminutive lemmas and tokens in ADS with the number of lemmas and tokens in CDS, reveals that the ratio of diminutives over the total number of nouns is higher in CDS. In the total input of Abel the percentages are 15% for noun lemmas and 15% for noun tokens, for Laura 26% and 19% and for Matthijs

24% and 18%, while in ADS we find a percentage of 11% for lemmas and 6% for tokens. The differences between ADS and CDS are significant for lemmas (CDS per child compared to ADS: Abel: $\chi^2(1) = 11.8$, $p < 0.01$; Laura: $\chi^2(1) = 103.9$, $p < 0.01$; Matthijs: $\chi^2(1) = 123.2$, $p < 0.01$). This means that indeed in CDS significantly more lemmas occur in their diminutivized form than in spontaneous adult-adult speech. This also holds for tokens: significantly more diminutivized word forms appear in CDS than in ADS (CDS per child compared to ADS: Abel: $\chi^2(1) = 416.8$, $p < 0.01$; Laura: $\chi^2(1) = 917.3$, $p < 0.01$; Matthijs: $\chi^2(1) = 1483.0$, $p < 0.01$). This confirms the idea that more diminutives can be found in CDS as compared to ADS.

As to the frequency of allomorphs a similar ranking of the frequencies in CDS and ADS is found. In Table 8, the distribution of diminutive allomorphs over nouns in adult speech is shown. As can be clearly seen, the allomorphs /jə/ and /tjə/ are the most frequent allomorph, followed by /ətjə/ and /i/. The other allomorphs, viz. /pjə/, /kə/, /kjə/, /əkə/, and /skə/ occur in less than 1% of the lemmas. The frequencies of the allomorphs in CDS are shown in Table 5. The allomorphs /jə/ and /tjə/ are the most frequent ones, followed by /ətjə/, /i/, and /pjə/ in that order. The allomorphs /kjə/, /kə/, and /əkə/ occur with a very low lemma frequency. Token frequencies provide a different picture in ADS: now /tjə/ is by far the most frequently used, followed by /jə/. /ətjə/ has a share of 6%, and all the other allomorphs are below 1%. This means that in ADS more lemmas take /jə/ in their diminutive form, but in actual speech, /tjə/ is the allomorph that occurs most frequently. In CDS on the other hand, /jə/ is the most frequent allomorph, followed by /tjə/, /ətjə/ and /i/. The other allomorphs occur with very low token frequencies. This result is quite unexpected: in ADS there are far more tokens of /tjə/ and more lemmas that take /jə/. In CDS type and token frequencies show the same picture: /jə/ is the most frequent allomorph, /tjə/ is less frequent. Not surprisingly, when statistically comparing the distributions of the various allomorphs in ADS and in CDS, no significant difference turn up when computed for lemmas (ADS – Abel-CDS: $\chi^2(5) = 6.31$, $p > 0.05$; ADS – Laura-CDS: $\chi^2(5) = 1.9$, $p > 0.05$; ADS – Matthijs-CDS: $\chi^2(5) = 2.01$, $p > 0.05$). But for tokens of diminutives, significant differences between ADS and the CDS directed to the three children do show up (ADS – Abel-CDS: $\chi^2(5) = 33.8$, $p < 0.01$; ADS – Laura-CDS: $\chi^2(5) = 12.0$, $p < 0.01$; ADS – Matthijs-CDS: $\chi^2(5) = 15.5$, $p < 0.01$). Although no clear explanation for the difference in token frequency between CDS and ADS has been found yet, it may point to a simplification strategy in CDS.

Table 8. Number of noun lemmas and tokens per diminutive allomorph as a percentage of total number of noun lemmas and tokens with a diminutive allomorph

Diminutive allomorphs in CGN	*lemmas %*	*tokens %*
/jə/	51.1	37.6
/tjə/	34.9	54.9
/pjə/	1.3	0.3
/kjə/	0.5	0.08
/ətjə/	7.7	6.0
/i/	3.2	0.9
/kə/	0.8	0.2
/əkə/	0.3	0.02
/skə/	0.1	0.02

7. Conclusion

In this chapter we analyzed the development of diminutives in the language of three Netherlandic Dutch speaking children between the age of 21 and 36 months. The children start out with a low frequency, which – after a period during which the input seems to provide more diminutive lemmas than the child produces – soon outnumbers the frequency in the input. By the age of three, the use of diminutives seems to have reached a ceiling and stabilizes.

One of the questions we asked in this chapter is whether diminutive formation is a productive process in the age period studied here. We argued that is it difficult to prove productivity here, since diminutive formation is a non-obligatory process and the contexts in which a diminutive may occur are not strictly determined. Therefore, we do not know whether a child is able to produce a diminutive form of a certain lemma in the data, since it is not mandatory for the child to produce the diminutive form.

As to the distribution of diminutive allomorphs we found that the distribution in the language of the children was similar to the one found in the input, except for the allomorphs /kjə/, /kə/, /əkə/, that do occur in the input (but not in the input of all children) and not in the output. The allomorphs that are not used by the children are very low frequent allomorphs, which may account for their non-occurrence in the language of the children. But in general, the order in which the allomorphs emerge in the children's language, reflects the frequency of the allomorphs in the parental input, and in addition also the children's frequency of usage reflects the frequency distribution found in their parents' language.

In the final section we compared the frequency of diminutives in CDS and ADS. We showed that the frequency of diminutives is significantly higher in CDS than in ADS. As to the distribution of allomorphs in CDS, we found that it does not differ from adult speech for lemmas, but shows significant differences for tokens, which may point to a simplification strategy in CDS.

Notes

1. This research was funded by the Research Foundation of Flanders, the Royal Academy of Dutch Language and Literature and a legacy to the University of Antwerp, Belgium.

2. The phonological base form of the allomorph is /tjə/; in actual pronunciation the cluster /tj/ is palatalized, which will be transcribed as [c]. This follows the trend in, at least, Italian, German, and English that diminutives involve " palatal vowels or palatalisation of vowels and consonants" (Dressler & Barberesi, 1994)

3. For more and alternative views on the diminutive morpheme and its allomorphs: Oostendorp (in prep); van der Hulst 1984; Gussenhoven & Jacobs 1998; Van de Weijer 2002; Huber 2004.

4. This description is based on Booij (1995), De Haas & Trommelen (1993), Booij & Van Santen (1995).

5. Note that in this environment a phonological rule inserts /ə/ between the liquid and the nasal, and thus this case is actually covered by the first clause: schwa plus /m/.

6. The ANS (Algemene Nederlandse Spraakkunst) is a standard Dutch grammar book, which is generally accepted as the descriptive reference grammar of Dutch.

7. We consider hypocoristics to be endearing and affectionate terms that refer to persons. In this sense, hypocoristics are a subset of diminutives.

8. This characteristic distinguishes them from other forms of adjective-to-noun conversion such as *gek - de gek - het gekje* ('crazy' - 'lunatic' - 'lunatic-DIM').

9. The data of the two triplets are also made available through CHILDES (MacWhinney 2000) and lemmatized, part-of-speech tagged, and morphologically coded in the same way as the data of Abel, Laura, and Matthijs.

10. Since it is the median that is shown in figure 3, the first and last months of the recordings of Laura as well as the first month of Matthijs is not shown in the chart.

11. Since the allomorph /i/ is not as phonologically restricted as the other allomorphs (lemmas that may occur with /jə/, /pjə/, or /kjə/, can also get /i/, for more information see section 1) we left this allomorph out of this analysis. The same holds for the low frequent allomorphs /kə/, /əkə/, and /skə/.

References

Bakema, P. 1998. *Het Verkleinwoord Verklaard.* PhD, KULeuven, Leuven.

Booij, G. 1995. *Phonology of Dutch.* Oxford: Clarendon Press.

Booij, G., and van Santen, A. 1995. *Morfologie: De Woordstructuur van het Nederlands.* Amsterdam: Amsterdam University Press.

Ceccherini, M., Bonifacio, S., and Zocconi, E. 1997. Acquisition of Diminutives in Italian. In *Studies in Pre- and Protomorphology*, W. U. Dressler (ed.), 157–164. Wien: Österreichischen Akademie der Wissenschaften.

Clyne, M.G. 1992. *Pluricentric Languages: Differing Norms in Different Nations*. Berlin: Mouton de Gruyter.

De Haas, W. and Trommelen, M. 1993. *Morfologisch Handboek van het Nederlands: Een Overzicht van de Woordvorming*. Den Haag: SDU Uitgeverij.

Den Os, E., and Harder, R. 1987. De Verwerving van de Regels voor Meervouds- en Verkleinwoordsvorming in het Nederlands. *De Nieuwe Taalgids* 80: 240–250.

Dressler, W., Gillis, S., Bertl, J., Korecky-Kröll, K., Laaha, S., Basbøll, H., and Rehfeldt Kofod, K. 2006. Core Morphology and its Acquisition: Plural Formation in Dutch, German and Danish. *Paper read at 12th International Morphology Meeting*, May 25–28, Budapest.

Dressler, W.U. and Merlini Barbaresi, L. 1994. *Morphopragmatics*. Berlin: Mouton de Gruyter.

Gillis, S. 1997. The Acquisition of Diminutives in Dutch. In *Studies in Pre- and Protomorphology*, W. U. Dressler (ed.), 165–179. Wien: Österreichischen Akademie der Wissenschaften.

Gussenhoven, C. and Jacobs, H. 1998. *Understanding Phonology*. London: Arnold.

Haeseryn, W., Romijn, K., Geerts, G., De Rooij, J. and Van den Toorn, M. 1997. *Algemene Nederlandse Spraakkunst*. Groningen/Deurne: Martinus Nijhoff/Wolters Plantyn.

Hinskens. F. 2001. Hypocoristische Vormen en Reductievormen in het Hedendaagse Nederlands. *Neerlandica Extra Muros* 39.3: 37–49.

Huber, D. 2004. Some notes about the Dutch diminutive suffix. *Leiden Papers in Linguistics* 2.4: 23–49.

Hulst, H. van der. 1984. *Syllable Structure and Stress in Dutch*. Dordrecht: Foris.

Kooij, J. and Van Oostendorp, M. 2003. *Fonologie: Uitnodiging tot de Klankleer van het Nederlands*. Amsterdam: Amsterdam University Press.

Kilani-Schoch, M. and Dressler, W.U. 2002. Emergence of inflectional paradigms in two French corpora: An illustration of general problems of pre- and protomorphology. In *Pre- and Protomorphology: Early Phases of Morphological Development in Nouns and Verbs*. M. D. Voeikova & W. U. Dressler (eds), 45–59. Munich: Lincom.

Laaha, S., Ravid, D., Korecky-Kröll, K., Laaha, G. and Dressler, W.U. 2006. Early noun plurals in German: regularity, production or default? *Journal of Child Language* 33.2: 271–302.

MacWhinney, B. 2000. *The* CHILDES *Project: Tools for Analyzing Talk*. Mahwah: Lawrence Erlbaum.

Snow, C.E., Smith, N.S. and Hoefnagel-Hohle, M. 1979. The Acquisition of Some Dutch Morphological Rules. *Journal of Child Language* 7: 539–553.

Stephany, U. 1997. Diminutives in Early Child Greek: A Preliminary Investigation. In *Studies in Pre- and Protomorphology*, W. U. Dressler (ed.), 145–156. Wien: Österreichischen Akademie der Wissenschaften.

Trommelen, M. 1983. *The Syllable in Dutch: With Special Reference to Diminutive Formation*. Dordrecht: Foris.

Van de Weijer, J. 2002. An Optimality Theoretical Analysis of the Dutch Diminutive. In *Linguistics in the Netherlands*. H. Broekhuis and P. Fikkert (eds), 199–209. Amsterdam/Philadelphia: Benjamins.

Van Oostendorp, M. in preparation. *Dutch Diminutives and the Question Mark*. Manuscript available from the Meertens Insituut, Amsterdam.

CHAPTER 8

Diminutives and Hypocoristics[1] in Austrian German (AG)[2]

Katharina Korecky-Kröll and Wolfgang U. Dressler

This paper intends to show how diminutives emerge in the corpus of two children who acquire a language which has productive diminutive formation, but where diminutives play a minor role due to low frequency; they do not serve as triggers or facilitators in the acquisition of German noun morphology. In addition, we will look into input-dependent inter-individual variation.

1. German adult language

We distinguish SG (common Standard German), ASG (Austrian Standard German), ACG (Austrian colloquial German = "Umgangssprache"), ADG (Austrian dialectal German of the Vienna region). A further category is Austrian German child-directed speech (CDS), whose characteristic use of diminutives and hypocoristics occurs also in pet-directed and lover-directed speech. The description is based on Dressler and Merlini Barbaresi (1994). It is, however, very reduced and simplified, because small children appear to have acquired very little of the adult Austrian German repertoire, both in morphotactics and (particularly) in morphosemantics and morphopragmatics.

German has neither augmentative nor pejorative affixes but there is a productive category of diminutives formed via a variety of productive[3] (but also unproductive) suffixes in German (cf. Dressler & Merlini Barbaresi 1994: 103–110):

DIM1 = *-i*	productive, especially for hypocoristics, for diminutives rather restricted to CDS
DIM2 = *-erl*	productive in ACG and ADG
DIM3 = *-chen*	productive, most frequent diminutive in Northern Standard German
DIM4 = *-lein*	productive, but less frequent, rather used in Southern literary German and ASG
DIM5 = *-ilein*	productive, rare, CDS, ACG, ADG
DIM6 = *-ili*	productive, rare, CDS, ACD, ADG
DIM7 = *-li*	productive, rare, CDS, ACD, ADG
DIM8 = *-l*	unproductive

Thus from *Weib* 'wife, woman', the following diminutives may be derived: *Weib-chen, Weib-lein, Weib-l, Weib-erl, Weib-i, Weib-i-li, Weib-i-lein.*

In hypocoristics, derived from names (especially first names), *-i* is the preferred suffix, whereas in Austria *-chen* is only literary. Moreover many conceivable derivations are blocked or simply do not exist, grammatical productivity is questionable. Thus from *Anna* 'Ann' we have (from most to least used): *Ann-i, Ann-erl, Ann-i-li, Ann-i-lein, Anna-lein*; only literary *Änn-chen*; **Ann-l*, **Ann-lein* are phonologically blocked. Hypocoristic diminutives of *Papa* 'dad' are: *Pap-i, Pap-i-lein, Pap-i-li*; *?Papa-lein, *Pap(a)-l, ?Päp-chen.*

All diminutive suffixes change the gender of the base into neuter gender, whereas gender is constant in hypocoristics and in hypocoristic diminutives of CDS, e. g.: *der Vater* 'father'→ *das Väter-chen/lein, Vater-l* vs. *der Vat-i(-li)* vs. *das Vat-i-lein.* Such CDS hypocoristics show typical truncation of final *-er*, which other diminutives do not share, and lack of umlaut (umlaut is normally triggered by *-chen* and *-lein*), cf. *Wasser* 'water' → *Wässer-chen/lein* vs. ACG, ADG *Wasser-l*, CDS *Wass-i.* Otherwise only word-final, unstressed *-e* and *-en* are truncated before all diminutive and hypocoristic suffixes, e. g. die *Katze* 'cat' → *das Kätz-chen* vs. ACG, ADG *Katz-erl*, CDS *Katz-i*; *der Klumpen* 'clot, lump' → *das Klümp-chen* vs. ACG, ADG *Klump-erl.* After word-final *-(e)l*, the suffixes *-l-* and *l-* suffixes are normally excluded, whereas word-final *-el* is truncated before ACG, ADG *-erl* and CDS *-i*, e. g. *der Vogel* 'bird' → *das Vögel-chen* vs. *das Vog-erl, Vog-i (exception: Vögelein* with fusion of word-final and suffix initial [l]).

As these examples show, the suffixes *-chen/-lein* trigger umlaut of the stressed stem vowel *-a/o/u/au-* to *-ä/ö/ü/äu-*. After final unstressed *-er*, the suffix *-erl* is haplologically replaced by *-l*, thus *die Mutter* → *das Mütter-chen/-lein, Mutter-l* (cf. *Wasser-l* above), *die Mutt-i.* Both processes reduce morphotactic transparency of diminutives.

Diminutive formation is productive only with nouns, the rare derivations from adjectives and numbers become nouns, e. g. ACG *g(e)scheit* 'clever' → *das Gscheit-erl* 'person that thinks to be always more clever than others', *zehn* 'ten' → ACG *das Zehn-erl* '(small) 10 Groschen piece'. In CDS, however, the word class of the base may be preserved, e. g. adj. *gscheit-i gscheit-i* 'clever clever', verbs *lieben* 'to love', *sitzen* 'to sit' → *lieb-el-n, sitz-erl-n, sitz-i*, interrogative *warum* 'why?' → *warump-erl denn?*, note also colloquial greetings, such as *hallo!* 'hello' → *hallo-chen.*[4]

Nearly all the few declension types of diminutives are productive, the respective plurals are zero for *-chen/-lein*, *-s* for *-i/-li*, slightly productive *-n* for *-erl/-l*: *das Häus-chen, Haus-erl, Haus-i*; *die Häus-chen, Haus-erl-n, Haus-i-s.*

The meaning of diminutives is primarily pragmatic, expressing a non-serious evaluation by the speaker, expressing playfulness, emotionality, sympathy, empathy, intimacy, and mitigation or simply referring to child-centered speech situations. The semantic meaning is "small" (much more in Dressler & Merlini Barbaresi 1994: 116–393, cf. 2001).

A calculation of the CELEX[5] frequencies shows the low type and token frequency of diminutives in German adult (non-child-directed) language.

Table 1. Diminutive frequency in CELEX

Diminutive types (no overt case marking)	210	Diminutive tokens (no overt case marking)	2776
Diminutive types (with overt case marking)	29	Diminutive tokens (with overt case marking)	123
Total of diminutive types	239	Total of diminutive tokens	2899
Noun types	34216	Noun tokens	1048212
% Diminutive types in respect to noun types	0,6985%	% Diminutive tokens in respect to noun tokens	0,277%

Table 1 indicates that only 0,7% of all noun types are diminutives, and even only 0,28% of all noun tokens are diminutives (including lexicalised diminutives, cf. § 7). One must add that the CELEX database is a sample of mainly Standard (Northern) German written and spoken language and does not exactly reflect the use of diminutives in Austrian Colloquial German (especially if one compares the different diminutive classes), which has the reputation of using diminutives much more often than Northern varieties (cf. Dressler & Merlini Barbaresi 1994: 103, 409). As we will see later on, diminutive frequencies in Austrian CDS are subject to considerable inter-individual differences.

2. The acquisition data

Our diminutive acquisition data are based on the longitudinal study of the Austrian boy Jan (aged 1;3 – 2;8; overview see table) and of the Austrian girl Katharina (aged 1;6 – 3;0).[6] Jan is an early talker, whereas Katharina is rather late. Most patterns of her noun morphology system emerge about 5 months later than Jan's. Nevertheless, she uses more diminutives than he does.

In the overview of table 2, imitations[7] are indicated separately from spontaneously produced diminutives; hypocoristics of proper nouns like *Pauli* and hypocoristic diminutives like *Mami* 'mummy', *Omi* 'granny' are included, but lexicalized diminutives like *Mädchen* ('girl') are not (cf. § 7).

During the total recording time of 1995 minutes, Jan produces only 28 different diminutive types and 184 tokens (including imitations). His spontaneously produced diminutives are limited to 24 different diminutive types and 167 tokens (the total of types in the table is calculated over all months). The relatively high token frequency in respect to the very low type frequency is due to the presence of 100 tokens of Jan's elder brother's nickname *Pauli*, a hypocoristic form of *Paul*. Without *Pauli*, there would be only 84 (including imitations) or 70 (spontaneous) diminutive tokens.

Table 2. Spontaneous and imitated diminutives in Jan's and Katharina's data

	Jan							Katharina				
Age	number of sessions	Total minutes	DIM types		DIM tokens		DIM types		DIM tokens		number of sessions	Total minutes
			Spont	Imi	Spont	Imi	Spont	Imi	Spont	Imi		
1;3	1	45	–	–	–	–						
1;4	1	30	–	–	–	–						
1;5	1	30	–	1	–	2						
1;6	1	30	1	–	1	–	–	–	0	–	2	36
1;7	1	30	–	–	–	–	–	–		–	–	–
1;8	4	240	4	1	13	1	–	–	0	–	1	33
1;9	4	240	6	2	28	3	–	–	0	–	1	20
1;10	3	180	6	–	14	–	–	–		–	1	28
1;11	4	240	3	–	10	–	1	–	1	–	3	56
2;0	4	240	5	2	12	2	4	1	32	1	4	77
2;1	3	90	4	3	46	4	3	–	19	–	3	33
2;2	3	90	3	3	8	5	3	–	19	–	2	32
2;3	3	90	4	–	8	–	7	1	85	3	3	92
2;4	3	90	1	–	7	–	9	–	40	–	2	60
2;5	3	90	4	–	9	–	5	–	26	–	2	60
2;6	3	90	1	–	2	–	5	–	58	–	3	90
2;7	3	90	4	–	4	–						
2;8	2	60	1	–	5	–	8	–	42	–	2	60
2;9							6	–	21	–	2	60
2;10							13	–	23	–	1	38
2;11							5	–	8	–	1	29
3;0							3	–	3	–	1	30
Total		1995	24	4	167	17	30	2	377	4		834

Katharina's diminutives emerge later (1;11) than Jan's (1;5 for the imitations; 1;6 for spontaneous productions) but increase more (from 2;0 onwards), especially for the tokens (377 in less than half of the recording time). But the number of noun lemmas, which take a diminutive ending, is about the same (Jan: 21, Katharina 24); i. e. Katharina's diminutives are less diverse in relation to the relatively high token frequency.

The following analysis is based on Jan's and Katharina's spontaneously produced diminutives: as there are relatively few diminutives, it is necessary to relate them to another measure, i. e. to the occurrence of nouns. In Jan's data, there is a top value of 6,67% of types at the age of 1;6 (i. e. in absolute numbers 1 diminutive type out of 15 noun types). Otherwise, the percentage never exceeds 6%. Katharina starts later but then uses more diminutives (8,38% for the types and even 28,16% for the tokens), whereas Jan's rate is 2,98% for the types and 2,84% for the tokens. Katharina's high token frequency is especially due to the hypocoristic diminutive *Mam-i* 'mummy' which she uses very frequently.

Table 3. Diminutives and nouns in Jan's and Katharina's spontaneous utterances and in the corresponding input

	Jan								*Katharina*							
Age	DIM typ	N typ	DIM typ (%)	Input typ (%)	DIM tok	N tok	DIM tok (%)	Input tok (%)	DIM typ	N typ	DIM typ (%)	Input typ (%)	DIM tok	N tok	DIM tok (%)	Input tok (%)
1;3	0	7	0	5,74	0	20	0	4,36								
1;4	0	12	0	4,41	0	50	0	2,18								
1;5	0	15	0	3,17	0	42	0	1,05								
1;6	1	15	6,67	1,85	1	76	1,32	1,78	0	1	0	14,29	0	1	0	20,69
1;7	0	18	0	1,41	0	36	0	0,91								
1;8	4	128	3,13	2,78	13	610	2,13	3,03	0	0		33,33	0	0		36,36
1;9	6	136	4,41	5,30	28	573	4,89	4,97	0	1	0	25,00	0	1	0	30,77
1;10	6	141	4,26	4,24	14	544	2,57	3,14				11,76				20,00
1;11	3	165	1,82	3,98	10	683	1,46	3,67	1	8	12,50	11,32	1	42	2,38	22,13
2;0	5	260	1,92	3,89	12	1150	1,04	1,88	4	20	20,00	13,68	32	93	34,41	25,22
2;1	4	122	3,28	2,66	46	421	10,93	4,65	3	32	9,38	9,20	19	87	21,84	13,59
2;2	3	104	2,88	2,19	8	384	2,08	1,66	3	17	17,65	6,98	19	62	30,65	10,11
2;3	4	114	3,51	2,50	8	274	2,92	3,32	7	64	10,94	7,21	85	197	43,15	25,65
2;4	1	109	0,92	2,39	7	243	2,88	3,43	9	57	15,79	9,66	40	122	32,79	15,28
2;5	4	105	3,81	1,36	9	263	3,42	1,91	5	40	12,50	8,33	26	81	32,10	20,46
2;6	1	102	0,98	4,41	2	236	0,85	2,75	5	63	7,94	8,99	58	165	35,15	19,06
2;7	4	71	5,63	3,54	4	115	3,48	3,67								
2;8	1	85	1,18	4,88	5	156	3,21	8,39	8	65	12,31	9,66	42	141	29,79	14,91
2;9									6	47	12,77	9,79	21	80	26,25	17,79
2;10									13	74	17,57	7,07	23	114	20,18	11,76
2;11									5	58	8,62	5,48	8	83	9,64	11,34
3;0									3	57	5,26	9,80	3	70	4,29	12,12
	24	806	2,98	4,02	167	5876	2,84	3,28	30	358	8,38	7,45	377	1339	28,16	19,00

These results correspond to the input frequencies to some extent: the diminutive rate of Katharina's mother is 7,45% for the types and 19,00% for the tokens, whereas Jan's mother uses less diminutive types (4,02%) and tokens (3,28%). Jan has a slightly lower token frequency (2,84%) than his mother, whereas Katharina has a much higher token frequency (28,16%) than her mother (19%), i. e. she extends the usage of an already frequent pattern of the input, and, as we will see in § 3, just of the productive child-specific *-i* DIM. Jan and his mother have a higher diminutive rate than the CELEX database for Standard German (0,7% types, 0,28% tokens)[8], but compared with other morphological patterns (e. g. compounding) is nevertheless low.

It is difficult to describe development of diminutives only based on these quantitative measures because diminutive usage depends very much on the context, note the great variations between Jan's adjacent months 2;1 (an outlier) and 2;2, and Katharina's months 2;10 and 2;11. Therefore, we have to look more closely on the emergence and distributions of the different diminutive classes as well as on qualitative aspects of diminutive acquisition such as semantics and pragmatics.

3. Distribution of the different diminutive classes

Which are the preferred diminutive classes in Austrian German child language? In the following table, Jan's and Katharina's spontaneous diminutives are arranged into diminutive classes. There is a preference for the productive ACG *-i* and *-erl* and ASG *-chen* diminutives. *-i* diminutives are especially frequent in both children because of hypocoristics ending in *-i*. Katharina has an even stronger preference for *-i* diminutives than Jan, whose diminutives are spread into more classes. The other occurring diminutives (*-lein* and *-li*) are extremely rare, and the classes 5, 6 and 8 are not found at all in the children's data.

The input shows a similar distribution, i.e., Jan and Katharina prefer the same diminutive classes as their mothers, but they do not use their mothers' rarest diminutive formations (Jan: classes 5, 6, and of 7 just one token; Katharina: classes 5, 6, 7, 8). Also note that the missing classes 5, 6 represent the only combinations of diminutive suffixes, another symptom of little productivity of most diminutives in the children's speech. Interestingly, Jan does not produce any form of the unproductive *-l* formation (DIM8), although his mother produced more tokens of it than of the productive *-lein* formation (DIM4), which Jan reproduces. Thus productivity seems to be more important than input frequency. Katharina's input lacks classes 7 and 8; otherwise the two inputs are comparable in distribution (but not in overall frequency, which is much higher in Katharina's input). Katharina's strong use of hypocoristic *-i* diminutives is motivated by the input, but she uses *-i* diminutives even more than her mother.

Katharina's mother generally has a more child-centered speech than Jan's mother: she frequently calls herself *Mami* (when talking about herself in the third person singular): e. g.

(1) (a) *Soll die Mami abdrehen?*
'Shall Mummy turn (the light) off?'
(b) *Die Mami tuts immer da hinein.*
'Mummy always puts it in there.'

Table 4. Emergence and frequency of diminutive classes in Jan's and Katharina's data

DIM class	Age of emergence JAN	JAN DIM types [% of noun types]	JAN DIM tokens [% of noun tokens]	Age of emergence KAT	KAT DIM types [% of noun types]	KAT DIM tokens [% of noun tokens]
DIM1 = -i	1;6: *Sessi* 'chair'-dim	8* [0,99%]	123** [2,09%]	1;11: *Vati* 'daddy'	21 [5,87%]	363*** [27,11%]
DIM2 = -erl	1;8: *Eiswagerl* 'ice cream car'-dim	9 [1,12%]	24 [0,41%]	2;4: *Vogerl* 'bird'-dim	4 [1,12%]	8 [0,60%]
DIM3 = -chen	[Imitation 1;5: *Hündse (=Hündchen)* 'doggie'] 1;8: *Mäulchen* 'mouth'-dim	4 [0,50%]	16 [0,27%]	2;5: *Lätzchen* 'bib'-dim	2 [0,56%]	2 [0,15%]
DIM4 = -lein	2;3: *Mäuslein* (pl.) 'mice'-dim	2 [0,25%]	3 [0,05%]	2;3: *Bäum(l)e(i)n*? 2;10: **Vogelein* 3;0: *Vögelein* 'bird'-dim	3 [0,84%]	4 (3 not completely correct) [0,30%]
DIM5 = -ilein	–	0	0	–	0	0
DIM6 = -ili	–	0	0	–	0	0
DIM7 = -li	2;1: *Ohrli* 'ear'-dim	1 [0,12%]	1 [0,02%]	–	0	0
DIM8 = -l		0	0	–	0	0

* including *Pauli* (without *Pauli* and genitive *Paulis*: 6 types)
** including 97 tokens of *Pauli* and genitive *Paulis* (without *Pauli* and *Paulis*: 30 tokens)
*** including 167 tokens of *Mami*, 56 tokens of *Moni*, 23 tokens of *Juli* (sisters' names)

Jan's mother never uses the diminutive *Mami* at all, and she rarely talks about herself in the third person singular. Katharina's mother also tends to use diminutives for toys and animals, whereas Jan's mother prefers diminutives for the child's body parts (which are less frequent). Furthermore, Katharina's mother calls all family members very often with *-i* diminutives (*Kathi, Moni, Juli, Papi*), which is the case in Jan's input only for *Pauli* and the very rare *Omi* 'granny'. Jan and his mother often talk about different sorts of vehicles. Diminutive formation of members of this semantic group is unusual, rare or even non-existing. This is not the case for Katharina who talks more about toys and people with her mother. But even in comparable situations, use of diminutives is higher in Katharina and her input.

Table 5. Input frequency of diminutive classes

Diminutive formation	**JAN input types [% of noun types]**	**JAN input tokens [% of noun tokens]**	**KAT input types [% of noun types]**	**KAT input tokens [% of noun tokens]**
DIM1 = -i	14* [0,74]	300** [2,14]	17 [2,50]	587*** [16,42]
DIM2 = -erl	25 [1,32]	64 [0,47]	19 [2,80]	26 [0,73]
DIM3 = -chen	25 [1,27]	57 [0,41]	16 [2,36]	46 [1,29]
DIM4 = -lein	2 [0,11]	4 [0,03]	9 [1,33]	10 [0,28]
DIM5 = -ilein	2 [0,11]	3 [0,02]	2 [0,29]	2 [0,06]
DIM6 = -ili	1 [0,05]	1 [0,01]	3 [0,44]	7 [0,20]
DIM7 = -li	2 [0,11]	4 [0,03]	0 [0,00]	0 [0,00]
DIM8 = -l	5 [0,26]	11 [0,08]	0 [0,00]	0 [0,00]

* including *Pauli* (without *Pauli* and genitive *Paulis*: 12 types)

** including *Pauli*, without *Pauli* and *Paulis*: 79 tokens

*** including *Kathi* (409 tokens), *Juli* (21 tokens) and *Moni* (36 tokens); without these and a few other hypocoristics, there are only 114 diminutive tokens of common nouns.

4. Frequency ranking of diminutives

The following table shows all spontaneously produced diminutive types in Jan's data with their token frequency and also with the token frequency of the corresponding simplex. Most lemmas are simplex-centered, but there are some exceptions with a more frequent diminutive: *Pauli, Mäulchen, Eiswagerl, Kofferwagerl, Zwergerl.*

Katharina's diminutive-centered lemmas are *Mami, Moni, Juli, Kathi, Schnulli, Jessi, Mausi, Kacki, Vogerl, Zopfspangis, Kugerl, Vögelein, Mutti, Vati, Lätzchen.* 8 of them are never used in their simplex form, in contrast to Jan who has only 4 diminutives without corresponding simplex. Differences between the children are also reflected in the tables 8 and 9 when the children's form oppositions are examined more in detail.

Table 6. Token frequency ranking of Jan's diminutives

	Diminutive	Dim. class	Dim. token freq.	Simplex	Simpl. token freq.	English translation/ explanation of diminutive
1	Pauli (incl. genitive Paulis)	1	97	Paul	11	Paul (Jan's elder brother, neighbour boy, boys in books)
2	Mami	1	15	Mama	120	mummy
3	Mäulchen	3	10	Maul	–	little mouth (of small animal, humorous also of small child)
4	Eiswagerl	2	8	Eiswagen	1	the ice-cream-man's little car
5	Kofferwagerl	2	7	Kofferwagen	–	little baggage car (used by employees of railway stations)
6	Bauchi Baucherl	1 2	4	Bauch	29	tummy
7	Popschi	1	3	Popsch/ Popo	1	botty
7	Vögelchen	3	3	Vogel	13	little bird
7	Mäuslein (incl. pl. Mäus-lein)	4	3	Maus	8	little mouse
8	Handi	1	2	Hand	29	little hand
8	Schüsserl	2	2	Schüssel	4	little bowl
8	Schwimmflügerl (sg. or pl.)	2	2	Schwimm-flügel	3	water wing(s)
8	Omi	1	2	Oma	7	(Jan's paternal) granny
8	Kätzchen (sg.)	3	2	Katze	42	little cat
8	Tropferl (incl. pl. Tropferln)	2	2	Tropfen	–	little drop
9	Ohrli	7	1	Ohr	3	little ear
9	Sessi	1	1	Sessel	24	little chair
9	Häschen (pl.)	3	1	Hasen (pl.)	1	bunnies
9	Würferln (=pl.)	2	1	Würfel (sg.)	5	little cube
9	Zwergerl	2	1	Zwerg	–	dwarf

Table 7. Token frequency ranking of Katharina's diminutives

	Diminutive	Dim class	Dim token frequency	Simplex	Simplex token frequency	English translation/explanation of diminutive
1	Mami	1	167	Mama	96	mummy
2	Moni	1	56	Monika	11	Monika (Katharina's sister)
3	Juli	1	54	Julia	23	Julia (Katharina's sister)
4	Kathi	1	28	Katharina	–	Katharina
5	Schnulli/Lulli	1	17	Schnuller	–	pacifier (baby talk)
6	Papi	1	9	Papa	9	daddy
7	Puppi	1	8	Puppe	9	little doll
8	Jessi	1	4	Jessica	–	Jessica
8	Mausi	1	4	Maus	1	little mouse
9	Ka(c)ki	1	3	Kaka	–	excrement (baby talk)
9	Luli	1	3	Lulu	9	urine (baby talk)
9	Vogerl	2	3	Vogel	2	little bird
9	Zopfspangis (Pl. ?)	1	3	Zopfspangen	–	little clips
10	Opi	1	2	Opa	4	granddaddy
10	Bäume(lei)n	4	2	Baum	8	little tree
10	Kinderwagerl	2	2	Kinderwagen	2	little baby carriage
10	Kugerl	2	2	Kugel	1	little ball, pellet, sphere
10	Vögelein (incl. 1 *Vogelein)	4	2	Vogel	2	little bird
10	Hundi	1	2	Hund	11	doggie
11	Mutti	1	1	Mutter	–	mummy
11	Vati	1	1	Vater	–	daddy
11	Blumi	1	1	Blume	5	little flower
11	Häuschen	3	1	Haus	14	little house
11	Körberl	2	1	Korb	1	little basket
11	Lätzchen	3	1	Latz	–	bib

5. Time course

5.1 Jan

If we put aside single examples without contrasting simplex forms, then we can identify *-i* and *-erl* diminutives (DIM1, DIM2) as Jan's earliest forms, which after their emergence (1;6 and 1;8 respectively, s. table 4 in § 3) recur nearly every month. Neither of the two suffixes provokes opacifying vowel umlaut.

Umlaut-provoking *-chen* forms (DIM3) first occur only in a single lemma (*Mäulchen* since 1;8), always without contrasting simplex (*Maul* 'mouth'), the second lemma to emerge is *Kätz-chen* 'cat-DIM' (at 2;2), then at 2;5 *Häs-chen* 'bunny' and *Vögel-chen* 'bird-DIM'. Equally umlaut-provoking *-lein* (DIM4) appears only in a single lemma *Mäus-lein* and only at 2;3.

These distributions in time do not allow a safe conclusion that morphotactic opacity slows down emergence of diminutives, because there exists an alternative explanation: the later emerging diminutive suffixes belong to the literary standard, the earlier emerging ones to Austrian colloquial German (*-erl*) or prototypically to CDS (*-i*). Note that the mother used the opacifying *-chen* suffix as often as the transparent *-erl* suffix (see table 6). Somehow Jan may have noticed a stylistic difference between uses of both suffixes and thus have preferred the colloquial *-erl* suffix, similar to the prototypically CDS *-i* suffix.

5.2 Katharina

Katharina also starts with CDS DIM1 *(-i)* at 1;11, which remains her favorite diminutive during the total recording time. At 2;3, there is a first potential DIM4 *(-lein)* *Bäume(lei)n* 'tree-DIM' (which is rather pronounced as a dative plural but interpreted as a diminutive by the mother), and only at 2;4 the productive and transparent DIM2 *Vogerl* 'bird-DIM' emerges. At 2;5, she produces the umlaut diminutive DIM3 *Lätzchen* 'bib' correctly. But Katharina has more problems in using the opaque umlaut diminutive DIM4 properly: **Vogelein* <-- *Vögelein* (once at 2;10).

6. Form oppositions and mini-paradigms

6.1 Jan's form oppositions

Form oppositions of the same lemma within the same month are good indicators for the acquisition of morphology (cf. Kilani-Schoch & Dressler 2002). The following table shows the emergence of first form oppositions in Jan's data.

Table 8. Form oppositions in Jan's diminutives

Age	Lemma = Simplex	DIM	Simplex-PL	DIM-PL
1;6	Sessel (1 token)	Sessi (1 token)		
1;9	Bauch (3)	Bauchi (2)		
1;9	Paul (3)	Pauli (18)		
1;10	Schüssel (2)	Schüsserl (3)		
2;0	Hand (7)	Handi (2)	Hände (5)	
2;0	Mama (4)	Mami (3)		
2;2	Katze (11)	Kätzchen (2)		
2;3			Mäuse (7)	Mäuslein (1)
2;5			Hasen (1)	Häschen (1)
2;5	Vogel (3)	Vögelchen (3)		
2;5			Mäuse (2), Mäusen* (3)	Mäuslein (2)

The first apparent contrast at 1;6 *Sessel* – *Sessi* 'chair' seems to be rather an example of phonological variation than of morphological opposition. At 1;9 Jan makes a clear phonological difference between *Bauch* and *Bauchi* 'tummy', but it is used in the same context. The variant *Bauch-erl* is produced much later (2;0). With *Paul* and *Pauli*, the situation is different, there seems to be a first contrastive use (see § 8). The context is equally different with *Schüssel* and *Schüsserl* 'bowl' at the age of 1;10 because they are two different bowls (one which is used as a toy, and one which is used as a dish),

At 2;0, there is even a 3-member mini-paradigm: *Hand* – *Handi* – *Hände* (simplex-pl.). The context is not always contrastive: The diminutive is always used in playful situations and denotes Jan's own hand, like *hallo Handi!* 'hello hand-DIM' or *guguck Handi!* 'look-look, hand-DIM', but the simplex may also be used in such playful situations as well as in other situations. The plural *Hände* is used in all plural contexts. There seems to be no contrastive use at all between *Mama* and *Mami* 'mummy', but at the age of 2;0 and especially at 2;1, Jan likes to use the diminutive (2;0: 4 tokens of *Mama*, 3 tokens of *Mami*; 2;1: 12 tokens of *Mami*, 1 token of *Mama*). This is interesting because nobody else calls mother *Mami*. This confirms that Jan has discovered diminutive formation and uses it in a productive way. *Katze* and *Kätzchen* 'cat' are used in contrastive contexts, as well as *Mäuse* and *Mäuslein* 'mice' (see § 8), but not *Hasen* – *Häschen* 'bunnies' and *Vogel* – *Vögelchen* 'bird'. The second 3-member mini-paradigm does not really count because it is only due to the wrong plural nominative *Mäusen*.

The analysis shows that despite the small percentage of diminutives there is relatively many form oppositions, which point to a productive use of diminutives.

6.2 Katharina's form oppositions

Despite the higher number of diminutives, Katharina has less form oppositions than Jan. Of course, the data-base is also smaller, but the fact that 4 of her 7 form oppositions (Jan: 2 of 11) concern hypocoristics and hypocoristic diminutives (maybe also *Puppi* in reference to her doll) and that all but one concern class 1 allow the conclusion that she only uses child-specific i-diminutives productively and in compensation, similar to inflectional imperialism (cf. Slobin 1985: 1216), more frequently than her mother and much more frequently than Jan (cf. § 4).

Table 9. Form oppositions in Katharina's diminutives

Age	Lemma = Simplex	DIM
2;0	Mama (8)	Mami (12)
2;2	Puppe (3) 'doll'	Puppi (2)
2;3	Papa (1)	Papi (4)
2;3	Julia (5)	Juli (9)
2;3	Monika (3)	Moni (10)
2;4	Lulu (1) 'urine'	Luli (3)
2;4	Vogel (1) 'bird'	Vogerl (1)

Plurals are not formed from hypocoristics or mass nouns, nor does Katharina produce plurals of *doll* and *bird*, and in general she produces less plurals than Jan, a property of a late developer. Thus her frequent use of diminutives, an intermediate category between prototypical inflection and prototypical derivation like plural formation (cf. Dressler 1989, Dressler & Karpf 1995), is all the more remarkable.

6.3 Form oppositions in the input

Table 10 shows that recording time is about the same (90 vs. 92 minutes) in this month in each corpus, therefore input data are comparable in quantity. Nevertheless there are twice as many diminutive tokens in Katharina's input (47 vs. 23 in Jan's input). But there is slightly more variation in Jan's input concerning filling of slots in form oppositions (different plural forms, once different case forms). In Katharina's input data, there are only simplex – diminutive oppositions, much more with hypocoristics than in Jan's input (due to the girl's conversation about persons, dolls and animals vs. the boy's conversation about cars), but in the case of *Katharina* – DIM1 *Kathi*, DIM6 *Kathili*, DIM3 *Katharinchen*, there is a variety of different diminutives.

Table 10. Form oppositions in the input (only child's age month 2;3)

JAN input SIMPL SG types (tokens)	JAN input DIM SG types (tokens)	JAN input SIMPL PL types (tokens)	JAN input DIM PL types (tokens)	JAN input other case	KAT input SIMPL SG types (tokens)	KAT input DIM SG types (tokens)
Stück 'piece' (2)	Stücki (2)				Mama (4)	Mami (18)
		Kuschelmäuse (1)	Kuschel-mäuschen (2)		Papa (5)	Papi (1)
Maus (2) 'mouse'	Mäuschen (1)	Mäuse (3)	Mäuslein (3)		Baum (1) 'tree'	Bäumelein (1)
		Ringe (4) 'rings'	Ringerln (2)	Ringen (1 dat-pl)	Haus (1) 'house'	Häuschen (1)
Paul (13)	Pauli (4)				Schnuller (1) 'pacifier'	Schnulli (17)
					Katharina (6)	Kathi (106), Kathili (1) Katharinchen (1)
					Julia (39)	Juli (2)
					Monika (9)	Moni (5)

7. Semantic groups of diminutives

Diminutives can be classified according to different semantic groups – most diminutives in Jan's and Katharina's speech fit into one of the following classes:

1. Hypocoristic diminutives: *Mami, Papi, Pauli, Juli, Moni, Jessi, Opi* 'granddad', *Omi* 'granny'
2. Toys: *Schnulli* 'pacifier', *Puppi* 'doll', *Schwimmflügerl* 'water wings', *Schüsserl* 'bowl', *Häuschen* 'house', *Kugerl* 'ball, sphere'
3. Body parts (only Jan): *Ohrli* 'ear', *Bauchi* 'tummy', *Popschi* 'botty', *Handi* 'hand'
4. Body functions (only Katharina): *Kacki* 'excrement', *Luli* 'urine'
5. Animals: *Vogerl, Vögelchen, Vögelein* 'bird', *Kätzchen* 'cat', *Hundi* 'dog', *Häschen* 'hare, rabbit', *Mausi, Mäuslein* 'mouse'
6. Vehicles: *Kofferwagerl* 'baggage car', *Eiswagerl* 'ice-cream car', *Kinderwagerl* 'baby carriage'

In both children's input, the same classes are important. The only significant difference to the children's output is that both mothers use more different hypocoristic forms when addressing their children, e. g. *Schatzi* 'darling', *Mausi* 'little mouse', *Bärli* 'little bear'. The children do not use such forms to address their mothers.

Diminutives can also be classified according to the degree of lexicalization. There are quite a lot of lexicalized diminutives in German: in the CELEX database, 20% of all diminutive types and even 61,3% of all diminutive tokens are lexicalized diminutives, which is another symptom of the rather low importance of productive diminutive formation.

There are cases where a diminutive suffix can be identified even within a completely lexicalized diminutive. Thus, *Maid* 'maid', the diachronic simplex base of *Mädchen* 'girl' is obsolete (and the derivational relation morphosemantically and morphotactically opaque). However, *Mädchen* has the synonyms *Mäd-erl, Mäd-(e)l* and in child/pet/lover-directed speech *Mäd-i*, alternations that are only possible with diminutive suffixes. This variation allows a diminutive interpretation of *-chen, -erl, -l, -i*. Thus these synonyms may be identified as acephalous diminutives, i. e. diminutives without an existing but only an abstract simplex base (cf. Malkiel 1970: 7).

This specific variation does not occur in our corpora, but in the following dialogue (2;0) Katharina substitutes her mother's *Zuck-erl* 'candy' (lexicalized diminutive of *Zucker* 'sugar') with more child-centered *Zuck-i*:

(2) *MUT: *ein zuckerl!*
%eng: a candy-DIM2.
*MUT: *was isn [: ist denn] das?*
%eng: what is this?
*KAT: *gucki@ [: zucki].*
%eng: candy-DIM1.
*MUT: *ein zucki?*
%eng: a candy-DIM1?
*KAT: *ja!*
%mor: CO:ass|ja!
%eng: yes
*MUT: *ein zuckerl!*
%eng: a candy-DIM2.

Alternations of the type *Zuck-erl/Zuck-i*, similar to *Mädchen*, are boundary cases between suffixes and pseudo-suffixes in adult language. If a child substitutes one variant with another, this is a stronger sign of diminutive-suffix awareness than in cases of replacement of clear diminutive suffixes.

8. Evidence for diminutive acquisition

8.1 Semantic and pragmatic evidence for diminutive acquisition in Jan's data

Despite the little number of diminutives in Jan's data, we argue that he starts to understand the concept of diminutives from about 1;9 onwards, which also supports our findings concerning the beginning of his protomorphological phase[9]. The first evidence is a backformation at the age of 1;9.23:

(3) *JAN: *muesli!*
%eng: muesli, cereals (lexicalized diminutive).
*MUT: *heast Jan du hast vorher semm(e)l gegess(e)n.*
%eng: come on, Jan, you ate a breadroll before.
*MUT: *wir ham [: haben] schon eine vormittagsjause xx.*
%eng: we have already xx a morning snack.
*JAN: *muesli!*
%eng: muesli, cereals.
*MUT: *du hast doch eine semm(e)l gegess(e)n!*
%eng: but you have eaten a breadroll.
*JAN: *ich will mues*!*
%eng: I want mues (= back-formation)!

In this situation, Jan is hungry and wants to eat his cereals. The mother says that he has already eaten enough and does not want to give him what he wants. As the time of asking in a friendly way (which is an adequate context for diminutives) is over in Jan's eyes, he vehemently demands now his *mues*, a simplex which does not exist. That shows that he has identified at least one pragmatic aspect of diminutive formation, i. e. the adequacy of its use in non-conflictual rather than conflictual speech situations.

One week later, another aspect of diminutive formation (i. e. the basic meaning of smallness) shows up in the following discussion with his mother:

(4) *MUT: *ja da [: der] Jan is(t) ein kleiner bub.*
%eng: yes (the) Jan is a little boy.
*MUT: *und die Evodie is(t) ein kleines maedchen.*
%eng: and (the) Evodie is a little girl.
*MUT: *und da [: der] Pauli is(t) ein grosser bub.*
%eng: and (the) Paul-DIM is a big boy.
*JAN: *Paul.*
*MUT: mhm.
*JAN: *Pauli.*
%eng: Paul-DIM1.
*MUT: *da [: der] Pauli is(t) ein grosser bub.*
%eng: (the) Paul-DIM1 is a big boy.

*MUT: *Pauli oder Paul.*
%eng: Paul-DIM or Paul.
*MUT: *kamma [: kann man] beides sag(e)n.*
%eng: you can say both.

As the mother says that his brother Pauli (the hypocoristic form) is a big boy, Jan seems to wonder about the contrast between the hypocoristic and the adjective *big* and corrects the mother by using the simplex form *Paul*. This is interesting because *Paul* has never been used in the recordings before for his brother's name but only very seldom for another boy's name in a book. Of course, Jan may have heard someone call his brother *Paul* as well, but in the family this is absolutely unusual. The mother agrees that Jan calls his brother *Paul*, but Jan offers a hypocoristic variant, as if he wants to elicit an explanation, but the only explanation he gets is that the simplex and the hypocoristic can both be used. He uses the simplex *Paul* immediately afterwards, which points to a possible semantic interpretation of the diminutive suffix, which runs counter a general assumption of the late emergence of the semantic meaning "small" of diminutives (cf. Dressler & Merlini Barbaresi 2001).

These examples show that even at the age of 1;9, Jan seems to have identified at least some aspects of diminutive formation despite the rareness of diminutive types. Maybe this has to do with the fact that he is often confronted with the hypocoristic of his brother's name and sometimes also with the base form *Paul*. This is the only diminutive or hypocoristic with high token frequency in input and output. Thus it may have served for him as a sort of trigger.

2;2.13:
(5) (a) *JAN: *mmh [/] mmh liebes kaetzchen.*
%eng: mmh mmh dear cat-DIM3.
(b) *JAN: *achtung bissige katze!*
%eng: attention vicious cat! (= be aware of the cat!)

At 2;2, this is a clearly contrastive example. Jan uses the diminutive for the cat when it is nice, but the simplex when it is vicious. Also recall (§ 6.1) that *Hand-i*, in contrast to the simplex *Hand* 'hand', is only used in playful situations, which fits to the pragmatics of prototypically child-centered *-i* diminutives.

2;3.16:
(6) *MUT: *maeuschen komm her zu mir!*
%eng: mouse-DIM3 come here to me!
*MUT: *meine kleinen kusch(e)lmaeuse.*
%eng: my little cuddly mice (= Jan and his brother).
*JAN: *hoppaladipoppaladi sag(e)n die maeuslein.*
%eng: oops say the mice-DIM4.

In this example, Jan uses another diminutive form of *Maus* than his mother which is also an evidence for productive use.

2;5.13:
Further evidence appears in:

(7)	*MUT:	*is(t) da ein baby maus?*
	%eng:	is there a baby mouse?
	*JAN:	*ja.*
	%eng:	yes.
	*MUT:	*oh das is(t) noch ziemlich klein.*
	%eng:	oh this is still rather small.
	*JAN:	*ja.*
	%eng:	yes.
	*JAN:	*baby ist noch ziemlich klein.*
	%eng:	baby is still rather small.
	*JAN:	*hab(e)n da auch eine maeuslein xx zweite maeuslein.*
	%eng:	(we/they) have there also a mouse-DIM4, second mouse-DIM4.

Mother and Jan both stress that the mouse baby is small, so it is appropriate to use the diminutive.

Jan uses more often the adjectives *klein* and *groß* 'small and big' (44 and 65 tokens) than Katharina (2 tokens for each), but apart from the examples cited above, there is no further clear opposition between use of *klein* + DIM diminutive vs. *groß* + simplex use. Never does he use *groß* with a diminutive. But he uses the adjective *klein* where others might use diminutives (e. g. *kleines Haus* 'small house' instead of *Häuschen, kleine Katze* instead of *Kätzchen* or *Katzerl*).

In contrast to productive diminutives of adult language, Jan did not produce any diminutive of the unproductive class 8 (*-l* suffix), although it is well represented in the input.

There are no overgeneralizations or analogies in Jan's data. The umlaut, which is frequent in diminutive class 3, is always correctly produced. There are just a few examples of missing or false gender shift, but since Jan's use of articles is always rather arbitrary before the age of 2;6 (see also Korecky-Kröll & Dressler, in prep.), we should not pay too much attention to these examples:

2;1:

(8)	*JAN:	*hat eine* maeulchen.*
	%eng:	has a(fem.) mouth-DIM3.
	%com:	a little rabbit in a book.

In this example, Jan uses a feminine article instead of the neuter *ein* which would be correct both for the simplex *Maul* as well as for the diminutive *Mäulchen*.

2;5:

(9) *JAN: *hab(e)n da auch eine* maeuslein xx zweite maeuslein.*
%eng: (they) have there also a (fem.) mouse-DIM4 xx second mouse-DIM4.

This is an example of missing gender shift. The simplex *Maus* is feminine, and Jan uses the feminine article also for the diminutive which requires neuter gender. Similarly, he does not shift from the masculine simplex to the neuter diminutive in:

(10) *JAN: und der # stein fresst* den* voeg(e)len@ [: voegelchen].
%eng: and the # stone eats (verb overgeneralization) the (masculine) bird-DIM.
JAN: # Heidi hat den voeg(e)lchen lieb.
%eng: Heidi loves the (masculine) bird-DIM.
The masculine accusative article *den* fits *Vogel*, but not *das Vögelchen.*

8.2 Semantic and pragmatic evidence for diminutive acquisition in Katharina's data

From 2;0 onwards, Katharina has a slight preference for using *Mama* instead of *Mami* in situations when either herself or the mother has just used a negation or contradiction which pragmatically shows lack of sympathy or empathy (but mostly, there are no clear oppositions). Of course, there are also several situations where the diminutive *Mami* seems to be used to demonstrate intimacy (e.g. at 2;4 when the mother says that she has a secret that she does not want to show to Katharina; thus Katharina apparently tries to have a look at the secret by flattering her *Mami*, i. e. already a rhetoric use). But as Katharina's default address form is *Mami* and as her pragmatic use of diminutives is less contrastive than e. g. Jan's use of *Müesli* and **Mües*, these cases should not be over-interpreted.

A first possible evidence for the acquisition of the semantic aspect of smallness appears at 2;3, when Katharina talks about a baby who sleeps (under a) *Bäumen** 'tree-?' (which, at first sight, looks like a dative plural but rather seems to be a not properly pronounced diminutive (class 3 or 4) *Bäumchen/Bäumelein.* The mother corrects her by saying *Bäumelein* but Katharina clarifies her utterance by adding *kleiner* Bäumen* 'small-masc.* sg. 'tree-DIM*' in order to be understood. Otherwise she uses the adjectives *klein* and *groß* 'small and big' extremely rarely, so that a connection to diminutive or simplex use or to replacement of diminutives by adjectives cannot be established.

In contrast to Jan, Katharina has a problem with the opaque umlaut diminutive 4: She uses **Vogelein* instead of *Vögelein* 'bird-DIM4' (2;10). She seems to prefer transparent diminutives, thus she produces only 7 umlaut diminutive tokens (1,86% of her diminutive tokens vs. Jan: 19 tokens = 11,38% of his diminutive tokens).

There is also one example of lack of gender shift (from masculine to neuter):

(11) *KAT: *Moni auch einen laetzen@ [: laetzchen].*
%eng: Moni also an-acc-masc* bib-DIM3.

9. Comparison of Jan's and Katharina's diminutives

The Austrian girl Katharina's data are scarcer in general but nevertheless interesting as far as diminutives are concerned: Katharina's mother uses considerably more diminutives (especially CDS diminutives ending in *-i*) than Jan's mother. Katharina's input has a diminutive rate of 7,45% for the types and 19% for the tokens whereas there are only 4,02% of diminutive types and 3,28% of diminutive tokens in Jan's input. Therefore we need not wonder that Katharina also has a higher diminutive rate than Jan (8,38% for the types, 28,16% for the tokens vs. 2,98% and 2,84%, over all months). The difference of diminutive frequency in the input might be due to the fact that parents often use more diminutives when addressing girls than when addressing boys (cf. Berko Gleason at al. 1990) but also simply to inter-individual differences. It is noteworthy that, in terms of both types and tokens, Jan uses even less diminutives than his mother, and analogously Katharina even more than her mother.

Katharina's most frequent diminutive lemma is *Mami* which becomes the standard address form to her mother from 2;0 onwards: before 1;11, Katharina only uses the simplex. Her diminutives are mostly ending in *-i*, the classes 2 and 3 (*-erl*, *-chen*) are underrepresented in comparison to Jan's, and she has no unproductive *-li* diminutive. In Jan's data, the classes 1, 2 and 3 emerge before age 2; in Katharina's data, this is only the case for the *-i* diminutives.

Katharina, who is a late talker in comparison to Jan, also starts later in acquiring diminutives: her first diminutive is the hypocoristic *Vati* 'daddy' which appears at 1;11, whereas Jan already starts at 1;6 with the unclear opposition *Sessel* – *Sessi* 'chair' (followed by other diminutives of class 2 and 3 at 1;8). Katharina's first form oppositions appear at 2;0 (*Mama* – *Mami* 'mummy'). From that time onwards, Katharina has a slight preference to use *Mama* instead of *Mami* in situations lacking sympathy of empathy. A first sign of Katharina's acquisition of the semantic aspect of smallness appears at 2;3 (Jan at 1;9, see section 8). Thus, as evidence for productivity, formal oppositions precede meaning contrasts in both corpora.

Although all plural formations of the diminutives of Jan's corpus are productive and transparent, their very low frequency disfavours any assumption of a role of diminutives in facilitating the acquisition of plural and case (see table 11).

In the input, there is a slight asymmetry between plurals of simplex and diminutive nouns (10,44% vs. 8,33%), but there is a striking asymmetry in Jan: he produces only 2,40% plurals of diminutives, but 9,68% plurals of simplex nouns. The same holds for case: There is no example for an inflectionally marked dative plural of a diminutive. Of course, inflectional dative plural marking is generally reduced to DIM classes 2 (*-erl*) and 8 (*-l*), because the other classes (ending in *-i*, *-chen*, *-lein*) are not marked for dative plural.

Also Katharina's high number of diminutives does not facilitate her acquisition of plural and case: she produces especially many CDS *-i* diminutives (which would take an *s* plural) but only once uses this *-s* plural (*Zopfspangis* 'hair clips'), otherwise she produces the dialectal zero form (*zwei Mausi-0* 'two mouse-DIM'). Moreover her frequently used hypocoristics in *-i* exclude the use of a plural.

Table 11. Relation of plural- and case-marked forms in simplex and diminutive nouns

	JAN			INPUT		
SIMPL-PL-TOK/ SIMPL-N-TOK	456	4709	9,68%	1365	13077	10,44%
DIM-PL-TOK/ DIM-TOK	4	167	2,40%	37	444	8,33%
SIMPL-DAT-PL-TOK/ SIMPL-N-TOK	10	4709	0,21%	86	13077	0,66%
DIM-DAT-PL-TOK/ DIM-TOK	0	167	0,00%	1	444	0,23%

Therefore, in both corpora, diminutive formation does not further plural and case formation, on the contrary, it impedes further inflection, even when productive diminutive formation of the target system and of the actual input is used productively by the child. Plausible reasons for disfavouring inflection of diminutives in the early acquisition phases of these children are 1) the optionality of diminutive use, 2) the lack of high token frequency in the input (clearly for Jan, but not for Katharina), 3) the fact that all diminutive patterns add a syllable to the base of inflection, thereby lengthening the word to be produced, 4) that they add a morpheme before inflection, thereby making morphological composition and decomposition more complex. Note, first, that in German inflection there is just one case where two inflectional suffixes are concatenated: the Dative plural, where the case suffix *-n* follows just two of the plural suffixes (*-e*, *-er*, besides after zero suffixes), and this suffix combination emerges late (cf. Korecky-Kröll & Dressler, in prep.). Second, note, that by the end of the acquisition periods documented in our study (2;8 for Jan, 3;0 for Katharina), no other pattern of derivational morphology is used productively by the two children (in contrast to compounding).

Despite the lower diminutive type and token frequency in Jan's input and output, the boy is faster in acquiring patterns of diminutive formation and use than the girl Katharina. Katharina's use is much more extensive, but also one-sided, i. e. focused on *-i* hypocoristics and diminutives.

10. Conclusion

Due to the small database, these conclusions are very tentative, but they fit results on other languages of the project.

Diminutives are rare in the German Standard language and not that frequent in Austrian German as certain stereotypes would make us believe. Diminutives are not even very frequent in CDS (although there are considerable inter-individual differences between Jan's and Katharina's input), but because of their productivity they are nevertheless acquired relatively early, both with pragmatic and semantic meanings. Early emergence of the suffixes *-i* and *-erl*, later *-chen*, appears to be favoured by productivity (vs. lack of emergence of the unproductive but frequent *-l* suffix), by input frequency (classes 1 – 4 vs. 5 – 7), but not necessarily by morphotactic transparency. The one example of backformation (Jan's *mues*) may be evidence for productivity, the lack of suffix combinations (classes 5 – 7) against.

Diminutives do not facilitate the acquisition of plural and case formation, they even make it more difficult, note the scarcity of plurals and oblique cases (cf. § 9).

Due to the pragmatic use of diminutives in CDS (as evidenced especially in Katharina's input), diminutive formation is also in Austrian German the first pattern of derivational morphology that is acquired, but this does not accelerate acquisition of morphology at large, as in other languages described in this volume.

However, the time of emergence of diminutives (in early protomorphology) and the symptoms of productivity discussed above allow the assumption that the detection of morphology in diminutive formation occurs simultaneously with the detection of morphology in compounds, plural formation and verb inflection (cf. Klampfer & Korecky-Kröll 2002; Dressler, Kilani-Schoch & Klampfer 2003). But the leading role (in emergence and speed of development) is with compound and plural formation, not with diminutive formation.

Whereas there is no clear evidence in adult language for a dual-mechanism model of diminutive formation in the sense of Clahsen (1999), Katharina's development of diminutives may be interpreted in terms of a dichotomy between productive use of a child-specific diminutive rule (*i*-suffixation) and lexical management of the other diminutives. On the other hand, many of these *i* diminutives are also sorts of lexicalized forms (e. g. the hypocoristics and hypocoristic diminutives), so this can only be a tentative conclusion.

The diminutive type and token frequency differences between Jan's and Katharina's input may reflect the phenomenon that parents tend to use more diminutives when talking to girls than when talking to boys. This frequency effect is reflected in the children's output: Katharina uses ten times more diminutive tokens than Jan. But low frequency does not necessarily result in less productive use or late acquisition, as can be seen in Jan's data.

Abbreviations

dial.	dialectal
imi	imitation
sgt.	singulare tantum
spont	spontaneous
tok	tokens
typ	types

Notes

1. The term "diminutive" can be used as a cover term for both diminutives and hypocoristics. But more specifically, hypocoristics are formed from names (e.g. *William → Bill, Billy*), diminutives from common nouns, name-like address forms, such as *daddy*, are in between. This intermediate category will be called hypocoristic diminutives. Nouns are usually given with their definite articles in order to signal gender: Sg. masc. *der*, fem. *die*, neuter *das*.

2. Thanks are due to Sabine Laaha and Maria Arduc (née Sedlak) for their work on Viennese child data, cf. the earlier presentation Dressler & Sedlak (1997).

3. For the concept of productivity see Dressler & Ladányi 2000.

4. A detailed description of nominal and non-nominal *-l* and *-erl* diminutives in the Graz variant of Austrian German see Glauninger (2003), for Vienna Öller (1994).

5. CELEX Lexical Database, Release 2, German Version 2.5, Max Planck Institute for Psycholinguistics, Centre for Lexical Information 1995.

6. These longitudinal studies have been financed by the Austrian Science foundation projects P-10250 and P-13681 SPR. We also thank Sabine Laaha for the morphological coding of the data.

7. Imitations are immediate repetitions of the mother's utterances or of parts of them.

8. The frequencies are not totally comparable: CELEX includes completely lexicalized diminutives (e.g. *Mädchen* 'girl') while the analyses on Jan and his mother do not. Nevertheless, their diminutive frequency is higher, which may be due to properties of both Austrian German and CDS.

9. The beginning of protomorphology can be dated around 1;8 when Jan starts with first simplex–compound and singular-plural oppositions (cf. Klampfer & Korecky-Kröll 2002). Compounds are extremely frequent in German, which makes them a good starting point for morphology.

References

Berko Gleason, J., Perlmann, R. Y., Ely, R. and Evans, D. W. 1990. The baby talk register: Parent's use of diminutives. In *Handbook of Research in Language Development using* CHILDES, J. L. Sokolov and C. E. Snow (eds), 50–76. Hillsdale, NJ: Lawrence Erlbaum Associates.

Clahsen, H. 1999. Lexical entries and rules of language: A multidisciplinary study of German inflection. *Behavioral and Brain Sciences* 22: 991–1060.

Dressler, W.U. 1989. Prototypical Differences between Inflection and Derivation. *Zeitschrift für Phonetik, Sprachwissenschaft und Kommununikationsforschung* 42: 3–10.

Dressler, W.U. and Karpf, A. 1995. The theoretical relevance of pre- and protomorphology in language acquisition. In: *Yearbook of Morphology 1994*, G. Booj and J. van Marle (eds), 99–122. Dordrecht: Kluwer Academic Publishers.

Dressler, W.U., Kilani-Schoch, M., and Klampfer, S. 2003. How does a child detect morphology? Evidence from production. In *Morphological Structure in Language Processing*, R. H. Baayen & R. Schreuder (eds), 391–425. Berlin: Mouton de Gruyter.

Dressler, W.U. and Ladány. M. 2000. Productivity in Word formation (WF): a morphological approach. *Acta Linguistica Hungarica* 47: 103–144.

Dressler, W.U. and Merlini Barbaresi, L. 1994. *Morphopragmatics*. Berlin: Mouton de Gruyter.

Dressler, W.U. and Merlini Barbaresi, L. 2001. Morphopragmatics of diminutives and augmentatives: on the priority of pragmatics over semantics. Diminutives and intensifiers in Italian, German, and other languages. In *Perspectives on Semantics, Pragmatics and Discourse*, I. Kenesei and R. Harnish (eds), 43–58. Amsterdam: Benjamins.

Dressler, W.U. and Sedlak, M. 1997. Diminutives and Hypocoristics in Austrian German (AG). Presentation at the Vienna workshop of the Crosslinguistic Project on Pre- and Protomorphology in Language Acquisition.

Glauninger, Manfred. 2003. Zu Form und Funktion der Deminutive auf -l und -erl im Grazer Deutsch. PhD dissertation, University of Graz.

Kilani-Schoch, M. and Dressler, W.U. 2002. Emergence of inflectional paradigms in two French corpora: An illustration of general problems of pre- and protomorphology. In *Pre- and Protomorphology: Early Phases of Morphological Development in Nouns and Verbs*, M.D. Voeikova and W.U. Dressler (eds), 45–59. Munich: Lincom.

Klampfer, S. and Korecky-Kröll, K. 2002. Nouns and verbs at the transition from pre- to protomorphology: a longitudinal case study on Austrian German. In *Pre- and Protomorphology: Early Phases of Morphological Development in Nouns and Verbs*, M.D. Voeikova and W.U. Dressler (eds), 61–73. Munich: Lincom.

Korecky-Kröll, K. and Dressler, W.U. in prep. The acquisition of number and case in Austrian German nouns. To appear in *Development of Nominal Inflection in First Language Acquisition, a Cross-Linguistic Perspective*, U. Stephany and M.D. Voeikova (eds).

Malkiel, Yakov. 1970. *Patterns of Derivational Affixation in the Cabraniego Dialect of East-Central Asturian*. Berkeley: University of California Press.

Öller, Wilfried. 1994. -l und -erl: Zwei Wiener Diminutive im semantischen und pragmatischen Vergleich. M.A. thesis, University of Vienna.

Slobin, Dan I. 1985. Crosslinguistic evidence for the language-making capacity. In: *The crosslinguistic study of language acquisition: Vol. 2. Theoretical issues*, D.I. Slobin (ed.), 1157–1256. Hillsdale NJ: Lawrence Erlbaum.

CHAPTER 9

Acquisition of diminutives in Hungarian[1]

Péter Bodor and Virág Barcza

The chapter presents a longitudinal study on the acquisition of diminutives in Hungarian from the age of two to three. The analysis shows that the two children in the study followed their own particular paths while acquiring diminutive suffixes. Grammatical productivity did not exert an unequivocal effect on the sequence of acquisition: both children started with unproductive suffixes such as *-u* and *-ó*, with the productive *-kA* and the semi-productive *-i*, whereas the grammatically most productive *-cskA* was produced later. Our analysis indicates that matching relevant functions to diminutive suffixes is probably a later development: diminutive suffixes did not convey the semantic meaning of "smallness"; a positive emotional evaluation as a pragmatic value of diminutives was not clearly present in the analyzed conversations either.

Introduction

Our primary aim in this chapter is descriptive: we want to describe the patterns of use of diminutives, and its change in time, by two Hungarian monolingual children. Furthermore, a set of more specific research questions will be addressed. What is the order of acquisition of the different suffixes of diminutives in Hungarian? Which diminutives are acquired first: the grammatically productive or non-productive forms? Can we detect in our children's language the semantic value of "smallness" frequently attributed to diminutives, or rather are they used to realize pragmatic information? We will also analyse the question whether acquiring diminutive forms could serve as bootstrapping device, due to the structural fact that they simplify noun suffixation, i.e. make it easier to acquire noun declension.

In our view, at least two main types of questions lie behind all psychological studies pertaining to human development, including linguistic development. The first is: *what are the possible mechanisms of development*? This means to identify the driving forces which make developmental changes occur, and which are responsible for development. The second set of questions is: *how does development proceed?* This means looking for the pattern of changes in the relevant aspect or aspects of conduct. These are the issues of "how to learn" and of "what to learn" (Bodor 2004: 73–74).

There are three main types of answers to the first question, to the question of the possible mechanism of development. Note furthermore, that an answer to this question is also an attempt to give an *explanation of development*. According to the innatist answer, developmental changes can be attributed to the individual's pre-programmed resources, to its biologically given capacities (e.g. Meisel 1995); according to the environmentalist answer, environmental shaping forces are responsible for developmental changes (e.g. Elman 2001); the interactionist view, which we tend to share, though will not argue for in this context, maintains that both the individual's epigenetically continuously changing resources and the environmental context are instrumental in bringing about developmental changes (e.g. Nelson 1996).

The question of how development proceeds can be analyzed in various ways. However, most researchers would endorse the claim that the process of acquisition involves a set of changes in the respective conduct with time. In other terms, while describing the process of development, perhaps all developmental studies are searching for a set of different patterns of conduct in time, and probably most would think that the relevant changes are qualitative ones. Answering this type of question amounts to offering a *description of development*. However, even qualitative changes do not qualify as developmental changes in themselves: nobody would consider regression as development, aphasia as language acquisition. Thus, it can be argued, that the developmentally relevant changes are directed toward some more or less clearly defined end-state, or end-states (Werner & Kaplan 1963; Kaplan 1992). In other terms, in our view, reconstruction of a developmental scenario necessarily involves teleological concerns. According to this view, development is more than mere change in time, it is directed to some target or targets, and consequently, description of development is a teleological enterprise. In this way, the telos of development, either tacitly or openly, must be identified by the researcher. Thus, for example, when the development of intelligence was analysed by Piaget, the target of development was his characterization of adult-like mental operations, what he called formal operations (Piaget 1947/2001). It is also widely known, that on the explanatory level, he used the dialectic triad of accommodation – assimilation – equilibration.

Human language development can be meaningfully analyzed as learning the use of appropriate form-function pairings characteristic of the given language community. In our case the target of development is the way adults use diminutives in Hungarian. Our paper is organized in four main points. First, we will start with a relatively detailed characterization of forms and functions of the respective linguistic devices: we will present the structural characterization of diminutive formation in the Hungarian language, and describe the functional role diminutives play for Hungarians. The grammatical morphemes of diminutives in Hungarian and their semantic and/or pragmatic roles will be discussed. Furthermore, as already Ferguson (1964) supposed, there are certain characteristics of baby talk, including the relative high frequency of diminutives, which may prove to be instrumental in language acquisition. According to a related, though more specific hypothesis, due to a structural fact present in a number of languages, namely that diminutivized nouns shift their classes of noun declension from less transparent to more transparent and/or from less productive to more productive classes, acquisition of diminutives may contribute to the ease of acquisition of noun inflection.[2] In order to prepare our related analysis whether the acquisition of diminutives contributes to the "ease" of acquisition of some noun inflection in Hungarian we will characterize the relevant aspects of the noun declension system of Hungarian as well. Second, we will introduce and characterize in general terms the two databases of our empirical analyses. Third, we will describe two Hungarian children's and their family's diminutive use and compare them. Here we will be oriented by such questions as how the different forms and functions of diminutives emerge. In this section we will also present our findings regarding the effect of diminutivization on the acquisition of noun inflection. Fourth, we will summarize and discuss our findings and their psycholinguistic implications.

1. Description of the adult language

1.1 Diminutive formation in Hungarian

Hungarian is a predominantly agglutinative language and it has a rather uniform manner of marking number and case (there is just one uniform suffix for plural and for each case both in singular and plural). Hungarian has both a productive and unproductive system of diminutive formation, both in terms of suffixation.

Usually in Hungarian grammars there is a differentiation between derivational suffixes used for forming diminutives (*-kA*,[3] *-(V)cskA)* and derivational suffixes used for forming hypocoristics (*-i*), but because in child language and colloquial speech *-i* is used widely and not only for forming hypocoristics, we treat it also as a diminutive suffix. However, there is a difference between *-i* used for deriving hypocoristics and *-i* used for deriving diminutives. Namely the first one is regarded as a productive way of derivation while the latter one is not, although it is spreading, but probably only analogically and not as a result of applying rules (Kiefer & Ladányi 2000; Kiefer 2003).

Table 1 shows the productive and unproductive diminutive suffixes in Hungarian with some examples partly also from our data.[4] Suffix *-i* is listed both among the productive and the unproductive suffixes; perhaps it can be coined as a semi-productive element. Despite the formal sameness, there is an essential difference between DIM3 and DIM4. While the former normally lacks any pragmatic function of typical diminutives and is largely conventionalized, DIM4 shares the pragmatic properties of DIM1 and DIM2.

Table 1. Diminutive suffixes in Hungarian

PRODUCTIVE SUFFIXES	
DIM1 = (V)*cskA*	orro***cska*** < orr 'nose', szeme***cske*** < szem 'eye', napo***cska*** < nap 'sun' vessző***cske*** < vessző 'tick'
DIM2 = ***kA***	malac***ka*** < malac 'pig', egér***ke*** < egér 'mouse'
DIM3 = ***i*** (+ truncation)	Ist***i*** < István, Józs***i*** < József, Kat***i*** < Katalin
UNPRODUCTIVE SUFFIXES	
DIM4 = ***i*** (+ truncation)	sün***i*** < sün 'hedgehog', csok***i*** < csokoládé 'chocolate', hus***i*** < hús 'meat'
DIM5 = ***csi*** (+ truncation)	pul***csi*** < pulóver 'pullover', Jul***csi*** < Júlia
DIM6 = ***ci*** (+ truncation)	na***ci*** < nadrág 'trousers', Mar***ci*** < Márton
DIM7 = ***u*** (+ truncation)	any***u*** < anya 'mother', ap***u*** < apa 'father'
DIM8 = ***us*** (+ truncation)	kuty***us*** < kutya 'dog', pel***us*** < pelenka 'nappy'
DIM9 = ***ó/ő*** (+ truncation)	nyusz***ó*** < nyuszi 'bunny', gaty***ó*** < gatya 'trousers', tes***ó*** < testvér 'sibling'
DIM10 = ***(i)kó***	Pal***kó*** < Pál, ágy***ikó*** < ágy 'bed', ház***ikó*** < ház 'house'
DIM11 = ***si*** (+ truncation)	jog***si*** < jogosítvány 'driving licence', ak***si*** < akkumulátor 'accumulator'

All the productive diminutives are productive just in the case of simplex nouns. However, it is possible to attach diminutive suffixes to adjectives also, but they are rather analogical forms and sometimes they are also lexicalized (*szegény+ke* 'poor', *okos-ka* 'clever', *butá-cska* 'stupid', *csúnyá-cska* 'ugly'). This is the case also with two pronouns (*valami+cske* 'something', *magá+cska* 'formal you') and an adverb (*kettecskén* 'the two of us'). In colloquial speech, recently, it is very common to use diminutivized forms of greetings and modifiers as well (e.g. *helló-ka, köszi-ke* 'thanks', *bocs-i* 'sorry').

The three productive diminutive suffixes are *-(V)cskA*, *-kA* and *-i*. *-(V)cskA* is the most productive diminutive suffix. Its form is *-cskA* when it is added to a word ending in a vowel. The epenthetic vowel used when the word is ending in a consonant can be *-a- (láb+acska* 'leg'*), -o- (kar+ocska* 'arm'*), -e- (szem+ecske* 'eye'*)* and *-ö- (ökr+öcske* 'bull'*)*.

The suffix *-kA* is less productive; its productivity is governed by phonological distribution. Two restrictions can be formulated in connection with suffix *-kA*. It cannot be used when the noun consists of one syllable and ends in a consonant (**lábka* 'leg') or when the noun ends in *-a/-e* (**kecskéke* 'goat') (Ladányi 2004).

In other cases it is possible to attach either *-(V)cskA* or *-kA*. *-(V)cskA* and *-kA* cannot be combined, nor *-i* and *-(V)cskA*. If the *-i* suffix is already attached to the stem, then *-kA* can be attached to it (*sünike*).

Word formation with *-i* is different from the majority of Hungarian derivation types, because *-i* is preceded by truncation. Truncation is a very rare phenomenon in Hungarian morphology, suffixes are attached usually to the complete word, not to a truncated form of it. Truncation appears also in connection with other, unproductive and much less frequent diminutive suffixes such as *-csi*, *-ci,- us* or *-si*.

Forming hypocoristics consists partly in employing the same strategies as in the case of diminutivizing common nouns. The most productive way of forming hypocoristics is attaching *-i* or *-kA* (or *-cskA* in the case of names ending in *-a/-e*) to the names. It is also possible to derive the *i* version first and then diminutivize it again by *-kA*. Hypocoristics can contain other, unproductive suffixes such as *-csi, -ci, -us, -kó*. There are some other, unproductive morphological processes in connection with hypocoristics that do not appear in forming diminutives from common nouns: the last syllable of the name is preserved or a consonant is added to the vowel-initial name, and then these are affixed with *-i*. Thus, from *Éva* and *István* we can form *Évi, Évike, Évácska, Vica, Vicus; Istvánka, Isti, Istike, Pista, Pisti, Pistike, Pistuka.*

Henceforward we will use four groups in the category of diminutives: diminutives derived from common nouns, hypocoristics derived from names, intermediate category (formed from kinship terms, such as *daddy* from *father*) and lexicalized forms (nouns that contain a diminutive suffix, but have no simplex counterpart or their simplex bases do not have the same meaning, for example *cukor* 'sugar', *cukorka* 'candy').

1.2 Declension of diminutives

Declension in Hungarian is less varied for diminutives than for their simplex bases. Diminutives inflect just in three (productive) declension classes, whereas their simplex bases in eight at least. It means that theoretically there is a possibility in Hungarian that diminutives may simplify the acquisition of the declension.

Table 2 shows Hungarian declension classes (Pöchträger, Bodó, Dressler & Schweiger 1998). We divided the classes into a productive and an unproductive group in order to be able to observe that diminutives appear only in productive declension classes. Some of the declension classes of simplex nouns are not listed here because of their rarity.

Diminutives ending in *-i, -u,* and *-ó/-ő* inflect according to class 1, diminutives ending in *-us* do so according to class 2, and diminutives ending in *-a/-e* inflect according to class 4. So it means that nouns belonging originally to an unproductive class are transferred to a productive class when taking any of the diminutive suffixes (for example *ló* 'horse' – Pl. *lov-ak*, Acc. *lov-at*, 1sgPoss. *lov-am*; *lovacska* 'horse-DIM' – Pl. *lovacská-k*, Acc. *lovacská-t*, 1sgPoss. *lovacská-m*).

Inflection is most transparent in class 1. Diminutives derived by *-i, -ci,- csi, -si, -u, -ó* and *-ő* from nouns belonging to another than class 1, inflect more transparently than their bases. Applying *-kA* or *-cskA* does not make the inflection more transparent, because stem-final *-A* lengthens before the majority of suffixes.

Table 3 shows for each combination of class of base and productive diminutive suffix, whether it increases productivity and makes the declension of the diminutive more or less transparent than that of the base. Some of the combinations exist only in theory due to the limited productivity of the suffix *-i* and the fact that names do not inflect in unproductive classes.

Table 2. Declension classes in Hungarian

Number of class	Description of class	Nouns belonging to the class	Pl.	Acc.	1sgPoss.
PRODUCTIVE CLASSES					
Class 1	nouns (and adjectives, etc.) without stem-internal alternation & no epenthesis in Pl., Acc. and possessive	*kicsi* 'small' *kapu* 'gate' *hajó* 'ship'	*kicsi-k* *kapu-k* *hajó-k*	*kicsi-t* *kepu-t* *hajó-t*	*kicsi-m* *kapu-m* *hajó-m*
Class 2	nouns without stem-internal alternation & no epenthesis in Acc., but epenthesis in Pl. and possessive after stem-final consonant	*kakas* 'cock' *ember* 'human being'	*kakas-ok* *ember-ek*	*kakas-t* *ember-t*	*kakas-om* *ember-em*
Class 3	nouns without stem-internal alternation but short mid insertion vowel in Pl., Acc. and possessive	*kalap* 'hat' *kép* 'picture'	*kalap-ok* *kép-ek*	*kalap-ot* *kép-et*	*kalap-om* *kép-em*
Class 4	nouns with stem-internal alternation: stem-final vowel lengthening of nouns ending in *a/e*	*jóga* 'yoga' *csésze* 'cup'	*jógá-k* *csészé-k*	*jógá-t* *csészé-t*	*jógá-m* *csészé-m*
UNPRODUCTIVE CLASSES					
Class 5	nouns without stem-internal alternation so called 'lowering stems': short low insertion vowel in Pl., Acc. and Poss	*ház* 'house'	*ház-ak*	*ház-at*	*ház-am*
Class 6	nouns with stem-internal alternation: vowel epenthesis in Nom. and before any suffixes except for the plural, accusative, superessive, and possessed forms	*bokor* 'bush' *szerelem* 'love'	*bokr-ok* *szerelm-ek*	*bokr-ot* *szerelm-et*	*bokr-om* *szerelm-em*
Class 7	nouns with stem-internal alternation: vowel shortening in a final closed syllable and low epenthetic vowel	*egér* 'mouse' *bogár* 'insect'	*eger-ek* *bogar-ak*	*eger-et* *bogar-at*	*eger-em* *bogar-am*
Class 8	nouns with stem-internal alternation: so called 'v-stems': *v* epenthesis between the stem-final vowel and the suffix-initial vowel with compensatory shortening	*ló* 'horse' *fű* 'grass'	*lov-ak* *füv-ek*	*lov-at* *füv-et*	*lov-am* *füv-em*

As to prosody, diminutive inflection in Hungarian is not necessarily more uniform than that of their simplicia. The majority of Hungarian case suffixes (e.g. Dat. *-nAk*, Iness. *-bAn*) increase the number of the syllables by one, because they constitute a syllable themselves. It means that the base is one syllable shorter than the inflected form both in diminutives and their base nouns (*ló* 'horse' – Dat. *lónak*, Iness. *lóban; lovacska* 'horse-DIM' – Dat. *lovacskának*, Iness. *lovacskában*). Therefore studying prosodic uniformity is more relevant in cases where the suffix consists of only one consonant (e.g. Acc. *-t*, Pl. *-k*) and does not necessarily increase the number of syllables. If a noun ends in a vowel (and does not belong to the class 8), then its inflection is as uniform as the inflection of a diminutive derived from it by *-i, -ci,- csi, -si, -u, -ó* or *-ő*. *-us* makes the inflection less uniform in the case of vowel-final nouns (*kutya* 'dog' – Pl. *kutyák*, Acc.

kutyát; *kutyus* 'dog-DIM' – Pl. *kutyusok*, Acc. *kutyust*). Nouns ending in a consonant, except for class 7, inflect prosodically in a less uniform way than their simplicia (*egér* 'mouse' – Pl. *egerek*, Acc. *egeret; egérke* 'mouse-DIM' – Pl. *egérkék*, Acc. *egérkét*).

It should be noted as well, that stress in Hungarian is always on the first syllable. In Hungarian there are no related categories such as pejoratives and augmentatives, but pejorative meaning can be expressed by diminutive suffixes.

Table 3. Comparing productivity and transparency of diminutives and their bases in the case of applying one of the productive diminutive suffixes (-i, -(cs)kA)

Class of base	Class of dim.		Productivity	Transparency of dim.
1	1	Ildikó > Ildi	same as base	same as base
1	4	kicsi > kicsike	same as base	less transparent
2	1	Gábor > Gabi	same as base	more transparent
2	4	ember > emberke	same as base	lengthening instead of insertion
3	1	Róbert > Robi	same as base	more transparent
3	4	kalap > kalapocska	same as base	lengthening instead of insertion
4	1	Andrea > Andi	same as base	more transparent
4	4	csésze > csészécske	same as base	same as base
5	1	láb > lábi	more productive	more transparent
5	4	ház > házacska	more productive	lengthening instead of insertion
6	1	történelem > töri	more productive	more transparent
6	4	bokor > bokrocska	more productive	lengthening instead of v-deletion
7	1	–	more productive	more transparent
7	4	egér > egérke	more productive	lengthening instead of shortening and insertion
8	1	–	more productive	more transparent
8	4	ló > lovacska	more productive	lengthening instead of *v*-insertion and shortening

1.3 Functional aspects of diminutives

The function of diminutive suffixes is considered usually as semantic and/or pragmatic. Regarding the semantic meaning of the above mentioned diminutive suffixes, only *-kA* and *-cskA* denote primarily smallness, but only in certain contexts (Kiefer 2003, 2004). At the same time they can acquire a pragmatic meaning as well. All the other diminutive suffixes have a purely pragmatic function: according to Dressler and Kiefer (1990) they determine the relationship between the speaker and the listener. We would rather consider diminutives as having an emotional function in the sense that they are used for expressing or realizing the speaker's evaluative relationship to the object/person spoken about (Bodor 1997, 2004). This conceptualization of emotion and emotional language were developed from a social constructionist account of emotions (Averill 1980, Coulter 1979, Sarbin 1989). Like in other languages, the use of diminutives and hypocoristics in Hungarian is typical in speech situations when it is important to express or realize emotions, characteristically in child-directed, lover-directed and pet-directed speech.

Considering the utterance as the unit of analysis, emotive speech-acts may realize this emotional function: linguistically realized emotional displays are performatives and can be coined as emotives. Various linguistic units may serve as device for carrying the illocutionary force of an emotive speech-act. Lexical units, such as emotional terms, for example 'love' or 'hate' can be taken as emotion specifiers, and as such they are constituents of *explicit emotive speech-acts*.[5] At the same time, other devices such as intonation (Bakhtin 1926/1985) or morphopragmatic units such as diminutives (Dressler & Merlini Barbaresi 1994) are devices carrying the action-value of *primary emotive speech-acts*. Under this description most emotion markers, including diminutive suffixes can be considered as emotion modulators as opposed to emotion specifiers (Ochs & Schieffelin 1989). Emotion modulators do not specify a particular emotional judgment in them;[6] rather, they contribute to the general evaluative character of the speaker's talk. Furthermore, usually the interlocutors share this evaluation; the participants presuppose it. In regard to diminutives this presupposed emotional evaluation or affective stance is positive as a default. Pejoratives as morphological units which carry negative evaluation are not present in Hungarian. However, diminutives may carry negative evaluation: when the default evaluation of an event or entity is positive, use of diminutives represents a negative evaluation on behalf of the speaker. For example, a perfectly intelligible common practice among Hungarians is to refer to disliked public figures (such as politicians) by diminutivized surnames, by hypocoristics. Similarly, you can get also a pejorative meaning in the case of nouns denotating professions: *költő – költőcske* ('poet' – 'an unimportant poet'), *elnök – elnököcske* ('president' – 'the president of an unimportant organization').[7]

2. Description of the databases

In order to establish an empirically grounded account of the emergence of diminutive use in Hungarian we analyzed and compared two databases (girl Panna and boy Miki). The formal and functional concerns of our analysis, in other terms, the telos of acquiring diminutives in Hungarian were described in the previous sections of our paper. Here we will describe briefly the empirical material utilized by our analysis, and some general characteristics of our analysis.

The two databases we analyzed according to the CHILDES standards (MacWhinney 2000). The first author collected Panna's data. Miki's data has been collected by Zita Réger and is partly available on the CHILDES database.

Both target children come from a similar background regarding the SES of their family and their parents' level of education. Furthermore, since both databases cover approximately one year (13 and 11 months), it allowed two longitudinal analyses and their comparison. Interestingly, apart from some pioneer cross-sectional studies such as MacWhinney (1974), Pléh, Vinkler and Kálmán (1996), and more recently Babarczy (2006) to our knowledge, there are no real longitudinal studies investigating the acquisition of Hungarian on the basis of transcribed conversations, i.e. studies which try to describe the emergence of one or more linguistic devices in time in one or more child productions.

2.1 Panna's database

Table 4. Description of the PANNA database: Number of recorded sessions and their "size" in number of words – Input, Child

Age of Child	No. of Sessions	Input - No. of Words (Type/Token)	Child - No. of Words (Type/Token)
2;00	2	1104 (543/1104)	185 (84 /185)
2;01	17	10658 (2170/10658)	4321 (645/4321)
2;02	11	7817 (1944/7817)	3592 (612/3592)
2;03	6	4429 (1215/4429)	2193 (440/2193)
2;04	8	5547 (1477/5547)	2585 (517/2585)
2;05	7	3791 (1223/3791)	2241 (519/2241)
2;06	3	2231 (799/2231)	1232 (384/1232)
2;07	2	986 (423/986)	412 (193/412)
2;08	2	1172 (553/1172)	449 (228/449)
2;09	3	1440 (534 /1440)	953 (369/953)
2;10	2	1259 (489/1259)	1086 (336/1086)
Total	63	40434 (6679/40434)	19249 (2786/19249)

Panna was born on 14 December 1992.[8] She comes from a middle class family living in Budapest. Her parents are native speakers of Hungarian. The Panna's database consists of 63 recordings, in which the girl was an active participant talking to her parents and other family members. The majority of these conversations were recorded at home. The recordings were transcribed in CHAT format and cover 11 months from age 2;0 to 3;0. The most important characteristics of the Panna's database are presented in Table 4. The table describes the number of recorded and transcribed sessions, and the number of "words" the target child, Panna, and her other family members produced during the recordings.

2.2 Miki's database

Table 5. Description of the MIKI database: Number of recorded sessions and their "size" in number of words – Input, Child

Age of Child	No. of Sessions	Input - No. of Words (Type/Token)	Child - No. of Words (Type/Token)
1;11	4	6324 (1463 /6324)	1859 (420/1859)
2;00	2	3355 (871/3355)	835 (248/835)
2;01	4	2277 (692/2277)	788 (314/788)
2;02	2	2509 (745/2509)	954 (331/954)
2;03	3	4375 (1078/4375)	1749 (521/1749)
2;04	1	1516 (472/1516)	674 (277/674)
2;05	2	2589 (758/2589)	1857 (593/1857)
2;06	2	3190 (869/3190)	1649 (539/1649)
2;07	2	3003 (932/3003)	1497 (584/1497)
2;08	2	4060 (1110/4060)	1837 (622/1837)
2;09	4	7615 (1834/7615)	3161 (910/3161)
2;10	2	2347 (727/2347)	1147 (402/1147)
2;11	1	1880 (642/1880)	1058 (399/1058)
Total	31	45040 (6483/45040)	19065 (3980/19065)

The principal child in Réger's database is a boy called Miki, born in 1990.[9] He comes from a middle-class family residing in Budapest. Miki's parents are native speakers of Hungarian. The Miki database consists of 31 recordings of Miki's conversations with his parents, his three siblings and other family members and friends. These conversations were recorded in natural settings, usually at home. The recordings were transcribed and are accessible in CHAT format. The transcribed conversations cover 13 months from approximately 2 to 3 years of age. One to four transcribed sessions are available for a month-long period. Some general characteristics of the Miki's database are described in Table 5.

2.3 The applied "data purification"

As in most cases of empirical analysis of language, we applied a "data purification" procedure as well. Items of diminutive forms used in *formulas* such as songs were identified and excluded from the analysis. The issue of *imitation* is an intricate and highly debated problem in language acquisition studies (cf. Ninio & Snow 1996). For our present purposes, we defined imitation on strictly formal bases: a token of diminutive use of Panna or Miki was taken as imitation, if exactly the same form was used by an adult or some other interlocutor in the previous utterance. Thus, if the child modified the morphological characteristics of the word it was not taken as an imitation, as the following example shows[10]:

(1) *MIK: *öldöke* [=? köldöke].
%eng: his (b)elly button:POSS.
*MOM: *pocija?*
%eng: his tummy-DIM:POSS [simplex: *pocak*]?
*MIK: *poci.*
%eng: tummy-DIM.
(1;11)

However, two qualifications were applied to this formal procedure of identifying imitations: First, if the adult already „imitated" the previous utterance of the child, as the following examples attest, they were not taken as imitations on behalf of the child.

(2) *PET: *ki van ott például?*
%eng: who is there, for example?
*PAN: *Sanyi, Panka.*
%eng: Sanyi:DIM, Panka-DIM.
*PET: *Sanyi és Panka?*
%eng: Sanyi-DIM and Panka-DIM?
*PAN: *Sanyi Panka igen.*
%eng: Sanyi-DIM Panka-DIM yes.
(2;4)

Second, when it was clear from the wider previous context that the child already acquired the specific linguistic device, i.e. s/he used it spontaneously, we did not consider it as imitation any more. Applying this procedure, four uses of the targeted forms proved to be imitations in the Panna database and six in Miki's speech. Although there were really few items of imitations, we excluded them from further analysis.

3. Description of the findings on Miki and Panna

3.1 Overall view of the children's use of diminutives in the corpuses

3.1.1 *Panna*

Altogether, Panna used 401 tokens of diminutives, which means that 2,08% of her words were diminutives. These words fell into 80 types in the corpus. It means, that she used two diminutives out of hundred words, and slightly less than three types of diminutives, 2,87 out of hundred types of words.

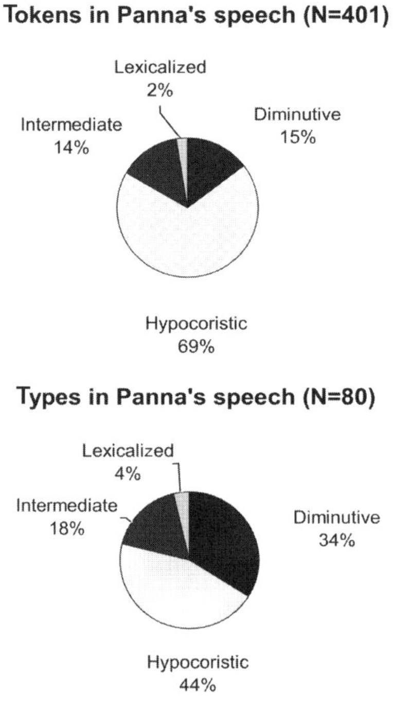

Figure 1. Diminutive types in Panna's data – type and token information

As the charts in Figure 1 show, the majority of her diminutives were hypocoristics, diminutive forms of personal names. The first diminutive in her data is a hypocoristic, her own name *Panni*, which appears at the age of 2;0. Her first real diminutive is *kupi* 'mess-DIM' at the age of 2;1, the first intermediate form is *apu* 'father-DIM' at the same age. The first lexicalized form (*popó* 'bottom-DIM') appears at the age of 2;1 as well.

3.1.2 *Miki*

Miki produced 829 diminutive items, somewhat more than 4 per 100 words (4,34%) during his recorded conversations. These words fall into 189 types, which mean 4,74% of all the types he uttered. Miki had several real diminutives (e.g. *cumika* 'pacifier-DIM', *motorka* 'motor-cycle-DIM', *vödörke* 'bucket-DIM') and hypocoristics (*Borika, Mikici, Levici)* already during the first investigated month (1;11). First intermediate forms from the same age are *anyu* 'mother-DIM', *anyuci* 'mother-DIM-DIM', *apu* 'father-DIM', *apuci* 'father-DIM-DIM' and first lexicalized forms are *apó* 'old man', *hami* 'food', *popó* 'bottom'. The following figures present the distribution of Miki's diminutives according to diminutive types.

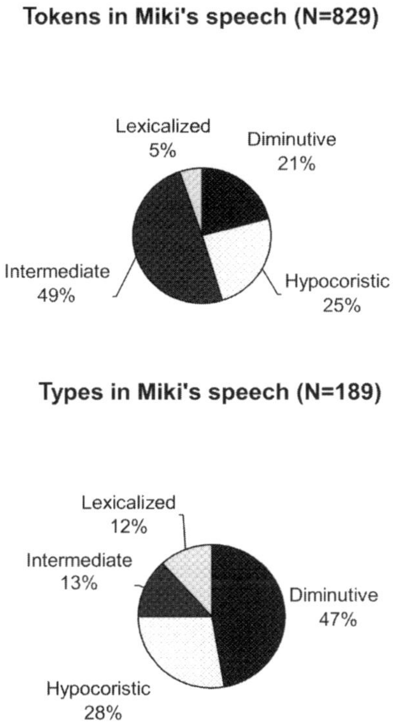

Figure 2. Diminutive types in Miki's data – type and token information

Figure 2 shows that Miki's favourite diminutives were what we called intermediate forms: mainly the respective forms of father and mother. One out of four diminutives he used were personal names, and only somewhat more than 20 percent of his diminutives were of common nouns.

3.1.3 *Comparing Panna's and Miki's use of diminutives*

From the comparison of Figures 1 and 2 it is clear that the number of types and tokens of diminutive use by the two investigated children are markedly different. Although less dramatically, the onset time of diminutive use is different for the two children as well: Miki used all four different types of diminutives roughly two months earlier than Panna did. Miki used approximately twice as many diminutive tokens as Panna did.

The respective numbers for the two morphologically productive endings of diminutive formation, for *-kA* and *-cskA,* are 1,29 per 100 words for Panna; 0,61 per 100 words for Miki; 1,12 per 100 words for all other speakers in the linguistic input of the two corpora. In our two corpora for all speakers this number is 1,07.

Consider that all of these figures are significantly greater than the frequency of "adult use" derived from the Hungarian National Corpus. Table 6 below shows the respective frequency of diminutives formed by *-kA* or *-cskA.*[11]

Table 6. Diminutive frequency in HNC: Hungarian National Corpus

diminutive types	3452	diminutive tokens	53631
noun types	705 377	noun tokens	59 000 000
% diminutive types in respect to noun types	0,489%	% diminutive tokens in respect to noun tokens	0,09%

In this way, the general wisdom that baby talk, or child-directed speech, just like child speech, contains more diminutives than other language use is supported by our data and proved to be valid for Hungarian as well.

What factors are responsible for the patterns of children's use of diminutives we found in our data? Clearly, the frequency of diminutive use depends on a great number of possible factors. Among these one can include structural, competence and social constituents alike. First the linguistic, structural factor can be mentioned in this context: languages are different in the richness of diminutivization, as other papers in the present volume attest. Second, the speaker's competence can influence production data as well. Third, contextually relevant social factors and attributes such as speech situation, the identity of speakers, even gender can influence the frequency of diminutive use. Thus, relatively frequent use of diminutives is considered as a feature of baby talk (Ferguson 1964) or child-directed speech. As we documented above, this is also true for Hungarian. Furthermore, Berko Gleason and her colleagues (1990) found, that girls are exposed to more diminutives than boys, which has been interpreted as socializing girls to be more emotional.

Naturally, structural and typological factors cannot be evoked for interpreting the difference in number of diminutive uses between Miki and Panna, since both speak Hungarian. Difference in competence is certainly playing a role in accounting for their difference in diminutive production: in general Panna was a relatively late talker compared to Miki. Consider moreover that both children's use of diminutives correlates with the frequency of diminutives they were exposed to – as figure 3 shows.[12] This indicates an effect of linguistic input on the production data, and possibly its effect on acquisition.

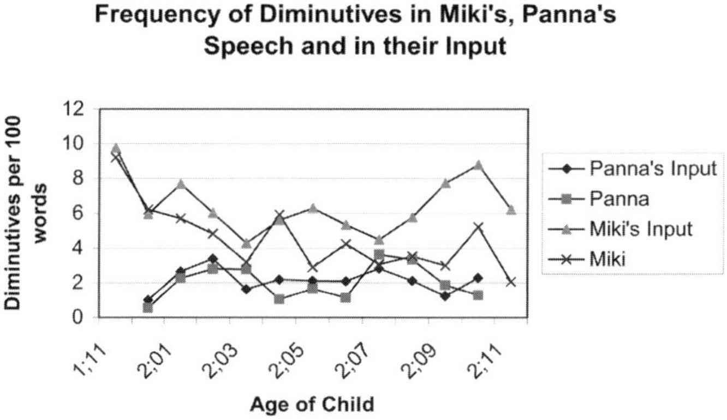

Figure 3. Frequency of diminutives in Miki's and Panna's speech and their input

More specifically, it seems that in our two cases something overwrites the effect of gender factor documented by Berko Gleason and her colleagues, since contrary to the prediction one may draw on the bases of their findings, in our data the boy's parents produced proportionally many more diminutives than the girl's parents. Thus, if we consider also the correlation which can be detected between the input and output, one may propose that something we may coin as "family culture" can be a relevant factor in this respect, i.e. can play a significant role in the amount of diminutives a particular child produces, and consequently, influence his/her acquisition process.

3.2 Distribution of different diminutive classes

In this section we will describe the distribution of different diminutive classes, in other terms, different diminutive suffixes in the two investigated children's speech and in their input.

Table 7 shows that the distribution of different diminutive classes is quite similar in Panna's input and output, apart from diminutive class 1 and the rarer classes DIM10, 8 and 6. The high token frequency in class 2 (in input and output) is due to the hypocoristic formed from Panna's name (*Panka*). According to our data *-cskA*, which is structurally the most productive diminutive suffix in Hungarian, despite its massive presence in the input, was not productive in Panna. The possible reason for the low frequency of diminutive class 1 in the child's speech is the difficult consonant cluster in the suffix -*cskA*. Indeed, for Panna the sequence -*cska* was difficult to pronounce in other contexts as well, thus, instead of *macska* 'cat' she occasionally used a shortened version:

(3) *PAN: *macs* [: macska] *baba xxx ott pici ga ott piszi ba.*
%eng: cat baby xxx there little there little baby.
(2;3)

Table 7. Frequency of diminutive classes in Panna's speech and in her input

Diminutive suffix	Panna (types)	Panna (tokens)	Input (types)	Input (tokens)
DIM1 = (V)cskA	1	1	21	46
DIM2 = kA	11	248	37	441
DIM3,4 = i	22	87	31	170
DIM5 = csi	1	8	1	10
DIM6 = ci	–	–	6	18
DIM7 = u	3	56	5	81
DIM8 = us	1	1	5	159
DIM9 = ó/ő	1	13	8	15
DIM10 = (i)kó	–	–	2	3

Table 8. Frequency of diminutive classes in Miki's data and in his input

Diminutive suffix	Miki (types)	Miki (tokens)	Input (types)	Input (tokens)
DIM1 = (V)cskA	5	24	25	85
DIM2 = kA	30	93	47	389
DIM3,4 = i	27	231	48	1831
DIM5 = csi	2	5	3	5
DIM6 = ci	8	83	10	208
DIM7 = u	2	327	4	407
DIM8 = us	2	17	4	28
DIM9 = ó/ő	2	12	4	27
DIM10 = (i)kó	2	13	3	26

The occurrence of different diminutive formations in the child's speech and the input correlate in Miki's case as well. The exception is the diminutive class 1 again, though the difference between the input and the child's speech is not as striking as in Panna's case. Otherwise Miki produced all the diminutive classes that were used in the input. The diminutive suffix -*ci* is relatively frequent for being unproductive. It seems to be characteristic of the mother's language use that she attaches -*ci* to the names of every family member, although this method is not the conventional way of forming nicknames.

3.3 Evolution of the children's diminutive use in time

Until now we presented solely aggregated data which were created from whole databases. In other terms, development as a gradually enfolding process was not considered. In this section we will describe the pattern of different diminutive suffixes in the speech of Panna and Miki in time.

Mastering different linguistic devices even with the same function may very well be a gradual process. Insofar acquisition of different diminutive suffixes is similar to climbing up a staircase, Panna's mastering of the Hungarian diminutive suffixes can be represented visually as follows.

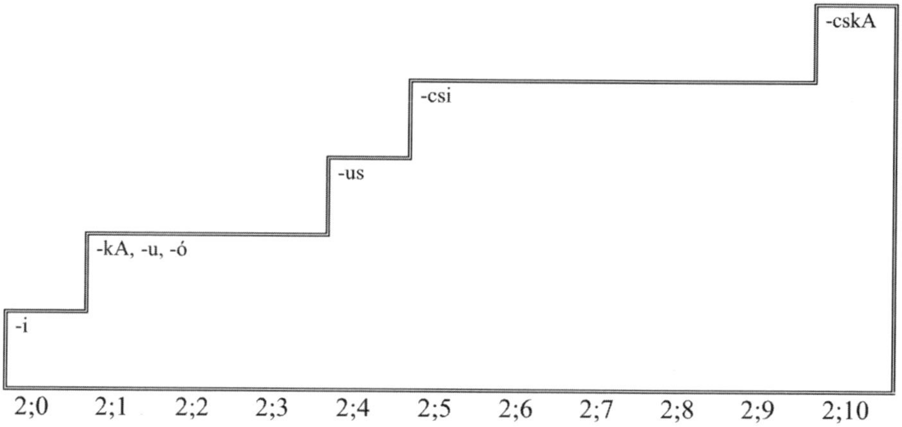

Figure 4. Panna's developmental staircase of diminutives: onset time for each particular suffix

Note, that the figure was compiled from data on onset time only. Further data on Panna's and Miki's use of different types of diminutive suffixes in time are included in Table 11 and 12 of the Appendix. These tables provide information on diminutive types and type/token information as well and qualify the developmental staircase above.

In Panna's speech the first diminutive suffixes occur in hypocoristics or intermediate forms. The first suffix to emerge also in common nouns is *-i* (DIM3, 4). Interestingly, this suffix is considered as being productive only in forming hypocoristics, but not for common nouns (see above under 1.1). *-kA* (DIM2) becomes productive around the age of 2;7–2;8 and *-cskA* (DIM1) appears in Panna's speech only at the end of the investigated period.

Regarding the time course, the situation is different in Miki's data. His developmental staircase is represented in Figure 5.

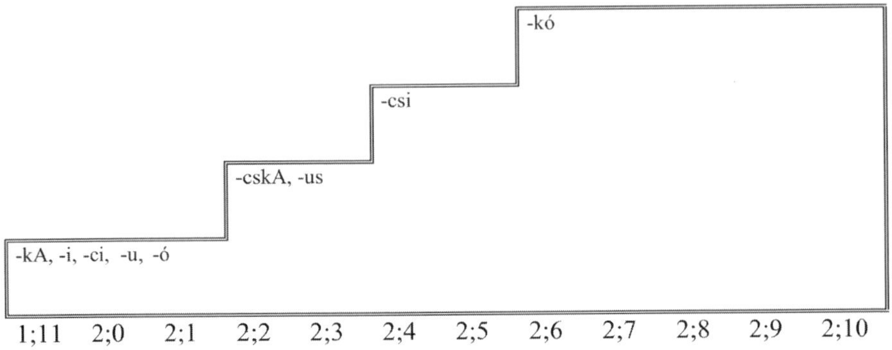

Figure 5. Miki's developmental staircase of diminutives: onset time for each particular suffix

Miki uses three diminutive suffixes (DIM2, DIM3, 4, and DIM6) in at least four different word types already during the first recordings. DIM1 emerges much earlier than in Panna's speech, at the age of 2;2, and subsequently he uses it in many different word types.

Although the two children approached diminutive formation in their own ways, some common features can be detected. Most interesting is perhaps that grammatical productivity did not exert a noticeable effect on their production: both of them started with some unproductive suffixes such as *-u* and *-ó* and with the productive *-kA* and the semi-productive *-i*, whereas the grammatically most productive *-cskA* was produced significantly later.

3.4 Emergence of diminutives and their simplex counterparts

Savickienė et al. (in press) argue that the acquisition of diminutives might simplify the nominal declensional system and thus facilitate its acquisition. Is it possible to detect some facilitating effect of change of noun class due to diminutivization on the acquisition of noun suffixation in our data? Different kinds of predictions follow from this structural possibility.

First, if it can be proved that, compared with a base-line, children prefer to shift to diminutive in case they are more transparent and/or productive than their respective base nouns, then we would prove: a) that children do differentiate between words belonging to productive versus unproductive, and transparent versus opaque declensional paradigms, and b) that children prefer the forms for which noun declension is simpler. This could be a prerequisite of the putative bootstrapping process, and as such it could be a marker of the facilitative effect of diminutivization on acquisition of noun declension. Indeed, an analysis of the data presented on Tables 9 and 10 below and performed by Savickienė et al. (in press) proves that children prefer diminutives as predicted. Thus, similar to the Croatian and Lithuanian data (see in this volume), they showed via a chi-square test that Panna relied significantly more on diminutives when the corresponding base nouns was less productive or less transparent. In our interpretation these results show that children are sensitive to the categories of productivity and transparency, and differentiate between them, quite like naturalist grammar predicts. Nevertheless, note that these figures only indirectly hint to the possible facilitative effect of diminutivization on acquisition by identifying one of its necessary precondition, but do not prove it.

In our view, there is a second, and more direct control of the relevant bootstrapping hypothesis: if some facilitative effect of diminutives on noun declension existed, noun suffixation would appear earlier on diminutivized nouns than on their simplex counterparts. In the remainder of this section we will deal with this possibility.

Table 9 shows the emergence of diminutives and their simplex counterparts with token numbers in Panna's data. First suffixed forms of diminutives and base nouns together with token numbers are included as well.

Panna's data contains 17 diminutive–simplex oppositions. In 8 cases neither the simplex nor the diminutive suffixed form could be detected during the investigated period. The remaining 9 pairs show the following distribution: simplex suffixed forms emerge earlier than diminutive suffixed forms in 5 cases, diminutive suffixed forms emerge earlier than simplex suffixed forms in the case of 3 nouns, and both suffixed forms emerge at the same time in the case of one noun. The age of emergence of suffixed forms is affected by token frequency in the input: in most cases the more frequent counterpart is the earlier one to be inflected.

In Panna's data there are only four nouns that are represented in both the nominative singular and a suffixed form of simplex and diminutive (*apa – apuka, maci –macika, kicsi – kicsike, egér – egérke*), thus, it is difficult to draw reliable conclusions on the effect of productivity and transparency in the time course of acquisition.

The next table (Table 10) shows the emergence of diminutives and their simplex counterparts with token numbers in Miki's data. First suffixed forms of diminutives and simplex base nouns together with token numbers are included as well.

Miki's data contains 37 diminutive–simplex oppositions. In 7 cases neither the simplex nor the diminutive suffixed form emerges during the investigated period. The remaining 30 pairs show the following distribution: simplex suffixed form emerges earlier than the diminutive suffixed form in 18 cases, the diminutive suffixed form emerges earlier than the simplex suffixed form in the case of 7 nouns and both suffixed forms emerge at the same time in the case of 3 nouns. Similarly to the findings on Panna's data, it holds true for Miki's data as well that in most cases the more frequent counterpart is the earlier one to be inflected.

Table 9. Emergence of diminutives and their simplex counterparts in Panna's data

DIM Nom. Sg. form	Age	Decl. class	SIMPL Nom. Sg. form	Age	Decl. class	DIM suffixed forms	Age	SIMPL suffixed forms	Age
Panka (208)	2;1	4	Panna (51)	2;1	4	–		Pannának:DAT (1)	2;9
Panni (3)	2;1	1	Panna (51)	2;1	4	–		–	
apu (14)	2;1	1	apa 'father' (316)	2;0	4	–		apáé:POSS (3)	2;2
Peti (5)	2;1	1	Péter (53)	2;2	2	–		–	
Nagypapi (2)	2;1	1	nagypapa 'grandpa' (5)	2;1	4	–		–	
anyu (12)	2;2	1	anya 'mother' (23)	2;1	4	anyunak: DAT (2)	2;7	–	
Tündi (1)	2;2	1	Tünde (45)	2;1	4	–		–	
Anyuka (10)	2;5	4	anya 'mother' (23)	2;1	4	anyukája: Px (5) (7)	2;8	–	
husi (1)	2;5	1	hús 'meat' (5)	2;1	2	–		–	
apuka (2)	2;6	4	apa 'father' (316)	2;0	4	apukát: ACC (1)	2;6	apáé:POSS (3)	2;2
macika (1)	2;7	4	maci 'teddy-bear' (68)	2;1	1	macikához: ALLAT (1)	2;9	macit:ACC (2)	2;1
Nyuszika (–)		4	nyuszi 'bunny' (14)	2;4	1	nyuszikám:Px (2)	2;8	nyuszit:ACC (2)	2;8
Sanyika (1)	2;8	4	Sanyi (4)	2;1	1	–		–	
kicsike (2)	2;9	4	kicsi 'little' (8)	2;2	1	kicsikét: ACC (2)	2;9	kicsit:ACC (2)	2;6
egérke (3)	2;9	4	egér 'mouse' (2)	2;5	7	egérkék: PL:NOM (5)	2;8	egeret:ACC (1)	2;9
Bodorka (1)	2;9	4	Bodor (21)	2;2	2	–		–	
Napocska (1)	2;10	4	nap 'sun' (10)	2;1	3	–		–	

Table 10. Emergence of diminutives and their simplex counterparts in Miki's data

DIM Nom. Sg. form	Age	Decl. class	SIMPL Nom. Sg. form	Age	Decl. class	DIM suffixed forms	Age	SIMPL suffixed forms	Age
anyu (242)	1;11	1	anya 'mother'(90)	2;1	4	anyut:ACC (4)	2;2	anyának:DAT (1)	2;2
anyuci (32)	1;11	1	anya 'mother'(90)	2;1	4	anyucit:ACC (1)	2;6	anyának:DAT (1)	2;2
Apu (29)	1;11	1	apa 'father' (6)	2;6	4	apuhoz:ALL (5)	2;3	–	
apuci (4)	1;11	1	apa 'father' (6)	2;6	4	–		–	
Mikici (24)	1;11	1	Miki (56)	1;11	1	–		Mikit:ACC (2)	2;2
Linci (6)	1;11	1	Lőrinc (2)	2;2	3	–		–	
cumika (2)	1;11	4	cumi 'pacifier' (18)	1;11	1	cumikát:ACC (1)	2;3	cumit:ACC (5)	2;2
kicsike (1)	1;11	4	kicsi 'small/little' (24)	2;2	1	–		kicsivel:INSTR (2)	2;2
poci (1)	1;11	1	pocak 'tummy' (1)	2;9	3	–		–	
vödörke (1)	1;11	4	vödör 'bucket' (1)	1;11	6	–		–	
Orsici (1)	1;11	1	Orsi (18)	1;11	1	–		Orsival:COM (10)	2;4
motorka (2)	1;11	4	motor 'motorcycle' (12)	1;11	2	–		motorral: INSTR (24)	2;0
macika (3)	2;0	4	maci 'teddy-bear' (26)	1;11	1	macikát:ACC (3)	2;3	macira: SUBLAT (14)	2;2
bilike (1)	2;0	4	bili 'potty' (1)	2;3	1	bilikébe:ILL (1)	2;1	bilibe:ILL (4)	2;2
süti (1)	2;1	1	sütemény 'cake' (1)	2;7	2	sütit:ACC (3)	2;1	–	
hamika (1)	2;1	4	hami 'food' (6)	1;11	1	–		hamit:ACC (5)	2;1
Mókuska (1)	2;1	4	mókus 'squirrel' (2)	2;1	2	–		–	
Lovacska (11)	2;2	4	ló 'horse' (3)	2;7	8	lovacskát:ACC (7)	2;2	lóra:SUBLAT (1)	2;7
anyuka (1)	2;2	4	anya 'mother' (90)	2;1	4	anyukája:Px (13)	2;2	anyának:DAT (1)	2;2
apuka (–)		4	apa 'father' (6)	2;6	4	apukája:Px (4)	2;2	–	
kutyus (6)	2;2	2	kutya 'dog' (6)	2;4	4	kutyust:ACC (1)	2;10	kutyát:ACC (1)	2;2
Napocska (2)	2;2	4	nap 'sun' (1)	2;7	3	–		–	
picike (1)	2;3	4	pici 'small/little' (24)	2;4	1	picikét:ACC (1)	2;3	picit:ACC (12)	2;1

halacska (1)	2;3	4	hal 'fish' (1)	2;4	5	–		halak:PL:NOM (3)	2;2
mozdonyka (1)	2;3	4	mozdony 'locomotive' (1)	2;3	2	–		mozdonyt: ACC (1)	2;3
bábuka (6)	2;3	4	bábu 'piece (in game)' (7)	1;11	1	–		bábuk:PL: NOM (5)	2;3
pulcsika (1)	2;4	4	pulcsi 'pullover' (2)	2;4	1	–		–	
nyuszika (3)	2;5	4	nyuszi 'bunny' (19)	2;5	1	nyuszikát:ACC (1)	2;6	nyuszit:ACC (7)	2;5
Anyucika (2)	2;5	4	anya 'mother' (90)	2;1	4	–		anyának:DAT (1)	2;2
házikó (4)	2;6	1	ház 'house' (3)	1;11	5	házikóban: INESS (8)	2;6	házban:INESS (5)	2;6
ágyikó (1)	2;6	1	ágy 'bed' (7)	2;3	5	ágyikómba: Px:ILL (3)	2;6	ágyra:SUBLAT (6)	2;3
madárka (1)	2;6	4	madár 'bird' (1)	2;6	7	–		madárnak (1)	2;11
Tamáska (1)	2;7	4	Tamás (9)	1;11	2	–		–	
Tomi (2)	2;8	1	Tamás (9)	1;11	2	Tomim:Px (2)	2;8	–	
Tesi (–)		1	testvér 'sibling' (–)		2	tesije:Px (1)	2;8	testvére:Px (1)	2;9
Orsika (1)	2;9	4	Orsi (18)	1;11	1	–		Orsival:COM (10)	2;4
gazdi (3)	2;10	1	gazda 'owner' (1)	2;5	4	gazdinak:DAT (1)	2;10	gazdájuk:Px (1)	2;5

3.5. Formal productivity

In the following we are going to discuss some phenomena that can indicate whether diminutive formation is productive in the two investigated children.

Although in Panna's data there are relatively few diminutives and she forms diminutives only from a small number of base nouns, around the age of 2;8 there are signs of diminutive formation being productive. The example below is a back-formation:

(4) *MOT: *Hát az állatok nem szeretik, ha az emberek fogdossák őket, csak a házi+állatok, mert azok már megszokták szegények.*
%eng: well, animals do not like when people keep touching them, only domestic animals, because they are used to it.
*PAN: *őzikék is.*
%eng: deers-DIM as well.
*MOT: *őzikék se házi+állatok.*
%eng: deers-DIM are not domestic animals either.

*PAN: *Házi+állatok, házi+őzi.*
%eng: domestic animals, domestic deer-DIM.
*MOT: *Házi+őzike nincsen.*
%eng: there is no domestic deer-DIM
(2;8)

Őz 'deer' is not used with only the suffix *-i* in adult language, its normative diminutive form is the double diminutive *őzike.* In the example above Panna deletes one diminutive suffix (*-kA*), thus producing a word that does not exist in adult language. This happens at the same age when other diminutives formed by *-kA* together with their corresponding base nouns appear in her data, so the use of this form might be productive.

It should be mentioned as well, that for Panna it was apparently impossible to produce diminutives formed by *-kA* or *-cskA* earlier. Possibly since words derived by them consist of at least three syllables, by concentrating on the stressed beginning of the word, she had problems with pronouncing words longer than two syllables. Miki, on the other hand, produced three-syllable words already in the first recording.

Miki diminutivizes many different words. This would indicate that his diminutive formation can be productive. Overgeneralization has not appeared in Miki's data, although the diminutive suffix *-ci* was more frequently used during the first recordings than it is usual in everyday speech. However, it can be characteristic of the whole family. It seems that Miki uses this suffix productively:

(5) a. *MOM: *vagy miki?*
%eng: or Miki-DIM?
*MIK: mik*ici.*
%eng: Mikici-DIM-DIM.
(1;11)

b. *MOM: *biztos orsi csönget vagy levi.*
%eng: it must be Orsi-DIM or Levi-DIM who is ringing.
*MIK: le*ici*?
%eng: leici-DIM-DIM.
*MOM: *levici.*
%eng: levici-DIM-DIM.
(1;11)

These examples above show another phenomenon as well, namely the variation between simple and combined hypocoristics, which also proves that diminutive formation is productive in his case.

3.6. Semantic and pragmatic aspects of diminutive acquisition

In contrasting environments both Miki and his mother use collocations of attributive adjectives and noun simplicia. There is no example in the data for using only a diminutive and its simplex counterpart for expressing difference in size.

In Panna's case collocations of the adjectives small/big with nouns are especially interesting, since they occur relatively early in the data (at the age of 2;1).

(6) a. *PAN: *nem pici baba na [=nagy] ba [= baba].*
%eng: (looking at a picture) not a small baby, big baby.
(2;1)

b. *PET: *és evőeszközt adsz a csacsinak?*
%eng: are you giving cutlery to the donkey?
*PAN: *hm pa nan [= nagy] ka [= kanál] pici ka [= kanál], nan [= nagy] ka [= kanál] pici ka [= kanál], nan [= nagy] ka [= kanál] pici ka [= kanál] na [=nagy] ka [= kanál] na [=nagy] ka [= kanál].*
%eng: big spoon small spoon big spoon small spoon big spoon small spoon big spoon big spoon.
(2;1)

Examples like these show that Panna has already captured the semantic meaning of smallness, although the diminutive suffix *-kA* appears in her data months later, around the age of 2;8. At this time she starts to apply *-kA* to different types of words, but her basic strategy for expressing smallness remains the use of collocations. It seems that the meaning of the suffix *-kA* is rather additional, it alone cannot carry the semantic meaning of smallness.

(7) a. *PAN: A nagy+*fiúknak # nad [: nagy] áduk [: ágyuk]* van.
%eng: big boys have big bed.
a few lines below
*PET: és a # *kis+fiúknak* milyen ágya van?
%eng: and small boys, what kind of bed do they have?
*PAN: *Kicsike.*
%eng: small-DIM.
(2;9)

b. *PET: *Menjünk sétálni?*
%eng: shall we go for a walk?
*PAN: *Igen, látogatóba a kis macikához.*
%eng: yes, let us visit the small/little teddy-bear-DIM.
(2;9)

In spite of the small number of diminutives in Panna's data, the example below shows that she has understood one important pragmatic aspect of diminutives. She is expressing her affection for bunnies. Her utterances can be interpreted as a modest request as well.

(8) *PAN: Ott, *szejetném [: szeretném] nusikám [: nyuszikám] lenne*, de szejetném [: szeretném].
%eng: there, I would like if I had a bunny-DIM:POSS, I would like it so much.
*MOT: *De szeretnéd?*
%eng: you would like it so much?
*PAN: *Ananos [: aranyos] nyuszikák*!
%eng: sweet bunnies-DIM!
(2;8)

In Panna's input usually both the semantic and the pragmatic meaning of diminutives are present: they are used because adults are talking to a child and at the same time they denote smallness as well. Diminutives occur in typical lexico-semantic groups in their speech: body parts, toys, animals and food.

It is very difficult to decide whether Miki acquires any semantic or pragmatic meaning of the diminutives during the studied period. We assume that this is due to the fact that his mother is not completely consequent in this aspect either. She often uses the diminutive form immediately after the simple base noun, denoting the same object and without any noticeable pragmatic difference between the two speech events.

(9) *MOM: *hol is van még macika*?
%eng: where were some more teddy-bears-DIM?
*MOM: *Miki, lehet, hogy nincs több maci*?
%eng: Miki, is it possible that there are no more teddy-bears?
(2;5)

This is characteristic also for Miki's use of diminutives:

(10) *MIK: *ho(l) van a # bábu*?
%eng: where is the piece (in a game)?
*MIK: *itt van a bábuka.*
%eng: here the piece-DIM is.
(2;3)

And a bit later during the same recording:

(11) *MIK: *nem bábut* kéjtem [=? kértem].
%eng: I didn't ask for a piece.
*MIK: *ho(l) van a bábuka*?
%eng: where is the piece-DIM?
(2;3)

However, some collocations of the adjective *kis* 'small' and a diminutive occur in Miki's data, around the same time when he starts using the collocations of the adjective small/ big and a simplex noun for expressing difference in size. This indicates that Miki has some sense of the semantic meaning of diminutives.

(12) *MIK: *abba(n) ilyen kis házikó.*
%eng: in that kind of small house-DIM
*MOM: *na és hol lakjon a madár?*
%eng: and where should the bird live?
*MIK: *madár?*
%eng: the bird?
*MIK: a *kis madájka* [=? madárka]?
%eng: the small bird-DIM?
(2;6)

The lexico-semantic groups of toys, food and animals occur relatively frequently as diminutives both in the input and in Miki's speech, the group of body parts and pieces of clothing only in the input.

4. Summary and conclusions

The major and rather descriptive aim of our research has been to describe how often and how early Hungarian children use diminutive forms. Thus, we investigated the occurrence of diminutives in Hungarian children's speech. The two children in the study used markedly different amounts of diminutives during the investigated period: somewhat more than 4 percent of all the words Miki used were diminutives, while Panna used half as many, roughly 2 percent. The productive suffixes (*-kA* and *-cskA*) were much more frequent in our data than the same suffixes in the "adult use" derived from the Hungarian National Corpus. Thus, the general wisdom that child-directed speech and the corresponding child speech contain more diminutives than other language use is supported by our data and seems valid for Hungarian.

Not only the frequency, but also the onset time of diminutive use was also markedly different for the two investigated children. One of them, Miki used all types of diminutives (i.e. hypocoristics, intermediate forms, lexicalized forms and real diminutives as well) from 1;11, from the first recorded sessions onwards. At the same time the other child, Panna started with hypocoristics at 2;0 which was followed by intermediate forms, lexicalized forms and real diminutives somewhat later, at 2;1. From the pattern of onset time for different diminutive endings we can propose the following tentative developmental scenario: The grammatically productive *-kA* and the semi-productive *-i*, are among the first diminutive suffixes acquired by Hungarian children. They are produced at the same time as *-u* and *-ó*, the two earliest unproductive diminutive suffixes. Interestingly, *-cskA*, which is considered as the most productive diminutive suffix, is acquired relatively late, apparently due to phonological difficulty.

Our data on the possible promoting effect of change of noun class due to diminutivization on the acquisition of noun suffixation is not decisive. If there is such an effect, it is not robust enough, at least in Hungarian. Nevertheless, the bootstrapping hypothesis is not falsified by our data. Naturally, diminutivization is not a necessary condition for mastering noun declension. Indeed, according to our data noun declension is frequently performed earlier on simplex than on its diminutivized counterparts.

In Hungarian, as in other languages, there are two major functional characterizations of diminutives: semantic and pragmatic. On the semantic level, diminutives may convey the proposition of "smallness". Our data shows, that both of the investigated children do have the corresponding big-small distinction, though they realize it by adjectives. At the same time, according to our data, Hungarian children between 2 to 3 years of age do not use diminutives for the same purposes, i.e. for expressing "smallness". It is highly possible that the semantic value of "small" for diminutives is secondary, and acquired later than three years of age by Hungarian children.

On the pragmatic level, in our understanding, diminutives serve to realize the speaker's evaluative stance toward the diminutivized entity by a linguistic device. In other terms we consider diminutives as emotives, which are modulating and not specifying the relevant emotional evaluation. This position is based on a social constructionist account on emotions.

In our understanding the primary function of diminutives is that of illocutory devices for positive emotion modulation. We can offer a speculative scenario on the transition from mere pragmatic to the semantic role of diminutive suffixes. Thus, if children are valued positively in a culture, and caretakers are striving for creating positive environment for their children in and through language as well, the relatively high frequency of diminutives in their child-directed speech should not be surprising. Insofar positively valued people, namely our children are small, the property of being kind to us and the property of smallness are co-extensive. What is more, this fact may serve as a bridge to create from the pragmatic value of positive evaluation the meaning of smallness in its neutral sense. Furthermore, at least in our cultures, children are surrounded by a "mini-world" which consisting of toys specifically created for children. This fact also can promote the relevant transition from the function of positive evaluation to the denotation of neutral size.

Be that as it may, the collocations we documented may serve as proper environment for diminutives in gaining the lexical meaning of "smallness". Further research relying on data from older children could certainly clarify these issues.

Some segments of the analysed conversations may very well be interpreted as children's realization of pragmatic function through diminutive use. Nevertheless, our data do not entitle us to claim that children between the ages of 2 to 3 do use diminutives for this purpose. Indeed, in a parallel case study on the lexical level of realizing emotions it was found that the first use of an emotion word with the function of the general marking of "good" versus "bad" characteristics of an event appeared only at age 3. "It seems that only after mastering the good (-bad) evaluation the possible emotional stances are further differentiated... GEN [genuine] use appears somewhat later (3;2.27)" (Bodor 2004: 125). It seems to us, that for some reason, children between the ages of 2 to 3 do not have the pragmatic competence (or perhaps the social right?) to evaluate and mark linguistically by diminutive use the relevant aspects of the situations on their own.

Appendix

Table 11. Panna's use of different types of diminutive suffixes in time

Age of Child	DIM1= cskA	DIM2= kA	DIM3,4= i	DIM5= csi	DIM6= ci	DIM7= u	DIM8= us	DIM9= ó	DIM10= (i)kó
2;0	0	0	+/– (*)	0	0	0	0	0	0
2;1	0	+/– (*)	+	0	0	+/– (*)	0	+/– (*)	0
2;2	0	+/– (*)	+	0	0	+/– (*)	0	0	0
2;3	0	+/– (*)	+	0	0	+/– (*)	0	0	0
2;4	0	+/– (*)	+/–	0	0	+/– (*)	+/–	0	0
2;5	0	+/– (*)	+	+/– (*)	0	+/– (*)	0	+/– (*)	0
2;6	0	+/– (*)	0	0	0	+/– (*)	0	0	0
2;7	0	+/–	+/– (*)	0	0	+/– (*)	0	0	0
2;8	0	+	+	0	0	+/– (*)	0	0	0
2;9	0	+	+/–	0	0	+/– (*)	0	0	0
2;10	+/–	+/–	+/–	0	0	+/– (*)	0	+/– (*)	0

o: no use
+: use
+/–: only one to three types of words are used with the suffix
(*): only hypocoristics and/or intermediate forms are suffixed

Table 12. Miki's use of different types of diminutive suffixes in time

Age of Child	DIM1= cskA	DIM2= kA	DIM3,4= i	DIM5= csi	DIM6= ci	DIM7= u	DIM8= us	DIM9= ó	DIM10= (i)kó
1;11	0	+	+	0	+ (*)	+/– (*)	0	+/–	0
2;0	0	+/–	+/–	0	+ (*)	+/– (*)	0	0	0
2;1	0	+	+	0	+ (*)	+/– (*)	0	0	0
2;2	+/–	+/– (*)	+	0	+ (*)	+/– (*)	+/–	0	0
2;3	+	+	+	0	+ (*)	+/– (*)	0	0	0
2;4	0	+/–	+	+/–	+ (*)	+/– (*)	+/–	+/–	0
2;5	+/–	+	+	0	+ (*)	+/– (*)	+/–	+/–	0
2;6	0	+/–	+	0	+ (*)	+/– (*)	+/–	0	+/–
2;7	0	+/–	+	0	+ (*)	+/– (*)	0	0	+/–
2;8	0	+	+	0	+/–	+/– (*)	+/–	0	+/–
2;9	+/–	+	+	0	0	+/– (*)	+/–	0	0
2;10	+/–	+/–	+	+/– (*)	+/–	+/–	+/–	0	0
2;11	+/–	+/–	+/–	0	0	+/– (*)	+/–	0	+/–

o: no use
+: use
+/–: only one to three types of words are used with the suffix
(*): only hypocoristics and/or intermediate forms are suffixed

List of abbreviations

Acc.	Accusative
Adess.	Adessive
Allat.	Allative
Com.	Comitative
Dat.	Dative
Ill.	Illative
Iness.	Inessive
Instr.	Instrumental
Nom.	Nominative
Pl.	Plural
Px.	Possessive Suffix on the possessed
Poss.	Possessive Marker on the possessor
Sublat.	Sublative

Notes

1. The authors are grateful to Ineta Savickienė and Wolfgang U. Dressler, to the editors of the present volume, for their continuous encouragement and extremely helpful commentaries. We are also thankful for István Kenesei's commentaries, we included them wherever we could. During the preparation of the study financial support was provided to the first author by the Hungarian Széchenyi Scholarship.

2. For a more detailed exposition of such naturalist concepts as transparency see the Introduction of the present volume.

3. *-kA* = *-ka* or *-ke*; *-cskA* = *-cska* or *-cske* according to palatovelar vowel harmony. In Hungarian most suffixes have a palatal and a velar variant form and their use depends on the quality of the vowels in the stem.

4. A few words about Hungarian pronounciation: accent above the vowel means that the vowel is long. Consonants: *cs* [tʃ]: voiceless alveopalatal affricate, *ny* [nj]:voiced palatalized nasal, *ty* [tj]: voiceless palatalized plosive, *sz* [s]: voiceless alveolar fricative, s [ʃ]: voiceless alveolapalatal fricative.

5. On the concepts of explicit and primary performatives see Austin (1962/1973).

6. Emotions considered as specific enthymemic judgements are detailed in Harré (1993).

7. For this observation we are thankful to Ferenc Kiefer.

8. These data were collected by Péter Bodor from his first daughter. Despite various attempts, the transcription and coding were not assisted financially by any Hungarian agencies. However, the presentation of our preliminary findings at the annual meetings of the Pre- and Protomorphology Project headed by W. Dressler, were supported by the Austrian Academy of Sciences. Anna Stibrányi, Éva Suba and Virág Barcza transcribed most of the recordings.

9. These data were transcribed and coded with financial assistance from the Child Language Strand, Study Centre on Language Contact, Netherlands Institute for Advanced Study (Coordinator: Annick De Houwer). The Hungarian members instrumental in transcription were Anna Babarczy and Szilvia Papp.

10. The relevant aspects of transcriptions are in italics.

11. The source of these statistics is the Hungarian National Corpus (http://corpus.nytud.hu/mnsz), a corpus of present-day standard Hungarian, which contains 153.7 millions words and represents different written text types, inter alia literature, scientific texts and discussions of an internet portal. There is information available from the HNC on the frequency of use of diminutives derived by -kA and -cskA, but not on the other types.

12. For Miki r=0,55, while for Panna r=0,46.

References

Austin, J. L. 1962/1973. *How to Do Things with Words*. Oxford: Oxford University Press.

Averill, J. R. 1980. A Constructivist View of Emotion. In *Emotion: Theory, Research and Experience. Vol. 1. Theories of Emotion*, R. Plutchik and H. Kellerman (eds), 305–341. New York: Academic Press.

Babarczy, A. 2006. Negation and word order in Hungarian child language. *Lingua* 116 (3): 377–392.

Bakhtin, M. M. 1926/1985. *A szó az életben és a költészetben.* [The Word in Life and in Poetry.] Budapest: Európa Könyvkiadó.

Berko Gleason, J., Perlmann, R. Y., Ely, R. and Evans, D. W. 1990. The baby talk register: Parent's use of diminutives. In *Handbook of Research in Language Development using* CHILDES, J. L. Sokolov and C. E. Snow (eds), 50–77. Mahwah NJ: Lawrence Erlbaum.

Bodor, P. 1997. On the Usage of Emotional Language: A Developmental view of the Tip of an Iceberg. In *The Language of Emotions*, R. Dirven and S. Niemeier (eds), 195–209. Amsterdam: Benjamins.

Bodor, P. 2004. *On Emotions: Developmental Social Constructionist Account.* Budapest: L'Harmattan.

Coulter, J. 1979. *The Social Construction of Mind.* Totowa, NJ: Rowman and Littlefield.

van De Weijer, J. 1989. The formation of diminutive names in Hungarian. *Acta Linguistica Hungarica* 39: 353–371.

Dressler, W. U. and Merlini Barbaresi, L. 1994. *Morphopragmatics: Diminutives and Intensifiers in Italian, German, and Other Languages.* Berlin: Mouton de Gruyter.

Dressler, W. U. and Kiefer, F. 1990. Austro-Hungarian morphopragmatics. In *Contemporary Morphology*, W. U. Dressler (ed.), 69–77. Berlin: Mouton de Gruyter.

Elman, J. L. 2001. Connectionism and Language Acquisition. In *Language Development – The Essential Readings*, M. Tomasello and E. Bates (eds), 295–307. Malden Mass: Blackwell.

Ferguson, C. A. 1964. Baby talk in six languages. *American Anthropologist* 66: 103–114.

Harré R. 1993. Towards an emotionology of local moral orders. *Common knowledge* 2 (3): 12–14.

Kaplan, B. 1992. Strife of Systems. Tension between Organismic and Developmental Points of View. *Theory & Psychology* 2 (4): 431–443.

Kiefer, F. 2003. Alaktan. In *A magyar nyelv kézikönyve*, F. Kiefer and P. Siptár (eds), 185–203. Budapest: Akadémiai.

Kiefer, F. 2004. Morphopragmatic phenomena in Hungarian. *Acta Linguistica Hungarica* 51: 325–349.

Kiefer, F. and Ladányi, M. 2000. Morfoszintaktikailag semleges képzések. In *Strukturális magyar nyelvtan 3. Morfológia*, Kiefer, F. (ed.), 165–214. Budapest: Akadémiai.

Ladányi M. 2004. Szinkrón összefüggések – elméleti, funkcionális és történeti magyarázatok (megjegyzések a -ka/-ke és -cska/-cske főnévképzőről). In *„...még onnét is ejutni túlra..." – Nyelvészeti és irodalmi tanulmányok Horváth Katalin tiszteletére*, Ladányi M., Dér Cs. and Hattyár H. (eds), 52–63. Budapest: Tinta Könyvkiadó.

Meisel, J. M. 1995. Parameters in Acquisition. In *The Handbook of Child Language.* P. Fletcher and B. MacWhinney (eds), 10–36. Cambridge Mass: Blackwell.

MacWhinney, B. 1974. How Hungarian Children Learn to Speak. Unpublished doctoral dissertation, University of California, Berkeley.

MacWhinney, B. 2000. *The CHILDES Project: Tools for analyzing talk.* Vol. 2: The Database. Mahwah, NJ: Erlbaum.

Nelson, K. 1996 *Language in Cognitive Development: The Emergence of the Mediated Mind.* Cambridge: Cambridge University Press.

Ninio, A. and Snow, C. E. 1996. *Pragmatic Development.* Boulder: Westview Press.

Ochs, E. and Schieffelin, B. 1989. Language has a heart. *Text* 9 (1): 7–25.

Piaget, J. 1947/2001 *The psychology of intelligence.* London: Routledge.

Pléh, Cs., Vinkler Zs. and Kálmán L. 1996. Early morphology of spatial expressions in Hungarian children: A CHILDES study. *Acta Linguistica Hungarica* 40: 129–142.

Pöchträger, M. A., Bodó, Cs., Dressler, W. U. and Schweiger, T. 1998. On some inflectional properties of the agglutinating type illustrated from Finnish, Hungarian and Turkish inflection. *Wiener linguistische Gazette* 62–63: 57–92.

Sarbin, T. R. 1989. Emotions as Situated Actions. In *Emotions in Human Development*. L. Cirillo, B. Kaplan and S. Wapner (eds), 77–101. Hillsdale, NJ: Lawrence Erlbaum.

Savickienė, I., Dressler, W. U., Barcza, V., Bodor, P., Ketrez, N., Korecky-Kröll, K., Palmović, M., Stephany, U. and Thomadaki, E. in press. Diminutives as Pioneers of Derivational and Inflectional Development – a Crosslinguistic Perspective. *Antwerp papers in linguistics*. Antwerp: Universiteit Antwerpen.

Werner, H. and Kaplan B. 1963. *Symbol Formation*. New York: Wiley.

CHAPTER 10

Diminutives in Finnish child-directed and child speech

Klaus Laalo

There are various means to form diminutives in Finnish, for example regular suffixation (e.g. *isä* 'father' + *i* > *isi* 'daddy') and modification of the stem possibly combined with suffixation (e.g. *kissa* 'cat' > *kisu* 'pussycat', *maha* 'stomach' > *masu* 'tummy'). The article first deals with the different types of Finnish diminutives and then examines the diminutives of two Finnish-speaking children.

In early child language, a trochaic bias is observed. In diminutive formation, there is a tendency towards transparent inflection: when forming diminutives by stem modification, different morphophonological alternations are eliminated and transparent inflection patterns are favoured.

1. Introduction

There are several types of diminutives in Finnish. They are used only infrequently in adult speech but more frequently in child-directed and child speech. The different types of Finnish diminutives are first presented (1–4), and after that the diminutives of two Finnish-speaking children are examined (5.1–5.3). From the speech of the girl, Tuulikki, as well as from the speech of the boy, Tuomas, there are both diary material and recordings. The paper ends in a short conclusion part (6).

1.1 Types of diminutives in Finnish

In many languages (e.g. in Austrian German, Lithuanian, Greek and Russian) there is a more or less clear-cut derivational category of diminutives. In some languages, diminutives are formed with a very regular derivational pattern (see e.g. Gillis 1997 for Dutch), but in Finnish there is no such clear-cut derivational category of diminutives. Instead, there are different ways to express diminutiveness:

a. various derivational suffixes (e.g. *kukka* 'flower' -> *kukka+nen* 'little flower')
b. shortening and modification of the stem (e.g. *kissa* 'cat' -> *kisu* 'pussycat')

c. to some extent, also compounding

Thus, in Finnish there are various types of diminutives formed by regular derivation, but the diminutives are also often constructed so that the stem is shortened and an affix-like element is attached. Most important among compounds which express smallness are those formed with *pikku-* and *pien-* (both meaning 'little'), e.g. *pikkumies* 'little man, boy' (cf. *mies* 'man'), *pikkuhuilu* 'piccolo' (cf. *huilu* 'flute'), *pikkubussi* 'minibus' (cf. *bussi* 'bus'), *pienasunto* 'small dwelling' and *pieneliö* 'micro-organism' (cf. *eliö* 'organism'). Many compounds beginning with *pikku-* are used also in colloquial speech, and some of them (e.g. *pikkumies* in the meaning of 'boy') are disposed to carry positive pragmatic effects typical of diminutives. The other *pikku*-compounds and the compounds beginning with *pien-* are mostly neologisms belonging to the matter-of-fact-style, and some of them have been invented to replace loanwords (e.g. *pikkubussi* 'minibus', *pieneliö* 'micro-organism').

1.2 Pejoratives and augmentatives

Many pejoratives in Finnish are based on sound symbolism. Diachronically, the youngest member of the Finnish vowel system is *ö*, and it is often used in descriptive vocabulary: in a few words with a positive connotation (e.g. *söpö* 'sweet, pretty'), in certain neutral descriptive words (e.g. *pörröinen* 'fluffy'), but especially in pejorative words (e.g. *hölmö, höpsö, pöhkö, törppö* all meaning 'stupid', *sökö* 'broken, out of order').

Augmentatives are formed by compounding: the adjectives *iso-* and *suur(i)-* (both meaning 'big, large') are used in such compounds as *isojyväinen* 'large-grained', *isomasto* 'main mast', *isoveli* 'big brother', *isoäiti* 'grand mother'; *suurjännite* 'high tension', *suurlakko* 'general strike', *suurmestari* 'grand master', *suursaavutus* 'great achievement' etc.

1.3 Hypocoristics

Hypocoristics derived from names belong mainly to the type of diminutives which are formed by shortening and modifying the stem, e.g. *Elina* -> *Ellu*, *Johanna* -> *Jossu*, *Tuomas* -> *Tompsu*, *Tuulikki* -> *Tuuti*. The modification often includes the attachment of a suffix-like element, e.g. *-u*.

On the border of diminutives and hypocoristics there are kinship terms, which include derivatives such as *isi* 'daddy' (< *isä* 'father' + the diminutive suffix *i*), *ukki* 'grandfather' (< *ukko* 'old man' + *i*), *veikka* (< *veli* 'brother' + the diminutive suffix *-kka*), *äitikkä* ~ *äitsykkä* (from *äiti* 'mother') and loan words such as *mummi* 'grandmother' (< Swedish *mormor* 'mother of mother') and *vaari* 'grandfather' (< Swedish *far* 'father').

2. Formal aspects of diminutives in Finnish

2.1 The simplex bases

Most bases for the Finnish diminutives are common nouns, but there are also some adjectives (e.g. *pyöreä* 'round' -> *pyörykkä* 'the little round one' and *kalpea* 'pale' -> *kalvakka* 'somewhat pale'), and some numerals (e.g. *yksi* 'one' -> *ykkönen, kaksi* 'two' -> *kakkonen* [to illustrate: there is on the Finnish TV-channel number two a popular child program called *Pikku kakkonen* 'the little two-DIM'] and *kymmenen* 'ten' -> *kymppi*; in the last case affixation is combined with shortening and modification of the stem). Some verbs may also be interpreted as diminutivized. These derivatives formed with *-ele-* express understatement, frequentativeness or sporadic occurrence: *nauraa* 'is laughing' -> *naureskelee* 'is laughing (quietly or repeatedly)' and *hyppii* 'is jumping' -> *hyppelee* 'is jumping (now and then)'.

2.2 Formation by regular affixation

Many Finnish diminutives are formed with derivational suffixes, for example with the following ones:

a. **-nen** e.g. *kala* 'fish' -> *kalanen* 'little fish'; *kirja* 'book' -> *kirjanen* 'booklet'; *kukka* 'flower' -> *kukkanen* 'little flower'; *tyttö* 'girl' -> *tyttönen* 'little girl'. This is the most productive diminutive suffix in Finnish; it can be attached to most noun stems. Many of the *nen*-diminutives have been lexicalized, e.g. *lehti* 'leaf; newspaper, journal' -> *lehtinen* 'leaflet'. (Note that a similar suffix is used in adjective derivation, and the resulting meaning is 'one of its kind' or 'made of', e.g. *kulta* 'gold' -> *kultainen* 'golden', *jää* 'ice' -> *jäinen* 'icy'.)

b. **-i** e.g. *isä* 'father' -> *isi*; *ukko* 'old man' -> *ukki* 'grandfather'

c. **-ke** e.g. *haara* 'branch'-> *haarake* 'little branch', *lahti* 'bay, gulf' -> *lahdeke* 'cove', *linna* 'castle' -> *linnake* 'fort(ress)', *niemi* 'cape' -> *niemeke* 'little cape', *saari* 'island' -> *saareke* 'little island'

d. **-kkA** e.g. *peni* 'dog' (archaic) -> *penikka* 'whelp, pup' with subtypes

d1. **-(U)kkA**, e.g. *nenä* 'nose' -> *nenukka* 'little nose', *lehti* 'leaf' -> *lehdykkä* 'little leaf', *pyöreä* 'round' -> *pyörykkä* 'the little round one', *soppi* 'corner' -> *sopukka* 'little corner'; used also as a hypocoristic affix, e.g. *isä* 'father' -> *isukka*; *äiti* 'mother' -> *äitsykkä*

d2. **-(i)kkA**, e.g. *kanta* 'base' -> *kannikka* 'crust', *musta* 'black' -> *mustikka* 'blueberry', *made* 'burbot' -> *matikka*, *vasa* 'fawn' -> *vasikka* 'calf'

e. **-kAinen** (= kkA + inen) e.g. *ainoa* 'the only one' -> *ainokainen* 'the dear only one', *kaunis* 'beautiful' -> *kaunokainen* 'the beautiful one', *keiju* 'fairy' -> *keijukainen*, *lapsi* 'child' -> *lapsukainen* 'dear/little child', *pieni* 'little' -> *pienokainen* 'little child'

f. **-O** e.g *emä* 'mother (archaic)' -> *emo* 'dam', *jänis* 'rabbit' -> *jänö* 'bunny', *tytär* 'daughter' -> *tyttö* 'girl' (also some adjectives, e.g. *iso* 'big' <- *isä* 'father')
g. **-U** e.g. *kissa* 'cat' -> *kisu* 'puss, little cat', *kulta* 'gold/dear' -> *kultu* 'little dear one', *maha* 'stomach' > *mas(s)u* 'tummy', *silmä* 'eye' -> *simmu* 'sweet little eye', *peukalo* 'thumb' -> *peukku*, *poika* 'boy' (inflection stem *poja-*) -> *poju*, *porsas* 'pig' -> *possu* 'piggie'; also adjectives: *pikku* 'little' < *-pikka-*, *virkku* (cf. *virkeä*) 'fresh, frisky'.
h. **-li(ini)** e.g. *ukko* 'old man' -> *ukkeli* (Standard Finnish), *purukumi* 'chewing gum' -> *purukumeli* (Tuomas 2;6); *vauva* 'baby' -> *vauveli* ~ *vauveliini* (Standard Finnish), *kissa* 'cat' -> *kissaliini* 'pussycat' (Tuulikki 1;10). Both *-li* and *-liini* obviously come from Anglo-Saxon *-ly*/*-lein*.

The productivity of these derivational suffixes has some variation. Usually, the suffix *-li* is not productive, but in certain families or in the use of certain children it can get productive; for example, Räisänen (1975: 261) mentions that his sons used such diminutives as *mummuli* 'grandmother' (<- *mummu* 'grandmother'), *soppali* 'soup' (<- *soppa* 'soup'), *Petrili* (<- the proper noun *Petri*), *sähköli* 'light, electricity' (<- *sähkö* 'electricity') etc. based on the model provided by the words *vauveli* 'baby' (<- *vauva* 'baby') and *haisuli* 'the little one who stinks' (<- *haisu* 'smeel. stink') used by the adults.

2.3 Formation of diminutives by stem modification

The diminutives formed by shortening and stem modification are typical of the Finnish child language and child-directed speech, and the formation of such diminutives includes often a change to a more transparently inflected stem-type. As one can see from the examples in f. and g. in 2.2 above, the diminutive suffixes *-O* and *-U* are not merely typical suffix elements which are added to the end of the stem, but the stem is often shortened and modified, as in *jänis* 'rabbit' > *jänö* 'bunny', *kissa* 'cat' > *kisu* 'pussycat', *peukalo* 'thumb' > *peukku*, and *porsas* 'pig' > *possu* 'piggie'.

This way of forming diminutives also includes a change of inflection class: the most transparent Finnish inflection type with a minimum of stem alternations and no variation in suffix morphology consists of two-syllabic stems with a final labial vowel, and transfering the word to a more transparent stem-type makes the inflection of the new derivatives easier. This morphophonological aspect is studied in detail in section 4 below.

The U-diminutives are used frequently in Finnish motherese (J. Toivainen 1972; K. Toivainen 1995: 289, 300–304). Also diminutives belonging to other stem types than O- and U-stems are formed in Finnish by truncation and accompanying sound modification, e.g. *hevonen* 'horse' > *heppa* 'horsey' and *varvas* 'toe' > *varppi*.

3. Semantics and pragmatics of diminutives

Different diminutives formed from the same simplex can have different meanings: *poika* 'boy' -> *poju* 'little boy' but *poika* 'boy' -> *poikanen* 'young animal'; *ukko* 'old man' -> *ukki* 'grandfather' but *ukko* 'old man' -> *ukkeli* 'old guy' and *ukko* 'old man' -> *ukkonen* 'thunder' (this comes from the euphemist name of the god).

Certain Finnish diminutives have almost exclusively the semantic meaning of smallness. Examples from derivatives mentioned in section 2.2 above are *kirjanen* 'booklet', *lehtinen* 'leaflet', *penikka* 'whelp, pup'. Certain other diminutives have a clear pragmatic meaning of intimacy, e.g. *lapsukainen* 'dear/little child', *simmu* 'sweet little eye'. But the suffixes themselves can not be divided to those carrying the meaning of smallness and others carrying the meaning of intimacy, because the meaning depends also on the stem to which the suffix is attached.

In Finnish child-directed and child speech, there are many diminutive formations that are used mainly for pragmatic purposes. From the morphological point of view, these diminutives are rather exceptional: they are not formed by regular suffixation but their derivational morphology is similar to certain affective formations in Finnish colloquial speech and slang. From the pragmatic point of view, they are clear diminutives expressing endearment, intimacy and warm feelings. From the morphophonological point of view, they exhibit a tendency to simplification and transparency of inflection: the simplex base is modified so that there occurs an inflectional class shift to a more productive and transparent class.

4. Morphophonological aspects of Finnish diminutives

The transparency of inflection, a minimum of stem alternations, is an advantage in early acquisition, because the child's attempts to recognize word-forms are made easier. Canonical word-forms have the same advantage; in the group of lexemes denoting to body parts there are diminutives which are linked to each other by a phonetic family resemblance, namely they all have stems ending in a nasal consonant + U: *nenu* 'little nose' (derived from *nenä* 'nose'), *simmu* 'little eye' (derived from *silmä* 'eye'; the cluster *-lm-* is simplified to *-mm-*), and *känny* 'little hand' (derived from *käsi* 'hand').

Morphophonological transparency is thus one factor which facilitates language learning. The morphophonological alternations in certain Finnish inflection classes are complex, but there is also the possibility to reduce this complexity by diminutive formation, because many Finnish diminutive types, especially those ending in a labial vowel, represent inflectional transparency. The corresponding non-diminutive nouns are inflectionally more complex, because they have more stem alternations: different stem variants are used in different case forms. For example, there are no stem alternations in the following diminutives (1a) but there are many different stem alternations in the corresponding simplex words (1b); from each word, the singular nominative, genitive and partitive forms and the plural partitive form are given:

(1a)	känny: känny+n: känny+ä: känny+j+ä	'sweet ~ dear little hand'
	possu: possu+n: possu+a: possu+j+a	'piggy'
	jänö: jänö+n: jänö+ä: jänö+j+ä	'bunny'
	heppa: hepa+n: heppa+a: heppo+j+a	'horsey'
(1b)	käsi: käde+n: kät+tä: käs+i+ä	'hand'
	porsas: porsaa+n: porsas+ta: porsa+i+ta	'pig'
	jänis: jänikse+n: jänis+tä: jäniks+i+ä	'rabbit'
	hevonen: hevose+n: hevos+ta: hevos+i+a	'horse'

The inflection type with a final labial vowel (*o*, *u*, *y* or *ö*) – and thus also the diminutive type *känny*, *possu* etc. – belongs to the most transparent stem-types in Finnish: there are no stem vowel alternations either in singular or plural. Contrary to this, when the plural suffix *i* is added, the illabial stem-final vowels are either dropped (e.g. in *ovi* 'door' -e+i = i, in *silmä* -ä+i = i, in *muna* -a+i = i) or changed (e.g. in *jalka* -a+i = oi, in *kuppi* -i+i = ei), as shown in the following examples:

(2)	NOMINATIVE SG.	INESSIVE SG.	INESSIVE PLURAL
	ovi 'door':	ove+ssa 'in the door':	ov+i+ssa 'in the doors'
	silmä 'eye':	silmä+ssä 'in the eye:	silm+i+ssä 'in the eyes'
	muna 'egg':	muna+ssa 'in the egg':	mun+i+ssa 'in the eggs'
	jalka 'leg':	jala+ssa 'in the leg':	jalo+i+ssa 'in the legs'
	kuppi 'cup':	kupi+ssa 'in the cup':	kupe+i+ssa 'in the cups'

The modification of the stem so that there occurs a final labial vowel is common both in Finnish child language and in child-directed speech. Labial vowels are favoured as stem-final vowels of diminutives, and there are some diminutives in which the vowel of the second syllable is changed to a labial vowel even if there are also other diminutive derivational elements, e.g. *lapsi* -> *lapsonen*, *lapsukainen* and *poika* -> *poitsukkeli* (= *poits-u-kkeli*, cf. also the diminutive *ukkeli* 'old man'). But for many nouns, including loan-words, no change is needed, because they already belong to a transparent inflection type, for example *auto* 'car', *karhu* 'bear', *kukko* 'cock', *lintu* 'bird', *norsu* 'elephant' and *poni* 'pony' (all these nouns are used in the recordings of Tuulikki and Tuomas).

5. Diminutives in the speech of two Finnish-speaking children

5.1 The material: classes of diminutives and the frequency of diminutives

The empirical data for this study were collected by the author from the speech of both his daughter and his son. The daughter, Tuulikki, was born in June 1991. The son, Tuomas, was born in May 1997. From the speech of both children there is diary material as well as recordings.

The diminutives used by the children can be grouped in three classes. The first consists of one regular derivative produced by the diminutive suffix *i*, namely *isi* 'daddy' = *isä* 'father' + *i*. The second class consists of diminutives produced by stem modification (which is often combined to shortening and possibly also to the attachment of a suffix-like element, e.g. -*u*), e.g. *heppa* 'horsey' < *hevonen* 'horse', *peukku* 'thumb' < *peukalo* 'thumb', *simmu* 'eye' < *silmä* 'eye', *sisko* 'sister' < *sisar* 'sister'. The third class consists of diminutive names of animals, often with unclear etymology, probably onomatopoetic, e.g. *hauva* 'bowwow', *pupu* 'bunny', *tipu* 'birdie' etc. The emergence of the different diminutive types in the transcripts is presented in Table 1.

Table 1. Three classes of Finnish diminutives

Diminutive class	Tuulikki: age of emergence in the transcripts	Tuomas: age of emergence in the transcripts
Class 1 (-i)	*isi* 'father' 1;7	*isi* 'father' 1;7
Class 2 (stem modification)	*heppa* 'horsey' 1;7 *hepo* 'horsey' 1;9 *masu* 'tummy' 1;9 *massu* 'tummy' 1;11 *simmu* 'eye' 2;1	*peukku* 'thumb' 1;7 *heppa* 'horsey' 1;8 *masu* ' tummy' 1;8 *peppu* 'behind' 1;8 *possu* 'piggie' 1;9 *sisko* 'sister' 2;1
Class 3 (mostly onomatopoetic)	*hauva* 'bowwow' 1;8 *pupu* 'bunny' 1;8 *tipu* 'birdie' 1;7	*hauva* 'bowwow' 1;7 *kaakka* 'bird' 1;8

There are certain lexico-semantic groups which attract diminutives (cf. Stephany 1997: 152–153; Dressler–Merlini Barbaresi 1994: 224). Examples from the speech of Tuulikki and Tuomas of diminutives belonging to these groups:

a. names of relatives: *isi* ~ *iskä* 'father', *äiti(kki)* 'mother', *sisko* 'sister'
b. body parts: *masu* ~ *massu* 'tummy', *nenu* 'nose', *peppu* 'bottom, behind', *peukku* 'thumb', *simmu* 'eye', *varppi* 'toe'
c. animals (also toy animals): *hauva* 'bowwow', *heppa* 'geegee', *kisu* 'pussycat', *possu* 'piggie', *pupu* 'bunny', *tipu* 'birdie'. Many of these animal names have an onomatopoetic origin, for example *hauv(v)a* 'dog' (from the onomatopoetic sound imitating

the barking of the dog, "hau-hau" or "hau-vau"), *pupu* 'bunny' (from the reduplicative onomatopoetic verb imitating the sound of a rabbit, *puputtaa*) and *tipu* 'birdie' (from reduplicative onomatopoetic words used for domestic fowl: *tipu tipu*).

Some diminutives which have the pragmatic connotation of intimacy occur in the child-directed speech (CDS). These diminutives typically refer to body parts (e.g. *masu* ~ *massu* 'tummy', cf. *maha* 'stomach'), living or toy animals (e.g. *heppa* 'horsey' from *hevonen* 'horse'), and family members (e.g. *isi* 'father' < *isä* 'father' + *i*). They are acquired early by the children and belong already to the first nouns in their vocabulary.

The frequencies of both diminutives and all nouns and the rate of diminutives in child-directed speech and in the speech of Tuulikki and Tuomas are presented in Tables 2 and 3, respectively.

Table 2. Frequencies of diminutives and all nouns in the recordings of Tuulikki

Age of	Child-directed speech (CDS)			Child speech		
Tuulikki	noun types/tokens	diminutive types/tokens	% of diminutives	nouns (typ/tok)	diminutives (typ/tok)	% of diminutives
1;7.28	85/129	3/14	10,8	72/113	3/9	7,9
1;8.06	113/172	3/3	1,7	67/92	4/5	5,4
1;8.13	54/114	2/15	13,1	41/104	3/10	9,6
1;9.14	37/57	3/17	29,8	36/66	3/11	16,7
1;9.17	64/91	4/15	16,4	37/71	4/13	18,3
1;10.11	18/21	–	0	28/66	1/4	6,0
1;11.16	22/31	1/3	9,6	8/9	1/1	11,1
1;11.23	38/50	1/5	10,0	22/39	2/7	17,9
2;01.17	32/60	1/2	3,3	18/35	–	0
2;01.19	35/74	2/4	5,4	59/106	4/11	10,3
2;2.18	38/72	2/4	5,5	31/47	4/11	23,4
2;3.20	144/199	4/8	4,0	56/95	4/12	12,6
2;3.21	79/113	1/2	1,7	46/70	2/4	5,7

In the recordings of Tuulikki, the rate of diminutive tokens of all word tokens ranges in adult speech from 0% to 29,8% and in child speech from 0% to 23,4%. Many diminutives occur repeatedly, e.g. *isi* is used in almost every recording. Most of the diminutives are words for (toy) animals: *hauva* 'bowwow', *heppa* 'geegee', *pupu* 'bunny', *tipu* 'birdie'. There is also one word for body part, namely *mas(s)u* 'tummy'.

There is no growth in the ratio of diminutives when Tuulikki gets older, but the ratio of diminutives both in CDS and in child speech varies according to the topic of conversation.

Table 3. Frequencies of diminutives and all nouns in the recordings of Tuomas

Age of	Child-directed speech (CDS)			Child speech		
Tuomas	noun types/tokens	diminutive types/tokens	% of diminutives	nouns (typ/tok)	diminutives (typ/tok)	% of diminutives
1;7	155/434	8/54	12,4	35/191	5/20	10,4
1;8	261/685	7/133	19,4	65/182	8/64	35,1
1;9	168/367	7/55	14,9	55/128	5/7	5,4
1;10	134/282	5/59	20,9	37/105	4/16	15,2
1;11	117/174	3/3	1,7	38/57	1/1	1,7
2;1	182/289	2/5	1,7	38/67	3/8	11,9
2;2	212/387	3/18	4,6	118/266	3/47	17,6

In the recordings of Tuomas, the proportion of diminutive tokens of all word tokens ranges in the input from 1,7% to 20,9% and in child speech from 1,7% to 35,1%. The highest frequency of both the adult and child diminutives is in the 1;8 recording, where two diminutives occur exceptionally often because of the recurrent topic: *hauva* 'bowwow' 17 times and *heppa* 'geegee' even 28 times. Without these two lexemes, the amount of diminutives would be 10,4% in child speech. This shows how much the rate of diminutives depends on the topic of conversation.

As in the case of Tuulikki, there is no systematic growth in the ratio of diminutives when Tuomas gets older, but the ratio of diminutives both in CDS and in child speech varies according to the topic of conversation.

In the tables above the rate of diminutives is quite high, especially in child speech in the Tuulikki-recordings 1;9.17 and 2;2 and in the Tuomas-recordings 1;8 and 1;10. This is partly due to the high frequency of some animal names in the recording situation. The high rate of diminutives is also due to the broad interpretation of diminutives adopted here: in addition to regular derivatives (*isä* 'father' + the derivative suffix *i* = *isi* 'daddy') and stem modifications (e.g. *hevonen* 'horse' > *heppa*, *sisar* 'sister' > *sisko*, *maha* 'stomach' > *massu*, *peukalo* 'thumb' > *peukku*) also such forms are counted as diminutives which have only a lexical non-diminutive counterpart, e.g. *hauva* 'bowwow' vs. *koira* 'dog', *pupu* 'bunny' vs. *jänis* 'rabbit', *tipu* 'birdie' vs. *kananpoika* 'chicken'. All these diminutives share the pragmatic connotations of intimacy and endearment and they are typical of Finnish CDS and child speech.

5.2 Tuulikki: diminutives in diary material and recordings

5.2.1 *The first diminutives and the trochaic bias*

At first Tuulikki used diminutives which truncate long words to two-syllables (e.g. *heppa* 'horsey' < *hevonen* 'horse') or transform words to a morphophonologically more transparent stem-type (e.g. *simmu* 'eye' < *silmä* 'eye'). These were all acquired as such from the input, as word-forms usually are during this early phase of premorphology. At the end of her second year, Tuulikki started to produce her own diminutive formations, which were individual neologisms. This is a sign of the child's own morphological processing, which is typical of the protomorphological period. Tuulikki started with an extension of the use of the self-invented *putti*-element, and a little later used canonical four-syllabic words ending in *-(l)iini*. Both *putti-* and *liini*-elements have the phonetic characteristics of typical iconic diminutives, i.e. palatal vowels (Dressler and Merlini Barbaresi 1994: 93).

The first diminutives of Tuulikki until the age of 1;8 were all rote-learnt from child-directed speech. The following words have the pragmatic connotation of intimacy which is typical of diminutives, and they are all based on child-centered speech. The age mentioned refers to the first occurrences in Tuulikki's speech:

(3) 0;8 *isi* 'father'
0;10 *hauv(v)a* 'bowwow' [avva], an onomatopoeic word; cf. Standard Finnish *koira* 'dog'
1;4 *heppa* 'geegee' [eppa], derived from *hevonen* 'horse'
1;5 *simmu* 'eye' [timmu], derived from *silmä* 'eye'
1;6 *possu* 'piggy' [posu], derived from *porsas* 'pig'
1;7 *essu* (< *esiliina* 'apron'); *tipu* 'birdie'
1;8 *massu* 'tummy' (< *maha* 'stomach'); *pottu* (< *potaatti* 'potatoe'); *varppi* 'toe' [vamppi] (cf. Standard Finnish *varvas* 'toe')

The early diminutives used by Tuulikki were all two-syllabic. In her speech before the age of 1;10, Tuulikki used only the two initial syllables of most word-forms. This way of reducing longer word-forms to two-syllables is a common strategy in the speech development of many children acquiring Finnish (Laalo 1994, 2001; Räisänen 1975: 256; Savinainen-Makkonen 2000). This shortening results in trochaic word-forms which are favoured by the Finnish stress pattern: the main stress is always on the first syllable. Many children acquiring other languages have also been observed to truncate word-forms to trochaic two-syllables (Wijnen et al. 1994; Gerken 1994; Jusczyk 1997: 107–108, 186–187, 225). The truncations of Finnish children are rather easily understood as representing certain word-forms, although they appear without most suffixes and derivational elements; in some languages the trochaic truncations may be more difficult to identify, because even the first syllable may be unstressed and can thus be deleted.

The trochaic formations can have more than two syllables. Some four-syllabic word-forms, mostly compounds, consisting of two trochaic parts are also typical of the two-syllabic period (Laalo 1994: 431, 2001: 212; Räisänen 1975: 256). Even more than four syllables are possible, but only seldom more than six; this prosodic pattern of word-forms consisting of more than one trochaic part (e.g. *bana-liini* 'banana-DIM', *etusormi-putti* 'forefinger-DIM') was also characteristic of the first diminutives formed by Tuulikki herself: these diminutives were at the same time her first neologisms in general.

5.2.2 *Tuulikki's own diminutive types in the diary material*

At the age of 1;8 Tuulikki used some very special compound-like diminutive formations for three fingers. These were her first diminutives occurring in explicit opposition to simplex words; her earlier diminutives were used without a simplex counterpart (one exception: *isä – isi* 'father'). The model for these formations was the compound-like diminutive of *peukalo* 'thumb', namely *peukaloputti*, and Tuulikki's first own diminutives were formed by segmenting the element *putti* (which has a pragmatic effect typical of diminutives) and adding it to the names of three other fingers. These fingers are *pikkurilli* 'little finger', *etusormi* 'forefinger' and *keskisormi* 'middle finger' (the fifth finger, which had no diminutive with *putti*-ending, is the three-syllabic *nimetön* 'nameless'; it does not fit the trochaic pattern). The diminutives *pikkulilli-putti*, *etutommi-putti* and *kekkitommi-putti* are analogical overextensions, Tuulikki's first individual type of spontaneous diminutive formations; an element with no denotative meaning, used as a diminutive element but normally attached only to the word *peukalo* 'thumb', was segmented and attached to the names of other fingers but did not occur with other stems.

Tuulikki's most productive type of spontaneous diminutive formations was the type of four-syllabic word-forms ending in *-(l)iini*. She started to produce them at the age of 1;10, and especially during that month this type was very productive. In order to attain these diminutives Tuulikki sometimes simply added the *liini*-element to the simplex, e.g. *kissa* 'cat' -> *kissaliini* 'pussycat', *pesu* 'washing' -> *pesuliini* and *kärryt* 'waggon' (plurale tantum in Finnish) -> *kärryliinit*. But often the neologisms were formed in a special way so that the combination of the base and the derivative element was modified to fit the trochaic pattern, e.g. at 1;10:

(4)	*kiisseli* 'thickened fruit juice'	+ *liini* => *kiisseliini*	(not *kiisseliliini)
	meloni 'melon'	+ *liini* => *meloniini*	(not *meloniliini)
	rypäle 'grape'	+ *liini* => *vypäliini*	(not *rypäleliini)
	banaani 'banana'	+ *liini* => *banaliini*	(not *banaaniliini)
	peruna 'potatoe'	+ *liini* => *penuliini*	(not *perunaliini)
	porkkana 'carrot'	+ *liini* => *ponkkaliini*	(not *porkkanaliini)
	tomaatti 'tomatoe'	+ *liini* => *tomaliini*	(not *tomaattiliini)
	paperi 'paper'	+ *liini* => *papeliini*	(not *paperiliini)
	tiski 'the dishes'	+ *liini* => *tikkaliini*	(cf. the verb *tiskata* 'to do the dishes')

This diminutive type has some possible models, above all the motherese diminutives *vauveliini* 'dear little baby' (<- *vauva* 'baby'), *pupuliini* 'little bunny' (<- *pupu* 'bunny'), *tuhmeliini* 'the little mischief' (<- *tuhma* 'naughty'), perhaps also the colloquial variant of the name *Nikitin*, namely *Nikitiini* (the name of Tuulikki's own doctor); these motherese words were used often in the adult speech directed at Tuulikki. Following the model of these formations, Tuulikki produced so many *liini*-diminutives that she seems to have developed a word-formation rule for them. The *-liini*-diminutives were not formed by as simple a surface analogy as *putti*-diminutives; rather, Tuulikki established her own productive type of diminutives, which she initially used very frequently. The productivity of this type was soon weakened, but still at the age of 6;2 Tuulikki derived a *liini*-diminutive of her newborn little brother *Tuomas*, namely *Tuomasliini*.

The third diminutive type used by Tuulikki was an analogical formation. In intimate speech, two variants of Tuulikki's name were used, namely *Tuuti* and *Tuutikki*. She segmented the *kki*-element (< *kka* + *i*) and used it in her own diminutive formations based on *äiti* 'mother' and *isi* 'father'. At the age of 2;2 Tuulikki combined the *kki*-element with the strong stem variant of *äiti* 'mother' and used the diminutive *Tuutikki* of herself. Thus these both words ended in a -*tikki*-scheme:

(5a) *Hyvä äiti.kki hyvä Tuutikki hyvä isi.kki.*
good mother-DIM good Tuutikki good father-DIM
'Well done mommy, well done Tuutikki, well done daddy.'

At the age of 2;4 Tuulikki combined the *kki*-element with the weak stem variant of *äiti* 'mother' (*äili-*) and used the non-diminutive variant *Tuulikki* of herself. These both words thus ended in a *likki*-scheme:

(5b) *Nii.len nimi ol.i Tuulikki ja äili.kki ja isi.kki.*
they-GEN name be-PAST Tuulikki and mother-DIM and father-DIM
'Their name was Tuulikki and mommy and daddy.'

5.2.3 *Tuulikki's diminutives in the recordings*

In the majority of cases, Tuulikki uses for one certain lexeme either the simplex or the diminutive form. There are just a few examples of the use of both diminutive and simplex. For example, in the recordings of Tuulikki, both the forms *isi* 'father-DIM' and *isä* 'father' are used, but in the recording made at the age of 1;9 the diminutive *isi* is used for Tuulikki's own father (example 6) and the non-diminutive *isä* is used for other fathers, e.g. about the father of a boy called Lauri (example 7):

(6) *Ammu nukku.u. Ei is.i häili* [: häiritse].
moo-cow sleep-3S Not father-DIM disturb
'The cow is sleeping, Daddy may not disturb.'

(7) *Ei Lauri.n isä häili [: häiritse] ammu.*
not Lauri-GEN father disturb moo-cow
'The father of Lauri may not disturb the cow.'

The Standard Finnish non-diminutive word for 'pig', *porsas*, was used by Tuulikki at 2;3 when speaking about a certain pig which was refered to with the compound *pummeliporsas*, but when speaking about other piggies the diminutive *possu* was used.

In the recordings of Tuulikki, there appear four diminutives only in the basic form nominative singular: *hauva* 'doggie', *masu* 'tummy', *possu* 'piggie' and *simmu* 'eye'. Inflected forms of three diminutives are used by Tuulikki in the recordings:

heppa 'geegee': the nominative *heppa*, adessive singular *hepalla* 'with the geegee' and adessive plural *hepoilla* 'with the geegees'
isi 'father': the nominative *isi*, genitive *isin*, allative *isille* 'to the father' and translative *isiksi* 'to [become] a father'
pupu 'bunny': the nominative *pupu*, genitive *pupun* and plural partitive *pupuja* 'the bunnies'

5.2.4 *Summary of Tuulikki's diminutives*

To sum up: during premorphology, Tuulikki used two-syllabic diminutives which were acquired as such from the input. At the onset of protomorphology, Tuulikki started to produce diminutive neologisms of her own, both derivatives (e.g. *liini*-derivatives and *kki*-derivatives) and compound-like formations (e.g. names of fingers combined with the *putti*-element).

There are only a few examples of the use of both simplex form and diminutive for the same lexeme: *isi* 'father-DIM' is used for Tuulikki's own father, *isä* 'father' for the male parents of both other children and (toy) animals; *porsas* 'pig' is used when it belongs to the name of a certain pig, *possu* 'pig-DIM' is otherwise used for pigs.

The diminutives are often inflected in a more transparent way than the corresponding simplex forms. An example of this advantage is the inflection *heppa* 'geegee': *hepa-lla* 'geegee-ADESS (with the geegee)': *hepo-i-lla* 'geegee-PL-ADESS (with the geegees)' in the Tuulikki-recording as compared to the corresponding inflection of the *hevonen* 'horse': *hevose-lla* 'horse-ADESS (with the horse)': *hevos-i-lla* 'horse-PL-ADESS (with the horses)'.

5.3 Tuomas: diminutives in diary material and recordings

The data of Tuomas consist of both diary material and recordings. Tuomas, in the same way as his sister Tuulikki, used many diminutives which are typical of the Finnish motherese and child speech: 1;1 *hauva* 'bowwow', 1;3 *heppa* 'geegee', 1;4 *pupu* 'bunny' etc. But unlike his sister, he produced only few diminutives of his own. At first there were some trochaic forms, e.g. at 1:4 *kaakka* 'bird' based on the onomatopoetic expression *kvaak* which is used to imitate the voice of ducks. The neologism *kaakka* was used by Tuomas frequently, and at the same age (1;4) he formed another neologism, namely *kiikki* 'cat' (= Standard Finnish *kissa*), apparently modified to fit the phonological model of *kaakka*. He also shortened the name of his sister *Tuulikki* to *Tuukki*, which fits the same CVVKKV-pattern.

In contrast to Tuulikki, Tuomas produced only a few longer diminutives with a contrasting simplex noun, but there were some isolated ones: (2;6) *mä haluun purukumin // mä haluun purukumelin* 'I want to have a chewing gum // I want to have a chewing gum-DIM', (3;4) *pättikäinen* 'mother' (the word formation chain is *äiti* 'mother' –> *ätti* [phonetic modification typical of small children] –> *pätti* + DIM). Both *purukumeli* and *pättikäinen* have a strong pragmatic connotation of intimacy. Tuomas also produced a diminutive adverb at the age of 3;8, namely *sipitittisen* 'very little'. This neologism has an obvious meaning component of smallness:

(8) *Tos on punasta vähän ja vihreetä vähän*
There is red-PARTIT little and green-PARTIT little
ja ihan sipitittisen mustaa.
and very little black-PARTIT
'There is some red colour, some green and only *sipitittisen* (= very very little) of black.'

In a similar way as his sister, also Tuomas uses the diminutive *isi* when speaking about his own father and the non-diminutive *isä* when speaking about other male parents.

In the recordings of Tuomas, three diminutives appear only in nominative singular: *kaakka* 'birdie', *peukku* 'thumb' and *possu* 'piggie'. Tuomas uses inflected forms from four diminutives:

hauva 'doggie': nominative *hauva*, partitive singular *hauvaa* and nominative plural *hauvat*
heppa 'geegee, nominative *heppa* and partitive *heppaa*
isi 'father': nominative *isi*, genitive *isin* and partitive *isiä* ~ *isii*
masu 'tummy': the illative *masuun* 'into the tummy'

To sum up: Tuomas used similar acquired diminutives as his sister but he did not produce so many own diminutives as she. The early own diminutives of Tuomas had the phonological pattern CVVkkV. Later he produced only a few diminutive neologisms, and they had a clear pragmatic connotation of endearment.

6. Conclusion

Diminutive formation has a morphopragmatic effect: the diminutives discussed in section 5 above have the pragmatic connotation of endearment. The semantic meaning of smallness belongs in a natural, inherent way to the diminutives referring to the body parts of the child (e.g. *masu* 'tummy') and to the toy animals. This meaning of smallness does not belong in the same way to kinship terms (*isi* 'father', *äitsykkä* 'mother', *ukki* 'grandfather' etc.) which are on the border of diminutives and hypocoristics. In the recorded material, the purely semantic meaning component of 'smallness' is most obvious in the compounds used by the adults, e.g. *pikkuauto* 'small private car' (Tuomas-recording 1:10) and *pienkone* 'small plane' (Tuomas-recording 1;11).

Diminutives in Finnish child-directed and child speech are interesting not only from the morphopragmatic perspective which Finnish shares with other languages but also from the more language-specific morphophonemic perspective: producing diminutives by shortening and modification of the stem is one way to avoid certain rather complex morphophonemic stem alternations, because the Finnish diminutives have usually a more simple and transparent inflection pattern than the nouns from which these diminutives have been derived. The diminutive derivation sometimes makes the nouns shorter than their simple base, for example *peukalo* 'thumb' -> *peukku*. In certain other languages, for example in Dutch, Lithuanian and Russian, diminutives also often have a more transparent inflection than their simplex bases, but this simplification of inflection is achieved by adding certain derivative elements which make the resulting diminutives longer than their bases (cf. Voeikova 1998 and the chapters by Savickienė and others in this volume).

In the Finnish derivation morphology there is much variation in the marking of diminutiveness: there is no single diminutive element. Finnish diminutives can be formed by regular affixation, but they are often formed by modifying the word: by shortening the original stem, eliminating difficult sounds and attaching an affix-like element, e.g. *porsas* 'pig' > *possu* 'piggie', *silmä* 'eye' > *simmu* and *käsi* 'hand' > *känny*.

In certain words the modification of the stem results in short diminutives which reflect the idea of smallness in an iconical way: *peukalo* 'thumb' > *peukku*, *kissa* 'cat' > *kisu*, *hevonen* 'horse' > *heppa*, *porsas* 'pig' -> *possu* 'piggie'. In these derivatives, adding the semantic feature 'small' is reflected iconically in the reduction of the sound substance, and the resulting word-form is shorter than the base. The actual reason for these short diminutives is the tendency to truncate longer words to trochaic forms (see section 5.2.1).

From the morphological point of view, many of the diminutives used in Finnish child-directed and child speech are rather exceptional: they are not formed by regular suffixation but their derivational morphology is similar to affective formations in Finnish colloquial speech. From the pragmatic point of view, they are diminutives expressing endearment, intimacy and warm feelings.

The empirical material includes some overextensions at the onset of productive diminutive formation. The girl, Tuulikki, started with diminutives formed by shortening and stem-type simplification which are also characteristic of the child-directed speech. From the age of 1;8 onwards, Tuulikki established some individual diminutive derivation types which seem to be at least partly based on adult models. These diminutives were her first productive type of neologisms, and especially the two-syllabic *liini*-suffix used in the derivation of four-syllabic trochaic diminutives was remarkably longer than other suffixes used at the same age. The boy, Tuomas, also used diminutives formed by shortening and stem-type simplification; these occur frequently in the child-directed speech as well. He produced only a few diminutive formations of his own. For both children, the pragmatic expression of endearment was important in the use of diminutives, and diminutives were used especially for family members, toy animals, body parts and certain favourite foods of the child.

References

Dressler, W. U. and Merlini Barbaresi, L. 1994. *Morphopragmatics: diminutives and intensifiers in Italian, German, and other languages*. Berlin: Mouton de Gruyter.

Gerken, L. 1994. A metrical template account of children's weak syllable omissions from multisyllabic words. *Journal of Child Language* 21 (3): 565–584.

Gillis, S. 1997. The acquisition of diminutives in Dutch. In *Studies in pre- and protomorphology*, Wolfgang U. Dressler (ed.), 165–179. Wien: Verlag der Österreichischen Akademie der Wissenschaften.

Jusczyk, P. W. 1997. *The discovery of spoken language*. Cambridge: The MIT Press.

Laalo, K. 1994. Kaksitavuvaihe lapsen kielen kehityksessä. (English summary: The disyllabic stage in language acquisition.) *Virittäjä* (Journal of the Mother Tongue Society) 97 (3): 430–448.

Laalo, K. 2001. The tendency to trochaic word-forms in Finnish child language. In *Congressus nonus internationalis fenno-ugristarum 7. - 13. 8. 2000 Tartu*, Tonu Seilenthal (ed.), Pars V: 209–214. Tartu: OÜ PAAR.

Räisänen, A. 1975. Havaintoja lastenkielestä. (English summary: Observations on child language). *Virittäjä* (Journal of the Mother Tongue Society) 79 (3): 251–266.

Savinainen-Makkonen, T. 2000. Learning to produce three-syllable words: a longitudinal study of Finnish twins. In *New Directions in Language Development and Disorders*, M. Perkins and S. Howard (eds), 223–231. New York, Boston, Dordrecht, London, Moscow: Plenum Publishing.

Stephany, U. 1997. Diminutives in early child Greek, a preliminary investigation. In *Studies in pre- and protomorphology*, Wolfgang U. Dressler (ed.), 147–156. Wien: Verlag der Österreichischen Akademie der Wissenschaften.

Toivainen, J. 1972. Suomen murteiden hoivasanasto. Lapsen fyysiseen rakenteeseen ja toimintaan viittaavat appellatiivit. Lisensiaatintyö. Oulun yliopiston suomen ja saamen kielen ja logopedian laitos. (Unpublished manuscript about motherese in the Finnish dialects).

Toivainen, K. 1995. Satakunnan hoivasanaston ominaispiirteitä. In *Kielen ja kulttuurin satakunta. Juhlakirja Aimo Hakasen 60-vuotispäiväksi 1. 11. 1995. Turun yliopiston suomalaisen ja yleisen kielitieteen laitoksen julkaisuja 51*, 287–308. Vammala. (Article about motherese in the dialects of Satakunta).

Wijnen, F., Krikhaar, E. and Den Os, E. 1994. The (non)realization of unstressed elements in children's utterances: evidence for a rhythmic constraint. *Journal of Child Language* 21 (1): 59–83.

Voeikova, M. 1998. Acquisition of diminutives by a Russian child: Preliminary observations in connection with the early adjectives. In *Studies in the acquisition of number and diminutive marking* [Antwerp papers in linguistics 95], S. Gillis (ed.), 97–113. Antwerpen: Universiteit Antwerpen.

CHAPTER 11

The (scarcity of) diminutives in Turkish child language*

F. Nihan Ketrez and Ayhan Aksu-Koç

This study reports that diminutive morphology is not one of the early acquisitions in Turkish child speech (1;3–2;0), although the language has a number of productive diminutive morphemes. Similarly the use of hypocoristic forms of nouns is not a typical property of Turkish child speech. We attribute the scarcity of diminutives and hypocoristic forms in child speech to their infrequent use in the input speech and the complexity of the diminutive formation in the language which does not have properties that could facilitate word learning.

1. Introduction

Diminutives are typical properties of child directed speech in many languages (Gillis 1997; Jurafsky 1996; Stephany 1997 among others). They are important also because they are the earliest productive derivational morphology recorded in various child languages (Slobin 1966 among others). Their frequent use in CDS and early emergence in child speech are attributed to their morphological and phonological simplification and regularization impact on nominal stems. In Spanish and Russian, for example, diminutives are argued to facilitate learning by simplification of the gender system; in Finnish and Lithuanian, the diminutive formation simplifies the case system and declension paradigms (Kempe & Brooks 2001; Kempe et. al. 2003; Melzi & King 2003; Laalo 1998; Savickienė 1998; Wojcik 1994 among others). Similarly, in English and Dutch, diminutives regularize the stress pattern and simplify word recognition (Gillis 1997; Jusczyk 1997). In this chapter, we present a description of the diminutive system in Turkish spoken in İstanbul, Turkey, and discuss the use of diminutives in the speech of a monolingual Turkish child and her mother between the ages 1;3 and 2;0.

Turkish is an agglutinative language in which word formation is realized mainly by suffixation. Inflectional and derivational systems are quite regular and suffixes obey the rules of vowel harmony and consonant alternations. There is no grammatical gender. Although the language has a number of productive diminutive morphemes, there has been no in-depth study of the diminutive formations in Turkish. It has not been studied from a language learning perspective either.

In this chapter, we show that although Turkish has a number of productive and semi-productive diminutive morphemes, nominals that bear the diminutive morphology constitute less than 5% of the nouns in our subject's speech. Thus, Turkish contrasts with other languages such as Russian, Lithuanian and Dutch with respect to the amount of diminutive use in child speech. We attribute the scarcity of diminutives in early Turkish to the following factors: 1. *Amount of diminutive use in* CDS. Turkish mothers do not use diminutives as frequently as the mothers speaking other languages. The simplex forms of the words that appear in diminutive form are used much more frequently. 2. *Increased complexity of diminutive-marked nominals.* The diminutive formation is not needed to simplify the system, which is already very salient and transparent for a learner (Aksu-Koç & Slobin 1985). Rather, it adds complexity to the semantics and the morphology of words. 3. *No contribution to the stress pattern.* The diminutive marker does not necessarily impact the stress pattern of words and it does not contribute to the regularization of a stress pattern. Moreover, its variable behavior in different lexical classes (nouns versus adjectives) adds complexity and irregularity to a simple and relatively regular phonological system.

Because diminutives do not contribute to the simplification or regularization of the morpho-phonological system in Turkish grammar and because they are not used frequently in adult speech directed to children, the scarcity of diminutive use in our subject's speech is not surprising, and more importantly, it is predicted by the nominal morphology theory defended in this volume.

2. Diminutives and hypocoristics in Turkish grammar

In this section, the forms and functions of the diminutives are presented and their morphological and phonological properties are discussed. Some affixes that do not appear in CDS are included as well, in order to present the complete system of diminutive formation in Turkish and also to show that the language provides many forms, but they are not all used in CDS.

2.1 -*CIK*

-CIK, which is the most productive diminutive suffix, can be attached to nouns (e.g., *kedi-cik* (cat-DIM) 'little/poor cat'), proper nouns (e.g., *Ayşe-cik* (Ayşe-DIM) 'little/poor Ayşe'), adjectives (e.g., *kısa-cık* (short-DIM) 'very short') and the cardinal number *bir* (e.g., *bir-i-cik* (one-DIM) 'the only/dear').[1, 2] It is possible to attach more than one -CIK to a stem to intensify the effect of the diminutive morpheme (e.g., *kısa* (short) > *kısa-cık* 'very short' > *kısa-cı-cık* 'very very short').

-CIK behaves differently according to the grammatical category of the stem it is attached to, with respect to not only morpho-phonological properties but also the intended meaning and function. The use of -CIK with common nouns and proper names is straightforward. No stem change is seen. The intended meaning is that of smallness in size or a feeling of affection. A word such as cat-DIM means 'little cat' or 'poor cat.' When it is attached to proper names, it usually expresses sympathy and affection as in the case of *Ayşe-cik* 'poor/dear Ayşe.' The behavior of -CIK with adjectives is different. Following are the differences.

First, -CIK results in a stem alternation. Those words that end in /k/ undergo final consonant deletion as in the case of *küçük* 'small' > *küçü-cük*. Such a deletion is seen in adjectives only. The language allows /k/ in this position when the word is a noun.[3] Compare *köpek* > *köpek-çik* 'dog-DIM' with *küçük* > *küçü-cük* 'small-DIM.' Another stem-change, in the form of vowel epenthesis, is observed in words such as the cardinal number *bir* 'one' and some other adjectives. *Bir* > *bir-i-cik* and *az* 'little' > *az-ı-cık* are some examples. Such a change is not observed in nouns or proper names. Contrast *kaz-cık* 'goose-DIM' and *Naz-cık* 'Naz-DIM' with *az-ı-cık,* for example. Secondly, when attached to a noun or a proper noun, -CIK gives a meaning of smallness, affection or sympathy. The meaning that it adds to adjectives, however, varies. When attached to an adjective such as 'small' or 'little,' which already has a dimensional meaning of smallness/shortness, it intensifies the meaning and makes the noun reference even smaller. In that sense, -CIK is more like an intensifier, rather than a diminutive, because it increases the smallness of the size. In contrast, when -CIK is attached to adjectives that do not denote smallness, it is either ungrammatical as in the case of *uzun* 'long' > **uzun-cuk*), or it results in a noun interpretation of the word ('the little long (one)') with a difference in the stress pattern, which will be discussed below. All these examples suggest that in contrast to the diminutive function in nouns, the function of -CIK in adjectives is that of an intensifier, rather than a true diminutive and thus it results in a diminutive meaning only in adjectives that already denote smallness by an increase in the degree of smallness.

The stress pattern of -CIK words varies due to the grammatical category of the word as well. In adjectives with the diminutive suffix, the stress falls on the first syllable (e.g., *kısá* 'short' > *kísacık* 'very short'). In nouns and proper nouns, the stress pattern does not change with the attachment of -CIK. In those words that have word final stress (e.g., *ayí* 'bear'), the stress passes onto the diminutive affix and the word final stress pattern is retained (e.g., *ayı-cík*). Such a stress-shift to the right is typical of all word-finally stressed words in Turkish. No stress-placement change is observed in those words that have non-final stress. The word *sandálye* > *sandálye-cik* is an example.[4]

In summary, -CIK does not have a unique pattern that simplifies or regularizes the word morphology in Turkish.[5] The stem change that it causes in some words is not governed by a simple mechanism and thus enhances the complexity of derivation. Various stress patterns of diminutive words show that the diminutive morpheme does not add any simplicity to the phonological system of the word. Moreover, various conflicting meanings that are associated with the diminutive morpheme add semantic complexity to the derivation, and present a potential challenge for a child.

2.2 Other diminutives (or other forms of -CIK)

The diminutive suffixes *-CIğIm*, *-CIğImA*, *-CIktA*, and *-CIktAn* are the other forms of -CIK diminutives. When -CIK is followed by the possessive marker (which is marked for person and number), it usually has a vocative function. *Deniz-ciğ-im* (Deniz-DIM-POSS&1sg) 'my dear Deniz' or *anne-ciğim* (mother-DIM-POSS&1sg) 'my dear mother' are two examples. The possessive form together with the diminutive marker expresses an endearment of the addressee. *Sonra-cığım-a* (after/later-CIK-POSS&1sg-DATIVE) is the only example where we can have the DIM+POSS&1Sg followed by the dative. Its meaning is 'and then' or 'after (that)' but with an informal tone. We can analyze the diminutive in this word as a marker that decreases formality. Those forms where the diminutive marker is attached to nouns and is followed by the locative or ablative case (-CIktA and -CIktAn) are used as adverbials. *Şaka-cık-tan* (joke-DIM-ABL) 'as a little joke/ let's pretend' is an example. *Şuracıkta*, derived from *şura* 'over there' refers to a (short) distance which is shorter and more accessible than the one indicated by *şura*.

-CA is a diminutive affix with four variants: *-ca, -ce, -ça, -çe*. It is less common and less productive than -CIK. It is attached to adjectives only (e.g., *büyük* 'big'> *büyükçe, ufak* 'small'> *ufakça)* and always has a diminutive or decreasing impact on the meaning of adjectives- even those such as *küçük* 'small' and *kısa* 'short.' Those words such as *büyük* that cannot enter into the derivation with -CIK *(*büyük-cük)* can be derived by -CA with a diminutive meaning: *büyük-çe* means 'not very big.'

-CA does not result in a stress-shift to the final syllable (e.g., *uzún* 'long' > *uzún-ca*, with no stress shift). Contrast the stress shift and the meaning change in the word *ufak* 'small' when derived with -CA versus -CIK: *ufák* > *ufák-ça* (with no stress shift) results in a decrease in the degree of smallness, meaning 'not very small' and *ufák* > *úfa-cık* (with a stress shift to the initial syllable) causes an increase in the degree of smallness meaning 'very small.'

-CA can be followed by -CIK in some adjectives and adverbs (e.g., *yavas-ça-cık*, 'slowly-DIM-DIM'). -CACIK is an example of a double-marking that does not have an additional semantic contribution to the diminutive meaning of the word but rather serves the pragmatic function of reflecting the attitude of the speaker (Dressler & Barbaresi 1994).

-CAnA is another form of -CA as seen in examples *eski-cene* 'old-DIM', *sulu-cana*, 'juicy-DIM' *fazla-cana* 'plenty-DIM' (Banguoğlu 1990: 350).[6]

The other diminunive suffix, *-CAğIz*, is attached to nouns (Lees 1961; Çotuksöken 1980), such as man, girl, woman and expresses a feeling of strong pity or sympathy. *Kadın-cağız* 'woman-DIM' means 'poor woman,' for example. It does not denote 'smallness' or a decrease in the property of being a woman, but expresses this meaning of disparagement by pragmatic extension from the connotative meaning of 'affection,' the actual reference of the derived word depending on knowledge of the world or speech situation (Dressler & Barbaresi 1994). -CAğIZ does not have an impact on the stress pattern of the word. No stem change occurs either.

2.3 *-Iş/-Oş* and other hypocoristics

Hypocoristics are formed by the attachment of an affix *-o, -i, -oş/-iş, -k* to a shortened form of the word. Lewis (1967) states that when the diminutive affixes are attached to a proper name, the first syllable of the name is retained and *-i, -o* or a syllable ending in *-ş* is added to the noun. *Fato* (derived from *Fat.ma*) and *İbo* (derived from *İb.ra. him*) are such examples.[7] However, the following examples suggest that the derivation is more complicated than it is described by Lewis (1967). In majority of the cases, the word is not shortened by the syllable boundary. In words such as *Murti* (derived from *Mur.ta.za*) or *Erci* (derived from *Er.cü.ment*) the diminutive affix *-i* is attached to the first syllable + the first consonant of the second syllable, that is the base is truncated to the longest legal closed syllable (*Murt* and *Erc*) and then the vowel is added.[8] *Mıs.tık* (derived from *Mus.ta.fa*) and *Fa.dik* (derived from *Fa.di.me*) are other examples, which are derived by another hypocoristic morpheme *-(i)k*, where the truncation occurs after the second syllabus. The final syllabus is omitted and *-(i)k* is added to the base.

Another addition to the complexity is vowel alternations. The choice between *-i* and *-o* is not predictable, and words derived from the same stem by both affixes also exist in the language (e.g., *Fatı* and *Fato* derived from *Fatma*). The names that are formed with *-o* are accented on the first syllable, while the others are accented at the final syllable (no stress-shift occurs).[9]

The affix *-Iş* can be attached to common nouns (*bebiş*, derived from *bebek* 'baby'; *ciciş* derived from the noun form of *cici* 'cute') as well as proper names (e.g., *Aliş*). Note the stem alternations (final vowel change or *k*-omission) in the examples above. *-Işko* is a variety of *-Iş* which has a restrictive use with words such as *babişko* (derived from *baba* 'father'). These words express sympathy, mutual closeness and are very informal. Lewis (1967) considers *-o* diminutives more familiar and socially less acceptable than those ending in *-[I]ş*.

In summary, as in the case of the other diminutive derivations with -CIK and its variants, hypocoristics, present a potential challenge to a Turkish child, as they do not have a predictable derivational pattern, and do not seem to contribute to the simplification of the word structure.

So far, we presented a description of adult grammar. In the sections that follow, we will present the production of diminutives in child speech and CDS and show that despite its productivity in the grammar, it is *not* a common word formation strategy in CDS and child speech.

3. Method

The study is based on the spontaneous speech samples of a monolingual Turkish girl, Deniz, recorded longitudinally between the ages 1;3,3 and 2;0,4. 20 minute-long recordings were done approximately twice a month. During the sessions, which were recorded by the mother at home, she was engaged in various natural everyday activities. The utterances were transcribed and coded morphologically according to the CHAT conventions of CHILDES (MacWhinney 2000). All the words that can potentially bear diminutive morphology were targeted for analysis.

4. Diminutives are rare in child speech

Table 1 presents Deniz's diminutive vocabulary together with the age of emergence, tokens and the simplex forms. The picture shows that diminutive is not a frequent word form in our subject's speech. As can be observed, simplex forms appear much earlier than their diminutive counterparts. They are used much more frequently and the proportion of the nouns marked with the diminutive morpheme is less than 2% of the total number of nouns. This proportion is higher for adjectives (25%), given that the total number of adjectives in Deniz's speech is very low. Considering all diminutivizable nouns and adjectives together for the whole period studied, the percentage of diminutives in Deniz' speech is about 1%.

Table 1. Diminutives and their simplex counterparts in child speech (To=tokens, CN=common noun, PN=proper noun, A=adjective/adverb)

Simplex	Gloss	Age	To	Diminutive	Age	To (%)	All To
ayı (CN)	bear	1;7,8	28	*ayı-cık*	1;9,1	**1 (0.4)**	239
					1;11,23	**2 (0.6)**	325
Kaan (PN)	Kaan	1;10,19	7	*Kaan-cığ-ım*	1;11,23	**1 (0.3)**	325
şaka (CN)	joke	-	-	*şaka-cık-tan*	1;11,10	**1 (0.6)**	172
minik (A)	small	1;8,11	3	*minnacık**	1;11,10	2 (25)	8

(*) failed attempt.

The earliest diminutive word *ayı-cık* (bear-DIM) 'little bear' appears at 1;9,1, two months later than the simplex form *ayı* 'bear' and it is produced only three times during the sessions, while the simplex form is recorded 28 times (13 times in bare form and 15 times marked with case and possessive markers). By the time the diminutive form appears (2), the simplex form of the word is already in use in the child's speech (1). However, we do not have the two forms attested at the same session, therefore, we do not have an evidence for productive use.

(1) MOT: Deniz bu ne? CHI: **ayı** (Age: 1;7,23)
'Deniz what is this?' 'bear'

(2) CHI: **a:-dık [:ayıcık]** yatağ-ı-na yat-mış. (Age: 1;9,1)
bear-DIM bed-POSS&2sg-DAT lie-PFV
'The little bear has lied /is down on her bed.'

The word *şakacıktan* (joke-DIM-ABL) 'as a joke/let's pretend' is the only example that is used only in the diminutive form. We do not have any evidence for the productive use of the diminutive marker on this word either. It is very likely that it is used as a non-analyzed form by the child.

In addition to *-CIK*, Deniz uses *-CIğIm* in one word in a role-play game with her mother. The word is used in the diminutive form by the mother all through the conversation, so we do not know whether the child is using the word to express sympathy, endearment or affection intentionally. That is, it is likely that she is copying the address form used by the mother, without analyzing its pragmatic function herself.

(3) MOT: beğen-di-n mi oyuncağ-ı **Kaan-cı(ğ)-ım**. (Age: 1;11,23)
like-PAST-1S Qu toy-ACC Kaan-DIM-POSS&1sg
'Did you like the toy, Kaan-DIM?'
(...)
CHI: **Kaan-dı-m** o-nu elle-me yap.[10]
Kaan-DIM-POSS&1sg that-ACC touch-NEG do
'Do(=say) Kaan-DIM, don't touch it'

In summary, the only grammatical diminutive morphemes that Deniz uses are *-CIK*, *-CIktAn* and *-CIğIm*. The other morphemes do not appear in her speech during the period analyzed. She does not form or use any hypocoristics either. In addition to the examples reported above, there is an overmarking error, recorded at the age of 1;11,10, which suggests that Deniz has analyzed the diminutive formation and is attempting to use the diminutive morpheme productively. Despite this error, it is difficult to understand whether she mastered the morpho-pragmatics of diminutives during the period we analyze due to the few number of diminutive morphology in her speech. In the next section, we discuss this error and the target form.

5. An error

In the error (4) that is observed in the production of the word *minnacık* 'very small' Deniz marks the adjective 'small' with a diminutive marker twice and does not omit the first /k/. The example shows that she detected the diminutive morpheme and attempts to use it productively.[11]

(4) CHI: Minna-dık*-cık (Age: 1;11,10)

Small-DIM-*DIM
Adult form: *minna-**cık*** or *minna-**cı-cık**.*

The word that she attempts to produce is not an easy one. Consider the paradigm in (5). In this paradigm, it is possible to have double marking of -CIK, but the derivation has restrictions. Moreover, in addition to double marking with -CIK, it is also possible to emphasize the smallness with *mini,* which is a borrowed form and appears in restricted contexts such as *mini fırın* 'mini owen' or *mini etek* 'mini skirt.' It does not appear as a free morpheme or word, but it appears in a reduplication *minimini* and functions as a modifier meaning very small. The word *minik* is an adjective meaning 'small.' *Minik* can be marked with the diminutive marker -CIK and just as it is the case with all the adjectives that end in /k/, it is pronounced as *minicik* with k-deletion. Note that *mini mini* can also be marked with -CIK and the outcome is *mini-mini-cik.* Both versions can take one more -CIK, and are pronounced as *mini-mini-ci-cik* or *mini-ci-cik.* Addition of another diminutive -CIK increases the effect of the diminutive marker. The word meaning small becomes smaller and smaller with the addition of each -CIK. The final-k of *minik* is omitted with the attachment of first -CIK and the final /k/ of -CIK is deleted by the attachment of the second -CIK. The result is mini-ci-cik (*mini-cik-cik). The word *minna-cık* can be analyzed as a variety of *mini-cik* or a reduced form of *miniminicik.* It can also be pronounced as *mini-minna:-cık.* The forms that are recorded in the CDS are marked with an arrow.

(5) The paradigm of *mini* in adult speech:
a. mini
b. mini mini
c. minik
d. mini-**cik** ←CDS
e. mini-**ci-cik**
f. mini-mini-**cik** ←CDS
g. mini-mini-**ci-cik**
h. minna:-**cık** ←CDS
i. minna:**cı-cık**
j. mini-minna:-**cık** ←CDS
k. *mini-**cik-cik** (without /k/-omission)
l. *minna:-**cık-cık** (without /k/-omission)

As shown in the paradigm, the mother does not use the double marking of -CIK, but rather increases the intensity of smallness with the usage of *mini.* Despite that, the double marking of -CIK appears in the child's speech. What Deniz is doing is legitimate but has morpho-phonological restrictions (i.e., /k/-omission). Considering the complexity of the paradigm, which is an exceptionally complex paradigm in Turkish, it is not surprising that the child fails in her attempt.

6. Scarcity of diminutives in CDS

The CDS is similar to Deniz's speech. The frequency of diminutives is relatively low despite the fact that the context of mother-child interaction has all the properties favorable to the production of diminutives: a female caregiver's child directed speech in a nurturing environment (Ferguson 1977) and Turkish has a number of diminutive suffixes that could be used.

Table 2. Proportion of diminutives in CDS (CN=common noun, PN=proper noun, A=adjective/adverb)

	Total			Diminutive					
Class	Lem	Type	To	Lem	%	Type	%	To	%
CN	565	1494	4744	17	3.0	18	1.2	35	0.7
PN	56	119	868	3	5.3	4	3.3	72	8.2
A	112	132	948	4	5.3	4	4.5	34	3.7
Total	733	1745	6560	24	3.2	26	1.4	141	2.1

Table 3. Diminutives, hypocoristics and their proportion in CDS

	Lemma	Type	Token	Diminutive %
-CIK/-CIğIm	11	15	117	83.5
-CIktAn/-CIğImA	2	2	8	5.7
-CAğIZ	1	1	3	2.1
-CA	1	1	1	0.7
Hypocoristics *-o/-iş*	8	9	11	7.8
Total	23	28	140	99.8

As seen in Table 2 and Table 3, only 2.1% of the nominal stems bear diminutive morphology in the mother's speech (based on tokens). Table 4, presents the diminutive forms, their simplex counterparts and the token frequency of each, and shows that the frequency of the diminutive words is much less than their simplex counterparts. There are exceptions such as *Kaan-cığım,* the diminutive form of which is used more often, and *kadıncağız* 'poor woman' as well as some frozen forms such as *tontiş, montiş,* that are used only with diminutive morphology. In general, however, the picture suggests that diminutive forms of the words are used *less* frequently. The most frequent diminutive word is the child's name *Deniz,* which is produced as *Deniz-ciğim,* with diminutive suffix 57 times. Its simplex use, however, is much more frequent (424 tokens) throughout the period recorded.

A difference between child speech and CDS is that, in Deniz's speech we have only -CIK, -CIktAn and -CIğIm, while the mother uses the other types of diminutive formations as well. Despite the variety, -CIK, -CIktAn and -CIğIm are the most frequently used ones in CDS. An inspection of the frequencies in Table 4 and Table 5 suggest that Deniz picks up the diminutive morpheme that is used most frequently (83.5%) in adult speech. This parallelism supports the hypothesis that the production of diminutives in child's speech reflects the use of diminutives in CDS. Due to the scarcity of diminutives in Deniz's speech, however, we are unable to put forth a strong claim about such a parallelism although this hypothesis seems to hold pretty much for many other structures, e.g., early use of TAM markers mirrors that of mothers in terms of frequency and verb type (Aksu-Koç 1998).

Table 4. Diminutives (word class between prentheses) and their simplex counterparts in CDS

	Diminutive	Gloss	To	Simplex	To	%
-CIğIm, -CIK	yavru-cuğ-um (CN)	child-dim-poss:1sg	2	yavru	1	66.6
	Deniz-ciğ-im (PN)	Deniz-dim-poss:1sg	57	*Deniz*	424	11.8
	Kaan-cığ-ım (PN)	Kaan-dim-poss:1sg	12	*Kaan*	6	66.6
	anne-ciğ-im (CN)	mother-dim-poss:1sg	3	*anne*	97	3
	ayı-cığ-ım (CN) *ayı-cık* (CN)	bear-dim-poss:1sg	11	*ayı*	95	10.3
	dede-ciğim (PN)	grandpa-dim-poss:1sg	1	*dede*	47	2.08
	(mini)mini-cik,(A) *(mini)minna-cık* (A)	small-dim mini-small-dim	16	*minik*	24	40
	biraz-cık (A)	alittle-dim	9	*biraz*	42	17.6
	tane-cik (CN)	piece/grain-dim	1	*tane*	33	2.94
	kedi-cik (CN)	cat-dim	2	*kedi*	49	3.9
	abi-cik(CN)	male child-dim	2	*abi*	78	2.56
	parça-cık(CN)	piece-dim	1	*parça*	9	10
-CIktAn	şaka-cıktan(CN)	joke-dim-abl	1	*şaka*	1	50
-CIğImA	*sonra-cığ-ıma* (A)	later-dim-poss:1sg-dat	7	*Sonra*	94	7.4
-CAğIz	*kadın-cağız* (CN)	woman-dim	3	*kadın*	0	100
-CA	*epey-ce* (A)	very-dim	1	*epey*	2	33.3

Table 5. Hypocristics (word class between parentheses) and their simplex counterparts in CDS

	Hypocristics	Gloss	To	Simplex	To	%
-o/-iş	*Hako, Hako-ya* (PN)	Hakan-*o*	3	*Hakan*	5	57.5
	*minnoş** (CN)	-	1	-	-	-
	*montiş-im** (CN)	-	1	-	-	-
	*tontiş** (CN)	-	1	-	-	-
	uykuş (CN)	sleep-*ş*	2	*uyku*	17	10.52
	popi-ş (CN)	bottom-*ş*	1	*popo*	2	33.3
	tatlı-ş (CN)	sweet-*ş*	1	*tatlı*	6	14.2
	tip-oş (CN)	type/sort-*ş*	1	*tip*	0	100

We propose that the scarcity of diminutives in the child's speech can be attributed to the scarcity of diminutives in CDS which may be related to the complex nature of the Turkish diminutive system.[12] It is important to note that, however, the scarcity of diminutives is not a property of Turkish CDS only. In adult-to-adult speech as well, we do not observe many diminutives in the variety of Turkish we are studying. Therefore, the infrequent use of diminutives should not be considered a simplification strategy that is peculiar to CDS.

Turkish has a transparent nominal declension system which does not need any further simplification. Thus there is no motivation for the early acquisition of this derivational process by the Turkish child. Early acquisition, instead, proceeds with the learning of the highly regular noun and verb inflection systems. Our subject is a precocious learner and by the age of 2;0,4 when our recordings end she is already in the morphological stage. She has almost mastered the inflectional paradigms in these domains (Aksu-Koç & Ketrez 2003; Ketrez & Aksu-Koç under review) and her speech provides evidence for derivational morphology. These findings, together with the present ones indicate that the diminutive system emerges relatively late in Turkish and will proceed along with other derivational processes. We may expect an increase in the frequency of use and variety of diminutives both in our subject's and her mother's speech in the subsequent phases of the morphological period. More specifically, we would expect the mother to accommodate her speech in response to the developments in the child's speech. Melzi and King (2003: 302) who investigated the use of diminutives in mother-child conversations in Spanish, report that children and mothers encourage the use of these forms by imitating each other's use: "imitation of diminutive forms by one interlocutor is highly correlated and serves as a strong predictor of total frequency of diminutive use by their interlocutor."

The present series of studies carried out in different languages show that the differences in the patterns observed in the input and the child speech may be related to differential functionality of diminutive formations in easing acquisition. Diminutives in

Turkish do not bring about syntactic, morphological and phonological simplification and thus in the case of Turkish their use and the age of emergence are more likely to be determined by semantic and/or pragmatic motivations such as endearment, expression of affection, and personal point of view.

7. Conclusion

In this chapter, we showed that in Turkish CDS diminutives are not used frequently and, in Turkish, diminutive formation is done through an application of complex pragmatic, lexical, phonological and morphological processes. It results in irregularity, rather than regularity. It makes the morphological system more complex, rather than turning it into a more learner-friendly form. Turkish diminutive contrasts with the forms and functions of the diminutives in other languages, therefore, it is not surprising to see that it is not a typical property of CDS. Due to its properties, and based on what we know about the use of diminutives in other languages, we hypothesized that our Turkish subject would not have many diminutive forms in her early speech. In this chapter, we showed that this was exactly what was borne out.

Notes

* The data analyzed in this study were collected for the project *A Longitudinal Study of the Acquisition of Turkish* (project no: 96S0017) that was supported by a grant to A. Aksu-Koç from the Boğaziçi University Research Fund. We would like to thank Barış Kabak and Fetiye Karabay for discussion on various aspects of diminutives presented in this chapter and two anonymous reviewers for the interesting questions they raised.

1. Upper-case characters indicate vowel and consonant changes due to vowel harmony and consonant assimilation. -CIK, for example, represents 16 possible forms (*-cik, -çik, cık, -çık, -cük, -çük, -cuk, -çuk, -ciğ, -çiğ, -cığ,-çığ, -cüğ ,-çüğ, -cuğ, -çuğ*).

2. -CIK cannot be attached to any other numeral.

3. Ülkü (1980) reports examples such as *bebek* 'baby' > *bebe-cik*, *köpek* 'dog' > *köpe-cik*, which are nouns and are produced with /k/-deletion, therefore, some varieties of Turkish allow /k/-deletion in nouns as well as adjectives. Whether the /k/ deletion is an optional or an obligatory process in these varieties needs further study. It would also be interesting to investigate whether /k/-deletion can apply to all nouns ending in /k/. While the examples above do not sound ungrammatical (they sound like a different variety only), in some other examples such as inanimate *tabak* 'plate,' or animate *inek* 'cow,' diminutive forms with /k/-deletion sound bad. It is also possible that those varieties have *bebe* or *köpe* as the noun forms (without /k/) and there is actually no /k/-deletion. *Köpe* sounds bad in isolation but it appears in some compound curse words in Turkish. *Bebe* appears alone in the language along with *bebek* and can be inflected by other nominal morphology (e.g., *bebe-ler*). The description in this chapter is the description of

the standard variety that the authors speak (which is the same variety as the subject in this study is acquiring) and the use of diminutives in other dialects is beyond the scope of the study.

4. It is likely that the reason behind the stress pattern difference in nouns and adjectives derived by -CIK is related to the different functions of -CIK in two grammatical categories. In nouns it is a true diminutive morpheme. In adjectives, however, it is more like an intensifier, and that is why it has the word initial stress. Note that another derivational affix, with a similar intensifier function, behaves in a similar fashion: Those words that undergo reduplication result in a stress-shift to the initial syllable. The word *uzún* 'long,' which is a word-final-stress word, becomes *úpuzun* 'very long' with a stress shift after the reduplication.

5. -CIK appears in some lexicalized words or idiomatic expressions too. *Mehmet* > *Mehmet-cik*, for example, refers to a Turkish soldier, or Turkish army in general. *Kitap-çık* 'book-DIM' meaning 'booklet' is another lexicalized example. While in the former example, the diminutive has a sympathy meaning towards the army, in the latter example, it expresses smallness in size. The word *gelincik* 'bride-DIM,' which literally mean 'little bride' and which is the Turkish name for the flower 'poppy,' is another lexicalized example. Therefore in the lexicalized forms too, the behavior of -CIK is similar to its behavior in non-lexicalized examples (sympathy with proper names, smallness in size with common nouns). -CIK also appears in place names such as *Yakacık* and *Gölcük*. In addition, it occurs in words derived from verbs. *Gül-* 'to laugh' > *gül-ü-cük* '(small) smile' and *öp-* 'to kiss' *öp-ü-cük* 'little kiss' are two examples (Ülkü 1980). Rather than analyzing -CIK as a morpheme that can be attached to both verbs and nouns, we can consider these examples as derived nominal stems. While *gül-ü* and *öp-ü* are not possible words in contemporary Turkish, there are words such as *kaz-* '(to) excavate' > *kazı* 'excavation' or *yaz* '(to) write' > *yazı* 'writing' in the language. Thus, it is possible to analyze *-ü* as a derivational affix that derives nouns from verbs, and the -CIK morpheme an affix that is attached to this derived noun.

6. As it is the case for the morpheme -CIK, -CA can appear in lexicalized or idiomatic words, too (Ülkü 1980). *İl* 'province'> *ilçe* 'administrative district in a province' is an example. In this derivation, too, the diminutive affix maintains its meaning of 'smallness.' As we reported above we observed the same behavior in lexicalized forms of the words derived with -CIK.

7. The symbol (.) stands for a syllable boundary.

8. Dressler (p.c.) notes that such a resyllabification operation is not peculiar to Turkish, it is observed in many other languages such as Hungarian (e.g., *cso.ko.la.de* 'chokolate' > diminutive *csok-i*, *Istvan* 'Steven' > hypocoristic *Pist-a*)

9. It is likely that the stress shift to the first syllable in *o*-diminutives is not peculiar to the diminutive formation, rather, it is a result of a general stress shift rule in the language. It is not very common to have *-o* in the final syllable of words in Turkish. Such words, which are limited in number, are restricted to borrowed words (e.g., *koro* 'chorus,' *depo* 'depot') and in a great majority of the cases they have the primary stress on the first syllable just as most other borrowed words in Turkish (Sezer 1983; Çakır 2000). Such an interpretation would explain why we do not have a similar kind of stress shift in all the hypocoristics.

10. In the word /kaandım/, the voiced alveolar affricate sound undergoes plosivization and is produced as a voiced denti-alveolar plosive.

11. We do not analyze this example as self-correction of the diminutive marker as the child produces the word as one single word, without having a pause between the two morphemes. If it

is a self-correction, it still shows that she is treating -CIK as a separate morpheme, and producing it as an individual morpheme.

12. An anonymous reviewer has drawn our attention to the fact that in the variety of Turkish spoken in Cyprus speakers use diminutive forms more frequently than they do in Turkey and children acquire them earlier. We do not have access to a comparative study of diminutives in other varieties of Turkish; therefore we do not know whether the description of the complex system we presented here reflects the facts for the Cypriot Turkish as well. It is apparent that the frequency of use in CDS is important. High amount of diminutives in Cypriot Turkish may be related to a possible language and culture contact with Greek-speaking Cypriots. Interestingly, the variety of Greek spoken on Cyprus is observed to have less diminutives than the one spoken in Greece (Terkourafi 2004). It is likely that the two communities accommodate to each other, one by increasing the diminutive use, and the other by decreasing it. We leave the investigation of this possible language contact issue and a comparative analysis of diminutives across different varieties of languages to a future study.

References

Aksu-Koç, A. 1998. Input and tense-aspect in Turkish. *First language* 18(3): 255–280.

Aksu-Koç, A. and Slobin, D. I. 1985. The acquisition of Turkish. In *The Crosslinguistic Study of Language Acquisition* [Vol.1], D. I. Slobin (ed.), 839–878. Hillsdale, N.J.: Lawrence Earlbaum Associates.

Aksu-Koç, A. and Ketrez, F. N. 2003. Early verbal morphology in Turkish: Emergence of inflections. In *Mini-paradigms and the emergence of verb morphology*, D. Bittner, W.U. Dressler and M. Kilani-Schoch (eds), 27–52. Berlin: Mouton de Gruyter.

Banguoğlu, T. 1990. *Türkçe'nin Grameri*. Ankara: TDK.

Çakır, M. C. 2000. On non-final stress in Turkish simplex words. In *Studies on Turkish and Turkic Languages*, A. Göksel and C. Kerslake (eds), 3–10. Turcologica 46. Wiesbaden: Harrassowitz Verlag.

Çotuksöken, Y. 1980. *Türkçe'de ekler, kökler, gövdeler*. İstanbul: Alaz Yayınları.

Demircan, Ö. 1996. *Türkçe'nin sesdizimi*. İstanbul: Der Yayınları.

Dressler, W. U. and Barbaresi, L. M. 1994. *Morphopragmatics*. Berlin: Mouton de Gruyter.

Ferguson, C. 1977. Baby talk as a simplified register. In *Talking to Children*, C. E. Snow and C. Ferguson (eds), 209–235. Cambridge: Cambridge University Press.

Gillis, S. 1997. The acquisition of diminutives in Dutch. In *Studies in Pre-and Proto morphology*, W.U. Dressler (ed.), 165–179. Wien: Österreichischen Akademie der Wissenschaften.

Jurafsky, D. 1996. Universal tendencies in the semantics of the diminutive. *Language* 72: 533–578.

Jusczyk, P. W. 1997. *The discovery of spoken language*. Cambridge, MA: MIT Press.

Kempe, V. and P. J. Brooks. 2001. The role of diminutives in the acquisition of Russian gender: Can elements of child-directed speech aid in learning morphology? *Language Learning* 51: 221–256.

Kempe, V., Brooks, P.J., Mironova, N. and Fedorova, O. 2003. Diminutivization supports gender acquisition in Russian children. *Journal of Child Language* 30: 471–484.

Ketrez, F. N. and Aksu-Koç, A. under review. Early Nominal Morphology: Emergence of Case and Number. In *The Development of Number and Case in the First Language Acquisition: A*

Cross-Linguistic Perspective, M. Voeikova and U. Stephany (eds). Berlin: Mouton de Gruyter.

Laalo, K. 1998. Diminutives in Finnish child-directed and child speech. In *Studies in the acquisition of number and diminutive marking* [Antwerp papers in Linguistics 95], S. Gillis (ed.), 137–148. Antwerp: Universiteit Antwerpen.

Lees, R. 1961. *The phonology of modern standard Turkish* [Uralic and Altaic Series, Volume 6]. Bloomington, IN: Indiana University Publications.

Lewis, G. L. 1967. *Turkish Grammar*. Oxford: Oxford Univ. Press.

MacWhinney, B. 2000. *The CHILDES project: Tools for analyzing talk*. Hillsdale, N.J.: Lawrence Earlbaum Associates.

Melzi, G. and King, K. A. 2003. Spanish diminutives in mother-child conversations. *Journal of Child Language* 30: 281–304.

Savickienė, I. 1998. The acquisition of diminutives in Lithuanian. In *Studies in the acquisition of number and diminutive marking* [Antwerp papers in Linguistics 95], S. Gillis (ed.), 115–135. Antwerp: Universiteit Antwerpen.

Sezer, E. 1983. On non-final stress in Turkish. *Journal of Turkish Studies* 5: 61–69.

Slobin, D. I. 1966. The acquisition of Russian as a native language. In *The genesis of language. A psycholinguistics Approach*, F. Smith and G.A. Miller (eds), 129–148. Cambridge, MA: MIT Press.

Stephany, U. 1997. Diminutives in early child Greek. In *Studies in Pre- and Protomorphology*, W.U. Dressler (ed.), 145–156. Wien: Österreichischen Akademie der Wissenschaften.

Terkourafi, M. 2004. Politeness in Cyprus: A coffee or a small coffee? In *Politeness in Europe*, L. Hickey and M. Stewart (eds), 277–291. Clevedon: Multilingual Matters.

Ülkü, V. 1980. *Affixale Wortbildung im Deutschen und Türkischen* [Dil ve Tarih-Coğrafya Fakültesi Yayınları 294]. Ankara: Ankara Üniversitesi Basımevi.

Wojcik, P. 1994. Some characteristic features of Lithuanian baby talk. *Linguistica Baltica* 3: 71–86.

CHAPTER 12

Acquiring diminutive structures and meanings in Hebrew

An experimental study

Anat Hora, Galit Ben-Zvi, Ronit Levie and Dorit Ravid

The chapter describes an experimental study of the acquisition of derivational diminutives in Hebrew. The study population consisted of 48 children in four age groups: 5–6, 7–8, 10–11, 12–13, and adults. Participants were administered two tasks: an explanation task, and a production task. The learning curves we uncovered begin in kindergarten, with less than one quarter correct productions and about one third correct explanations, and they rise steadily from age 7–8 throughout grade school, especially between ages 9–12. Only from age 12 do Hebrew speakers show that they have mastered the morphological, semantic, pragmatic, and cognitive factors that interact in understanding and producing diminutive forms. Diminutive derivational morphology is thus part of what is termed 'later language development', that is, linguistic acquisition during the school years.

1. Introduction

Diminutives have attracted considerable attention in recent research. Documenting over 80 languages, Jurafsky (1996) identified "child-relatedness" as the core meaning of the diminutive derivation from which all other meanings and uses are derived. Semantically, diminutives mark 'small' or 'young,' while pragmatically they can mark affection, playfulness, endearment or contempt.

Diminutive forms occur early in child language at a period when morpho-syntax is not yet well established and morphological operations are largely absent (Clark 1993; Dressler 1994; Gillis 1997). One reason that diminutives facilitate acquisition is that in many languages they regularize irregular aspects of inflectional morphology. Moreover, diminutives occur with high frequency in CDS (Kempe, Brooks & Gillis, this volume), another facilitating factor in language acquisition. Diminutives are more frequent in languages where they lead to greater morphophonological transparency in gender marking (Kempe & Brooks 2001; Kempe, Brooks & Pirott 2001). Dressler

(1994), Dressler and Karpf (1995) demonstrate that extra-grammatical operations in the formation of diminutives characterize children's early productions, before the emergence of morphological rules at a stage when children rely on cognitive rather than specifically grammatical knowledge. Independent support for this idea is provided by data from different languages reported by Clark (1985, 1993).

Although diminutive formation in Hebrew is neither as central nor as rich and varied as in some languages (Ceccherini, Bonifacio & Zocconi 1997; Gillis 1997; Stephany 1997), diminutive devices constitute an established and well-documented part of Modern Hebrew morphology and lexicon in both spoken and literary usage (Sagi 1997). Besides, Hebrew is of interest in this respect since it has diverse means for diminutive formation, ranging from forms typical of early CDS to genuinely derivational processes that reflect key morphological properties of the language.

1.1 Borrowed Hebrew diminutives

Diminutive forms in Hebrew derive from two sources – foreign and native. Hebrew has borrowed diminutive suffixes mainly from languages with dominant diminutive systems such as Russian, Yiddish and Judeo-Spanish (Sagi 1997). Foreign-suffixed diminutives (such as *-uš, -le, -ka*) may be attached to both non-native and native bases. For example, Russian *-čik* occurs in both foreign-based *pónčik* 'doughnut-DIM [baby's nickname]' and native-based *šaménčik* 'fat-DIM' from *šamen* 'fat'; Judeo-Spanish *-íko* is attached to Hebrew *kof* 'monkey' to yield *kofíko* 'monkey-DIM' (Avineri 1964; Bolozky 1994), and is widely used to create nicknames such as *Físko* from *Yosef(íko), Saharíko* from *Sahar*[1]. The main function of these loan diminutives is to express familiarity, informality and endearment in child-directed and child-centered speech (Dressler & Merlini-Barbaresi 1994; Stephany 1997). They are not, however, productive beyond certain frozen forms, and are also restricted to the ethnic groups that make up Israeli society. The current study focuses on the acquisition of native Hebrew diminutives.

1.2 Native Hebrew diminutives

Native Hebrew diminutives are of special interest because they fall into two different classes, *juvenile* and *conventional-derivational*, which together represent the range of meanings typical of diminutives. The category that emerges initially in the speech of young children – *juvenile* diminutives – is a simplex morphological device constituting a bridge between inflection and derivation. In contrast, *conventional-derivational* diminutives emerge much later and employ well-established, quite general Hebrew morphological devices.

The chapter starts with by summarizing Ravid's (1998) study of juvenile diminutives in early child Hebrew (Section 1.2.1) and then outlines the *conventional derivational* diminutive morphology of concern to the present study (1.2.2). Sections 2 and 3 describe an experimental study of the acquisition of conventional derivational diminutives in Hebrew.

1.2.1 *Juvenile diminutives*

Ravid's (1998) analysis of longitudinal data from eight normally developing, native Hebrew-speaking children between the ages of 1;5 to 5;6 showed that the overwhelmingly favored diminutive option among Hebrew-speaking toddlers is suffixation of nouns and adjectives by (unstressed) *-i* as in *xatúli* 'cat-DIM', *gadóli* 'big-DIM', or *masa'íti* 'truck-DIM' (see also Ravid & Nir 2000). This is the diminutive form, which, as in other languages, occurs early on in child language development, at a period when, as noted before, morpho-syntax is not yet well established. As in other languages, hypocoristic use (i.e. as an endearment or pet name) of unstressed diminutive *-i* is common in early child directed speech or baby talk, well-suited to conveying the intimate, playful atmosphere of endearment and attachment typical of a caregiver / child relationship (Berman 1985: 341–342; Stephany 1997). The interchanges in (1) and (2) are typical examples from the Berman and Ravid corpora.

(1) Sahar and his mother talking about his diaper [Ravid corpus]:
Sahar, 1;4.06
*SAH: *itúli [xitúli]* [cf. adult *xitul*]
diaper-DIM
*MEI: *xitúli xitúli meod ratuv.*
diaper-DIM, diaper-DIM very wet
'Diaper, diaper (is) very wet'

(2) Leor playing with his grandmother [Berman corpus]:
Leor, 2;0
*LEO: *sáfti torídi* [cf. adult *sáfta*]
%mor: N-DIM V,Imp
granny-DIM take-down:FM
'Granny, take (it) down'

(3) Hagar asks for her bottle [Berman corpus]:
Hagar 2;01
*HAG: *ten ta^babúki [: et ha^bakbúki]* [cf. adult *bakbuk*]
%mor: V P:ACC AR N-DIM
give:Msc the-bottle-DIM
'Give (me) the bottle'

(4) Smadar describes a visit to the playground [Berman corpus]:
Smadar, 2;01
*SMD: *hayínu ba^gan ša'ašuim ha^gadóli, ve ve sixáknu ba^ ba^xol,*
%mor: V P&AR N+N A-DIM CONJ CONJ V P&AR P&AR N
ve hitgalášnu ve hitgalášnu, ve az nasánu

%mor: CONJ V CONJ V CONJ! V
were,1st in-the-garden play the-big-DIM, and and played,1st,Pl in-the-sand, and slid,1st,Pl and slid,1st,Pl, and then drove,1st,Pl
'We were in the big playground, and and we played in the sand and we slid and slid, and then we drove'

Like most vocabulary items in young children's emerging lexicons, the nouns to which -*i* diminutives attach refer to people, animals and concrete, often countable objects (e.g., *ball, balloon, beetle, bottle, duck, elephant, kitty, clown, granny, pacifier, plastic bag, truck, sea*). They also attach to basic adjectives (*big, small, sweet*). The survey in Ravid (1998) shows that diminutivization by -*i* constitutes a transient, juvenile pathway into word formation in a number of senses. First, it is more pragmatic than semantic, taking the child's specific point of view and familiar context into account. The semantic change in forms such as *xitúli* 'diaper-DIM' is negligible; it almost amounts to calling it 'my dear diaper to which I am very much attached'. This inflection-like change is non-varying and predictable, and it can be applied to any singular noun without any of the restrictions of derivation. As noted by Gillis (1997:168), juvenile diminutives are gender-neutral: the suffix -*i* is equally applicable to masculine and feminine nouns as well as to adjectives. Moreover, juvenile diminutives have a special status in morphology as an operation that induces no category change beyond the shift from X to "small X" and "falls midway between inflection and derivation" (Anderson 1982; Spencer 1991:197).

Second, -*i* diminutives are context-bound in a very specific sense – the fact that the process applies to a particular item in a class, rather than to a whole category. For example, Leor referred to any grandma (such as the one in the story "Red Riding Hood") by general *sáfta*, and reserved the diminutivized form *sáfti* to his own grandmother. All innovative productions of *i*-diminutives are restricted in the same way and are in fact semantically under-extended (Barrett 1995): *masa'íti* 'truck-DIM' [cf. *masa'it*] is not any truck but 'my own beloved toy', and even the big-DIM [*gadóli,* cf. *gadol*] playground in Smadar's description is a specific, familiar playground. Diminutivization by -*i* may thus be regarded as a *personalizing* device, with the diminutivized item appropriated personally by of the interlocutor. This is probably why *i*-suffixed diminutive nouns are not pluralizable: while many are proper names (e.g., *Miryámi, Pútsi, Múši*), others acquire a unique proper-noun denotation with the attachment of -*i,* e.g., *barvázi* 'duck-DIM', *píli* 'elephant-DIM', and their plural counterparts are ungrammatical.

Structurally, too, *i*-diminutivization is marked as a juvenile strategy. Hebrew linear operations on nominal stems overwhelmingly shift stress to the final syllable. Diminutivization by final -*i,* in contrast, leaves the original stem stress intact, and therefore makes no stem changes, e.g., *leycan* / *leycáni* 'clown / clown-DIM', *gamad* / *gamádi* 'dwarf / dwarf-DIM'. Preserving the original structure and stress pattern of the nominal stem is an early, well-attested childhood strategy in Hebrew (Ravid 1995).

From all points of view, juvenile -*i* diminutives thus constitute an immature morphological device that generates almost no phonological, grammatical or semantic change in base forms. Juvenile *-i* serves first and foremost as a personalizing device for children (rather than denoting smallness and immaturity), and may thus facilitate the acquisition of noun and adjective reference. Given its extra-grammatical nature, juvenile *-i* may also serve as a channel into more conventional morphology (Dressler & Merlini-Barbaresi 1994; Kempe, Brooks & Gillis, this volume; Kempe, Brooks, Mironova & Fedorova 2003; Kempe, Brooks, Mironova, Pershukova & Fedorova 2005). Kempe (p.c.) has recently proposed that diminutives are guided by low-level prosodic processes that prefer coda-avoidance in the input to and speech of young speakers. This observation captures the essence of the Hebrew juvenile *-i* diminutive: By attaching to the ends of words, diminutive *-i* initiates a process of re-syllabification that allows for coda avoidance, and since this final CV is not stressed, it draws toddlers' attention to the preceding syllable which is both stressed and lengthened and often carries important lexical and inflectional information.

1.2.2 *Conventional-derivational diminutives*

The focus of the present study is on diminutive devices that emerge later in acquisition and constitute part of the conventional derivational system of Hebrew, rather than on the early-emerging diminutive forms reviewed above. Hebrew employs two structural devices in expressing conventional-derivational diminutivization – linear formation and reduplication (Avineri 1964; Schwarzwald 2004).

Linear formation

There are two productive diminutive suffixes in Hebrew that attach to noun and adjective bases: Feminine *-it* (e.g., *sak / sakit* 'sack / (plastic) bag') and masculine *-on* (e.g., *géšer / gišron* 'bridge / little bridge'), with the feminine variant *-ónet* (e.g., *kubiya / kubiyónet* 'small block'). Many of the forms created by linear suffixation by *-it* and *-on* predictably and transparently express a smaller object or a younger animal e.g., *mapa / mapit* 'tablecloth / napkin', *dégel / diglon* 'flag / small flag', *kélev / kalbon* 'dog / puppy'. They may also convey a lesser amount of a property, sometimes in deprecatory, informal, familiar sense, e.g., *tipeš / tipšon* 'fool / little fool' (compare Dressler & Merlini-Barbaresi 1994; Stephany 1997).

These linear diminutivizers are, however, typical nominal derivational constructs in their unpredictable scope, non-automatic semantics, and nominal morphology (Bolozky 1994). They go beyond mere depreciation in amount, age, formality or seriousness of the base, and are clearly derivational in nature, and thus require familiarity with the Hebrew lexicon. Note the unpredictable meanings of the diminutivized nouns in Table 1, taken from Bolozky (1994) and Nir (1993). They all share the feature of 'smaller than the base form', but their conventional meanings are far from simply 'base + DIM'.

Table 1. Conventional-derivational linear diminutive suffixes in Hebrew

Base form	Gloss	Base + suffix *-it*	Gloss
kaš	straw	*kašit*	drinking straw
tav	musical note	*tavit*	tag
mapúax	bellows	*mapuxit*	harmonica
aron	closet	*aronit*	locker
kruv	cabbage	*kruvit*	cauliflower
Base form	**Gloss**	**Base + suffix *-on***	**Gloss**
gan	kindergarten	*ganon*	nursery school
sahar	moon	*saharon*	Crescent-shaped jewelry
pakid	clerk	*pkidon*	bureaucrat
gag	roof	*gagon*	roof-rack
maxšev	computer	*maxševon*	pocket calculator

In fact, *-it* and *-on* are the two most productive suffixes in Hebrew (Nir 1993), and designate a number of semantic categories, such as instruments (*xalal / xalalit* 'space / spaceship', *safa / sfaton* 'lip / lipstick', *itur / iturit* 'tracing / pager'), and collective nouns (*milon* 'dictionary' from *mila* 'word' and *še'elon* 'questionnaire' from *še'ela* 'question'). The diminutive meaning of bases suffixed by *-it* and *-on* is more readily accessible, but not always conventional. For example, *tiyulon* from *tiyul* 'hike' could in principle refer to a short trip and is often used to convey this meaning, but it conventionally designates a baby stroller.

Unlike juvenile diminutives, conventional diminutives such as *barvazon* 'duck-DIM' and *pilon* 'elephant-DIM', the conventional terms for a baby duck and a young elephant, are ordinary common nouns, and are pluralizable. Even as diminutivized nouns, they are not personalized and made unique. Moreover, linear diminutive suffixes, like all productive nominal suffixes and unlike *-i* diminutives, are stress-assigning. As a result, the stem may undergo the same morphophonological changes as those entailed by other nominal suffixes. For example, *kaf* 'spoon' undergoes stop / spirant alternation when pluralized (*kaf / kap-ot* 'spoon / spoons), when assigned genitive case (e.g., *kaf / kapo* 'spoon / his spoon'), or when diminutivized ('*kaf / kap-it* 'spoon / teaspoon').

Of the two, Bolozky (1994) and Sagi (1997) claim that the unmarked or default Modern Hebrew diminutive device is *-on* or its feminine counterpart *-ónet* rather than *-it*. This seems to be true, since *-it* suffixation tends to designate highly specific meanings (Table 1), while *-on / -ónet* nouns and adjectives quite typically designate smaller versions of the base (e.g., *tipa / tipónet* 'drop / small drop', *dira / dirónet* 'apartment / small apartment') and express affection or depreciation (*metuka / metukónet* 'sweet:FM / little sweety'), as in other languages (1994:55).

Reduplication

A second adult conventional-derivational diminutive device is reduplication, e.g., *zkankan* 'short / sparse beard', from *zakan* 'beard', *kalil* 'airy, feathery', the diminutivized form of *kal* 'light' (Schwarzwald 2004). Reduplication is a non-concatenative morphological process in which some part of the base – consonants and vowels, syllables, morphemes, or the whole word – is repeated to the left, to the right, or inside the base, e.g., Agta *ulu* / *ululu* 'head/s'. It is a productive and varied process in many of the world's languages (Spencer 1991: 150–156).

Hebrew reduplication is a minor process in two senses:[2] First, it differs from the major word-internal morphological processes – nonlinear and linear affixation – in using material from the base itself as an extra morpheme instead of joining together two morphemes. Second, left-to-right reduplication is generally restricted to diminutive expression in nouns and adjectives, e.g., *xatul* / *xataltul* 'cat / kitten', *sagol* / *sgalgal* 'purple / purplish' (Nir 1993).[3] The latter process takes a variety of forms, including reduplicating the last stem consonant (compare *kal* / *kalil* 'light / very light' above) and reduplicating root components, such as the last root consonant (e.g., *kidrer* 'dribble' with quadriliteral root *k-d-r-r* extracted with reduplication from *kadur* 'ball') or two consonants (e.g. *difdef* 'glance through a book' with reduplicated root *d-f-d-f* extracted from *daf* 'page'; *hidhed* 'to echo' extracted from *hed* 'echo'; *kivkev* ' to draw a dotted line' extracted from *kav* 'line'). These denominal verbs whose bases have two consonants denote a durative or repetitive action (Ussishkin 1999). The only current reduplicated template that resembles a non-linear pattern is the typically diminutive pattern $\mathrm{CC}_1a\mathrm{C}_2\mathrm{C}_1a\mathrm{C}_2$, as in *ktantan* 'tiny' from *katan* 'small', and its feminine version $\mathrm{CC}_1a\mathrm{C}_2\mathrm{C}_1\acute{o}\mathrm{C}_2et$ (Bolozky 1994; Nir 1993). According to Bolozky (1999) the productivity of nominal reduplication is low. Howevwer, Graf (2002) has suggested that the principles operating behind nominal reduplication (templatic derivation) are very much active in the nominal system and in the language as a whole. Graf (2002) claims that the number of reduplicated tokens for adjectival items is much larger than the number of reduplicated tokens for noun items. From a semantic point of view there is no suffixal option for adjectives as attested for nouns with the diminutive meaning denoted by the reduplication pattern (reduplicated template). Note that diminutives can be stacked, with a linear diminutive suffix attached to a reduplicated stem, e.g., *znavnavon* or *znavnávčik* 'tail-DIM-DIM' reduplicated and suffixed respectively by Hebrew *-on* and foreign *-čik*, 'tail-DIM-DIM' from *zanav* 'tail'.

According to Bat-El (2004), reduplication is a strategy for word/stem formation in Hebrew, which has four such patterns: $\mathrm{C}_1\,\mathrm{VC}_2\,\mathrm{VC}_{2C}$; $\mathrm{C}_1\mathrm{VC}_2\mathrm{C}_3\mathrm{VC}_{3C}$; $\mathrm{C}_1\mathrm{VC}_2\mathrm{C}_{1C}\mathrm{VC}_2$; $\mathrm{C}_1\mathrm{C}_2\mathrm{VC}_3\mathrm{C}_{2C}\mathrm{VC}_{3C}$ (C stands for COPY). Contrary to Bolozky's (1999) claim that reduplication designates diminutives, Bat-El denies that the process is semantically predictive, since for her, structural similarity between semantically related forms does not necessarily entail a shared semantics. For example, the nominal suffix *-on* may carry a variety of semantic meanings (cf. *iton* 'newspaper' from *et* 'time' versus *dubon* 'teddy-bear-

DIM' from *dov* 'bear'). On the other hand, Bat–El acknowledges that the bulk of words in the pattern $c_1c_2vc_3c_{2C}vc_{3C}$ (e.g., *zkankan* 'beard-DIM') are indeed diminutives.

To the best of our knowledge, no systematic study has been carried out to date regarding the acquisition of Hebrew conventional-derivational diminutives. The current paper aims to provide initial information on children's perception and learning of linear and reduplicated diminutives.

2. Method

This is a first, and in a sense, exploratory experimental study of the acquisition of diminutive constructions in Hebrew. Hebrew diminutives, as explained above, are derivational entities, and therefore not expected to emerge in very young children, unlike *-i* diminutives of the type described in Ravid (1998). Since there is no systematic data available about the development of either the constructions or their meanings, we decided to focus on school-aged children as the domain of study.

2.1 Population

The study population consisted of 48 children in four age groups: kindergarteners aged 5–6, 2nd graders aged 7–8, 4th graders aged 10–11, 6th graders aged 12–13, and a control group of 13 adults. All participants were monolingual Hebrew speakers from middle-high SES background (the adults were all university graduates).

2.2 Research tasks and procedure

Participants were tested orally and individually in familiar surroundings. Each was administered two tasks in a fixed order. First, the *explanation task*, which required participants to explain the difference between two nouns (α=.714). This consisted of 12 items – six task items and six distracters – each in the form of a pair of nouns: a base noun and its morphologically related diminutive form (see Table 2). For example, **What is the difference between *zanav* 'tail' and *znavnav* 'tail-DIM'?** Every two pairs of task items were interspersed with a distracter item, where participants were required to explain the difference between two nouns related either morphologically or semantically, e.g., **What is the difference between *boreg* 'screw' and *mavreg* 'screwdriver'? What is the difference between *tapuax* 'apple' and *agas* 'pear?** The distracter items were inserted to prevent participants from realizing the aim of the study and -- although they yielded fascinating responses – they were not analyzed in the current framework. The explanation task was preceded by one training non-diminutive item.

Table 2. The Explanation Task

Task item		Gloss	Targeted Response
		What is the difference between…	
1.	*dag* and *dagig*	Fish and fish-DIM	*dag* is big / adult, *dagig* is smaller / younger, the young of the species
2.	*kélev* and *klavlav*	Dog and puppy (dog-DIM)	*kélev* is big / adult, *klavlav* is smaller / younger, the young of the species
3.	*séret* and *sirton*	Film and short film (film-DIM)	*séret* is longer / the full feature, *sirton* is shorter
4.	*zanav* and *znavnav*	Tail and tail-DIM	*zanav* is of ordinary length, *znavnav* is smaller / shorter
5.	*kaf* and *kapit*	Spoon and teaspoon (spoon-DIM)	*kaf* is of normal size, *kapit* is smaller and is used for tea, coffee
6.	*axbara* and *axbarónet*	Mouse:FM and Mouse, FM-DIM	*axbara* is big / adult, *axbarónet* is smaller / younger, the young of the species

The *production task* was administered after the completion of the explanation task (α=.816). Participants were asked to produce a diminutive form for an existing noun. This task also consisted of 12 items – six task items and six distracters. Task items consisted of a noun phrase describing a small or hypocoristic noun, and required participants to name it in one word (Table 3). For example, **what would you call / how would you say in one word <u>a small chair</u>?** Every two pairs of task items were interspersed with a distracter item, which required participants to produce different types of deverbal nouns following the design of Clark & Berman (1984), e.g., **What / how would you call in one word <u>a tool that breaks things</u>?** The distracter items had the same function of concealing the aim of the study, and were not analyzed in the current framework. The production task was preceded by one training on a non-diminutive item.

Table 3. The Production Task

Task item		Gloss	Targeted Responses
		What would you call / How would you say in one word…	
1.	*kise katan šel bubot*	A small doll's chair	*kis'on*
2.	*xovéret ktana*	A small booklet	*xovrónet*
3.	*xatul tinok*	A baby cat	*xataltul, xatulon*
4.	*mišehi kcat šmena*	Somebody:FM who is a bit fat:FM	*šmanmónet*
5.	*kubiya ktana ve-xamuda*	A small and cute cube / block	*kubiyónet*
6.	*zakan katan*	A small beard	*zkankan*

2.3 Analysis

Scoring scales were constructed by the four authors for each of the tasks. The scales were adjusted until they accommodated all response types. All four authors rated 100% of the responses on the scoring scales. Inter-judge agreement was 91%. Cases in dispute were discussed until agreement was reached.

(i) Explanation scale. Explanation responses were rated on a 6-point scale:

0 – No response, repetition, irrelevant response. For example, *I don't know*

1 – No comparison, comparison on a non-linguistic basis. For example, *The fish-*DIM *is the fish's friend; you can eat a fish and you can't eat a fish-*DIM*; There is no difference: a tail-*DIM *is the same as a tail.*

2 – Comparison on an inappropriate linguistic basis; hinted diminutive element. For example, *a film-*DIM *is maybe a cartoon; a film-*DIM *is one and a film is lots.*

3 – Ungrammatical structure of explanation or absence of comparative structure; bizarre element compared. For example, *the spoon-*DIM *has a thick round edge and spoon has a wider circle; small – big; a mouse:*FM-DIM *is less disgusting than a mouse:*FM.

4 – Hypocoristic diminutive used in explanation; comparison of non-canonical element; infelicitous or partial comparative structure. For example, *a dog is bigger, a dog-*DIM *is a cute puppy; A film-*DIM *is shorter; a tail-*DIM *is a short tail and a tail is a tail; a mouse:*FM-DIM *is a baby and a mouse:*FM *is a mother.*

5 – Correct response containing a full comparison of the canonical element. For example, *a spoon is larger than a spoon-*DIM*; the size, the age; Tail-*DIM *sounds like a short tail; a film is long – something like an hour or two, a film-*DIM *is a short film like a commercial.*

(ii) Production scale. Production responses were rated on a 6-point scale:

0 – No response, repetition, irrelevant response. For example, *I don't know.*

1 – Syntactic instead of morphological form; inflection instead of derivation. For example, *chairs; a little bit fat; beards; a short beard.*

2 – Extant word, diminutive onomatopoeia. For example, *diary* (for small booklet); *miau – miau, sweety* (for baby cat); round (for a bit fat); *moustache, špic* 'pointy form' (for small beard).

3 – These responses all exhibited some serious structural lacunae: Non-derivational constructions (e.g., compounding, juvenile diminutives); infelicitous word structure. For example, *kise teatronim* (theatre-chair, for small doll's chair); *kóbi* (shortened *kubiya,* for small block); *xatúli* (childish *-i* added to *xatul,* for baby cat); *xavéret* (ill-formed *xovéret,* for small booklet).

4 – These responses were all appropriate, yet not complete. They included ungrammatical derivational forms; blendings; inappropriate suffix; ill-formed base; wrong inflection. For example, *ksinson* (ill-formed reduplicated *kise), barbise* (blend of *Barbi* and *kise,* for small doll's chair); *mini-buk* (for small booklet); *xatoltol* (ill-formed *xataltul,* for baby cat); *šmananit* (ill-formed reduplicated

šmena, with a diminutive suffix), *šmanmuda* (blend of *šmena* 'fat:FM' and *xamuda* 'cute:FM', for a bit fat); *kubibub* (blend of *kubiya* and *buba* 'doll', for small block); *zakóni* (ill-formed double diminutive on *zakan*), *zaknun* (ill-formed reduplicated *zakan* for small beard).

5 – Correct response: targeted response or any other appropriate response with a diminutive device and a well-formed base obeying Hebrew morphophonological constraints. For example, *kis'ončik* (double diminutive for small doll's chair); *xovrónet, xovrit* (for small booklet); *xataltul, xataltulon* (for baby cat); *zkankan, ziknon* (for small beard).

2.3 Predictions

We assumed that the acquisition of conventional derivational diminutives is part of later, school-age linguistic development in Hebrew, and hence that kindergarteners would have only an initial and limited ability to explain and produce such diminutives. We further expected that morphological diminutive forming devices and their semantic and pragmatic functions would be more accessible to children as a function of age and schooling. We expected the explanations of older age groups to focus on the morphological link between item pairs, with more explicit reference to the diminutive device. We expected diminutive production in older age groups to follow Hebrew lexical conventions and to adhere to its morphophonological constraints. We expected the reduplicated form CC*a*CC*a*C to emerge later than the more transparent suffixes *-it* and *-on*.

3. Results

Responses were analyzed in two ways: (i) a *lenient analysis* – by calculating success as an average on the scale. This analysis reveals children's morphological strategies in producing and analyzing diminutives; and (ii) a *stringent analysis* – by calculating success as the correct response only (5). This analysis examines the morpho-lexical knowledge necessary to produce and analyze correct diminutive forms. In both analyses, scores were converted into percentages.

3.1 Study tasks

Table 4 presents lenient and stringent scores on the two study tasks – explanation and production.

Table 4. Mean percentages and standard deviations of success (lenient and stringent analyses) on the Explanation and Production tasks, by age group.

	Explanation		Production	
Age group	**Lenient scores**	**Stringent scores**	**Lenient scores**	**Stringent scores**
Kindergarten 5-6	62.05 (20.03)	37.18 (28.18)	54.1 (24.35)	23.08 (25.94)
2nd grade 7-8	78.49 (18.34)	56.06 (23.89)	65.46 (23.86)	39.39 (21.44)
4th grade 9-10	86.94 (15.53)	63.89 (29.16)	75.56 (21.43)	44.44 (28.72)
6th grade 11-12	88.61 (11.59)	59.72 (29.69)	91.11 (7.43)	72.22 (19.24)
Adults	85.64 (12.28)	66.67 (25.46)	78.72 (21.41)	58.97 (40.03)

Two-way analyses of age group (5) x task type (2) were conducted on the data in Table 4. The *lenient analysis* revealed an effect for age group ($F(4,56)=7.89$, $p<.0001$). The post-hoc Scheffé procedure (α =.05) showed that kindergarteners (5–6), with the lowest scores, differed from all age groups above second grade (7–8). There was also an effect for task ($F(1,56)=7.95$, $p<.008$), showing that the explanation task scored higher (M=80.35%) than the production task (M=72.99%). No interaction emerged.

The *stringent analysis* revealed an effect for age group ($F(4,56)=4.87$, $p<.003$). The post-hoc Scheffé procedure (α =.05) showed that kindergarteners (5–6), with the lowest scores, differed from the two oldest age groups, with the highest scores. There was also an effect for task ($F(1,56)=5.08$, $p<.03$), showing that the explanation task scored higher (M=56.7%) than the production task (M=47.62%). No interaction emerged.

3.2 Further analyses

We examined the responses on the two study tasks for possible factors that might affect performance.

3.2.1 *Explanation: animacy*

A possible factor affecting success in the explanation task was item animacy, e.g., *fish* vs. *spoon,* with the idea that animate items might be easier to explain than inanimate ones. We focused on the lenient score (Table 5), since the stringent score did not permit such an in-depth analysis.

Table 5. Mean percentages and standard deviations of success (lenient analysis) on the Explanation task, by age group and animacy

Age group	Animate items	Inanimate items
Kindergarten 5-6	68.21 (29.46)	55.9 (14.54)
2nd grade 7-8	73.33 (22.31)	83.64 (17.73)
4th grade 9-10	88.89 (16.41)	85.0 (18.67)
6th grade 11-12	91.11 (11.13)	86.11 (14.06)
Adults	88.72 (16.19)	82.56 (16.45)

A two-way analysis of age group (5) x item animacy (2) was conducted on the data in Table 5. There was an effect for age group ($F(4,56)=6.04$, $p<.0001$), but no effect for animacy. However, a close-to-significant interaction of age group x animacy emerged ($F(4,56)=2.36$, $p=.065$), depicted in Figure 1.

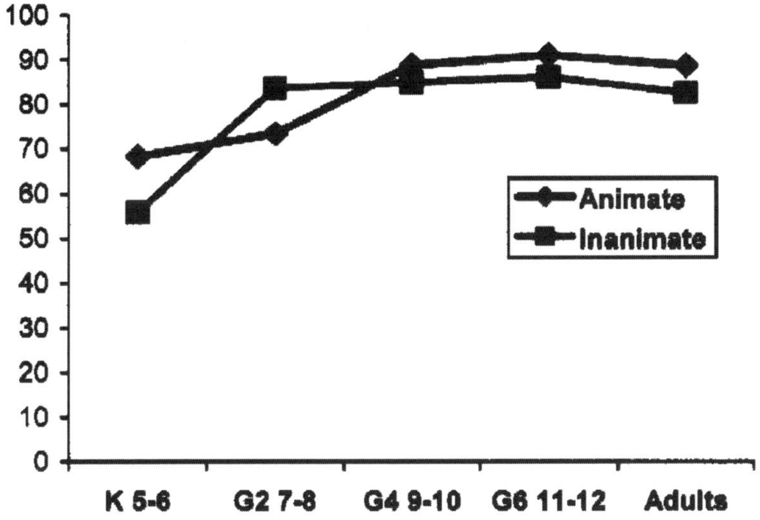

Figure 1. Interaction of age group and item animacy in the explanation task

3.2.2 *Explanation: dimensions*

Two of the diminutives on this task – *tail* and *film* – are best explained in terms of length (though in different senses); three others – *dog, fish,* and *mouse* – share the element of size or age; *spoon* is explained on the dimension of volume. A three-way analysis of age group (5) x item dimension (3: length, size/age, volume) was conducted on the data in Table 5. In addition to the effect for age group ($F(4,56)=5.63$, $p<.002$), there was an effect for dimension ($F(2,112)=11.04$, $p<.0001$): items differing in length (M=73.67%) proved to be harder than those differing in size/age (M=82.05%) and volume (M=88.59%). The interaction of age group x dimension ($F(8,112)=3.99$, $p<.0001$), depicted in Figure 2, showed that it derives from the youngest group's performance on length items.

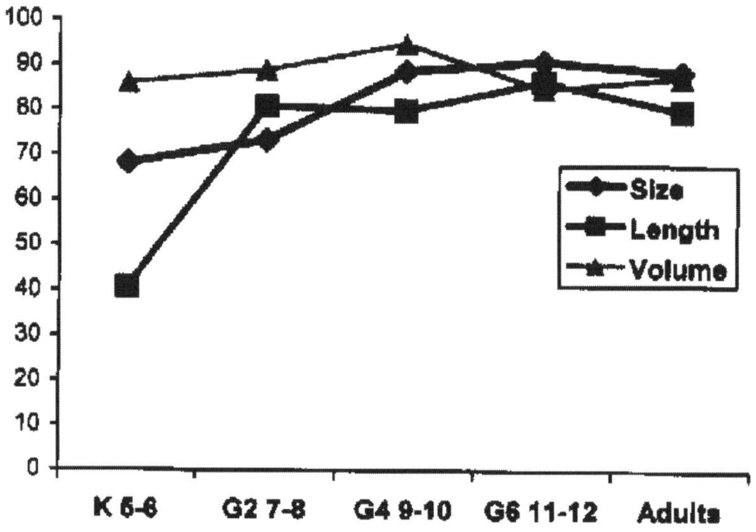

Figure 2. Interaction of age group and item dimension in the explanation task

Table 6. Mean percentages and standard deviations of success (lenient analysis) on the Production task, by age group and lexicalization

Age group	Lexicalized items	Non-lexicalized items
Kindergarten	54.87	53.33
5-6	(28.82)	(23.41)
2nd grade	55.76	75.15
7-8	(37.15)	(20.66)
4th grade	74.44	76.67
9-10	(26.49)	(25.35)
6th grade	87.78	94.44
11-12	(11.66)	(7.43)
Adults	76.92	80.51
	(21.88)	(25.31)

3.2.2 *Production: Lexicalization*

A possible factor affecting success in the explanation task was item lexicalization, i.e., whether there was an extant diminutive form for that item in Hebrew. The idea was that lexicalized items might be easier to produce than non-lexicalized ones. We focused on the lenient score (Table 6), since the stringent score did not permit such an in-depth analysis.

A two-way analysis of age group (5) x item animacy (2) was conducted on the data in Table 6. There was an effect for age group ($F(4,56)=5.67$, $p<.002$), and a close-to-significant effect of lexicalization ($F(1,56)=3.68$, $p=.06$), showing that the *non-lexicalized* items task scored higher (M=76.02%) than the *lexicalized* ones (M=69.96%). There was no interaction.

4. Discussion

This is the first empirical investigation known to us of the development of conventional-derivational diminutives in Hebrew-speaking kindergarteners and school children compared with adults. Participants were administered an explanation task comparing base nouns and their diminutive forms, and then a production task which required them to produce the diminutive forms of base nouns. Analyses were conducted both on the average score on the scale (lenient analysis), as well as on the correct responses alone (stringent analysis).

On the whole, our results indicate that knowledge of conventional-derivational diminutive structure and meaning is indeed not an early acquisition in Hebrew. Unlike juvenile *-i* diminutives, the structures investigated in this study emerge in later childhood and improve with age and schooling. The learning curves we uncovered begin in kindergarten, with less than one quarter correct productions and about one third correct explanations, and they rise steadily from 2nd grade (age 7–8) throughout grade school, especially between 4th and 6th grade. In fact, only from age 12 do Hebrew speakers show that they have mastered the morphological, semantic, pragmatic, and cognitive factors that interact in understanding and producing diminutive forms. Diminutive derivational morphology is thus part of what is termed 'later language development', that is, linguistic acquisition during the school years (Berman 2004; Ravid & Zilberbuch 2003). Like acquisition of other derivational processes of word-formation, conventional diminutivization depends on both morphological and lexical knowledge, which require a long developmental route (Ravid 2004).

Both analyses – lenient and stringent – revealed that the explanation task was easier than the production task in most age groups. This appears counter to results of other studies reporting meta-linguistic explanation tasks, where young participants often found it easier to produce morphological forms than to explain them (Ravid & Malenky 2001; Seidman 2000). Even language teachers have been shown to be challenged by the requirement to provide explanations for linguistic phenomena in comparison to actually performing linguistic tasks (Ravid & Gillis 2002). However, in this particular case explaining diminutive semantics seems to be easier than producing a full range of Hebrew diminutive forms. We propose that unlike other derivational categories learned during the school years such as place, collective, and abstract nominalization (Ravid & Avidor 1998; Ravid, Avivi-Ben Zvi & Levie 1999), the semantics of diminutives is readily accessible to school-age children since it is scaffolded by the earlier juvenile 'proto-diminutive'. The long developmental history of diminutive production revealed in the current study can thus be attributed mainly to the array of formal diminutive options in Hebrew and to the need for mapping diminutive semantics on these different alternatives.

4.1 The explanation task

The meta-linguistic explanation task required participants to explicitly state the relationship between the members of a pair of basic and diminutive nouns, for example, to specify the difference between *dag* 'fish' and *dagig* 'fish-DIM'.

Even the youngest group in the study, kindergarteners aged 5–6, revealed an awareness of the morphological relationship between nouns and their diminutive counterparts. Their responses in attempting to state this relationship, however, often veered towards number, the most expected inflectional property of the Hebrew noun, with plurality assigned either to the base or to the diminutive noun. Thus kindergarteners (and a few second graders) said (1) *dagig* (fish-DIM) *are many in the water and dag* (fish) *is one in the water;* (2) *dag is one and dagig is two / a few / many';* (3) *zanav* (tail) *is one and znavnav* (tail-DIM*) is two tails';* (4) *znavnav is a cute name and zanav is many znavnav;* (5) *sirton* (film-DIM) is one and *séret film is many*. Two conflicting accounts come to mind here. On the one hand, the children who produced examples 1–3 may have been relating to the fact that diminutives are longer words due to either reduplication or suffixation, and thus might express a larger number than the base nouns (similarly to what was found for preschoolers' writing – Levin & Korat 1993). On the other hand, such responses might be precursors of the prototypical *big* (base) / *small* (diminutive) relationship expressed by members of the pair. By assigning plural number to the base form our participants might be expressing its larger size.

Yet another phenomenon underscored developmental changes. Three of the task items were animate – *fish, dog, mouse*, and three – *tail, spoon, film* – were inanimate. The statistical analysis (Figure 1) revealed a changing pattern in development: Kindergarteners (5–6 year olds) found animate diminutives easier to explain than inanimate, while second graders (7–8 year olds) did better on inanimates. From 4th grade (9–10) up, there was no difference between the two semantic classes. A tentative explanation might be young children's sensitivity to animate objects, leading them to frame animate diminutives in terms of kinship relationships (*mommy, granny, daughter, cub*) and hypocoristics (*when you love somebody you say klavlav 'puppy'*). Older children's responses, in contrast, could reveal a growing perception of the fact that diminutives may also apply to properties of inanimate objects. Thus, participants in the older age groups did not refer to animate diminutives in terms of kinship relations, but characterized them along the more objective lines of age (*young / adult*) and size (*small / big*).

The three inanimate items elicited a broader array of responses, demonstrating how diminutive semantics diversifies and becomes multi-layered with age and schooling, pointing at interesting structural and semantic directions for further studies of diminutivization in Hebrew. The reduplicated diminutive *znavnav* 'tail-DIM' was clearly strange for children and often elicited laughter and puzzlement (e.g., *I have never heard that word*). While kindergarteners (5–6) spoke of *znavnav* in hypocoristic terms, 2nd graders (7–8) were already able to relate to the size of a tail, but not to its length – the dominant feature from 4th grade on. The familiar household objects *kaf / kapit* 'spoon / teaspoon [spoon-DIM]' elicited only size-related responses up to 4th grade (9–10-year-olds), with function-related responses emerging in 6th grade (12-year-olds): "A teaspoon is for cornflakes, a spoon is for soup". But only adults explicitly related to the properties of volume and depth as differentiating between a spoon and a teaspoon. The item *séret / sirton* 'film / film-DIM' was especially difficult for kindergarteners, who could only relate to the screening context as a possible indirect expression of size: *séret is on TV / in the cinema, sirton is on the computer.* By grade school, children were able to relate directly to *duration*, the conventional difference between the members of this pair (*séret is long, sirton is short*), although a few second graders still referred to length by size, with a less specific term (*séret is big, sirton is small*), as in *zanav / znzvnav* 'tail / tail-DIM' above. Finally, *séret* is ambiguous in Hebrew between *film* and *ribbon*: A few kindergarteners preferred the more concrete sense of an article of clothing (*you put a ribbon on your head*) to the less concrete sense of *film* as a product that can be measured temporally.

From another perspective, we found that the semantic dimension along which the items differed affected diminutive acquisition: Diminutives differing in length, a cognitively and lexically specific dimension (*tail* and *film*), were more difficult than those differing in size (*dog, fish, mouse,* and *spoon*), although the kindergarteners alone found length (*long* vs. *short*) to be harder than the more general dimension of size (*big* vs. *small*). Moreover, recall that length was concrete in *tail* and temporal in *film*, suggesting an interesting direction for future research.

Older school children provided meta-linguistic commentary that testified to increasing cognitive abilities of executive control (Kluwe & Logan 2000; Rubinstein, Meyer & Evans 2001) and the effect of formal school instruction. When they reached the third item on the Explanation task, 4th graders (9–10 year olds) often made comments indicating their ability to extract the principle underlying all items, e.g., *again, it's the same – small, big; as I said before…; it's like 2, 6, 8… it's the same point…* By 6th grade (ages 11–12), children's responses contained terminology that clearly derived from formal school instruction, such as comments on the morphological structure of the task items (*axbara* [mouse:FM] *is in feminine form; the word itself lets you understand that this is a short tail; it's the same word, it's just a general name, a general word;*

séret / sirton ['film / film-DIM'] – *you can't say it's smaller, though we learned in Hebrew class that it means smaller.*

The formulation of explanations identified an interesting developmental contrast between adults and the rest of the age groups. Most responses took the form of a classical Aristotelian definition (Hull 1992): In response to a question such as *What is the difference between a fish (dag) and a fish-DIM (dagig)?* most participants would respond with a full proposition consisting of the given referent and a novel predicating adjective, e.g., *a fish is older and a fish-DIM is young*. It was only members of the adult group who were able to succinctly sum up the difference by an abstract nominal specifying the superordinate category, e.g., *the size, the volume, the depth, the length…* – instantiated by the task items, an ability that depends on both mature command of executive control as well as knowledge of abstract nominalization.

4.2 The production task

Participants' responses highlight the developmental path taken by Hebrew speakers in learning to express diminutive dimensions. Even the youngest age group avoided producing juvenile *-i* forms in response to target items – although they did so for some of the distracter items, where they produced forms such as *šokoládi* 'chocolaty', and *ayfáni* 'tiredy'. It seems that even kindergarteners are aware of the fact that conventionally derived diminutives do not include *-i*, which they use only when they feel called upon to innovate on items with no conventional target diminutive. Instead, they produced numerous non-derivational responses involving inflection (*beards, chairs, blocks*) and syntactically periphrastic constructions (*a lady who's a bit fat, pregnant fat, toy chair*).

Two response types emerged in grade school. One involved double diminutives marked by two devices, usually internal reduplication and an external suffix, e.g. *zkankon* for *zkankan* 'beard-DIM', or *kubkubit* for *kubiyónet* 'block-DIM' – some of them in fact acceptable as diminutive options in Hebrew, e.g., *xataltulon* 'tiny kitten' and *kis'ončik* 'chair-DIM' with two diminutive suffixes – Hebrew and foreign. Older grade schoolers and adults also employed blending for diminutivization (Berman 1989) – *kubikat* (*kubiya* 'block' + *kat)* and *kaskat* (*kise* 'chair'+ *kat)* involving the high-register word for 'small' *kat; mini-xovéret, minivéret, (mini* + *xoveret* 'booklet'), *minikise* (*mini*+ *kise* 'chair') and *barbise (barbi* 'Barbie doll' + *kise* 'chair'). This finding, too, is consistent with previous indications that blending is a later language acquisition in Hebrew (Ravid 1990).

The only statistically significant difference in the production task was related to lexicalization: The three lexicalized items (*cat-kitten, fat-fatso, beard-small beard or goatee*) scored lower than the three non-lexicalized items (chair-small chair, booklet-small booklet, block-small block). Though no interaction emerged, Table 6 shows that the kindergarteners, with lowest scores, were the only group that was not adversely affected by item lexicalization. Two explanations are suggested for this finding. One is the nature of the task, which called for morphological operations on the stem rather than lexical retrieval. Thus, even those participants who knew the conventional diminutives tended to perform creative, innovative manipulations on the given stem (e.g., adult blend *šmanmuda* – a combination of *šmanmónet* 'fatso' and *xamuda* 'cute').

A second explanation relates to the fact that the three lexicalized items had reduplicated forms (*xataltul* 'cat-DIM', *šmanmonet* 'fat-DIM-DIM'), and *zkankan* 'beard-DIM') – which is the least accessible diminutive structure. Reduplication, as noted, does not take either of the major word-formation forms in Hebrew: It does not resemble linear formation, where a suffix attaches at the end of a stem (e.g. *pax-it* 'can-DIM'), nor can it be considered non-linear formation, where a consonantal root is combined with a pattern (e.g., *p-r-k* 'part' + CéCeC, cf. *pérek* 'chapter'). Reduplication works more like a prosodic than a morphological process, by amplifying word segments such as syllables and single consonants (e.g., *xalak* 'smooth' – *xalaklak* 'slippery'). Reduplicated segments do not have morphological status, since no morpheme boundaries can be identified in reduplicated structures. This makes reduplicated diminutive structures a different class of items than more mainstream diminutive structures, and hence less accessible to children, who do not have an overview of word-formation processes in Hebrew.

On the other hand, use of reduplication emerged quite early. A qualitative analysis of responses tentatively points at two age-related levels of reduplicated production interacting with item familiarity (i.e., the extent to which children were familiar with the lexical item). Younger, less linguistically adept language users (mostly kindergarteners and 2nd graders), produced innovative, ill-formed reduplicated diminutives that fail to follow the conventional CCaCCaC or CCaCCóCet structures – both for target items requiring reduplicated and non-reduplicated structures. Examples of this strategy include: *xavarbaronit* and *xovréret* from *xovéret* 'booklet', for target *xovrónet* 'booklet-DIM'; *kobikobi* from *kubiya* 'block', for target *kubiyónet* 'block-DIM'; *xatoltol* from *xatul* 'cat', for target *xataltul* 'cat-DIM'; *zaknanon* from *zakan* 'beard', for target *zkankan* 'beard-DIM'; and *šmenanit, šmanmena,* and *šmanmanmónet* from *šmena* 'fat', for target *šmanmónet* 'fat-DIM'. Interestingly, in a study of deverbal noun coinages, Berman (2000) found that 4-year-olds – more than younger or older children – often used this same device for innovating nouns. In contrast, older, more sophisticated and literate participants were able to perform correct reduplication on items where this was required. Mature Hebrew speakers might be more aware of prosodic restrictions on Hebrew reduplication, which prevent its application to longer words such as *xovéret* and restrict it to bi-syllabic words such as *zakan* (thanks to Irit Katzenberger for this insight).

Reliance on lexical items from the established lexicon was evident among both kindergarteners and adults, but in different ways. Kindergarteners occasionally produced concrete lexical alternatives for the required diminutives, e.g. *maxbéret* 'notebook' for *xovéret* 'booklet', or *gur* 'baby animal' for *kitten* and *puppy*. But adults produced lexically specific and appropriate items such as *pinkas* 'small notebook', *yoman* 'diary', or *alon* 'flyer', in some cases giving words that are structurally related to diminutives, e.g., *šrafraf* 'stool', a reduplicated form, or *alonit* 'flyer-DIM' for *xovéret.*

Here, too, older participants made meta-linguistic comments about the task, especially 4th and 6th gradeschoolers. For example *I'll look for something with mini-*(6th grade); *šmanmana* 'fat-DIM', *but it doesn't count as making it up* (4th grade); *cute directs me towards the suffix-on, kubiyónet* 'block-DIM' (adult).

Item familiarity interacted with other factors in the production task. Of the three lexicalized and reduplicated items, *zkankan* 'beard-DIM', the least common and most high-register item, was also the hardest, eliciting many alternative ill-formed responses such as *zakikon* (kindergarten), *zakóni* (2nd grade), *zakon* (2nd & 6th grade), *zaknan* (2nd & 4th grade), and extant *safam* 'moustache'. Of the three non-lexicalized items, all taking the suffix *-on*, the most difficult was *xovrónet* 'booklet-DIM': It likewise elicited many non-conventional responses such as *xovran, xavéret, xovróti* (a combination of plural and juvenile diminutive), as well as *maxbéret* 'notebook' from the same root.

Finally, the qualitative analysis of participants' responses indicates that Bolozky (1994) is correct in viewing *-on* rather than *-it* as the structure most identified with diminutive meaning in Hebrew. As noted earlier, both *-on* and *-it* have other derivational meanings such as instrument and collective. Nonetheless, responses with *-it* were fewer and emerged relatively later than *-on* (and reduplicated) responses, e.g., *kubit* 'block-DIM' for *kubiyónet* and *xovrit* 'booklet-DIM' for *xovrónet*. Hebrew speakers evidently tend to regard *-on* suffixation and reduplication, both of which have masculine and feminine versions, as target devices for expressing diminutive semantics, whereas *-it* remains strongly associated with feminine marking (e.g., in common girls' names like *Ronit, Dorit, Galit*) and only marginally connected with diminutiveness.

Notes

1. Stress is marked only penultimately.
2. Thought historically well established, deriving from Mishanic Hebrew, spoken in the Second Temple era (Avineri 1964).
3. Reduplication is enabled in the verbal system in extracting consonantal skeletons from words and creating a new root by reduplicating the third and last consonant, e.g. root *?-v-r-r* in *ivrer* 'brought fresh air in' from *avir* 'air'; root *t-x-n-n* in *tixnen* 'planned' from *toxnit* 'plan'. The result is not diminutive, although the process originally carried a diminutive function (Sagi 1997).

References

Anderson, S.R. 1982. Where's morphology? *Linguistic Inquiry* 13: 571–612.

Avineri, Y. 1964. *Yad ha-lashon*. Tel Aviv: Yizre'el. [in Hebrew]

Bat- El, O. 2004. Consonant identity and consonant copy: The segmental prosodic structure of Hebrew reduplication. In *Perspectives on language and language development,* D. Ravid and H. Bat-Zeev Shyldkrot (eds), 25–34. Dordrecht: Kluwer Academic Publishers.

Barrett, M. 1995. Early lexical development. In *The handbook of child language*, P. Fletcher and B. MacWhinney (eds), 362–392. Oxford, UK: Blackwell.
Berman, R.A. 1985. *Acquisition of Hebrew.* Hillsdale NJ: Earlbaum.
Berman, R.A. 1989. The role of blends in Modern Hebrew word-formation. In *Studia linguistica et orientalia memoriae Haim Blanc dedicata*, P. Wexler, A. Borg and S. Somekh (eds), 45–61. Wiesbaden: Harrassowitz.
Berman, R.A. 2000. Children's innovative verbs vs. nouns: Structured elicitations and spontaneous coinages. In *Methods for studying language production*, L. Menn, and N. Bernstein-Ratner, (eds), 69–93. Mahwah NJ: Erlbaum.
Berman, R.A (ed.). 2004. *Language development across childhood and adolescence: Psycholinguistic and crosslinguistic perspectives.* Amsterdam: Benjamins.
Bolozky, S. 1994. On the formation of diminutives in Modern Hebrew morphology. *Hebrew Studies* 35: 47–63.
Bolozky, S. 1999. *Measuring productivity in word formation: The case of Israeli Hebrew.* Leiden: Brill.
Ceccherini, M., Bonifacio, S. and Zocconi, E. 1997. Acquisition of diminutives in Italian (Sara). In *Studies in pre- and protomorphology*, W.U. Dressler (ed.), 157–163. Wien: Österreichischen Akademie der Wissenschaften.
Clark, E.V. 1985. The acquisition of Romance, with special reference to French. In *The crosslinguistic study of language acquisition,* D.I. Slobin (ed.), 687–782. Hillsdale NJ: Erlbaum.
Clark, E. 1993. *The lexicon in acquisition.* Cambridge: Cambridge University Press.
Clark, E. and Berman, R.A. 1984. Structure and use in acquisition of word-formation. *Language* 60: 542–590.
Dressler, W.U. 1994. Evidence from the first stages of morphology acquisition for linguistic theory: extragrammatical morphology and diminutives. *ALHafn* 27: 91–108.
Dressler, W.U. and Karpf, A. 1995. The theoretical relevance of pre- and protomorphology in language acquisition. In *Yearbook of Morphology 1994*, G. Booij and J. v. Marle (eds), 99–122. Dordrecht: Kluwer Academic Publishers.
Dressler, U.W. and Merlini-Barbaresi, L. 1994. *Morphopragmatics: diminutives and intensifiers in Italian, German, and other languages.* Berlin: Mouton de Gruyter.
Gillis, S. 1997. The acquisition of diminutives in Dutch. In *Studies in pre- and protomorphology*, W.U. Dressler (ed.), 147–156. Wien: Österreichischen Akademie der Wissenschaften.
Graf, D. 2002. A Study of Nominal Reduplication in Modern Hebrew. Proceedings of the 18th meeting of The Isaraeli Association of Theoretical Linguistics. Bar-Ilan University.
Hull, D.L. 1992. The effect of essentialism on taxonomy: two thousand years of stasis'. *The Units of Evolution*: 199–225.
Jurafsky, D. 1996. Universal tendencies in the semantics of the diminutive. *Language* 72: 533–578.
Kempe, V. and Brooks, P. J. 2001. The role of diminutives in Russian gender learning: Can child-directed speech facilitate the acquisition of inflectional morphology? *Language Learning* 51: 221–256.
Kempe, V., Brooks, P. J. and Pirott, L. 2001. How can child-directed speech facilitate the acquisition of morphology? In *Research on Child Language Acquisition: Proceedings of the 8th conference of the International Association for the Study of Child Language,* M. Almgren, A. Barrena, M.J. Ezeizabarrena, I. Idiazabal, and B. MacWhinney (eds), 1237–1247. Medford, MA: Cascadilla Press.

Kempe, V., Brooks, P.J., Mironova, N. and Fedorova, O. 2003. Diminutivization supports gender acquisition in Russian children. *Journal of Child Language* 30: 1–15.

Kempe, V., Brooks, P. J., Mironova, N., Pershukova, A. and Fedorova, O. 2005. Playing with the endings of words: The effect of switching between simplex and diminutive forms of a noun on morphology acquisition in Russian. Paper presentation, IASCL conference, July 25–29, Berlin.

Kluwe, R. and Logan, G.D. (eds.). 2000. Executive control. [Special issue]. *Psychological Research* 63 (4).

Levin, I. and Korat, O. 1993. Sensitivity to phonological, morphological, and semantic cues in early reading and writing in Hebrew. *Merrill-Palmer Quarterly* 39: 213–232.

Nir, R. 1993. *Word-formation in Modern Hebrew*. Tel Aviv: The Open University. [in Hebrew]

Ravid, D. 1990. Internal structure constraints on new-word formation devices in Modern Hebrew. *Folia Linguistica* 24: 289–346.

Ravid, D. 1995. The acquisition of morphological junctions in Modern Hebrew: the interface of rule and rote. In *The development of morphological systematicity: a cross-linguistic perspective*, H. Pishwa and K. Maroldt (eds), 55–77. Tubingen: Gunter Narr.

Ravid, D. 1998. Diminutive -i in early child Hebrew: an initial analysis. In *Studies in the acquisition of number and diminutive marking*, S. Gillis (ed.), 149–174. Antwerp: Universiteit Antwerpen.

Ravid, D. 2004. Later lexical development in Hebrew: derivational morphology revisited. In *Language development across childhood and adolescence: Psycholinguistic and cross-linguistic perspectives*, R.A. Berman (ed.), 53–82. Amsterdam: Benjamins.

Ravid, D. and Avidor, A. 1998. Acquisition of derived nominals in Hebrew: Developmental and linguistic principles. *Journal of Child Language* 25: 229–266.

Ravid, D. and Gillis, S. 2002. Teachers' perception of spelling patterns and children's spelling errors: A cross-linguistic perspective. In *Consistency in writing systems*, M. Neef, A. Neijt and R. Sproat (eds), 71–95. Tübingen: Niemeyer Verlag.

Ravid, D. and Malenky, A. 2001. Awareness of linear and nonlinear morphology in Hebrew: A developmental study. *First Language* 21: 25–56.

Ravid, D. and Nir, M. 2000. On the development of the category of adjective in Hebrew. In *From sound to sentence: Studies on first language acquisition*, M. Beers, B. van den Bogaerde, G. Bol, J. de Jong, and c. Rooijmans (eds), 113–124. Groningen: Center for Language and Cognition.

Ravid, D. and Zilberbuch, S. 2003. Morpho-syntactic constructs in the development of spoken and written Hebrew text production. *Journal of Child Language* 30: 395–418.

Ravid, D., Avivi-Ben Zvi, G. and Levie, R. 1999. Derivational morphology in SLI children: structure and semantics of Hebrew nouns. In *New directions in language development and disorders*, M. Perkins and S. Howard (eds), 39–49. New York: Plenum.

Rubinstein, J.S., Meyer, D.E. and Evans, J.E. 2001. Executive control of cognitive processes in task switching. *Journal of Experimental Psychology: Human Perception and Performance* 27: 763–797.

Schwarzwald, O.R. 2004. Comments on Hebrew reduplication. *Mehkerey morashtenu* 2–3: 251–261. [in Hebrew]

Seidman, O. 2000. Morphological and phonological perception and the development of writing from kindergarten to first grade. MA thesis, Department of Communications Disorders, Tel Aviv University.

Sagi, H. 1997. Selected morpho-syntactic changes in literary translations of Sholom-Aleichem from Yiddish into Hebrew: a study of the influence of Yiddish on the structure of Modern Hebrew. Unpublished doctoral dissertation, Bar Ilan University.

Spencer, A. 1991. *Morphological theory.* Oxford, UK: Blackwell.

Stephany, U. 1997. Diminutives in early child Greek, a preliminary investigation. In *Studies in pre- and protomorphology,* W.U. Dressler (ed.), 147–156. Wien: Österreichischen Akademie der Wissenschaften.

Ussishkin, A. 1999. The inadequacy of the consonantal root: Modern Hebrew denominal verbs and output-output correspondence. *Phonology* 16: 401–442.

CHAPTER 13

Diminutives provide multiple benefits for language acquisition

Vera Kempe, Patricia J. Brooks and Steven Gillis

This chapter explores the hypothesis that diminutive usage in child-directed speech may provide multiple benefits for language acquisition. We summarize a series of experiments that exposed naïve English-speaking adults to Dutch or Russian diminutives, and tested their ability to isolate words in fluent speech or acquire gender categories. Across studies, adults benefited from exposure to diminutives over their simplex counterparts, supporting the hypothesis that diminutives simplify word segmentation and morphology acquisition, by increasing word-ending invariance, regularizing stress patterns, and decreasing irregularity in morpho-syntactic categories. A similar diminutive advantage is observed in experimental studies of first language acquisition: Preschool children produce fewer gender agreement and case marking errors with diminutives than with simplex nouns across several languages (Russian, Serbian, Polish, Lithuanian).

Introduction

Peter Jusczyk's seminal studies of the development of infant speech perception have spurred intense interest in exploring the learning processes that enable young children to discover the linguistic structures of their native language(s) (e.g., Jusczyk & Aslin 1995; Jusczyk & Hohne 1997; Jusczyk 1997, 2002). One hypothesis, receiving renewed attention, is that general-purpose associative learning mechanisms play a crucial role in the acquisition of linguistic categories and structures (Gomez & Gerken 2000; Seidenberg & McDonald 1999). At present there is considerable evidence that infants and children are successful in tracking distributional patterns and regularities at a number of levels of linguistic analysis, including prosodic, phonological, morphological, and syntactic (e.g., Brooks & Zizak 2002; Gomez & Gerken 1999; Saffran, Aslin & Newport 1996; Saffran & Wilson 2003). This work, which suggests that language acquisition involves the implicit learning of probabilistic regularities extracted from highly complex input, makes the particular distributional characteristics of the speech directed to children a topic of considerable interest, both from applied (e.g., Hoff 2003; Huttenlocher, Vasilyeva, Cymerman & Levine 2002; Weizman & Snow 2001), and theoretical perspectives (e.g., Bates & MacWhinney 1987; Elman, Bates, Johnson, Karmiloff-Smith, Parisi & Plunkett 1996). There now is a sizeable body of research suggesting that child-directed speech (CDS) might simplify, regularize, and highlight relevant linguistic structures and, thereby, might facilitate the language acquisition process (e.g., Kuhl et al. 1997; Golinkoff & Alioto 1995; Morgan & Demuth 1996; Tamis-LeMonda & Bornstein 2002, but see also Fernald & McRoberts 1996, for a note of caution). In this chapter, we will focus on one feature of CDS, the use of diminutives: Starting with a cross-linguistic comparison of the frequency of diminutives in CDS, we will show how diminutives may exert simplifying and regularizing effects on different levels of linguistic structure and in different languages. Specifically, we will present empirical evidence from two typologically diverse languages, Dutch and Russian, to show how diminutives aid in two major language-learning tasks, word segmentation and grammatical gender acquisition. We report on experiments demonstrating that exposure to elements resembling Dutch and Russian diminutives facilitates word segmentation in adult language learners. We also report studies showing that Russian diminutives lead to advantages in the acquisition of grammatical gender, both in Russian children as well as in second language learners. For brevity, we omit the outcomes of the statistical tests but report only on findings that were statistically significant. We will end the chapter with some thoughts on why diminutives differ in their frequency across CDS registers of various languages, and what factors may account for the pervasiveness of beneficial forms in CDS in general.

1. The pervasiveness of diminutives in CDS

Diminutives are morphological derivations that express smallness, and connote affection and endearment. In some languages, diminutives are also used in a pejorative way. Quite obviously it makes semantic sense to use diminutives in CDS as they are well suited to adjust the meanings of words to the smaller world of the child. Indeed, an analysis of the semantics of diminutives in over 80 languages has identified child-relatedness as the core meaning of the diminutive derivation (Jurafsky 1996). Still, to speakers of English, our focus on diminutives as a major regularizing and simplifying force in children's language input might seem unwarranted given that in this language, the productivity of diminutives is extremely limited.[1] English diminutives can be derived from proper names as in *Billy*, *Patty* and *Johnny*, names of relatives as in *mommy*, *daddy* and *auntie*, and some names of animals as in *doggie*, *horsy*, and *birdie* (but not much beyond these, as ill-formed examples like **sheepy*, or **cowie* attest). A few additional English diminutives comprise child-related or other small objects such as *binkie*, *bootie*, *cookie*, and *panties*. In all cases, the diminutive appears to be derived from a monosyllabic stem or base noun, creating a bi-syllabic noun with a trochaic stress pattern.

Unlike English, many other languages have a much wider range of diminutive productivity. Thus, in languages as diverse as Dutch, German, Finnish, Lithuanian, Spanish, Serbian and Russian, diminutives can be derived from almost any concrete noun, and in some languages (e.g., Spanish, Russian, Serbian) even from adjectives and adverbs. The latter fact clearly suggests that diminutive usage is governed not just by semantic factors to convey the meaning of smallness, but seems to be primarily a pragmatic device[2] to express endearment and affection. Clearly, on pragmatic grounds, it seems reasonable to expect a higher frequency of diminutives in CDS than in adult-directed speech (ADS). Indeed, there is quite a lot of evidence for the pervasiveness of diminutives in CDS. Table 1 lists the estimated frequency of diminutivized nouns in the CDS registers of a number of languages. The estimates are provided for nouns only, to account for the fact that modifiers can only be diminutivized in some languages.[3]

Table 1. Estimated frequency of diminutivized nouns in CDS registers of a number of languages obtained from corpora of one mother-child dyad in each language

language	% diminutivized nouns	source
Lithuanian	30-40	Savickienė (1998), (2003)
German	3	Kempe, Brooks & Pirott (2001)
	3	Korecky-Kroell &Dressler (2004)
Dutch	20-30	Gillis (1997)
Spanish	42	Kempe, Brooks & Pirott (2001)
Russian	45	Kempe, Brooks & Pirott (2001)
Polish	20	Haman (2003)

Unfortunately, direct comparisons between CDS and ADS within the same language, or, even more informatively, within the same speakers of a language, are rare. Most of the estimates stem from recorded mother-child interactions, and fail to include an ADS baseline to which the frequency of diminutives in CDS can be compared. Thus, one might argue that a high frequency of diminutives may just be a peculiarity of certain registers in a particular language, and does not have to be a pervasive feature of just the CDS register. This argument has often been invoked with respect to Dutch, a language that is characterized by pervasive use of diminutives in colloquial speech.

In order to get direct evidence for an increase of diminutives in CDS, we recorded conversations of twelve Russian mothers with their 23-month-old children (range 18 – 28 months), and compared those to conversations of the same mothers with an adult interlocutor (Kempe, Brooks, Mironova, Pershukova, & Fedorova, in press). In the CDS samples, the mothers were engaged in normal daily activities like eating, dressing, going for a walk, and playing, and were asked to audio-tape their interactions with their child. No other person was present during the interactions with the child. To obtain samples of ADS, the mothers were asked to engage in a conversation with an adult researcher in the absence of their child, which was audiotaped as well. The researcher prompted them to talk about various past events of their life avoiding child-related topics. Since the researcher was an acquaintance in all cases these conversations tended to be relatively informal thus providing estimates of diminutives from adult-directed colloquial speech. To obtain preliminary estimates of the frequency of diminutives, and due to feasibility limitations for analysing the entire conversational episode, we analyzed just the first 100 nouns from each interaction. The frequency of productive diminutives was 45% (range 13% – 81%) in CDS, and 3% (range 1% – 8%) in ADS, and the difference was highly significant. This estimate provides strong evidence that, in Russian, the frequency of diminutives is much higher in CDS than in ADS. Clearly, corroborating evidence from other languages is needed to show that increased frequency of diminutives in Russian CDS is not an isolated phenomenon. However, given the rather impressive rates of diminutives in Lithuanian, Spanish, and other languages (see table 1), it seems reasonable to assume that the frequency of diminutives increases in CDS registers as much as the diminutive productivity of a given language permits.

As stated earlier, the use of diminutives in CDS seems to be primarily pragmatically motivated. How can a pragmatic device aid language acquisition on various other levels of linguistic analysis? The answer lies in the fact that any frequently occurring morphological derivation may increase regularity at several different levels of analysis. In the case of diminutives, firstly, there is a tendency to regularize metric stress patterns, which makes it easier to detect word boundaries, thereby aiding the task of segmenting the stream of uninterrupted speech into discrete words. Secondly, diminutives increase the invariance of word endings, which provides an additional word segmentation cue. Thirdly, diminutives may serve as word class markers thereby making it easier to distinguish nouns or modifiers from other parts of speech. Finally, in many languages, diminutives have a tendency to regularize irregular aspects of inflectional morphology thereby facilitating the acquisition of morpho-syntax. Below we will focus on the effects of frequent diminutive usage on word segmentation and morphology acquisition by presenting empirical evidence from Dutch and Russian.

2. Diminutives aid word segmentation

One of the major challenges of language acquisition is to segment the incoming stream of continuous speech into discrete meaningful units. A large body of research has demonstrated that many different sources of information may serve as word segmentation cues such as utterance boundaries (Brent & Siskind 2001), phonotactic regularities (e.g., Mattys & Jusczyk 2001b), transitional probabilities between phonemes or syllables (e.g., Saffran, Aslin & Newport 1996), context- or position-sensitive allophony (e.g., Jusczyk, Hohne & Bauman 1999; Mattys & Jusczyk 2001a), as well as rhythmic and prosodic patterns (e.g., Morgan & Saffran 1995; Morgan 1996; Jusczyk, Houston & Newsome 1999). There is evidence that CDS is much richer in word segmentation cues than ADS due to its exaggerated stress patterns, shorter utterances, and longer and more frequent pauses (Redford, Davis & Miikkulainen 2004). Not surprisingly, computational word segmentation models have shown superior performance with CDS input as compared to ADS input (Aslin, Woodward, LaMendola & Bever 1996; Brent & Cartwright 1996; Christiansen, Allen & Seidenberg 1998; Batchelder 2002).

In this context, frequent use of diminutives in CDS serves to increase the availability of word segmentation cues. This idea was first expressed by Jusczyk (1997) and Echols, Crowhurst and Childers (1997) who suggested "...that many diminutive forms in English that are used in addressing infants have strong/weak patterns ... (e.g., "daddy," "mommy," "doggie," "cookie," "kitty," etc). Consequently, it is not implausible that infants in English-speaking environments might develop a bias for trochaic patterns..." (Jusczyk 1997: 108). Since diminutives are often derived by adding unstressed suffixes to word stems, it is possible that stress regularization is a general phenomenon in languages with frequent diminutives in CDS. For example, Dutch diminutives comprise about 20–30% of all child-directed noun tokens (Gillis 1997), which increases the frequency of stressed/unstressed nouns in CDS to 74% of multi-syllabic word types (Taelman & Gillis 2000). For Russian, connectionist simulations of word boundary detection based on metrical stress of the 200 most frequent nouns show superior performance when the networks are trained on the diminutive rather than simplex forms of these nouns (Kempe, in preparation). This suggests that the complex metrical stress pattern typical for Russian becomes simplified and regularized in diminutive nouns, for example, by eliminating word-final stress. In Spanish, many words with atypical stress assignment (e.g., *teléfono* [telephone] with stress on the second syllable) have regular penultimate stress when diminutivized (e.g., *telefonito* [small telephone]).

Cutler and Norris (1988) and Cutler (1994) proposed the use of a metrical segmentation strategy which implies that listeners rely on knowledge about predominant rhythmic patterns in their language to detect word boundaries. For example, in English, stressed syllables are important cues for word onsets, which are utilized by both infants and adults, with phonotactically familiar (Echols et al. 1997; Jusczyk et al. 1999) as well as unfamiliar (Houston, Jusczyk, Kuijpers, Coolen & Cutler 2000; Kempe, Brooks & Gillis 2005) language input. Stress regularization through diminutivization obviously facilitates the use of metrical stress as a word segmentation cue.

However, stress regularization is not the only benefit for word segmentation that arises from frequent use of diminutives. In fact, this cue is inevitably confounded with increased word ending invariance. Since languages contain a limited number of diminutive suffixes, diminutivized words tend to have similar endings. For example, *daddy*, *mommy*, *doggie*, *cookie*, and *kitty* all end in the same vowel. In languages with more complex diminutive derivations, the invariant segment can be even longer. For instance, Spanish diminutives end in *-ito* /ito/ or *-ita* /ita/, depending on gender, German diminutives end in *-chen* /Xən/ or *-lein* /lajn/, and Dutch diminutives end in *-tje* /tjə/ or one of its allomorphs.

In Experiment 2 of Kempe et al. (2005), we investigated whether invariance in word endings introduced by diminutives facilitates word segmentation over and above the effects of regular trochaic (strong/weak) stress. We used Dutch materials because Dutch is a language with frequent and productive diminutive suffixation. Almost all Dutch concrete nouns can be diminutivized by adding the unstressed suffix *-tje* /tjə/, or its variants *-etje* /ətjə/, *-pje* /pjə/, *-kje* /kjə/, or *-je* /jə/, to simplex nouns such as chair (*stoel* /stul/ > *stoeltje* /stultjə/), glass (*glas* /Γlas/ > *glaasje* /Γlasjə/) or window (*raam* /ram/ > *raampje* /rampjə/). Thus, Dutch diminutive suffixes consist of a consonant cluster containing an affricate and a schwa ending. We varied the invariance in the consonant cluster and the vowel ending systematically to examine the independent contributions of consonant and vowel invariance found in Dutch diminutive affixes.

We utilized an incidental-learning paradigm, which originally was developed for the study of transitional probabilities between phonemes (Saffran, Newport, Aslin, Tunick & Barrueco 1997). Eighty-four adult English speakers with no prior knowledge of Dutch were randomly assigned to one of four conditions, and presented with continuous speech comprising 300 randomized repetitions of six bi-syllabic nonsense words as targets. The nonsense words were synthesized to ensure equivalent levels of co-articulation between syllables (both word internally and across word boundaries), and to eliminate other word boundary cues (e.g., pauses). The four conditions differed in the degree of ending invariance of the final syllable: The *low onset/low rhyme invariance* condition resembled Dutch bi-syllabic simplex nouns by combining the stems with six different consonant/vowel combinations, which were all dissimilar from each other (e.g., *knoochtie, steefkeu*). The *low onset/high rhyme invariance* condition resembled the degree of rhyme invariance of Dutch diminutives by combining the same second syllable consonant clusters with a schwa as the final vowel (e.g., *knoochte, steefke*). The *high onset/low rhyme invariance* condition resembled the degree of onset invariance of Dutch diminutive affixes by combining the onset of the three most frequent allomorphs of the Dutch diminutive, viz. glide /j/ and the obstruent glide clusters /tj/ and /pj/ (Booij 1995), and the full vowels used in the low onset/low rhyme invariance condition (e.g., *knoochjie, steefjeu*). Finally, the *high onset/high rhyme invariance* condition modeled the maximal ending invariance characteristic for Dutch diminutives by combining all stems with the three most frequent diminutive allomorphs -je /jə/, -tje /tjə/, and -pje /pjə/ (e.g., *knoochtje, steefje*). All nonsense words were presented as trochees, which allowed us to investigate the effect of ending invariance over and above the effect of metrical stress on the first syllable. After listening to the speech stream for eighteen minutes, participants were given a forced choice task to determine whether there was better recognition of the target strings over foils. The foils were created by recombining the target syllables in such a way that the second syllables of the targets were followed by first syllables. The syllable combinations of the foils did occasionally occur in the speech stream but with much lower frequency than the syllable combinations of the targets. All targets and foils are listed in table 2. Finally, to obtain a baseline measure for incidental a-priori familiarity and segmentability of the targets, another eighty-four participants were presented with a no-training condition, in which they completed the forced choice task only, but had no prior exposure to the speech stream.

Table 2. Targets and foils used in the word segmentation experiment (from Kempe, Brooks & Gillis 2005)

	Rhyme Invariance			
	low		high	
Onset Invariance	targets	foils	targets	foils
low	knoochtie	tieflijm	knoochte	teflijm
	steefkeu	keuvraul	steefke	kevraul
	schraamloo	loogluin	schraamle	legluin
	flijmsaa	saaknooch	flijmse	seknooch
	gluinfee	feeschraam	gluinfe	feeschraam
	vraulpuu	puusteef	vraulpe	pesteef
high	knoochjie	jieflijm	knoochje	jeflijm
	steefjeu	jeuvraul	steefje	jevraul
	schraampjoo	pjoogluin	schraampje	pjegluin
	flijmpjaa	spjaknooch	flijmpje	pjeknooch
	gluintjee	tjeeschraam	gluintje	tjeschraam
	vraultjuu	tjuusteef	vraultje	tjesteef

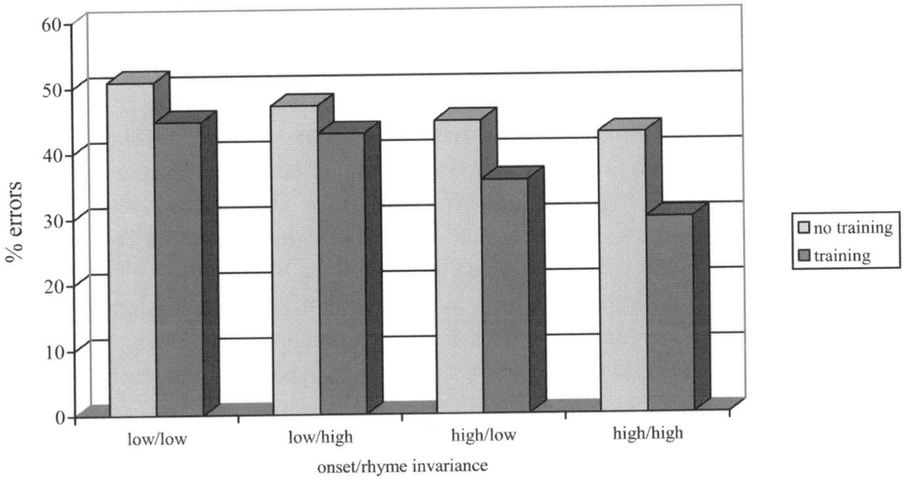

Figure 1. Percent errors in the forced-choice task in the word segmentation experiment (from Kempe, Brooks & Gillis 2005)

The results, depicted in figure 1, showed that participants were able to recognize the targets above chance in all conditions except for the two no-training conditions that contained variable final syllable onset consonant clusters (e.g., *knochtie, steefkeu* etc. and *knochte, steefke* etc.). This suggests that onset invariance, specifically the presence of the affricate in the final syllable onset, acts like a marker for the upcoming word ending, even without any exposure to the targets. It also shows that after 18 minutes of listening to the speech stream, participants learned to recognize all types of targets, even those which contained variable final syllable onsets and rhymes. This is due to the fact that all targets were trochees, and, as expected, stress on the first syllable was being used as a word onset cue. The most important finding, however, was related to the distribution of error rates. We observed an interaction between training and onset invariance. Thus, although performance generally improved after training, this interaction indicated that performance improved more in conditions with invariant consonant clusters containing the affricate typical for Dutch diminutives. Participants exhibited by far the best performance (70% correct) after listening to targets with maximal ending invariance, i.e., targets modeled after Dutch diminutives.

This experiment demonstrated that ending invariance induced by diminutives improves word segmentation performance over and above the benefits from regular trochaic stress. So far, we have presented evidence for only one language, Dutch. In general, however, any type of ending invariance induced by a morphological change that applies to word endings could facilitate word segmentation. Thus, there is no reason to assume that similar effects could not be obtained from regularly occurring plural morphemes or inflectional endings on verbs. We believe, however, that diminutives are especially helpful, just because the diminutive derivation tends to be particularly long and salient, as it often comprises one or even multiple syllables (e.g., Russian: *vodichechka* [water-Dim-Dim]). Indeed, a new set of experiments has provided cross-linguistic evidence for this claim by showing that targets modeled after Russian masculine nominative diminutives exert a similarly facilitating effect compared to targets resembling Russian masculine nominative simplex nouns (Kempe, Brooks, Gillis & Samson, in press).

But what if word endings remain variable due to inflectional changes as it would happen, for example, with the case-marked forms of Russian masculine nouns? Adding the diminutive suffix *-ik* may result in word endings like *-ika* (gen. sg.), *-iku* (dat. sg.), *-ike* (loc. sg.), *-iki* (nom. pl.) or *-ikam* (dat. pl.) etc., depending on number and case of the noun. Thus, ending invariance here is confined to the final syllable onset while the rhyme changes systematically according to whatever inflectional paradigm the noun belongs to. Would usage of diminutives in CDS still facilitate word segmentation in highly inflected languages where the diminutive suffixes precede systematically changing inflectional morphemes? The interaction between training and onset invariance in the word segmentation experiment described above suggests that invariant phonemes or phoneme clusters right before the inflectional endings might be sufficient to support the discovery of word boundaries. Based on this finding, we would predict that diminutivization should aid word segmentation even in highly inflected languages.

3. Diminutives aid morphology acquisition

In addition to learning to segment the speech stream into words, language acquisition entails mastering the complexities of the underlying structure governing the use of these words. This encompasses learning the regularities within words, i.e., the domain of morphology, and the regularities of how words are combined together, i.e., the domain of syntax. Below we want to focus on how diminutives may aid the acquisition of morphology.

In order to appreciate the potential impact of diminutives on morphology acquisition it is important to have an understanding as to what the particular challenges in this domain are. Morphology acquisition has been at the center of hot theoretical debates regarding the architecture of language representation in the brain, and the developmental processes shaping this architecture. Unfortunately, much of this debate has been informed by a fairly narrow empirical basis constrained to the study of a few languages, the most prominent being English with its rather impoverished morphological structure. The two aspects of English inflectional morphology that have received most of the attention are past tense formation in verbs and plural formation in nouns. Both of these structures consist of a regular pattern of high type frequency and a small number of irregular exceptions. Consequently, there is a research tradition that describes the acquisition of inflectional morphology in terms of two qualitatively distinct processes: a procedural route underlying the acquisition of a rule governing the formation of the regular pattern, and a memory-driven process accounting for the representation of the irregular exceptions in the lexicon (Pinker 1999). However, as soon as researchers started looking beyond the confines of simple English morphology by studying more complex morphological systems in which frequency and regularity are not confounded (e.g., German plural formation), the situation became more complicated: In such systems, the learner may have to acquire a multitude of inflectional patterns all of which differ in frequency, phonological similarity and neighborhood density (Hahn & Nakisa 2000; Plunkett & Nakisa 1997). Although there are assertions that even complex systems inevitably have a regular default pattern at their core, even if it is a low frequency pattern, (Marcus, Brinkmann, & Clahsen 1995), it is clear that in many instances the simple rules vs. exceptions dichotomy does not apply (Dąbrowska 2004). Unfortunately, research on the acquisition of more complex inflectional systems is scarce, and our understanding of the processes underlying their acquisition is just emerging. In this context, investigating the effects of a form as pervasive as the diminutive may shed light on the acquisition of complex morphological systems.

Diminutivizing a word means that the morphological status of that word may be altered. This implies that inflectional changes applying to the simplex and to the diminutive form of a word may not be identical. Consider the Russian noun *mysh'* 'mouse', a feminine noun of the third declension type which is the rarest declension type in Russian used only with a small class of feminine nouns, many of which end in palatalized consonants. Case-marked forms of the nominative *mysh'* are *myshi* for genitive, dative, and locative, and *mysh'ju* for instrumental. In contrast, the diminutive *myshka* uses the second declension type, which is much more frequent and results in forms like *myshki* (genitive), *myshke* (dative), *myshku* (accusative), *myshkoj* (instrumental) and *myshke* (locative). Two points are noteworthy with respect to this example: Firstly, the diminutive *myshka* has an ending that clearly identifies it as feminine nominative since most feminine nominative nouns in Russian end in *-a* or its allomorph *-ja*. If a noun contains the dominant form of feminine noun endings it should be easier to select the appropriate gender agreement. Gender agreement in Russian is important as it is obligatory for adjectives, past tense verbs and pronouns. Secondly, the declension applying to the diminutive *myshka* clearly differentiates all six Russian cases thus making it easier to identify the underlying semantic role of the noun, unlike its simplex counterpart for which three cases (genitive, dative, and locative) take one ending, two cases (nominative and accusative) take the null morpheme, and only the instrumental case has a unique ending (*-ju*). Clearly, this creates much more ambiguity as the noun form itself does not provide reliable information about case. Consequently, high frequency of diminutives in the input of Russian children should facilitate the acquisition of gender and case marking.

Table 3. Familiar and novel simplex and diminutive nouns used in the Russian gender elicitation experiment (Kempe et al. 2003) (Stressed syllables are marked by capitalized letters. All nouns were counterbalanced across two lists except the items marked by asterisks which remained the same in both lists. One half of the children were presented with list 1 and the other half with list 2)

masculine		feminine	
simplex	diminutive	simplex	diminutive
	familiar nouns		
jozh [porcupine]	jozhik	belka [squirrel]	belochka
zhiraf [giraffe]	zhirafik	lisa [fox]	lisichka
zhuk [beetle]	zhuchok	obez'jana [monkey]	obez'janka
slon [elephant]	slonik	ptica [bird]	ptichka
kit* [whale]	petushok* [roosterDIM]	cherepakha* [turtle]	babochka* [butterfly]
	novel nouns		
zurUn	zurUnchik	mYrva	mYrochkva
zhabUl	zhabUl'chik	vIgla	vIglochka
pusOt	pusOtik	sUra	sUrochka
cOkor	cOkorik	krjOfa	krjOfochka
farzjAk	farzjAchik	tImza	tImzochka
narAp	narApchik	gljUsha	gljUshechka

We have studied the effects of diminutives on the acquisition of Russian gender (Kempe, Brooks, Mironova & Fedorova 2003). In a gender agreement elicitation experiment, we presented forty-six Russian children (age 2,9 to 4,8) with 24 novel and familiar simplex and diminutive nouns (see table 3). We used only masculine and feminine nouns as the neuter category is much smaller thus making it difficult to select balanced stimulus materials. Also, masculine and feminine nouns are of particular interest as it is these gender categories within which a significant degree of irregularity exists: Most Russian masculine nouns tend to end in consonants, feminine nouns in *-a* or its allomorphs, and neuter nouns in *-o* or its allomorphs. But there is also the abovementioned class of nouns ending in palatalized consonants that can be either masculine (*pen'* 'stump', *gost'* 'guest') or feminine (*pech'* 'oven', *mysh'* 'mouse') because the nominative does not contain any morpho-phonological features providing cues to gender category membership. Based on estimates from the 200 most frequent Russian nouns (Zasorina 1977), these non-transparent nouns comprise about 10% of noun types. In the gender elicitation study, children were presented with the names of familiar and unfamiliar animals, along with pictures of the animals. Children were encouraged to talk about each animal, with the experimenter carefully avoiding any use of gender agreement in their own speech, so that the only cue to the gender of the animal was its name. The first instance of gender agreement produced by the child in their description of the animal, which tended to be either pronominal agreement or adjective agreement, was coded and analysed for errors. The error rates are depicted in figure 2.

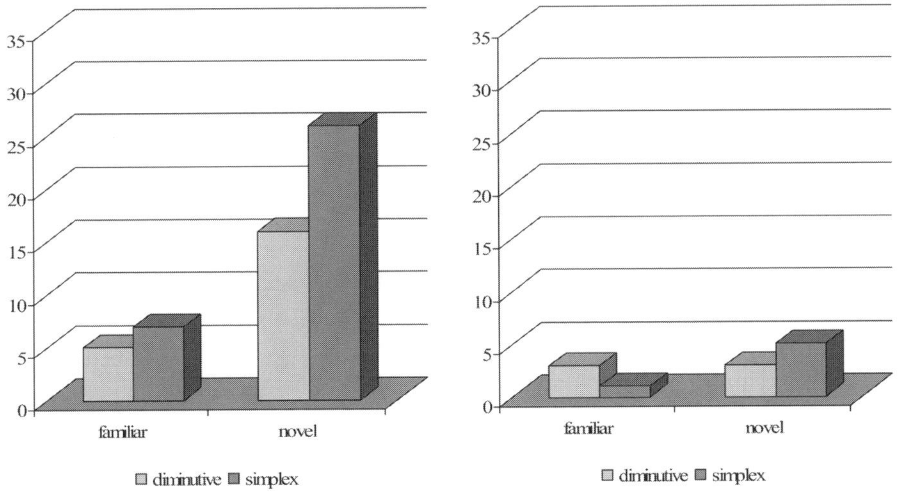

Figure 2. Percent gender agreement errors in Russian children in the gender elicitation task for feminine (left panel) and masculine (right panel) nouns (Kempe et al. 2003)

The results of this experiment demonstrated that Russian children made more agreement errors after novel nouns than after familiar nouns, and after feminine nouns than after masculine nouns. The novelty effect was mainly due to the feminine nouns, as indicated by an interaction between novelty and gender, suggesting that the masculine gender may be the unmarked form that is acquired first. Another possible reason for an advantage of masculine nouns is that one of the most frequent forms of gender agreement, agreement with adjectives, results in shorter and morphologically less complex masculine forms (e.g., *sinij* 'blue:MAS') compared to the feminine forms (e.g., *sinjaja* 'blue:FEM'). Most importantly, the findings showed a clear difference in errors between simplex and diminutive nouns, such that the children made significantly fewer gender agreement errors when presented with diminutive nouns. Thus, the experiment confirmed the existence of a diminutive advantage with respect to gender acquisition and productive use of gender agreement in 2- to 4- year-old Russian children. We attribute this phenomenon to the pervasiveness of diminutives in Russian CDS: A high frequency of diminutives in the input increases the overall degree of regularity in the gender-marking system because it increases the relative frequency of transparently gender marked nouns, and reduces the relative frequency of non-transparently gender marked nouns. At the same time, a higher frequency of diminutives introduces a very prominent sub-cluster of nouns that is characterized by high phonological similarity due to the overlap in diminutive suffixes.

More recently, Kempe, Brooks, Mironova, Pershukova and Fedorova (in press) demonstrated a similar diminutive advantage in children's production of Russian case marking. Preschool children were introduced to a variety of novel objects, with their nonce names introduced in the diminutive form, the simplex form or both (i.e., a 'word-play' condition). To elicit dative and genitive case marking, children were asked questions concerning the movements of an elephant towards or away from the object. Russian children produced a higher percentage of correctly case-inflected forms for nouns heard in the diminutive form, with best performance in the 'word-play' condition. Dąbrowska (2006) also reported a diminutive advantage for children acquiring Polish case marking, and argued that the diminutive advantage in morphology acquisition be attributed to children's acquisition of low-level schemas. That is, children tend to acquire inflectional changes first for salient sub-clusters of nouns before generalizing to a wider range of noun types. The results of the gender-agreement elicitation experiment described above may reflect the operation of both tendencies: increased frequency of regular gender marking and increased frequency of a phonologically similar sub-cluster of nouns that constitutes a prominent low-level schema. To tease apart these two consequences of increased diminutive frequency in the input, we conducted a micro-genetic gender-learning experiment contrasting an entirely regular system consisting solely of diminutives with input consisting of both regular and irregular patterns (Kempe & Brooks 2001). Obviously, contrasting these two situations is not possible in the study of first language acquisition. Thus, in order to systematically control the input, and to follow the trajectory of learning in the laboratory, we tested adult native speakers of English learning a subset of Russian noun morphology.

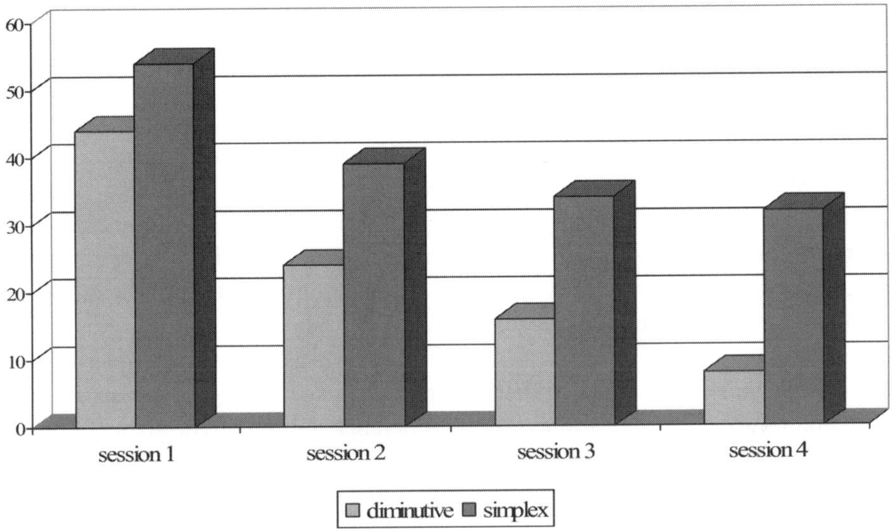

Figure 3. Percent gender agreement errors in L2-learners for transparent nouns over 4 sessions of training (Kempe & Brooks 2001)

Thirty-six adult native speakers of English with no prior knowledge of Russian were taught the gender of 30 Russian nouns. The training set consisted of 15 masculine and 15 feminine Russian nouns and their corresponding pictures. Five masculine and 5 feminine nouns were non-transparent with respect to gender marking, i.e., they ended in a palatalized consonant. In the diminutive training group, all nouns were presented as diminutives, thus rendering the entire set transparent with respect to gender marking in that all feminine nouns ended in *-a*, and all masculine nouns ended in a non-palatalized consonant. In the non-diminutive training group, the corresponding simplex forms were presented which resulted in a training set consisting of two-thirds transparently gender-marked nouns and one-third non-transparent gender-marked nouns. All nouns were combined with the color adjectives *zholtyj/zholtaja* 'yellow: MAS/yellow:FEM' and *krasnyj/krasnaja* 'red:MAS/red:FEM'. In the training sessions, participants engaged in three tasks designed to expose them to gender agreement and to elicit production of gender agreement. During the Listen and Repeat task, they were shown a red or yellow line drawing of the object and the corresponding adjective-noun phrase which they simply had to repeat. During the Color Choice task, they saw a red and a yellow drawing of the same object, and listened to an adjective-noun phrase denoting one of the colors and the object (e.g., *krasnyj domik* 'red house-DIM'). Participants were asked to select the appropriate drawing corresponding to the named color via button press. The rationale behind this task was to provide additional exposure to the correct adjective-noun gender agreement under the pretence of learning the color words. Finally, in the Production task, participants were shown a red or yellow drawing of the object, and heard just the noun. Their task was to produce the correct color word, e.g., the Russian word for 'red' or 'yellow'. In doing so, they also had to supply some form of gender agreement at the end of the adjective, which was coded and served as indicator for their mastery of gender. The results indicated that participants in the diminutive training group learned gender agreement faster than participants in the non-diminutive training group (see figure 3). When comparing performance just on the 20 transparently gender-marked nouns, the diminutive group reliably outperformed the non-diminutive training group over the course of training. Furthermore, performance across training sessions improved faster in the diminutive group than in the non-diminutive group.

The crucial question is whether learners were able to generalize the gender-marking pattern to novel nouns indicating that they had extracted the regularities in the input. To examine this, participants were given a generalization test after the fourth session, which utilized the same color-adjective Production task, only this time with a different color adjective, i.e., the one that was not presented during training (e.g., if the noun was presented in yellow during training, it was presented in red during testing and vice versa). For generalization, ten additional nouns and pictures were presented together with the 30 familiar nouns. The ten non-transparent nouns from the training set were presented in their simplex form, which was the form familiar to the non-diminutive group while the diminutive group had encountered these nouns as diminutives. Ten of the transparent nouns were presented in their diminutive form, which was the familiar form for the diminutive group while the non-diminutive group had encountered the simplex form of these nouns. The other ten transparent nouns were presented in their simplex form, which was the familiar form for the non-diminutive group while the diminutive group had encountered these nouns in their diminutive form. All ten novel nouns were transparent with respect to gender marking, and were presented in their simplex form. The rationale behind this test was to see whether the diminutive group could generalize gender agreement to the simplex form of the familiar nouns and to novel transparent nouns, and whether the non-diminutive group could generalize to diminutive forms of the familiar simplex forms as well as the novel nouns. The results are depicted in figure 4. For the diminutive nouns, the diminutive group was clearly superior in producing gender agreement. This was expected given that these were exactly the noun forms encountered by this group during training. For the familiar transparent nouns, we also found superior performance in the diminutive group. Notice that in this condition, participants in the diminutive group actually had to supply gender agreement for noun forms they had not encountered before in their simplex form. For the non-transparent nouns, we found an effect of noun gender, which was due to more errors in feminine non-transparent nouns. Recall that in Russian, most feminine non-transparent nouns end in a palatalized consonant, and, thus, resemble the overall phonological shape of masculine nouns. Consequently, in this experiment, participants treated them as masculine nouns 42% of the time. This finding suggests that participants in both groups did not memorize the association between gender and the word stem or the word meaning but were relying on the morpho-phonological marking of gender at the ends of words. Finally, in the novel transparent nouns, the diminutive training group exhibited a smaller error rate although the difference between diminutive and non-diminutive training group fell just short of significance.

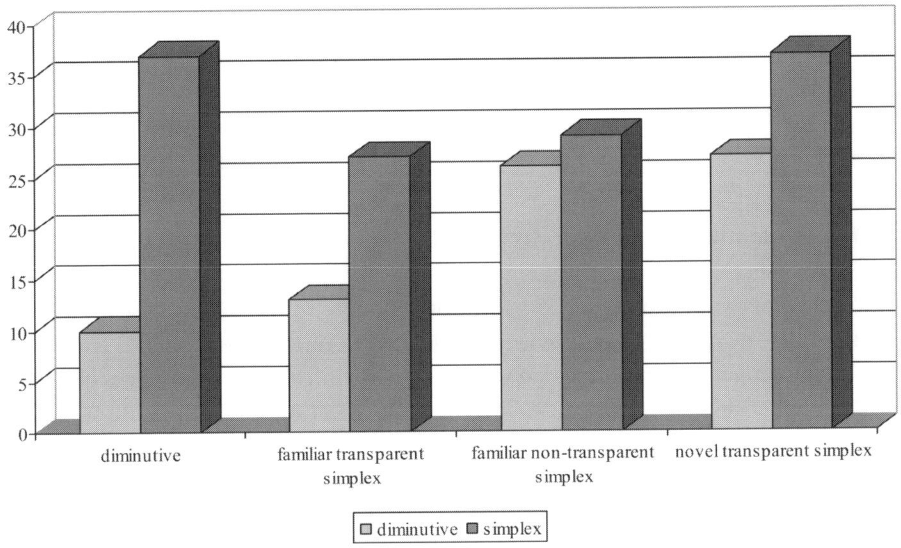

Figure 4. Percent gender agreement errors of L2-learners in the various noun types in the generalization task (Kempe & Brooks 2001)

Given the overall superior performance of the diminutive group, this experiment suggests that encountering input that is completely regular with respect to gender marking leads to faster learning and better generalization to novel nouns. Note that in the diminutive group, learners could not have isolated a salient sub-cluster of words to be learned first as all the nouns were diminutives and, thus, phonologically very similar to each other. Thus, the crucial difference between the two groups pertains to the regularity of the system the learners encountered: the diminutive group acquired gender based on an absolutely regular system whereas in the simplex group, participants encountered a training set comprising two-thirds regular nouns and one-third irregular exceptions. This clearly demonstrates that regularity supports learning. Note also that the diminutive group outperformed the non-diminutive group despite the fact that the longer and phonologically more complex diminutives should present more of a challenge to adult learners who are not familiar with Russian phonotactics.

The experiments described in this section show that when diminutives regularize an inflectional pattern this provides an advantage for the learner. However, in the case of Russian gender marking, regularity and frequency are confounded: Diminutives increase the frequency of the already more frequent regular pattern of gender marking, and this does improve learning. It does, however, not exclude the possibility, that Russian children, who encounter both simplex and diminutive nouns in their language input, may start to apply inflectional patterns to diminutives first because diminutives are a perceptually very salient cluster of nouns (Dąbrowska 2006). This supports item-based views on language learning: Children appear to move from learning morphological patterns for single words, to learning morphological patterns applying to narrow clusters of fairly similar words, and eventually to wider generalizations (Lieven, Pine & Baldwin 1997; Tomasello 1992, 2003), encompassing groups of words commonly labeled as grammatical categories.

4. Why so many diminutives? Towards an explanation of the nature of CDS

In this chapter, we summarized some of our research on the beneficial effects of diminutives in CDS on language learning. We have described evidence from Dutch and Russian showing that diminutives aid word segmentation and morphology acquisition. Similar predictions have been formulated for the effect of diminutives in other languages. For example, in Finnish, diminutivization results in a reduction of allophony associated with the case marking of nouns, thus rendering the declension system more transparent (Laalo 1998). In Lithuanian, diminutives fall into only three declension types out of twelve possible ones, thus exposing the learner to a simplified case-marking system (Savickienė 2003). At present, the claim that diminutives aid morphology acquisition has been tested in several other languages, including Serbian (Ševa, Kempe, Brooks, Mironova, Pershukova & Fedorova, in press), Lithuanian (Savickienė, Kempe & Brooks submitted), and Polish (Dąbrowska 2006), with consistent observations of better performance for diminutives over their simplex counterparts.

However, the conclusion that diminutives aid morphology acquisition does not hold universally across languages. The language that stands out as a counterexample is German. German diminutive nouns, which are formed by adding the suffixes *-chen*, *-lein*, *-le* (found in some German dialects) and *-ie*, are infrequent in CDS although diminutivization of nouns is as productive as in Russian, Dutch or Spanish. In Kempe, Brooks and Pirott (2001), we compared the frequency of diminutives in CDS between a Russian, a Spanish, and a German mother, and found that only about 3% of nouns were diminutivized in German CDS, in comparison to 44% of Russian nouns and 42% of Spanish nouns. Similarly, Korecky-Kroell and Dressler (2004) also found only 3% nouns produced as diminutives in German CDS, despite the fact that their sample was based on a Southern German dialect that is considered to use diminutives more widely than other German dialects. In terms of pragmatic usage, one would not expect differences in diminutive frequency across languages, assuming that German mothers are as keen to express endearment and affection towards their children as mothers who speak other languages. Furthermore, productivity of the German diminutive derivation is not a limitation: German diminutives can be derived from a large number of inanimate and animate nouns and are comparable in productivity potential to Russian or Spanish diminutives. So what then accounts for the cross-linguistic differences?

One candidate explanation is that German diminutives change the gender of nouns to neuter thereby, in essence, obscuring gender differences. This should hinder gender acquisition as the system becomes more difficult to learn because (a) the frequency of masculine and feminine nouns decreases, and (b) learners have to cope with changing gender for similar word stems depending on the noun's morphological status (simplex vs. diminutive). A system in which diminutivization alters the gender class of a noun, has been reported for other languages such as Dizi and Swahili (Corbett 1991). Unfortunately, no data on the frequency of diminutives are available for those languages. Thus, we have no means of verifying whether the morphological repercussions of the diminutive derivation are linked to the frequency of this form in CDS. In other words, are diminutives more frequent in the CDS registers of languages where they contribute to the simplification and regularization of some aspect of the morphological system, and less frequent in languages where the morphological system is being rendered more complex and irregular? The answer to this question is complicated for a number of reasons. Firstly, diminutivization obscures gender differences not just in German but also in Dutch, where all diminutives are neuter. But Dutch is a language with a high frequency of diminutives in CDS, as we have argued above. We can only speculate that the difference between these two languages may be related to the fact that in Dutch, gender agreement is not as pervasive as in German. For example, German case marking follows the gender distinction, and is ubiquitous in the language while Dutch does not have case marking. Furthermore, German requires gender agreement with adjectives while Dutch does not. Thus, one could argue, grammatical gender is a more important feature in German than in Dutch, and obscuring the gender distinction may therefore have more detrimental consequences for language learning in German. Secondly, as we have tried to show, diminutivization may exert effects on other aspects of language learning besides morphology such as word segmentation or word class categorization. It is difficult to assess what the net gain or net loss of frequent use of diminutives for the learner in any given language might be. German diminutives, even though they obscure gender distinctions, still may be beneficial for word segmentation as they may have the potential to regularize metrical stress patterns and provide substantial ending invariance. At the same time, they may hinder learning of noun classes as they do not represent typical German noun forms. Unlike in Dutch, where diminutives end in unstressed schwas, and unstressed vowels are typical Dutch noun endings, the diphthong in the German *-lein*, the fricative in the German *-chen*, and the long vowel in the German *-ie* all represent atypical German noun endings. This may be an additional factor that renders German diminutives unhelpful for the language learner. However, these explanations have to be tested empirically in future research.

Despite the many open questions, we want to conclude this chapter with a few thoughts on the factors responsible for diminutive usage, and the beneficial nature of CDS in general. The explanation we have pursued so far was based on the assumption that the net benefit of any given linguistic form for language acquisition may be responsible for the frequency of that form in CDS. Aside from the fact that more evidence is needed to support this assumption, it leads to the question as to why adult speakers shape CDS the way they do, and whether they are aware of the potential effects of their way of speaking on the child. In a recent study, Burnham, Kitamura and Vollmer-Conna (2002) demonstrated that mothers show the same changes in vocal features such as raised pitch and increased pitch range when speaking to their pets, and when speaking to their children. This can be taken as support for the idea that CDS has evolved as an affective register (Fernald 1992). Interestingly, however, the mothers tested in the Burnham et al. (2002) study hyper-articulated vowels only when speaking to their children but not when speaking to their pets. Hyper-articulation is another feature that may aid language acquisition as it helps learners to discriminate phonemes (Kuhl et al. 1997). This finding suggests that when speaking to children, adults employ features that benefit language learning, thus providing a form of didactic support. But how do they know which features are helpful in their language? Surely, it is unlikely that parents routinely engage in the kind of elaborate structural analyses of their language of the sort presented here. With respect to diminutives, it has been suggested that the frequency of diminutives in CDS in languages like Russian, Polish or Spanish can largely be attributed to the adults' attempts at imitating the child (Dąbrowska 2006; King and Melzi 2004). Thus, in a recent analysis of CDS of Peruvian mothers of 3- and 5-year-olds, King and Melzi (2004) observed that the frequency of diminutives in mothers' speech was best predicted by the frequency of diminutives in their child's speech and vice versa. Most interestingly, however, was their finding that mothers imitated the diminutive use of the child more frequently than the children imitated the diminutive use of the mother. The authors suggest that these mother-to-child imitations represent an attempt on the mothers' part to maintain emotional responsiveness and rapport with the child, which, in turn, has been demonstrated to benefit language development (Nicely, Tamis-LeMonda & Bornstein 1999; Tamis-LeMonda, Bornstein, Baumwell 2001). Still, what is unclear is how children come to prefer diminutives in the first place so as to produce a linguistic form that then can be imitated by the adult interlocutor to maintain discourse coherence and rapport. We would like to propose the following account, which can offer a tentative explanation for the frequent occurrence of beneficial linguistic forms in CDS.

From the outset, parents develop a close emotional attachment to their child. In their interactions, they use a speech register that is characterized by vocal expressions of positive affect (Trainor, Austin & Desjardins 2000; Singh, Morgan & Best 2002) and loaded with linguistic forms that have strong affective connotations. This affective mode of communication may have evolved to regulate infant emotion and arousal (Fernald 1992) in order to maintain contact with the child over physical distances (Falk

2004). As the parents produce such highly affectively colored speech, the child, using associative and statistical learning mechanisms (Gomez and Gerken 2000) will start to extract whatever distributional regularities the language input contains. If some of the affectively colored linguistic features, such as diminutives, happen to increase statistical regularity on any level, they will have a greater chance of being extracted and ultimately produced in the first utterances of the child. The adult caretaker, then, in an attempt to maintain emotional involvement, rapport, and communicative continuity with the child, will start imitating those features as they elicit greater responsiveness from the child. Thus, we propose that it only takes a small initial statistical benefit from some affectively colored element of speech to engage a communicative feedback loop that will amplify the frequency of that feature in subsequent adult-child conversation. If, on the other hand, an affectively colored feature slightly deviates from dominant patterns of statistical regularity, as in the case of German diminutives, it is less likely to be extracted and produced by the child and, consequently, less likely to be imitated by the parent thus fading into communicative oblivion despite its positive affective connotations. Such a dynamic view emphasizing mutual influences between language learning and adult-child interaction can explain why features that are beneficial from a learner's point of view may be amplified in CDS without any deliberate didactic attempts or even conscious awareness on the side of the adult speaker. In addition, as these patterns of interaction will tend to be similar across different speakers, they might ultimately become conventional in the speech register of a community of speakers. This would enable any speaker to use basic elements of the CDS register without much effort or prior interactions with a child. On this account, if, in a given language, diminutives regularize, simplify or highlight important structural aspects, they will end up being more frequent in CDS than in ADS.

From this perspective, diminutives provide a unique window into the interaction of affective, pragmatic, structural and statistical features of CDS, and the way the interaction between adult and child fosters the development of linguistic and communicative abilities. The view outlined above is compatible with a view that postulates a primacy of affective communication (Locke 2001) and echoes approaches that try to understand development as emerging out of the non-linear dynamic properties of the interaction between the developing organism and the environment (Thelen & Smith 1994). However, much more research is needed to get a full understanding of the factors shaping CDS in general, and diminutive usage in particular, and the mechanisms underlying their effect on language learning. Firstly, researchers need to broaden the cross-linguistic evidence for descriptions of CDS. So far, all data, including those presented in this chapter, stem from mostly a handful of Indo-European languages. Secondly, these descriptions of CDS need to include systematic comparisons with ADS to differentiate the sociolinguistic and cultural norms in a language community from features that are truly unique to CDS. Thirdly, descriptions of CDS should include interactions with children of various ages to map out the trajectory of changes of language input and interaction patterns over the course of language development. And finally, more empirical evidence is needed to demonstrate specific effects of CDS on the process of language learning. This empirical evidence should be gathered not only from child first language learners but also from adult second language learners, as the latter studies allow the systematic manipulation of input to test its effect on learning. Together, this research will improve our understanding of the dynamic nature of CDS as being shaped by and shaping the child in a way that is optimal for language learning and development.

Acknowledgements

Research reported in this chapter was supported The Spencer Foundation, PSC-CUNY, British Academy, *Language Learning – A Journal of Research in Language Studies*, and NATO Collaborative Linkage grants.

Notes

1. Diminutive frequency appears to vary considerably across English dialects with greater prevalence in Australian English, than in American or British English.

2. Note that all these languages also possess a set of lexicalized diminutives, i.e. diminutive nouns or modifiers which have no simplex counterpart like the Russian *banka* 'can' or diminutives the meaning of which has shifted away from the simplex such as in the Russian *vodka* which denotes the well-known spirit rather than being the diminutive form of the simplex *voda* 'water'. In what follows we will only consider productive, i.e. non-lexicalized diminutive forms.

3. Melzi and King (2003) estimated the frequency of diminutive usage in Spanish as 9% of all diminutivizable words including nouns, adjectives and adverbs. However, as they do not provide the total number of nouns, it is impossible to compare their and our estimates directly. Another reason for potential differences in the estimates for Spanish might have to do with the fact that Melzi and King based their calculations on data from 32 mothers speaking to three-year-old children in Limeño Spanish whereas in Kempe, Brooks and Pirott (2001), we used data from one mother speaking Mexican Spanish.

References

Aslin, R. N., Woodward, J. Z., LaMendola, N. P. and Bever, T. G. 1996. Models of word segmentation in fluent maternal speech to infants. In *Signal to syntax: Bootstrapping from speech to grammar in early acquisition*, J. L Morgan and K. Demuth (eds), 117–134. Mahwah, NJ: Erlbaum.

Batchelder, E. O. 2002. Bootstrapping the lexicon: A computational model of infant speech segmentation. *Cognition* 83: 167–206.

Bates, E., and MacWhinney, B. 1987. Competition, variation, and language learning. In *Mechanisms of language acquisition*, B. MacWhinney (ed.), 157–193. Hillsdale, NJ: Erlbaum.
Booij, G. 1995. *The phonology of Dutch*. Oxford: Oxford University Press.
Brent, M. R. and Cartwright, T. A. 1996. Distributional regularity and phonotactic constraints are useful for segmentation. *Cognition* 61: 93–125.
Brent, M. R. and Siskind, J. M. 2001. The role of exposure to isolated words in early vocabulary development. *Cognition* 81: B33-B44.
Brooks, P. J. and Zizak, O. 2002. Does pre-emption help children learn verb transitivity? *Journal of Child Language* 29: 759–781.
Burnham, D., Kitamura, C. and Vollmer-Conna, U. 2002. What's new, pussycat? On talking to babies and animals. *Science* 296: 1435.
Christiansen, M. H., Allen, J. and Seidenberg, M. S. 1998. Learning to segment speech using multiple cues: A connectionist model. *Language and Cognitive Processes* 13: 221–268.
Corbett, G. 1991. *Gender*. Cambridge: Cambridge University Press.
Cutler, A. and Norris, D. G. 1988. The role of stressed syllables in segmentation for lexical access. *Journal of Experimental Psychology: Human Perception and Performance* 14: 113–121.
Cutler, A. 1994. Segmentation problems, rhythmic solutions. *Lingua* 92: 81–104.
Dąbrowska, E. 2004. Rules or schemas? Evidence from Polish. *Language and Cognitive Processes* 19: 225–271.
Dąbrowska, E. 2006. Low-level schemas or productive rules: The role of diminutives in the acquisition of Polish case inflections. *Language Sciences* 28: 120–135.
Echols, C. H., Crowhurst, M. J. and Childers, J. B. 1997. Perception of rhythmic units in speech by infants and adults. *Journal of Memory and Language* 36: 202–225.
Elman, J. L., Bates, E. A., Johnson, M. H., Karmiloff-Smith, A., Parisi, D. and Plunkett, K. 1996. *Rethinking innateness: A connectionist perspective on development*. Cambridge, MA: MIT Press.
Falk, D. 2004. Prelinguistic evolution in early hominins: Whence motherese? *Behavioral and Brain Sciences* 27: 491–541.
Fernald, A. 1992. Human maternal vocalizations to infants as biologically relevant signals: An evolutionary perspective. In *The adapted mind: Evolutionary psychology and the generation of culture*, J. Barkow, L. Cosmides, and J. Tooby (eds), 391–428. New York: Oxford University Press.
Fernald, A. and McRoberts, G. 1996. Prosodic bootstrapping: A critical analysis of the argument and the evidence. In *Signal to syntax: Bootstrapping from speech to grammar in early acquisition*, J. L. Morgan and K. Demuth (eds), 365–388. Mahwah, NJ: Erlbaum.
Gillis, S. 1997. The acquisition of diminutives in Dutch. In *Studies in pre- and protomorphology*, W. Dressler (ed.), 165–179. Wien: Verlag der Österreichischen Akademie der Wissenschaften.
Golinkoff, R. M. and Alioto, A. 1995. Infant-directed speech facilitates lexical learning in adults hearing Chinese: Implications for language acquisition. *Journal of Child Language* 22: 703–726.
Gomez, R. L. and Gerken, L. A. 1999. Artificial grammar learning by one-year-olds leads to specific and abstract knowledge. *Cognition* 70: 109–135.
Gomez, R. L. and Gerken, L. A. 2000. Infant artificial language learning and language acquisition. *Trends in Cognitive Sciences* 4: 178–186.
Hahn, U. and Nakisa, R. C. 2000. German inflection: Single route or dual route? *Cognitive Psychology* 41: 313–360.
Haman, E. 2003. Early productivity in derivation: A case of diminutives in the acquisition of Polish. *Psychology of Language and Communication* 7: 37–56.

Hoff, E. 2003. The specificity of environmental influence: Socioeconomic status affects early vocabulary development via maternal speech. *Child Development* 74: 1368–1378.

Houston, D. M., Jusczyk. P. W., Kuijpers, C., Coolen, R. and Cutler, A. 2000. Cross-language word segmentation by 9-month-olds. *Psychonomic Bulletin and Review* 7: 504–509.

Huttenlocher, J., Vasilyeva, M. Cymerman, E. and Levine, S. 2002. Language input and child syntax. *Cognitive Psychology* 45: 337–374.

Jurafsky, D. 1996. Universal tendencies in the semantics of the diminutive. *Language* 72: 533–578.

Jusczyk, P. W. 1997. *The discovery of spoken language*. Cambridge, MA: MIT Press.

Jusczyk, P. W. 2002. How infants adapt speech-processing capacities to native-language structure. *Current Directions in Psychological Science* 11: 15–18.

Jusczyk, P. W. and Aslin, R. N. 1995. Infants' detection of sound patterns of words in fluent speech. *Cognitive Psychology* 29: 1–23.

Jusczyk, P. W. and Hohne, E. A. 1997. Infants' memory for spoken words. *Science* 277: 1984–1986.

Jusczyk, P. W., Hohne, E. A. and Bauman, A. 1999. Infant's sensitivity to allophonic cues for word segmentation. *Perception and Psychophysics* 61: 1465–1476.

Jusczyk, P. W., Houston, D. M. and Newsome, M. 1999. The beginnings of word segmentation in English-learning infants. *Cognitive Psychology* 39: 159–207.

Kempe, V. in preparation. Regularising effects of diminutiviziation on Russian metric stress patterns.

Kempe, V. and Brooks, P. J. 2001. The role of diminutives in Russian gender learning: Can child-directed speech facilitate the acquisition of inflectional morphology? *Language Learning* 51: 221–256.

Kempe, V., Brooks, P. J. and Gillis, S. 2005. Diminutives in child-directed speech supplement metric with distributional word segmentation cues. *Psychonomic Bulletin and Review* 12: 145–151.

Kempe, V., Brooks, P. J., Gillis, S and Samson, G. in press. Diminutives facilitate word segmentation in natural speech: Cross-linguistic evidence. *Memory and Cognition*.

Kempe, V., Brooks, P. J., Mironova, N. and Fedorova, O. 2003. Diminutivization supports gender acquisition in Russian children. *Journal of Child Language* 30: 471–485.

Kempe, V., Brooks, P. J. Mironova, N., Pershukova, A. and Fedorova, O. in press. Playing with word endings: Morphological variation in the learning of Russian noun inflections. *British Journal of Developmental Psychology*.

Kempe, V., Brooks, P. J. and Pirott, L. 2001. How can child-directed speech facilitate the acquisition of morphology? In *Research on Child Language Acquisition: Proceedings of the 8th conference of the International Association for the Study of Child Language*, M. Almgren, A. Barrena, M.-J. Ezeizabarrena, I. Idiazabal, and B. MacWhinney (eds), 1237–1247. Medford, MA: Cascadilla Press.

King, K. and Melzi, G. 2004. Intimacy, imitation and language learning: Spanish diminutives in mother-child conversation. *First Language* 24: 241–261.

Korecky-Kroell, K. and Dressler, W. 2004. Austrian German diminutives. Paper presented at the 11th International Morphology Meeting. Vienna, Austria.

Kuhl, P.K., Andruski, J.E., Chistovich, I.A., Chistovich, L.A., Kozhevnikova, E.V., Ryskina, V.L., Stolyarova, E.I., Sundberg, U., and Lacerda, F. 1997. Cross-language analysis of phonetic units in language addressed to infants. *Science* 277: 684–686.

Laalo, K. 1998. Diminutives in Finnish child-directed and child speech. In *Studies in the Acquisition of Number and Diminutive Marking* [Antwerp Papers in Linguistics, 95], S. Gillis (ed.), 137–148. Antwerp: Universiteit Anwerpen

Lieven, E. V., Pine, J. M., and Baldwin, G. 1997. Lexically-based learning and early grammatical development. *Journal of Child Language* 24: 187–219.

Locke, J. L. 2001. First communication: The emergence of vocal relationships. *Social Development* 10: 294–308.

Marcus, G. F., Brinkmann, U. and Clahsen, H. 1995. German inflection: The exception that proves the rule. *Cognitive Psychology* 29: 189–256.

Mattys, S. L. and Jusczyk, P. W. 2001a. Do infants segment words or recurring continguous patterns? *Journal of Experimental Psychology: Human Perception and Performance* 27: 644–655.

Mattys, S. L. and Jusczyk, P. W. 2001b. Phonotactic cues for segmentation of fluent speech by infants. *Cognition* 78: 91–121.

Melzi, G. and King, K. 2003. Spanish diminutives in mother-child conversations. *Journal of Child Language* 30: 281–304.

Morgan, J. L. and Demuth, K. (eds.). 1996. *Signal to syntax: Bootstrapping from speech to grammar in early acquisition*. Mahwah, NJ: Erlbaum.

Morgan, J. L. and Saffran, J. R. 1995. Emerging integration of sequential and suprasegmental information in preverbal speech segmentation. *Child Development* 66: 911–936.

Morgan, J. L. 1996. A rhythmic bias in preverbal speech segmentation. *Journal of Memory and Language* 35: 666–688.

Nicely, P., Tamis-LeMonda, C. S. and Bornstein, M. H. 1999. Mothers' attuned responses to infant affect expressivity promote earlier achievement of language milestones. *Infant Behavior and Development* 22: 557–568.

Pinker, S. 1999. *Words and rules: The ingredients of language*. New York: Basic Books.

Plunkett, K. and Nakisa, R. C. 1997. A connectionist model of the Arabic plural system. *Language and Cognitive Processes* 12: 807–836.

Redford, M.A., Davis, B.L. and Miikkulainen, R. 2004. Phonetic variability, and prosodic structure in mothers. *Infant Behavior and Development* 27: 477–498.

Saffran, J. R., Aslin, R. N., and Newport, E. L. 1996. Statistical learning by 8-month-olds. *Science* 274: 1026–1928.

Saffran, J. R., Newport, E. L., Aslin, R. N., Tunick, R. A. and Barrueco, S. 1997. Incidental language learning: Listening (and learning) out of the corner of your ear. *Psychological Science* 8: 101–105.

Saffran, J. R and Wilson, D. P. 2003. From syllables to syntax: Multilevel statistical learning by 12-month-old infants. *Infancy* 4: 273–284.

Savickienė, I. 2003. *The acquisition of Lithuanian noun morphology*. Wien: Verlag der Őstereichschen Akademie der Wissenschaften.

Savickienė, I. 1998. The acquisition of diminutives in Lithuanian. In *Studies in the Acquisition of Number and Diminutive Marking* [Antwerp Papers in Linguistics, 95], S. Gillis (ed.), 115–135. Antwerp: Universiteit Anwerpen.

Savickienė, I., Kempe, V. and Brooks, P. J. submitted. Acquisition of gender agreement in Lithuanian: Exploring the effect of diminutive usage in an elicited production task.

Seidenberg, M. S. and MacDonald, M. C. 1999. A probabilistic constraints approach to language acquisition and processing. *Cognitive Science* 23: 569–588.

Ševa, N., Kempe, V. Brooks, P. J., Mironova, N., Pershukova, A. and Fedorova, O. in press. Crosslinguistic evidence for the diminutive advantage: Gender agreement in Russian and Serbian children. *Journal of Child Language.*

Singh, L., Morgan, J. and Best, C. T. 2002. Infants' Listening preferences: Baby talk or happy talk. *Infancy* 3: 365–394.

Taelman, H. and Gillis, S. 2000. Gebruiken kinderen abstracte prosodische representaties? Een analyse van truncaties in het Maarten-corpus. *Antwerp Papers in Linguistics 99.* Antwerp: Universiteit Anwerpen.

Tamis-LeMonda, C. S. and Bornstein, M. H. 2002. Maternal responsiveness and early language acquisition. In *Advances in child development and behavior*, Vol. 29, R. Kail and H. W. Reese (eds), 89–127. San Diego, CA: Academic Press.

Tamis-LeMonda, C. S., Bornstein, M. H. and Baumwell, L. 2001. Maternal responsiveness and children's achievement of language milestones. *Child Development* 72: 748–767.

Thelen, E. and Smith, L. B. 1994. *A dynamic systems approach to the development of cognition and action.* Cambridge, MA: MIT Press.

Tomasello, M. 1992. *First verbs: A case study of early grammatical development.* Cambridge: Cambridge University Press.

Tomasello, M. 2003. *Constructing a language: A usage-based theory of language acquisition.* Cambridge, MA: Harvard University Press.

Trainor, L. J., Austin, C. M. and Desjardins, R. N. 2000. Is infant-directed speech prosody a result of the vocal expression of emotion? *Psychological Science* 11: 188–195.

Weizman, Z. O. and Snow, C. E. 2001. Lexical input as related to children's vocabulary acquisition: Effects of sophisticated exposure and support for meaning. *Developmental Psychology* 37:265–279.

Zasorina, L. N. E. 1977. *Častotnyj slovar' russkogo jazyka.* Moscow: Russkij Yazyk.

Conclusions

Ineta Savickienė and Wolfgang U. Dressler

1. In most of the languages studied, diminutive formation is the first pattern of word formation to emerge. The main reason for this seems to be the pragmatic functions of endearment, empathy, and sympathy, which make diminutives particularly appropriate for child-centered communication. This is especially true for things belonging to the child's world, which the caretakers tend to refer to using diminutives.

2.1 The present cross-linguistic study of the development of diminutives has dealt with the inflecting-fusional languages Lithuanian, Russian, Croatian, Greek, Italian, Spanish, German and Dutch as well as with the agglutinating languages Turkish, Hungarian and Finnish and with introflecting Hebrew. These languages, in addition to their different proximity to the three ideal language types, differ in various aspects, with repercussions for the acquisition of diminutives.

2.2 Data from the languages investigated show that, in addition to the acquisition of diminutives, other evaluative (alterative) categories are involved as well, i.e. augmentatives (Russian, Croatian, Italian and Greek) and/or pejoratives (Italian, Russian). Invariably augmentatives and pejoratives emerge after diminutives (in Croatian and Greek these evaluatives do not appear until the end of the recordings of our corpora). It is only in the phase that we call morphology proper, though, that examples of augmentatives increase in frequency (at least in Russian and Italian, where a few examples appear even before 2;0) This is in line with the unmarked status of diminutives as opposed to augmentatives and pejoratives within the system of alteratives. It also shows in the implication that no language may have augmentatives without having diminutives (but not vice-versa).

2.3 Token frequency of diminutives varies enormously across languages. Moreover, certain languages are stereotypically considered to be more diminutive-prone than others, e.g. Slavic and Mediterranean languages (more than other European languages), as well as Hungarian and Austrian German (cf. Dressler & Merlini Barbaresi 1994: 409ff). The latter claim that diminutives are frequent in Hungarian and Austrian German, however, was not confirmed for adult or child language, as the respective chapters of this volume show.

Among the languages represented in this volume, Dutch has the highest frequency in ADS, whereas in CDS Lithuanian appears to have the highest frequency of diminutive and hypocoristic usage. In both languages, CS is particularly rich in diminutives. The other languages are in the frequency order of diminutives in our child-language corpora: Russian, Croatian, Italian, Greek, Spanish, Hungarian, German, Finnish, and Turkish. The scarcity of Turkish diminutives in CS as well as in CDS can be attributed to the complex nature of the Turkish diminutive system and to factors discussed below (§ 5.5).

2.4 The observed cross-linguistic variation in frequency was smaller for hypocoristics than for diminutives. It appears that if a language uses fewer diminutives, the relative percentage of hypocoristics, in comparison to that of diminutives, is higher, as is the case for German and Turkish. On the other hand, hypocoristics seem to be noticeably rare in Italian CDS and CS.

2.5 Obviously there may be considerable inter-individual variation in CDS, as observed even when only two children were investigated for a given language, and this variability is echoed in the relative frequency of diminutives and hypocoristics in corresponding CS, as the children investigated in German, Greek, Hungarian, Italian, Russian and Spanish were compared. In fact, correlations between inter-individual variation in CDS and CS can deliver the best evidence on the degree of input-output dependency in language acquisition (Bates et. al. 1988; Lieven et al. 1997; Peters 1997; Tomasello 2003).

In many of our longitudinal corpora the frequency of diminutives appeared to decrease in the input as child age increased. Perhaps this trend suggests that some caretakers no longer treat their developing children as prototypical small children (cf. Melzi & King 2003: 300). Some corpora, such as Italian, Finnish, and Greek indicated a clearly decreasing frequency of diminutives in the input in morphology proper (or after the age of 3;0), whereas the input of other languages still contained a high number of diminutives or showed no significant signs of decrease (with German, Hungarian and Russian data showing differing results for different children).

3.1 Adult diminutives have two different basic meanings, the semantic meaning of smallness and a pragmatic meaning indicating endearment, sympathy, empathy, pleasure, but also irony. Diminutives furthermore mark child-centered speech situations and serve the mitigation of face-threatening speech acts and the like. Do acquisition data shed light on the still debated question of whether the semantic meaning of smallness or the pragmatic meaning is basic (e.g. Bates & Rankin 1979; Kiefer 2004 vs. Dressler & Merlini Barbaresi 1994, 2001)?

3.2 As far as CS is concerned, no differentiation in meaning between diminutives and their base forms was identifiable prior to the emergence of contrasts within the same lemma. Importantly, even after a child had acquired both diminutive and simplex forms of the same lemma, observers were often unable to ascertain any difference in meaning in the child's output between a diminutive and its simplex counterpart used in the same speech situation, and this was the case for several children acquiring Croatian, German, Greek, Hungarian, Italian, Lithuanian and Spanish over periods extending several months.

3.3 An important question is whether children produce diminutives alternating with their base forms just for the sake of playfulness. The assumption that diminutive usage simply marks a child-centered speech situation would seem to pose a problem for Eve Clark's principle of contrast (1993, 1995). This principle predicts that children should rapidly construct a distinction in meaning as they acquire diminutives and their base forms alongside. But this was not generally the case for the languages investigated. A further problem for Clark's principle of contrast lies in the children's apparently indiscriminate use of multiple diminutives and hypocoristics derived from the same base, as in Croatian, German, Greek, Italian, Lithuanian, Russian (mostly in hypocoristics). All these instances render the principle of contrast problematic for early phases of the acquisition of diminutives, especially, if it is restricted to semantic meaning. If one includes pragmatic meaning into the scope of Clark's principle of contrast, then the crucial period of indiscriminate use decreases but still remains problematic.

3.4 Pragmatic effects on the use of diminutives versus simple nouns in speech acts were first detected within the Finnish, German, Greek, Hungarian, Italian, Lithuanian, Russian and Spanish corpora before the age of 3;0, with some examples suggesting a pragmatic meaning of diminutives even before the age of 2;0. The Turkish data, however, did not provide any evidence for a pragmatic function of diminutives. Thus, contrary to what is claimed in the literature (Bates & Rankin 1979; Avrutin 1999; Ladegaard 2003), at least first pragmatic strategies can emerge in children well before the age of three (cf. Stephany 1997). These pragmatic values are endearment, affection, playfulness or attenuation. For this reason we conclude that in an early phase of child language acquisition the diminutive may be an exclusively pragmatic device. This may be regarded to offer developmental support for the general pragmaticist claim on pragmatics having priority over semantics. As Bodor and Barcza propose in the conclusion of their Hungarian chapter, the semantic meaning of diminutives may emerge after a pragmatic one due to coextension of pragmatic meanings with smallness in the child's world, as addressed by caretakers.

3.5 The semantic meaning of smallness is at first most often expressed by adjectives (cf. Bates & Rankin 1979: 37) or by diminutivized adjectives (which denote smallness, whereas their diminutive suffix appears to have a pragmatic meaning), as in Croatian, Italian, Lithuanian, Spanish and only later by adjectives accompanying diminutivized nouns and/or by nominal diminutives without adjectives denoting smallness, at least as far as our German, Greek, Hungarian, Italian, Lithuanian, Russian and Spanish data are concerned. Thus, rather late, diminutives begin to be used as an explicit formal device for marking the meaning of smallness.

Some exceptional evidence for the early emergence of the semantic meaning of smallness appears in one token each in German, Hungarian and Russian at an age before 2;0. Note that two of these three exceptions come from a hypocoristic name where the semantic dimension of smallness is usually irrelevant. A more general exception might be represented by diminutives referring to young animals, as observed, for example, in Greek. It should be noted, however, that this is a special lexical class whose subordinate semantic meaning of youngness might not be generalized to the superordinate meaning of smallness. In the Greek corpora, these diminutives were not accompanied by contrasting base forms, which might have provided more conclusive evidence for a semantic contrast. Moreover, because such diminutivized animal names referred to toy animals on most occasions, it is not at all clear whether the meaning of the diminutive is primarily a semantic (i.e., a reference to youngness) as opposed to pragmatic one (i.e., a reference to the world of the child).

4. A main topic of the volume is the relation of emergence and early development between diminutives and other types of word formation and inflection.

Is there any evidence for or against item-based acquisition (cf. Tomasello 2003: 117-121) as opposed to across-the-board acquisition? Clearly the emergence of diminutives belongs first to the domain of item-based acquisition. But later on, at least some of our data suggest that a single-route model of acquisition (Bybee 1995; Tomasello 2003), where all morphologically complex or derived words and word forms are considered to be rote learned for at least a long time period or expanded by analogy, may have problems explaining an acquisition process which becomes highly productive in a short period of time. The evidence from Finnish, Italian, Spanish supports the assumption of a productive use of the diminutive-formation rule and of across-the-board learning rather than item-based learning, which is supported by Greek and Russian. The acquisition of morphology based on rule or pattern extraction, as proposed by Clahsen (1999), Clahsen et al. (2003) might explain better the potentiality of the system, and seems to better account for the early acquisition of productive rules. Our claim is that, once morphological rules are detected in diminutive morphology, they act as bootstrapping elements in the development of other domains of morphological development.

The schema approach (cf. Introduction § 2.6) has only been discussed in the chapters on Greek and Russian, probably because in none of the other languages diminutive morphology represents a homogeneous schema. In Greek, if one diminutive suffix is considered to represent the strongest diminutive schema, this might also be handled with the notion of a weak default (cf. Introduction § 3.3).

5.1 The frequency of diminutives in the input as well as in the output of children clearly depends on the pragmatic role of diminutives in the respective language. In addition, their greater degree of morphological productivity and transparency, as well as their phonological saliency, favours the use of diminutives. In this case diminutives might facilitate the acquisition of inflection.

5.2 Statistical analysis[1] of productivity for Croatian, Hungarian, Italian and Lithuanian CS shows that there is a clear preference for the shift from base form to diminutive if the base form belongs to an unproductive class. Thus at least in four languages there is a significant main effect, and children appear to prefer to switch from base forms to diminutives, when this involves a switch from an unproductive to a productive inflection class. A similar trend is postulated for Russian.

5.3 Similar results for transparency/opacity show a significant main effect for Croatian and Hungarian, whereas Italian and Lithuanian show only an insignificant trend for switching from an opaque inflection of base forms to transparent diminutive inflection. For Lithuanian and Italian transparency is of lesser importance, because generally noun inflection is already transparent, except in a few cases, and in these cases almost always the more transparent diminutives are preferred. The most direct evidence for the relevance of transparency and for its facilitation effect in the acquisition of inflection comes from the experimental study of Russian gender acquisition, summarized by Kempe et al. in this volume.

5.4 Therefore, wherever more productive and transparent diminutives are systematically preferred to their unproductive and opaque base nouns, we can assume that the acquisition of diminutives may simplify the declensional system and thus facilitate its acquisition. In other words, we can assume that diminutive formation may be a derivational bootstrapping device (cf. Weissenborn & Höhle 2001) for the acquisition of nominal declension.

5.5 If, however, the base noun and the respective diminutive belong to the same productive and transparent class, no such bootstrapping effect is possible. This is the case with Turkish, which has a productive diminutive system. Despite its productivity, though, diminutive formation makes the morphological system more complex, rather than easier. Turkish contrasts with all the other languages with respect to the amount and function of diminutive use in child speech since in the acquisition of the highly regular and transparent nominal morphology diminutives add rather than reduce complexity. Because of their greater length and higher morphological complexity in comparison with their bases, diminutives prove to be a "disadvantage" for acquisition. Thus, in Turkish, diminutives were found to develop more slowly than simple nouns, due to the strongly agglutinating character of this language (as opposed to less agglutinating Hungarian) and their infrequent use in the input speech.

German diminutives do not facilitate the acquisition of declension either, although they are more productive and transparent than base nouns at large, because their use is, presumably due to pragmatic reasons, too infrequent in the input.

6. Unlike the so far mentioned longitudinal studies on diminutive acquisition, the experimental investigation on Hebrew deals with a much longer period of acquisition. It shows that the mastery of conventional-derivational diminutive structure and meaning (as designated as the latest acquisition phase in Berman 2004) does not emerge early on. Unlike juvenile-canonical *-i* diminutives, the structures investigated in this study emerge in later childhood and improve with age and schooling in Hebrew speakers. In fact, only from age 12 do Hebrew speakers master the morphological, semantic, pragmatic, and cognitive factors, which interact in diminutive formation.

7. It has been suggested that diminutivization might regularize patterns of metric stress thereby simplifying the problem of word segmentation (Jusczyk 1997) and of identifying structural patterns at the right edge of words, making them more salient. This would render diminutives easier to identify than simplex nouns. No extra sali-

ence can be assumed for Hungarian with its general and obligatory word-initial stress and its non-homogeneous prosodic make-up of diminutives. However, in all the other languages of our sample except Croatian, diminutives represent word-final trochees, at least in the base forms and most case forms, and are thus easily identifiable. This could be an additional factor responsible for the greater frequency of diminutives in CDS than in ADS. Experimental results on Dutch and Russian, reported by Kempe et al. in this volume, support the facilitating effect of such salience of diminutive suffixes for word segmentation.

8. Whereas this factor of salience is linked to the typology of prosodic phonology, the above-mentioned dimensions of productivity and transparency appear to be related to morphological typology: it is typical for inflecting-fusional languages to have a variety of both productive and unproductive or transparent and opaque declension classes. Thus a shift from base nouns to diminutives may enhance productivity and transparency, with its consequences for the acquisition of inflection. This is impossible in a strongly agglutinating language such as Turkish.

9. One note of precaution is in order before we close. No far-reaching generalizations with respect to the acquisition of diminutives can be put forward at this point, due to the fact that the longitudinal studies of our volume have analyzed the data of mostly only one or two children per language. More data and more research is needed in order to establish which features in the process of diminutive acquisition are truly universal, which are language-specific and which just point to some idiosyncratic usage patterns on the part of a particular child. In this respect, future research is especially needed to expand the cross-linguistic evidence to additional non-Indo-European languages.

Finally, investigation of the pragmatics of CDS versus ADS should be deepened into socio-linguistic aspects to go beyond cross-linguistic to truly intercultural studies.

Note

1. Other languages are not included into the statistics because the numbers of tokens are too small to be of statistical weight. The statistic analysis for Hungarian has been done in Savickienė et al. (in press).

References

Avrutin, S. 1999. *Development of the Syntax-Discourse Interface*. Dordrecht: Kluwer Academic Publishers.

Bates, E. and Rankin, J. 1979. Morphological development in Italian: connotation and denotation. *Journal of Child Language* 6: 29–52.

Bates, E., Bretherton, I. and Snyder, L. 1988. *From first words to grammar: Individual differences and dissociable mechanisms*. New York: Academic Press.

Berman, R. A. 2004. Between emergence and mastery: The long developmental route of language acquisition. In *Language Development across Childhood and Adolescence*, R. Berman (ed.), 9-34. Amsterdam: Benjamins.

Bybee, J. 1995. Regular morphology and the lexicon. *Language and Cognitive Processes* 10: 425–455.

Clahsen, H. 1999. Lexical entries and rules of language: A multidisciplinary study of German inflection. *Behavioral and Brain Sciences* 22: 991–1060.

Clahsen, H., Sonnenstuhl, I. and Blevins, J. P. 2003. Derivational morphology in the German mental lexicon: A dual mechanism account. In *Morphological Structure in Language Processing*, H. R. Baayen and R. Schreuder (eds), 125–155. Berlin: Mouton de Gruyter.

Clark, E. 1993. *The Lexicon in acquisition*. Cambridge, England: Cambridge University Press.

Clark, E. 1995. Later lexical development and word formation. In *The handbook of the child language*, P. Fletcher and B. MacWhinney (eds), 393–412. Oxford: Blackwell.

Dressler, W. U. and Merlini Barbaresi, L. 1994. *Morphopragmatics. Diminutives and intensifiers in Italian, German, and other languages*. Berlin: Mouton de Gruyter.

Dressler, W. U. and Merlini Barbaresi, L. 2001. Morphopragmatics of diminutives and augmentatives: on the priority of pragmatics over semantics. Diminutives and intensifiers in Italian, German, and other languages. In *Perspectives on Semantics, Pragmatics and Discourse*, I. Kenesei and R. Harnish (eds), 43–58. Amsterdam: Benjamins.

Jusczyk, P. W. 1997. *The discovery of spoken language*. Cambridge, MA: MIT Press.

Kiefer, F. 2004: Morphopragmatic phenomena in Hungarian. *Acta Linguistica Hungarica* 51: 325–349.

Ladegaard H. J. 2003. Politeness in young children's speech. Context, peer group influence and pragmatic competence. *Journal of Pragmatics* 36: 2003–2022.

Lieven, E. V., Pine, J. M., and Baldwin, G. 1997. Lexically-based learning and early grammatical development. *Journal of Child Language* 24: 187–219.

Melzi, G. and King, K. A. 2003. Spanish diminutives in mother-child conversations. *Journal of Child Language* 30: 281–304.

Peters, A. 1997. Language typology, prosody, and the acquisition of grammatical morphemes. In *The crosslinguistic study of language acquisition, Vol. 5. Expanding the contexts*, D. I. Slobin (ed.), 136–197. Hillsdale, NJ: Lawrence Erlbaum Associates.

Savickienė, I., Dressler, W. U., Barcza, V., Bodor, P., Ketrez, N., Korecky-Kröll, K., Palmović, M., Stephany, U. and Thomadaki, E. in press. Diminutives as Pioneers of Derivational and Inflectional Development – a Crosslinguistic Perspective. *Antwerp papers in linguistics*. Antwerp: Universiteit Antwerpen.

Stephany, U. 1997. Diminutives in early Greek. In *Studies in Pre- and Protomorphology*, W. U. Dressler (ed.), 145–156. Wien: Österreichischen Akademie der Wissenschaften.

Tomasello, M. 2003. *Constructing a language: A usage-based theory of language acquisition*. Cambridge, MA: Harvard University Press.

Weissenborn, J. and Höhle, B. (eds.). 2001. *Approaches to bootstrapping: Phonological, syntactic and neurological aspects of early language acquisition*. Amsterdam/Philadephia: Benjamins.

Subject Index

A
across-the-board learning 141, 149, 346
adjectives 15, 73, 90, 128, 138, 161, 175, 187, 208, 280
adult-directed speech (ADS) 1, 8, 18, 136, 204, 321, 343, 348
adverbs 15, 45, 161, 188
allomorphs 156, 183–190, 195–204, 324, 328–329
alteratives 1, 127, 344
alternations 8, 16, 48, 177, 221, 263, 267–268, 276, 279, 283
augmentatives 48, 50–51, 62, 70, 77, 92, 120, 126–127, 145, 207, 264
Austrian German 8, 207, 212, 228–229, 263, 344
see also German

B
baby talk (BT) 1, 232, 244, 261, 297
see also child-directed speech (CDS)
see also input
Baltic 6, 32
Bantu 2, 125
bootstrapping 177, 347

C
canonical word-forms 267
caretakers 3, 6, 44, 100–101, 119, 129, 148, 257, 344–346
child-directed speech (CDS) 1–2, 7–9, 18, 50, 68, 78, 113, 126–127, 155, 158, 183–184, 207, 244, 266, 277, 279, 287, 297, 319–320
see also baby talk (BT)
see also input
child speech (CS) 1, 7–8, 26, 62, 104, 113, 135, 183, 190, 244, 256, 263, 267, 283–284
compounds 8, 127, 149, 187, 212, 227–229, 264, 273, 274, 275, 290, 304
connotative meaning 128, 144, 283
conventional-derivational diminutives 296, 302, 309
Croatian 1, 6–7, 73–74, 77, 343–347
cross-sectional studies 239

D
declension 4, 13–14, 26, 46–47, 50–51, 56, 62–63, 92–93, 208, 231, 233, 235, 257, 279, 289, 334
declension class 4–7, 13, 15, 21, 26, 46–47, 59–60, 67–69, 93, 235
declension patterns 63, 67–68, 95
derivational morphology 71, 316, 350
dialect 76–78, 84, 230
diminutives 4, 7, 13, 18, 54, 63, 68, 93, 101, 127, 146, 150, 156, 184–185, 194–195, 233–234, 242–244, 276, 295–296, 309
Dizi 335
double suffixation 15, 23, 46, 61
dual-mechanism hypothesis 5, 228
Dutch 1, 8–9, 158, 190, 194, 198, 200–204, 263, 277, 280, 319–326, 334–335, 344

E
early emergence 189, 228
emotions 4, 13–14, 34, 44, 51, 86, 174, 238, 257
experiment(al) 316, 324, 342
explanation task 307, 311

F
Finnish 6, 8, 263–265, 321, 334, 344–347
Finno-Ugric 6
form oppositions 193, 217, 218, 219, 220
frozen diminutives 202

G
gender 2, 15, 32, 54, 74, 108, 126–128, 135, 177, 188, 208, 244–245, 279, 295, 298, 319–320, 323, 343
German 1, 3, 6, 8, 71, 117, 120, 212, 217, 221, 315, 321, 327, 337, 350
Germanic 6
Greek 1, 6–7, 32, 89, 117–118, 343–346

H
Hebrew 1, 3, 6, 9, 32, 117, 119, 295–302, 305, 309–312, 344
Hungarian 1, 5–6, 8, 233, 235, 343–347
hyper-articulation 336
hypocoristics 3, 15, 33, 46, 77, 91–92, 96–97, 113, 134, 208, 220, 235, 264, 283, 304

I
illocution 257
Indo-European 3, 6, 13, 337, 349
input 3, 8, 36, 48, 50, 59, 62, 108, 110, 136, 139, 157, 160, 211–214, 244–246, 255–256, 289, 299, 320, 323, 328, 330, 343, 345, 347
introflecting 3, 6, 344
Italian 1–2, 6–7, 32, 118–119, 125, 128, 343–346
item-based model 50, 111, 126, 140, 346

J
juvenile diminutives 119, 297, 347

L
Latvian 1, 32
lemmas 8, 44, 56–57, 59, 69, 80–81, 140, 147–148, 164, 177, 183, 186, 189–195, 197–199, 201–204, 210, 214
lexicalization 91, 98, 309
lexico-semantic groups 14, 32, 41, 143, 157, 220, 255

linear formation 299
Lithuanian 1, 6, 13–26, 41, 157–158, 160, 163, 167, 169, 175, 248, 263, 277, 319, 334, 344–347
longitudinal 2, 6–8, 18, 68, 89, 125, 155, 158, 183–184, 188, 195, 209, 229, 239, 297, 345
low-level schemas 2, 10, 330
see also schemas

M
microclass 15–16, 21
mini-paradigms 147, 164–166, 292
modularized morphology 136, 150
morphophonology 167, 181

N
numerals 15, 128–129, 187, 265

O
opaque 4–5, 14, 25–26, 45, 63–64, 125, 128, 136, 148, 217, 221, 225, 248
overextensions 277
overregularization 180

P
paradigm 2, 6, 13, 16, 40, 46, 66, 76, 81–82, 90–91, 107, 127, 134, 146–147, 177, 218, 286, 324, 326
pejoratives 7, 46, 48–49, 74, 77, 91, 207, 237–238, 264, 320
phase 2, 17–19, 44, 56, 126, 130, 134–135, 140, 144, 146, 163, 272, 344, 346
Polish 2, 117, 319, 330, 334, 336
politeness 293, 350
pragmatic 2, 4, 6–8, 13–15, 27–28, 32–34, 43, 49, 58–59, 62, 65–66, 68–69, 95–96, 117–118, 141–146, 155–157, 169–177, 195, 208, 222, 225, 228, 254–255, 257, 264, 267, 270–273, 275–277, 290, 295, 309, 321–322, 334, 337, 344–348, 350
premorphology 2, 134, 150, 158
production task 306, 308, 332
productive suffixes 3, 14, 15, 22, 78, 84, 256, 300
productivity 25, 110, 152, 230
protomorphology 2, 70, 126, 150, 350

Q
quantitative 1, 4, 6–7, 13, 18, 55, 77, 79, 148, 157, 161, 168, 191, 212

R
reduplication 301, 313
Romance 6, 315
rule-based models 126, 148, 171
Russian 1, 6–7, 32, 43–44, 54, 59–60, 117–118, 156–158, 160, 163, 175, 263, 277, 280, 296, 319–323, 326–336, 341, 343–347

S
schemas 2, 109–110, 330, 347
see also low-level schemas
semantics 26, 48, 59, 95, 141, 171, 220, 222, 225, 254, 267, 350
Semitic 6
Serbian 319, 321, 334, 343
Spanish 1, 6–7, 118, 167, 169–171, 173, 175, 279, 289, 296, 344–347, 350
Spoken Dutch Corpus 8, 184, 202
Swahili 335

T
token frequency 190, 215, 216, 344
transparency 4, 267, 348
trochees 24, 134, 146, 324, 326, 348
truncation 2, 234
Turkish 1, 3, 5, 279–281, 290, 343–344, 347–348

U
umlaut 208, 217, 224, 225
unproductive 4–5, 7–8, 14, 16, 25–26, 47, 93, 128–129, 147–149, 207, 226, 228, 231, 233–235, 246, 248, 256
usage-based models 104, 109

In the series *Language Acquisition and Language Disorders* the following titles have been published thus far or are scheduled for publication:

A complete list of titles in this series can be found on the publishers' website, *www.benjamins.com*

43 **SAVICKIENĖ, Ineta and Wolfgang U. DRESSLER (eds.):** The Acquisition of Diminutives. A cross-linguistic perspective. 2007. vi, 352 pp.

42 **LEFEBVRE, Claire, Lydia WHITE and Christine JOURDAN (eds.):** L2 Acquisition and Creole Genesis. Dialogues. 2006. viii, 433 pp.

41 **TORRENS, Vincent and Linda ESCOBAR (eds.):** The Acquisition of Syntax in Romance Languages. 2006. viii, 422 pp.

40 **DEEN, Kamil Ud:** The Acquisition of Swahili. 2005. xiv, 241 pp.

39 **UNSWORTH, Sharon, Teresa PARODI, Antonella SORACE and Martha YOUNG-SCHOLTEN (eds.):** Paths of Development in L1 and L2 acquisition. In honor of Bonnie D. Schwartz. 2006. viii, 222 pp.

38 **FRANCESCHINA, Florencia:** Fossilized Second Language Grammars. The acquisition of grammatical gender. 2005. xxiv, 288 pp.

37 **MONTRUL, Silvina A.:** The Acquisition of Spanish. Morphosyntactic development in monolingual and bilingual L1 acquisition and adult L2 acquisition. 2004. xvi, 413 pp.

36 **BARTKE, Susanne and Julia SIEGMÜLLER (eds.):** Williams Syndrome across Languages. 2004. xvi, 385 pp.

35 **SÁNCHEZ, Liliana:** Quechua-Spanish Bilingualism. Interference and convergence in functional categories. 2003. x, 189 pp.

34 **OTA, Mitsuhiko:** The Development of Prosodic Structure in Early Words. Continuity, divergence and change. 2003. xii, 224 pp.

33 **JOSEFSSON, Gunlög, Christer PLATZACK and Gisela HÅKANSSON (eds.):** The Acquisition of Swedish Grammar. 2004. vi, 315 pp.

32 **PRÉVOST, Philippe and Johanne PARADIS (eds.):** The Acquisition of French in Different Contexts. Focus on functional categories. 2004. viii, 384 pp.

31 **MARINIS, Theodoros:** The Acquisition of the DP in Modern Greek. 2003. xiv, 261 pp.

30 **HOUT, Roeland van, Aafke HULK, Folkert KUIKEN and Richard J. TOWELL (eds.):** The Lexicon–Syntax Interface in Second Language Acquisition. 2003. viii, 234 pp.

29 **FERNÁNDEZ, Eva M.:** Bilingual Sentence Processing. Relative clause attachment in English and Spanish. 2003. xx, 294 pp.

28 **SHIMRON, Joseph (ed.):** Language Processing and Acquisition in Languages of Semitic, Root-Based, Morphology. 2003. vi, 394 pp.

27 **SALABERRY, M. Rafael and Yasuhiro SHIRAI (eds.):** The L2 Acquisition of Tense–Aspect Morphology. 2002. x, 489 pp.

26 **SLABAKOVA, Roumyana:** Telicity in the Second Language. 2001. xii, 236 pp.

25 **CARROLL, Susanne E.:** Input and Evidence. The raw material of second language acquisition. 2001. xviii, 461 pp.

24 **WEISSENBORN, Jürgen and Barbara HÖHLE (eds.):** Approaches to Bootstrapping. Phonological, lexical, syntactic and neurophysiological aspects of early language acquisition. Volume 2. 2001. viii, 337 pp.

23 **WEISSENBORN, Jürgen and Barbara HÖHLE (eds.):** Approaches to Bootstrapping. Phonological, lexical, syntactic and neurophysiological aspects of early language acquisition. Volume 1. 2001. xviii, 299 pp.

22 **SCHAEFFER, Jeannette C.:** The Acquisition of Direct Object Scrambling and Clitic Placement. Syntax and pragmatics. 2000. xii, 187 pp.

21 **HERSCHENSOHN, Julia:** The Second Time Around – Minimalism and L2 Acquisition. 2000. xiv, 287 pp.

20 **KANNO, Kazue (ed.):** The Acquisition of Japanese as a Second Language. 1999. xii, 180 pp.

19 **BECK, Maria-Luise (ed.):** Morphology and its Interfaces in Second Language Knowledge. 1998. x, 387 pp.

18 **KLEIN, Elaine C. and Gita MARTOHARDJONO (eds.):** The Development of Second Language Grammars. A generative approach. 1999. vi, 412 pp.

17 **ARCHIBALD, John:** Second Language Phonology. 1998. xii, 313 pp.

16 **HANNAHS, S.J. and Martha YOUNG-SCHOLTEN (eds.):** Focus on Phonological Acquisition. 1997. v, 289 pp.

15 **BRINKMANN, Ursula:** The Locative Alternation in German. Its structure and acquisition. 1997. x, 289 pp.

14 **CLAHSEN, Harald (ed.):** Generative Perspectives on Language Acquisition. Empirical findings, theoretical considerations and crosslinguistic comparisons. 1996. xxviii, 499 pp.

13 **ALLEN, Shanley E.M.:** Aspects of Argument Structure Acquisition in Inuktitut. 1996. xvi, 244 pp.

12 **JUFFS, Alan:** Learnability and the Lexicon. Theories and second language acquisition research. 1996. xi, 277 pp.

11 **YIP, Virginia:** Interlanguage and Learnability. From Chinese to English. 1995. xvi, 247 pp.

10 **LAKSHMANAN, Usha:** Universal Grammar in Child Second Language Acquisition. Null subjects and morphological uniformity. 1994. x, 162 pp.

9 **ADONE, Dany:** The Acquisition of Mauritian Creole. 1994. xii, 167 pp.

8 **HOEKSTRA, Teun and Bonnie D. SCHWARTZ (eds.):** Language Acquisition Studies in Generative Grammar. 1994. xii, 401 pp.

7 **MEISEL, Jürgen M. (ed.):** Bilingual First Language Acquisition. French and German grammatical development. 1994. vi, 282 pp.

6 **THOMAS, Margaret:** Knowledge of Reflexives in a Second Language. 1993. x, 234 pp.

5 **GASS, Susan M. and Larry SELINKER (eds.):** Language Transfer in Language Learning. Revised edition. 1992. x, 236 pp.

4 **ECKMAN, Fred R. (ed.):** Confluence. Linguistics, L2 acquisition and speech pathology. 1993. xvi, 260 pp.

3 **EUBANK, Lynn (ed.):** Point Counterpoint. Universal Grammar in the second language. 1991. x, 439 pp.

2 **HUEBNER, Thom and Charles A. FERGUSON (eds.):** Cross Currents in Second Language Acquisition and Linguistic Theory. 1991. viii, 435 pp.

1 **WHITE, Lydia:** Universal Grammar and Second Language Acquisition. 1989. xii, 198 pp.